7/19

The New Comparative Economic History

The New Comparative Economic History

Essays in Honor of Jeffrey G. Williamson

Edited by Timothy J. Hatton, Kevin H. O'Rourke, and Alan M. Taylor

The MIT Press
Cambridge, Massachusetts
London, England

MIT Press books may be purchased at special quantity discounts for business or sales promotional use. For information, please e-mail ⟨special_sales@mitpress.mit.edu⟩ or write to Special Sales Department, The MIT Press, 55 Hayward Street, Cambridge, MA 02142.

This book was set in Times New Roman and Syntax on 3B2 by Asco Typesetters, Hong Kong, and was printed and bound in the United States of America.

Library of Congress Cataloging-in-Publication Data

The new comparative economic history : essays in honor of Jeffrey G. Williamson / edited by Timothy J. Hatton, Kevin H. O'Rourke, and Alan M. Taylor.
   p.   cm.
Includes bibliographical references and index.
ISBN: 978-0-262-08361-4 (hardcover : alk. paper)
1. Economic history—19th century. 2. Economic history—20th century. I. Williamson, Jeffrey G., 1935– II. Hatton, T. J. III. O'Rourke, Kevin H. IV. Taylor, Alan M., 1964–
HC53.N49   2007
330.9′034—dc22   2006032219

10 9 8 7 6 5 4 3 2 1

This book is dedicated to Jeffrey G. Williamson

Contents

Acknowledgments

This volume brings together papers presented at a conference entitled "The New Comparative Economic History," held on November 4–5, 2005, at Harvard University, and it serves as a Festschrift for Jeffrey G. Williamson, Laird Bell Professor of Economics at Harvard University. Our first acknowledgment is therefore to Jeff himself for all that he has given to us and to the field.

On behalf of all the conference participants, we would like to thank Harvard University for generously hosting this event at the Barker Center and Faculty Club. We are especially grateful for the financial support of the David Rockefeller Center for Latin American Studies, the Weatherhead Center for International Affairs, and the Dean of the Faculty of Arts and Sciences. Local arrangements for the conference were faultless, and for that we owe a great debt to our man on the spot, John Coatsworth, who took care of so much planning while the editors stayed, at all times, a minimum of 3,000 miles away. Translating plans into action, John was ably assisted by Monet Uva and Edwin Ortiz. We must also give thanks to the staff of the Faculty Club for a memorable evening, and especially to François Braun for his handling of the salamanzar. Nor shall Peter Lindert be forgotten for his smooth work as the master of ceremonies; he also gets an Oscar for video production.

We were very fortunate that Lawrence H. Summers, the President of Harvard University, was able to address the conference. His remarks, delivered with warmth and wit, spoke to the importance of economic history as a field and to the remarkable personal and professional contributions by Jeff Williamson that have benefited not just the advancement of scholarship but also have helped and inspired an enormous group of scholars from around the world. President Summers's address is reproduced here as an afterword.

Bringing the papers together as an edited volume has been made very easy by MIT Press. The editors wish to thank the editorial team, referees, copy editors, typesetters, and all others who made it all possible, but most of all we thank Elizabeth Murry and Deborah Cantor-Adams for their guidance throughout the project.

The New Comparative Economic History

Introduction: The New Comparative Economic History

Timothy J. Hatton, Kevin H. O'Rourke, and Alan M. Taylor

The cliometric revolution in economic history is now nearly half a century old. By applying formal economic methodology to historical questions, it marked a sea change in the way that issues such as slavery or the Industrial Revolution were debated, and thus fully deserves its revolutionary label. This book's purpose is to showcase a more recent trend in economic history, which is an evolution rather than a revolution but which still represents a distinct change in the way that many economic historians view their role, do their work, and interact with the broader economics profession.

As the label suggests, the New Comparative Economic History reflects a belief that economic processes can best be understood by systematically comparing experiences across time, regions, and, above all, countries. As such, it differs from much traditional work in cliometric history in the nature of the questions it asks and in the nature of the answers it provides. But like cliometrics, it has a long ancestry. It draws inspiration from such giants as Simon Kuznets, W. Arthur Lewis, and Douglass North, all three Nobel laureates. For pioneers like these, comparative thinking was so central, so natural, and so ingrained that it hardly needed to be mentioned as a point of reference and warranted no special rhetorical logo. From these towering intellectual figures and their many followers emerged what we might call—only with the benefit of hindsight—the old comparative economic history. In its time a flourishing new intellectual direction, this field set out some of the big questions and the earliest pieces of evidence on which today's scholarship builds. The New Comparative Economic History has taken up some of these earlier themes, brought in new perspectives, and built on the achievements of the earlier pioneers. But the transition from the old to the new has taken time, and it needed the evolution of economic history—and just as important, of economics—to set the stage for a second and quite distinctive burst of comparative economic history.

Cliometrics initially cut its teeth on questions that had emerged from national historiographies, and thus it had two limitations: it was national in scope, and it sought questions from the historian's agenda rather than from the economist's agenda. The aim of early cliometrics was to show that these questions could be better understood by using economic theory and rigorous quantification. As such, the lessons to be learned were largely of interest to other economic historians, who were usually focused on their own country's experience.

By contrast, the New Comparative Economic History is motivated by questions being posed by economists that are less nation-specific in scope—questions such as the sources of economic growth, the importance of institutions, and the impact of globalization. For example, its practitioners are less interested in the first, British Industrial Revolution as a specific historical episode than in what it tells us about the nature of economic growth. If the latter is the motivating question, then it makes sense to study not just this episode but other transitions to modern economic growth (and just as important, failures to achieve such transitions) as well. To take another example, New Comparative Economic History practitioners will tend to be interested in the impact of specific economic, political, or cultural institutions, such as slavery, democracy, or religion, not just in and of themselves, but also in how institutions influence economic development. As such, it makes sense to exploit the fact that history provides an immense variety of institutional arrangements that allows us to arrive at conclusions with a general validity, rather than simply improving our understanding of an institution embedded in a particular time and place.

The New Comparative Economic History is motivated by current debates among academic economists and policymakers rather than following agendas set by historians. At the same time, it aims to convince the rest of the economics profession that they have a lot to learn from taking history seriously. History can inform current debates by focusing on long-run trends rather than on short-run ups and downs in economic activity. As a result, it can provide an antidote to analysis that looks only at the present or the very recent past. It also provides a powerful reminder that one model may not fit all circumstances, because economic relationships that may seem immutable to economists familiar only with the present may in fact be highly time- or place-specific.

A good example of this concerns the relationship between openness and economic growth. While many studies have shown that the two are positively correlated for the post-1950 or post-1960 period, Clemens and Williamson (2004b) find that the correlation was reversed in earlier epochs and (to complicate matters further) that it differed across geographical regions. In turn, such findings can help economists think more carefully about what are the underlying assumptions driving their models' predictions and the changing regimes driving their econometric results. Economists are also reminded that the political, institutional, and economic environment can play an important role in shaping the relationships between policies and outcomes. This institutional sensitivity, a distinguishing feature of economic history in general, is finding a receptive audience among today's mainstream growth, development, and international economists.

Three other closely related features of the New Comparative Economic History have been its emphasis on the interactions between economies, the economic mechanisms driving aggregate correlations in the data, and political economy questions. Consider, for example, the issue of whether economic growth leads to country or regional convergence (Williamson 1965; Abramovitz 1986). A vast literature has tried to answer this question by exploring regressions of country-specific growth rates on initial income, trying to uncover evidence of unconditional, or possibly conditional, convergence. This methodology implicitly assumes that each country is an island, with its growth rate determined by a series of country-specific variables. At best, openness to trade or some other indicator of integration with the rest of the world will appear in the equation as a country-specific right-hand side variable.

However, economic intuition, common sense, and experience all tell us that whether poor countries catch up with rich countries will depend critically on the nature of the economic interactions between them, on the extent to which capital, more productive technology, better policies, and more efficient institutions are transferred to backward countries, or on the nature and extent of commodity trade and labor migration. In this light, no country is an island, and thus the researcher's attention is drawn irresistibly to the study of international capital flows, migration, trade, technological transfer, and the diffusion of good public policy. In turn, studying these flows can tell us a lot about what drove economic convergence (and divergence) between poor and rich regions at particular times and in particular parts of the world. Thus, economic convergence between poor and rich countries in the late nineteenth-century Atlantic economy was mostly driven by labor migrations (Hatton and Williamson 1998; O'Rourke and Williamson 1999; Taylor and Williamson 1997). Capital flows occasionally played a supporting role (as in the case of Sweden) but more often were a force for divergence rather than convergence. This leads to the historical questions, Why has capital never flowed more systematically to poor countries (Clemens and Williamson 2004a)? And why has migration not played the pro-convergence role in the twentieth century that it played during the nineteenth (Hatton and Williamson 2005)? The latter question is obviously one that requires a political economy explanation. Indeed, policy is clearly one of the key drivers of economic integration between countries, and it can help explain cross-country variations in economic performance more generally. Why the New Comparative Economic History is concerned with political economy issues is thus easily understood.

The New Comparative Economic History not only asks different questions from those posed by earlier cliometricians; it also differs in the type of answer it provides. One key rule is never to throw away information; history is the only laboratory we have, and it is important to exploit any variation in the data that can be found there. One important characteristic of the field, therefore, is its constant tendency to expand the range of countries being explored, from Great Britain and the United States (Williamson 1974; 1985; 1990), whose histories inspired the first cliometricians, to Japan (Kelley and Williamson 1974), the Atlantic economy (Hatton and Williamson 1998; O'Rourke and Williamson 1999; Taylor and Williamson 1997), Latin America (Coatsworth and Williamson 2004; Bértola and Williamson 2006), and the wider world (Hatton and Williamson 2005; Williamson 2006). In particular, the developing world is not only where most people live, but it comprises a variety of countries with different institutions and endowments whose economic histories are full of lessons for policymakers and growth economists. Uncovering these lessons has been and will continue to be one of the key tasks of the New Comparative Economic History.

If long-run cross-country variation is a key to understanding long-run economic processes, and consequently individual country experiences, then that has implications for the methodologies that economic historians will tend to use. Cliometrics became famous for its use of counterfactual analysis, and this made sense in a field where economists were asking country-specific questions, such as what was the impact of railways in the United States? The answer could be found by comparing the United

States as it actually was with a counterfactual United States without the railroad. Of course, such an approach implied that the researcher had to commit to some theoretical model, because otherwise the counterfactual comparator would remain forever unobserved. A lot of cliometrics thus involved theory with numbers, calibrating models ranging from back-of-the-envelope partial equilibrium models to full-scale general equilibrium models.

By contrast, the New Comparative Economic History instinctively tries to compare actual economies, not with counterfactuals but with each other—a different solution to the specification problem (Fogel 1967). If they wanted to explore the impact of railroads, its practitioners' first thought would be to exploit the fact that railroads were introduced at different times into different economies; they would be aware of the possibility that railroads would have had different effects in each because of differing geographies, different patterns of specialization, different political contexts, or other factors. Thus, comparative or counterfactual statements are closely linked to the range of historical experience. By allowing the data to speak in this manner and by avoiding theoretical assumptions that might narrow the range of possible answers, researchers can move away from the tyranny of the Harberger triangle, which always produces the answer "small," or the tyranny of partial equilibrium, which ignores the interaction between markets, or any other theoretical tyranny that imposes prior restrictions on the analysis and thus the answers.

We would not wish to exaggerate or oversimplify. It is not the case that the New Comparative Economic History never uses counterfactual analysis or computable general equilibrium models. The field is methodologically catholic, as the chapters in this book illustrate. Traditional cliometrics always made wide use of econometric analysis, relying on comparisons across time, agents, or place, as its 1970s British moniker, "econometric history," clearly indicates. Economic history, including cliometric history, has certainly produced comparative work in the past, such as the classic comparisons of French and British economic development (O'Brien and Keyder 1978; Crouzet 1991). Clearly, we are dealing with tendencies here. Nonetheless, it seems to us that there has been a discernible shift toward more comparative work in recent years. For example, economic history research and training networks have sprung up in Europe that are devoted explicitly to exposing students to other countries' experience. The move away from narrowly national economic history to broader approaches is further symbolized by the recent *Cambridge Economic History of Latin America* (Bulmer-Thomas, Coatsworth, and

Cortés-Conde 2006), which stresses a comparative approach. The contributors to the present volume have all been actively involved in comparative economic history projects over the years, ranging from comparative banking history, to comparative famine history, to even broader comparative questions about growth and development.

This trend toward comparative economic history was probably inevitable. After all, cliometrics required data, and data tend to be gathered at a national level. Early cliometric efforts were thus largely devoted to collecting these data and analyzing them systematically, starting with the construction of national income aggregates. This enterprise implied, almost by definition, a nation-specific approach to economic history. The barriers to entry for would-be comparative cliometricians were for a long time prohibitively high. Now, however, a broad range of comparative data is easily available, partly as a result of the extraordinarily cooperative tendencies of the worldwide cliometrics community, and partly as a result of collaborative data-gathering projects, such as those devoted to the systematic compilation of comparable wage and price data across as many countries and time periods as possible, illustrated by projects led by Robert Allen, Jan Luiten van Zanden, and Peter Lindert. With the barriers to entry falling, it is small wonder that the number of cliometricians doing serious comparative work has been rising over time.

There is a second reason for the growth in comparative work in recent years, and that is the intellectual leadership of Jeffrey G. Williamson. His influence across the world has been immense, particularly in regions such as Europe or Latin America, where economic historians have had no alternative but to take seriously the open-economy thinking that has characterized so much of his work. He has been a generous supporter of attempts to build up the cliometric profession in continental Europe, Latin America, Asia, and elsewhere, attending summer schools, giving keynote lectures, collaborating with local economic historians, and providing encouragement to those academic communities. In Europe he has been a much-valued supporter of the European Historical Economics Society, and he was crucially involved in the debates that led to the setting up of the society's journal, the *European Review of Economic History*, on whose editorial board he has served.

The immense regard in which he is held across Europe is reflected in the large number of European contributions to this book. In Latin America, Jeff has worked with numerous scholars, inspired many students in training, and traveled extensively to help develop and encourage new networks, conferences, and research projects, and in doing so, he has played an invaluable role in promoting the recent growth of Latin American economic history as a field. Through frequent visits to Australia, he has injected new vitality into a discipline that had been in retreat there. And through his insistence on the importance of Asia to global economic history, he has helped to foster comparative work in that region, too. Indeed, he plans to pursue an economic history program beginning in the Philippines. The fact that the New Comparative Economic History exploits such a wide range of experience has boosted interest in countries and regions previously considered to be peripheral to the main story. More than anyone else, Jeff has carried this message to all corners of the globe.

Most of all, as the many references cited here indicate, Jeff has led by example, helping to shape the intellectual agenda that others are now following. His own career has anticipated broader trends within the profession, its focus moving from U.S. and other single-country studies to globalization and comparative economic history more generally. He has influenced the New Comparative Economic History directly, through his work with students and collaborators, and indirectly, via his many writings. He is a giant in the field and in economic history more generally, and this volume is gratefully dedicated to him.

References

Abramovitz, A. 1986. Catching Up, Forging Ahead, and Falling Behind. *Journal of Economic History* 46: 385–406.

Bértola, L., and J. G. Williamson. 2006. Globalization in Latin America before 1940. In *The Cambridge Economic History of Latin America*. Vol. 2, *The Long Twentieth Century*, ed. V. Bulmer-Thomas, J. H. Coatsworth, and R. Cortés Conde. New York: Cambridge University Press.

Bulmer-Thomas, V., J. H. Coatsworth, and R. Cortés-Conde, eds. 2006. *The Cambridge Economic History of Latin America*. New York: Cambridge University Press.

Clemens, M. A., and J. G. Williamson. 2004a. Wealth Bias in the First Global Capital Market Boom, 1870–1913. *Economic Journal* 114: 311–344.

———. 2004b. Why Did the Tariff-Growth Correlation Reverse after 1950? *Journal of Economic Growth* 9: 5–46.

Coatsworth, J. H., and J. G. Williamson. 2004. The Roots of Latin American Protectionism: Looking before the Great Depression. In *Integrating the Americas: FTAA and Beyond*, ed. A. Estevadeordal, D. Rodrik, A. Taylor, and A. Velasco. Cambridge, Mass.: Harvard University Press.

Crouzet, F. 1991. *Britain Ascendant: Studies in British and Franco-British Economic History*. Cambridge: Cambridge University Press.

Fogel, R. W. 1967. The Specification Problem in Economic History. *Journal of Economic History* 27: 283–308.

Hatton, T. J., and J. G. Williamson. 1998. *The Age of Mass Migration: Causes and Economic Impact*. New York: Oxford University Press.

————. 2005. *Global Migration and the World Economy: Two Centuries of Policy and Performance.* Cambridge, Mass.: MIT Press.

Kelley, A. C., and J. G. Williamson. 1974. *Lessons from Japanese Economic Development: An Analytical Economic History.* Chicago: University of Chicago Press.

O'Brien, P. K., and C. Keyder. 1978. *Economic Growth in Britain and France: Two Paths to the Twentieth Century.* London: Allen and Unwin.

O'Rourke, K. H., and J. G. Williamson. 1999. *Globalization and History: The Evolution of the Nineteenth Century Atlantic Economy.* Cambridge, Mass.: MIT Press.

Taylor, A. M., and J. G. Williamson. 1997. Convergence in an Age of Mass Migration. *European Review of Economic History* 1: 27–63.

Williamson, J. G. 1965. Regional Inequality and the Process of National Development: A Description of the Patterns. *Economic Development and Cultural Change* 13: 3–84.

————. 1974. *Late Nineteenth Century American Development: A General Equilibrium History.* Cambridge: Cambridge University Press.

————. 1985. *Did British Capitalism Breed Inequality?* London: Allen and Unwin.

————. 1990. *Coping with City Growth during the British Industrial Revolution.* Cambridge: Cambridge University Press.

————. 2006. *Globalization and the Poor Periphery before the Modern Era: The 2004 Ohlin Lectures.* Cambridge, Mass.: MIT Press.

1 India in the Great Divergence

Robert C. Allen

Economic historians try to explain why some nations are rich and others poor. The question was first pursued in a European context—Why did the Industrial Revolution happen in Britain rather than France?—but in recent years the discussion has broadened to the whole world, and the question has become, When and why did Europe pull ahead of Asia? Broadening the question is very illuminating because it increases the variation in institutions, culture, policies, and economic structure. Not only do we learn why some countries have experienced little economic growth; we also learn more about the sources of Western success.

The classical economists posed the growth question in global terms. One indicator of success was the real wage. Adam Smith (1776, 74–75, 91, 187, 206) was typical; he saw the world in terms of a wage ladder on which workers in northwestern Europe had the highest standard of living and workers in Asia had the lowest. "In Great Britain the wages of labour seem, in the present times, to be evidently more than what is precisely necessary to enable the labourer to bring up a family." Workers' living standards were even a bit better in the Low Countries: "The wages of labour are said to be higher in Holland than in England." Within Britain, England was above Scotland: "Grain, the food of the common people, is dearer in Scotland than in England. . . . The price of labour, on the contrary, is dearer in England than in Scotland." However, in Scotland, "labour is somewhat better rewarded than in France." Asia lagged far behind Europe: "The real price of labour, the real quantity of the necessaries of life which is given to the labourer . . . is lower both in China and Indostan . . . than it is through the greater part of Europe." Smith saw the maritime centers of southern England and the Low Countries as having the highest real wages. Real wages were lower on Britain's Celtic fringe. Most of continental Europe also lagged behind the mercantile leaders, and Asia was at the bottom of the wage ladder. That was where wages were at the physiological minimum, in the classical view.

During the nineteenth century, the mainstream explanation of these facts was demographic. Malthus believed that population expands until birth and death rates are equal. The wage that corresponded to that outcome was the "subsistence" wage, which was just enough to allow parents to raise children and for the population to reproduce itself without expanding. In the original, positive check version of his theory, the birth rate was always at its maximum while mortality declined as wages rose. Under these circumstances, the subsistence wage had to be low enough to push mortality up to equal the high birth rate. In the later, preventive check version of the theory, fertility also declined as income dropped, and this modification meant that births and deaths equaled each other at a higher subsistence wage. The wage in a society, therefore, depended on whether the positive or the preventive check predominated. That was a question of marriage customs, law, and what Malthus called habit.

Malthus (1803, 116, 124, 251–252) applied the model by arguing that "habits" differed between Europe (in particular, England) and Asia. In England "the preventive check to population operates with considerable force throughout all the classes of the community." The sons of farmers and tradesmen deferred marriage "till they are settled in some business or farm, which may enable them to support a family." Even the laborer "will hesitate a little before he divides that pittance [of a wage] among four or five" family members. Late marriage restrained fertility and kept the English wage high. In Asia, on the other hand, several customs led to early and universal marriage, and that practice meant that the positive check reigned, and wages were lower than in Europe. Ancestor worship, the expectation that children would support their parents in old age, and infanticide all meant that China was "more populous, in proportion to its means of subsistence, than perhaps any other country in the world." Malthus entertained the possibility that Hindu asceticism depressed fertility (a preventive check) but concluded, "From the prevailing habits and opinions of the people there is reason to believe that the tendency to early marriages was still always predominant." As a result, "the lower classes of people [in India] were reduced to extreme poverty. . . . The population would thus be pressed hard against the limits of the means of subsistence, and the food of the country would be meted out to the major part of the people in the smallest shares that could support life." Disaster was never far away. "India, as might be expected, has in all ages been subject to the most dreadful famines."

Radicals, on the other hand, explained the income ladder in terms of geography, technology, social structure, and political organization. Marx (1853, 339) saw irrigation as "the sine qua non of farming in the East" for two reasons. First, there were "the vast tracts of desert, extending from the Sahara, through Arabia, Persia, India and Tartary, to the most elevated Asia highlands." These dry lands could be made fertile if water were supplied, so "artificial irrigation by canals and waterworks" became "the basis of Oriental agriculture." Second, in river valleys "as in Egypt and India" as well as China, periodic "inundations were used for fertilizing the soil." Water was periodically released on the land, and for that "advantage is taken of a high level for feeding irrigative canals" (331). Thus, both the potentially fertile deserts and the rich river valleys required extensive and elaborate water control systems to achieve maximal fertility. In the West the need for irrigation or water control "drove private enterprise to voluntary association, as in Flanders and Italy." However, in Asia, "where civilization was too low and the territorial extent too vast to call into life voluntary association, the interference of the centralizing power of government" was called into play. The state in Asia took on the job of administering a vast system of public works, which required a class of civil servants, notably the mandarins in China.

The state administration of irrigation had two effects, both of which were detrimental to economic growth. First, the production of agriculture and thus the economy as a whole depended on the performance of the bureaucracy. "In Asian empires we are quite accustomed to see agriculture deteriorating under one government and reviving again under some other government. There the harvests correspond to good or bad governments, as they change in Europe with good or bad seasons" (Marx 1853, 332). In Asia agriculture "is not capable of being conducted on the British principle of free competition, of laissez-faire and laisser-aller" (332). The result was a certain passivity: "The Hindu...like all Oriental peoples" left "to the central government the care of the great public works, the prime condition of his agriculture and commerce" (333).

Marx saw Asian society as composed of atomistic villages under the sway of a despotic state that determined their prosperity by the quality of its administration. Each village combined agriculture with textile production through hand processes. "Those family-communities were based on domestic industry in that peculiar combination of hand-weaving, hand-spinning and hand-tilling agriculture which gave them self-supporting power" (335). These villages were the "solid foundation of Oriental despotism," and they also stifled the rational acquisitiveness that propelled capitalism forward: "They restrained the human mind within the smallest possible compass, making it the unresisting tool of superstition, enslaving it beneath traditional rules, depriving it of all grandeur and historical energies" (335). But there was cause for hope: The "old Asiatic society" would be destroyed by "English steam and English free trade." Modern capitalism would drive India forward (335, 337).

Whichever explanation is favored, the classical view presumed that there were large and persistent differences in preindustrial living standards. This mattered because they cumulated. Prosperity in Europe guaranteed that most people had a small surplus that could be invested in human or physical capital formation. These investments explain the rise of the West (Jones 1981).

Recently, however, this view has been challenged by World System theorists (Frank 1998; Blaut 1993) and the California School of economic historians. Pomeranz (2000), Laveley and Wong (1998), Wong (1997), and Lee and Wang (1999) question both the traditional explanations for Europe's lead and the existence of the lead itself. In a provocative observation Pomeranz (2000, 49), for instance, speculated: "It seems likely that average incomes in Japan, China, and parts of southeast Asia were comparable to (or higher than) those in western Europe even in the late eighteenth century." These revisionists generally affirm that there were no important differences between Asia and Europe in demography, market institutions, or property rights. The great divergence is usually traced to the advantages Europe received from its colonies in the Americas. Had the Americas not existed—a geographical accident—the great divergence would not have happened.

While China has been the main battleground of the revisionists, India has also figured in the discussion. K. N. Chaudhuri (1985), Bayly (1989), and Prakash (1998) extolled India's highly developed commercial culture and extensive trade. These features of preindustrial economic organization are often assumed to cause "Smithian growth" and high incomes. In an important contribution to measurement, Parthasarathi (1998, 82) claimed that "South Indian labourers had higher [real] earnings than their British counterparts in the eighteenth century and lived lives of greater financial security."

These contributions have set the terms of the debate, and a debate there has been. On the one hand, Allen, Bengtsson, and Dribe (2005) reported income and demographic results that support the revisionist view. Clingingsmith and Williamson (2005) charted and explained India's deindustrialization in the eighteenth century, and Keller and Schiue (2004a; 2004b) compared the degree of market integration in eighteenth century Europe and China and found them roughly comparable. On the other hand, Broadberry and Gupta (2006) denied that the standard of living in India and England were similar, as did Bassino and Ma (2004) in comparing Japan and Europe, and Allen et al. (2005) in comparing China and Europe. It is fair to say that many more salvos will be fired before the issue is decided.

There are two types of problems that make it difficult to gauge the performance of preindustrial Asian economies, and this chapter addresses both in the context of India. A basic problem is lack of data. There is a long tradition of writing price histories of cities in Europe, and these provide one of the fundamental types of information for measuring European performance (another type being anthropometric evidence). To make progress on Asia, we need to put together comparable figures. These include the prices of major commodities in the various regions of the subcontinent as well as factor returns like wages, salaries, land and house rents, and interest rates. This chapter makes a start, for it is based on a data set of the prices of the principal foodstuffs and other consumer goods. These are used to measure the real incomes of unskilled laborers and textile workers. While this information is more extensive than has been used previously to address quantitative questions in Indian economic history, there are many gaps in the series, and they tend to fade into sporadic information as one moves back in time. Much work, therefore, remains to be done to complete the price and wage history of India. The present chapter represents a progress report based mainly on published material, albeit often from obscure sources.

The calculations reported here highlight a second, conceptual problem in the assessment of Indian economic performance, and that is the definition of the standard of living. The nub of the problem is that Asians and Europeans consumed very different baskets of goods, in particular, food. Not only were the basic starches different—wheat and rye versus rice and millet—but Europeans ate foods that were either naturally more expensive sources of nutrients (e.g., meat versus beans) or were more expensive because they were more highly processed (e.g., beer). Did these differences arise because Asians had a "taste for vegetarianism," or were Asians simply poorer than Europeans? A lot turns on the answer because it has a big impact on relative living standards.

Wages in Europe and Asia

Before we can compare real wages, we must establish the levels of nominal wages in India and Europe. The most widely available European wages are those of building craftsmen and laborers. I have collected their wage rates for a large sample of cities from the Middle Ages to the nineteenth century (Allen 2001). For international comparison, these must be expressed in a uniform standard, so I have converted all the wages to their silver equivalent. This is normal practice as silver coins were the most common medium of exchange in Asia as well as Europe.

Wages have been collected for India from a variety of secondary and governmental sources.[1] I have divided India into four regions—east, south, west, and north. The east is Bengal, the south is the Coromandel region around Madras and Pondicherry, the west includes Bombay, Puna, and vicinity, and the north refers to Rajasthan, Gujarat, Agra, and Delhi. Wages of unskilled occupations, variously called laborers, coolies, and peons, and so forth, are included as well as the earnings of weavers, which were very similar to the others. The wages of agricultural laborers are excluded because they frequently included food, whose value was not recorded. (In this regard it is important that the earnings of the weavers, who were paid entirely in cash, were very close to the wages of the other workers in the unskilled category.) All the wage quotations in each region were pooled to form four regional series of unskilled wages.

From 1873 onward, the four regional series could be extended into the twentieth century with the wages reported annually for about 220 administrative districts in *Prices and Wages in India*. Usually, the wages of an agricultural laborer, a horse keeper, and a carpenter were reported for each district. A representative district was chosen for each of the four regions, and the wage of the horse keeper was taken as representative of the wage of unskilled workers. In this way, we can trace the history of unskilled wages from the seventeenth century—indeed for Agra from 1595—to the twentieth.

Wages in India were quoted in two currencies. The most common was the rupee, which was used in the east, north, and west. It was a silver coin containing 10.78 grams of silver throughout the period. Computing silver wages from rupees was therefore simple. In southern India, however, wages and prices were denominated in pagodas, which was a gold coin. East India company exchange rates were used to convert pagodas to rupees and silver (K. N. Chaudhuri 1978, 471).

There were differences between Europe and India relating to the usual term of employment. In Europe workers were hired by the year, in which case they received most of their income as room and board, which is very hard to value, or by the day, when they were often paid entirely in cash.

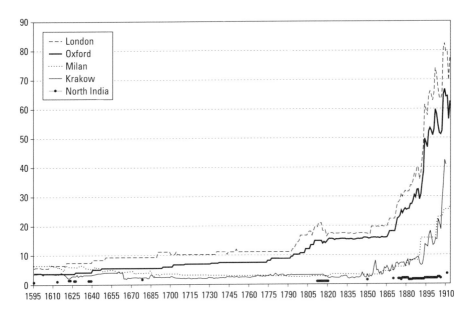

Figure 1.1
Nominal wages (grams of silver per day), Europe and India, 1595–1913.

Here I am concerned only with the latter. When annual earnings are computed for welfare comparisons, a full year's work is taken to be 250 days.
In India wages were typically quoted per month rather than per day.
Comparison with the few daily quotations suggests that monthly earnings
were 30 times the daily wage. Fortunately, the number of days that someone worked per month is not necessary for most calculations of this chapter, which focus on full-time earnings per year. These were assumed to be
12 times the monthly earnings.

Figure 1.1 establishes the broad outlines of the history of nominal
wages. The figure shows the daily wage of laborers in grams of silver.
One Indian series (for northern India) is shown, and the daily wage is
computed from the monthly quotations assuming that all 30 days were
worked. Several features stand out:

• Silver wages were lower in India than in Europe. Wages were highest in
the economically advanced parts of northwestern Europe (Oxford and
especially London) and lower in the backward regions (Krakow and
Milan). Wages in those cities were still double those in northern India,
although that premium would be cut if one assumed the Indian wage
applied to fewer than 30 days.

• The premium that northwestern Europe enjoyed over the rest of Europe and India widened over time, presumably as productivity growth accelerated (Broadberry and Gupta 2006).

• There was comparatively little trend in the Indian series. There was mild inflation in the seventeenth century and some deflation in the second half of the eighteenth and early nineteenth. Wage inflation became important only from 1870 onward.

Comparison with Europe indicates that India was a low-wage and rather static economy.

The series of northern Indian wages shown in figure 1.1 is broadly representative of India as a whole, although there were differences between regions. To greatly oversimplify the matter, between 1600 and 1850 the typical Indian laborer earned 3 rupees per month, which works out to about 1 gram of silver or 2 British pence per day. Wages tended to be lower than this—on the order of 0.8 grams of silver per day—in Bengal and the Coromandel. Wages were higher than 1 gram, occasionally as much as 1.5 grams, in western India. Wages tended to rise slowly in most regions in India between the seventeenth and mid-nineteenth centuries. After 1870 wage inflation increased.

A regression analysis was used to explore patterns in the wage data (table 1.1). The analysis is confined to the period before consistent annual

Table 1.1
Regression Analysis of Indian Wages, 1595–1870

	Regression 1	Regression 2	Regression 3
Constant	1.3505	1.3604	1.3832
	(44.216)	(50.869)	(32.85)
North	−0.1739	−0.1915	−0.1970
	(−2.875)	(−3.614)	(−3.675)
East	−0.5261	−0.5354	−0.5535
	(−9.739)	(−11.326)	(−10.271)
South	−0.1437	−0.1908	−0.2031
	(−2.887)	(−4.348)	(−4.293)
Date	0.0014	0.0012	0.0011
	(5.501)	(5.437)	(3.974)
Datesq			−0.00000216
			(−0.702)
Parthas		1.3397	1.3290
		(8.865)	(8.741)
R^2	.43	.57	.57

Note: The dependent variable is the daily wage or daily earnings in grams of silver. T-ratios are in parentheses. There are 258 observations in all regressions.

data were collected by the government of India and before the rapid inflation that began in 1870. In regression 1, the daily wage was regressed on
dummy variables representing the regions East, North, and South; the
dummy for the west is excluded, so its mean value is captured by the intercept, and the coefficients of the three regional dummies in the regressions represent deviations from the western level. These variables all
proved significant and had plausible coefficients. Wages were systematically highest in the west and lowest in the east. Also included is a time
trend called Date, which is equal to the year minus 1750. Its coefficient
indicates slow wage inflation throughout the period. To test whether inflation was accelerating or decelerating, Datesq, the square of Date, is
included in regression 3. However, Datesq always proves to be statistically insignificant, indicating no rise or fall in the rate of wage inflation.

Equations 2 and 3 also include a variable Parthas, equal to 1, for the
earnings quoted by Parthasarathi in support of his view that weavers in
India could purchase as much grain as weavers in England. The weavers
that he describes were in south India. He reports earnings in the eighteenth century from 1.5 to 2.5 pagodas per month. These figures correspond to 1.7 to 3.2 grams of silver per day on a 30-day month.
Comparison with other wages suggests that these were very high figures.
That impression is confirmed by the large and statistically significant
coefficient of Parthas in equations 2 and 3. Parthasarathi (1998; 2001)
attributes the high earnings of Coromandel textile workers in the first
half of the eighteenth century to the profusion of buyers of cloth—Asian
merchants plus the East India companies of several European countries—
and the collective organization of the weavers. By the end of the century,
England's defeat of France in the Seven Years' War and extension of the
English East India Company's hegemony in the region reduced competition on the demand side of the cloth market and broke the power of the
weavers' organizations. The East India Company was undoubtedly
pleased to be able to drive labor earnings in the Coromandel down to
the level in Bengal.

Welfare Ratios with a European Basket

Did the high silver wages of European workers translate into a higher
standard of living than in India? To answer that question, we need to
know the quantities and prices of the goods workers consumed. We can
approach this from both high-wage and low-wage perspectives, and they
both prove illuminating.

Table 1.2
Consumer Price Index: Basket of Goods, India

		Nutrients/Day	
	Quantity/Person/Year	Calories (g)	Protein (g)
Bread	182 kg	1,223	50
Beans/peas	52 L	160	10
Meat	26 kg	178	14
Butter[a]	5.2 kg	104	0
Cheese	5.2 kg	53	3
Eggs	52 each	11	1
Beer[a]	182 L	212	2
Soap	2.6 kg		
Linen	5 m		
Candles	2.6 kg		
Lamp oil	2.6 L		
Fuel	5.0 M BTU[b]		
Total		1,941	80

Source: Allen (2001).
Notes:
a. Where oil and wine were consumed instead of butter and beer, 5.2 liters of olive oil were
substituted for the butter, and 68.25 liters of wine for the beer. 5.2 liters of olive oil yields
116 calories per day and no protein; 68.25 liters of wine yields 159 calories per day and no
protein.
b. Millions of BTUs.

I begin with the northern European consumption basket shown in table
1.2. It was originally developed for comparisons within Europe and was
inspired by European budgets and the weights conventionally used in
cost-of-living indices.[2] The diet is "medieval" in that it does not include
New World crops like potatoes, sugar, or tobacco. The budget in table
1.2 defines a "respectable" standard of living; it was relatively high-
wage, and many people survived on less. Nevertheless, the budget provides a starting point for comparing the purchasing power of wages
across Europe. To do that, some modifications are required to reflect
local tastes and food availability: rye bread was used in eastern and central Europe, whereas wheat bread was used elsewhere; beer was used in
northern Europe and wine in southern Europe. The guiding principle in
these substitutions was to keep the calorie, protein, and alcohol content
the same.

We can extend the framework to India, but we rapidly run into difficulties, for consumption patterns were very different. Indians ate little ani-

mal protein, and that was mainly confined to fish. Also, Indians did not consume much alcohol, nor did they buy bread from bakers, which was the way that urban Europeans got their main carbohydrate. Rice was the staple in eastern and southern India. Wheat was grown in the north and west, but it was a luxury item; common people consumed millet. Beans were widely consumed and were an important protein source. Some foods (e.g., cheese, beer, wine) and many of the nonfoods shown in table 1.2 did not feature in spending. On the other hand, most Indians consumed sugar.

The consumption pattern of the Indians is manifest in the prices that historians can find. The commodities whose prices were most readily available include rice, wheat, millet (jowar and bajra), beans (gram, boot gram, dal), sugar, mustard oil, and ghi (clarified butter). In no case do we have a continuous time series from 1595 to 1913, but the series were most complete in the regions where the commodity was most widely consumed. In addition, some series for some regions in restricted periods could be compiled for barley, mutton, fish, eggs, and firewood. The prices of these goods relative to more common products in India could therefore be established. I have found no prices for wine, beer, spirits, soap, or cheese. Information on the price of coarse cotton cloth (baftas) was also available for Gujarat and Bengal. Presumably prices were similar elsewhere in India in view of the low cost of shipping cloth relative to its value.

The next step in comparing standards of living in Europe and India was to compute the cost in India of the basket shown in table 1.2. This is a hazardous exercise because so many of the prices had to be estimated. Indian prices of bread and beer are not available. It was necessary to estimate them using regressions on European data. Allen (2001), for instance, reported a "bread equation" in which the price of bread was expressed as a function of the price of wheat or rye and the skilled wage rate. This equation was evaluated with India wheat prices and wages in order to calculate the price at which European-style wheat bread could have been produced on the subcontinent. Similarly, a "beer equation" was estimated from European data and used to estimate the price at which beer might have been produced in India in view of the country's prices of grain and labor. Meat, cheese, and eggs were assumed to sell at the same price per kilo, and missing values of these prices, of which there were many, were estimated from the price of meat and eggs relative to grains, where that could be established. The price of firewood was dealt with similarly. Cloth prices were assumed to be the same in all regions of India.

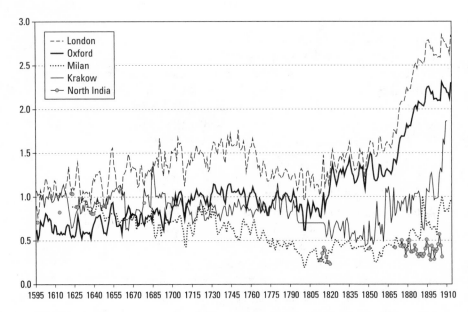

Figure 1.2
Welfare ratios (European respectability), Europe and India, 1595–1913.

In constructing a price index, we must bear in mind its intended use. In this study, we want to know whether a man employed full-time over a year could earn enough to support himself and his family. The basket in table 1.2 defines a standard of consumption that specifies "enough." The basket provides 80 grams of protein and 1,941 calories per day, which is taken as the nutritional norm for an adult male European. More nutrition was needed to support his wife and several children. Based roughly on the calorie requirements for men and women of different ages, the standard of consumption for a family is taken to be three baskets like table 1.2. Raising the cost of the basket by 5 percent to allow for rent implies that the cost of supporting a family at a standard of living like that of a man consuming the basket in table 1.2 is 3.15 times the cost of that basket.

Were laborers' wages in Europe and India high enough to allow them to purchase the lifestyle of table 1.2? The answer is in figures 1.2 and 1.3, which show welfare ratios for regions of Europe and India. A welfare ratio is equal to full-time, full-year earnings divided by the cost of living for a family for a year (i.e., 3.15 times the cost of the basket in table 1.2). Welfare ratios greater than 1 indicate that laborers were prosperous enough to buy that lifestyle, whereas ratios less than 1 indicate insufficient purchasing power. As figure 1.2 indicates, wages were high enough in

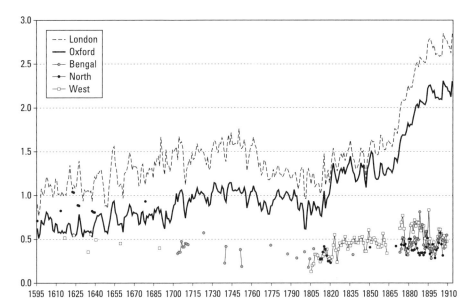

Figure 1.3
Welfare ratios (European respectability), England and India regions, 1595–1913.

London at all times and in Oxford in the eighteenth century for laborers to buy the lifestyle of table 1.2. In Milan and Krakow wages were insufficient. This pattern generalizes: laborers in the booming maritime centers of Britain and the Low Countries had welfare ratios over 1 in the eighteenth century, whereas their counterparts elsewhere on the continent did not.

Figure 1.2 shows the welfare ratio of laborers in northern India, and the situation in other regions is shown in figure 1.3. Two conclusions stand out. First, in the seventeenth century, Indian workers came close to being able to buy the lifestyle defined in table 1.2. Indeed, their standard of living was like that of workers in Europe. Second, the situation changed in the eighteenth century as real earnings slumped on much of the European continent while remaining steady or rising in northwestern Europe. Indian wages also slumped, and the decline in northern India, for instance, closely followed the pattern in Milan. Consequently, a substantial gap emerged between living standards in northwestern Europe in the early nineteenth century and those in central and eastern Europe and India. The gap widened in the late nineteenth century as real wages took off in Europe. In India they rebounded, but only to their seventeenth-century level.

Welfare Ratios with a Subsistence Basket

How did Indians and Europeans survive with welfare ratios below 1? The answer is that they shifted their diets to cheaper grain and cut their protein consumption. "It appears from contemporary accounts that the articles in the diet of the common people in most parts of India consisted chiefly of rice, millets and pulses" (Raychaudhuri and Habib 1982, I, 164). Palsaert, who visited India in the early seventeenth century, called the Indian diet "monotonous." In the Delhi-Agra region the people "have nothing but a little kitchery [kedgeree] made of green pulse mixed with rice ... eaten with butter in the evening, in the day time they munch a little parched pulse or other grain." The workmen "know little of the taste of meat." Indeed, pigs, cattle, chickens, and eggs were all taboo. Where available, fish was the only source of animal protein. It was a similar story in western India. Wheat was not eaten by the laboring population, whose main source of carbohydrates was millet. This was ground into a coarse flour and fried up as chapatis that were eaten with pulses and vegetables. Lockyer (1711, 258), who toured Asia in the early eighteenth century on the East India Company ship *Streatham*, observed of the Arab sailors in the Indian Ocean, "They serve for small Wages, and are Victual'd at a much cheaper Rate than our Ship's Companys: Salt-fish, Rice, Gee, and Doll, with a few Fowls, being all the Provisions they care for. Doll is a small Grain, less than Fetches, contains a Substance like our white Peas, and being boil'd with Rice makes Kutcheree."

The restricted character of consumption was also pronounced in other areas. Generally, Indians went barefoot. Contemporary accounts emphasize "the scantiness of clothing." For much of the year, men wore little more than a loin cloth and women a sari. Houses were mud huts with thatched roofs. The peasants and workers had few furnishings besides bamboo mats and cots. Metal pots and utensils were rare, and much cooking was done in earthen pots (Raychaudhuri and Habib 1982, I, 459–462). It was hard to spend less money on one's lifestyle than this.

It was a similar story in Europe. The poor narrowed their spending to food, went without meat, and ate "inferior grain." In the eighteenth century in northern Europe that was often oats, the cheapest source of carbohydrates. Oats, eaten both as bread and porridge, predominated in the low-wage parts of Britain, the northern English counties and Scotland. Dr. Johnson exaggerated only a little when he remarked that oats were "a grain which in England is generally given to horses but in Scotland

Table 1.3
Subsistence Income: Baskets of Goods, India

	Rice			Millet		
	Quantity/ Person/ Year	Nutrients/Day		Quantity/ Person/ Year	Nutrients/Day	
		Calories (g)	Protein (g)		Calories (g)	Protein (g)
Oats						
Rice	164 kg	1,627	34			
Millet				209 kg	1,731	63
Bread						
Beans/peas	20 kg	199	11	10 kg	100	5
Meat	3 kg	21	1	3 kg	21	1
Butter/ghi	3 kg	72	0	3 kg	72	0
Cheese						
Eggs						
Beer						
Sugar	2 kg	21	0	2 kg	21	0
Soap						
Cotton	3 m					
Candles						
Lamp oil						
Fuel						
Total		1,940	46		1,945	69

supports the people." That was what they could afford on their miserable incomes.

To see if shifting the diet to the cheapest grain was a viable survival strategy, we need to specify the spending pattern exactly and cost it out. Consider Indian workers first, for they suffered from very low welfare ratios in the early nineteenth century. To see how they survived, a subsistence budget is defined in table 1.3. Superfluous purchases have been eliminated, and the food is mainly confined to the cheapest cereals—rice in east and south India, millet in north and west India. Each diet, however, still gives about 1,941 calories per day. Protein intake is less with the other diets: 69 grams per day in the case of the millet-based diet and 46 grams with the rice-based diet. These protein levels, however, are adequate in terms of twenty-first-century norms. The U.S. Recommended Daily Allowance for protein is 0.8 grams per day per kilogram of ideal body weight. An Indian man who was 165 cm tall and who had a body-mass index of 20 (in the middle of the normal range) would have weighed

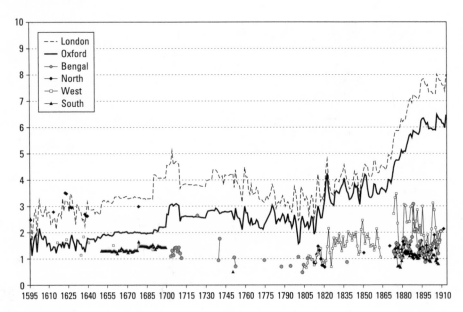

Figure 1.4
Welfare ratios, subsistence baskets, 1595–1913.

54.45 kg and required 43.56 grams of protein per day. The lower protein intake, therefore, does not signal malnutrition in India but extraordinarily high protein consumption in the prosperous parts of northwestern Europe.

Could Indian workers have purchased the subsistence diet? The test is to see if the welfare ratio, computed with respect to the subsistence budgets in table 1.3, equaled 1. Figure 1.4 shows Indian welfare ratios computed in this way. These ratios are all higher than those in the previous graphs because the subsistence diet cost less than the others. The same secular trends are apparent here: relatively high values in the seventeenth and early eighteenth century followed by a decline into the early nineteenth century and then a return to the seventeenth-century levels by the 1870s. No long-term improvement here. Laborers' incomes were clearly adequate to purchase the subsistence diet in the seventeenth century and the late nineteenth. In the early nineteenth century, the welfare ratio fluctuated around 1, indicating that in good years there was more than enough money to purchase the consumption basket, but in bad years there was not. Taken at face value, figure 1.4 suggests that in bad years Indian laborers borrowed in order to stay alive and then paid back the loans in the good years. The graph suggests that this system worked—just.

What figure 1.4 indicates is that Indian wages in the early nineteenth century were high enough for Indians to remain alive. Since the calories and grams of protein they consumed were similar to European levels, one might conclude that the standard of living of Indians and Europeans was the same, making allowance for different cultural preferences with respect to food. That would appear to be the import of figure 1.4, but it is a conclusion that misses many aspects of the standard of living.

The subsistence diet was specified to minimize the cost of getting 1,941 calories per day. The European diet in table 1.2 was not constructed in the same way, for it reflected what Europeans actually ate and not the least-cost way of surviving. What would a European subsistence diet have been? It would have relied on oats, the cheapest grain. The oats would have been eaten as a gruel or porridge rather than ground and baked into bread, for boiling the whole grain would have avoided nutritional losses in milling. The subsistence diet would also probably have included legumes, as in India. This diet is not fantastical because many Europeans living in peripheral, backward areas—the Scottish highlands, for instance—ate like that. Even in northern England and Wales in the first half of the eighteenth century, most bread was made of oats, barley, or rye; wheat bread was scarce (Deane and Cole 1969, 63–64).

Table 1.4 specifies a European subsistence diet that is the counterpart of those shown for India. It supplies the same number of calories, and indeed slightly more protein, than the meat- and beer-laden diet in table 1.2 because oats are protein-rich.

The cost implications of the oat-based diet are extreme: it cost about one-third of the cost of the "normal" European diet we began with. The cost savings emphasize the high cost of bread, beer, meat, and cheese as sources of calories and proteins. Since it was so cheap, English workers had no trouble purchasing this diet; indeed, in the seventeenth century, their income was double the cost of the subsistence diet. By the twentieth century, income was about eight times subsistence.

Comparison of Indian and English living standards with subsistence income baskets reinforces the conclusions implied by the European respectability baskets in figures 1.2 and 1.3. A very important point is that Indian and English living standards were similar in the seventeenth century. The highest earners (those in London and north India) had incomes three or four times subsistence; workers in Oxford and west India reached welfare ratios of about 2. Starting in the mid-seventeenth or early eighteenth century at the latest, Indian welfare ratios fell behind English ratios, and by the mid-eighteenth century, Indian ratios dropped to about

Table 1.4
Subsistence Income: Basket of Goods, Europe

		Nutrients/Day	
	Quantity/Person/Year	Calories (g)	Protein (g)
Oats	166 kg	1,774	77
Rice			
Millet			
Bread			
Beans/peas	5 kg	47	4
Meat	5 kg	34	3
Butter/ghi	3 kg	60	0
Cheese	3 kg	31	2
Eggs			
Beer			
Sugar			
Soap	2.6 kg		
Linen	5 m		
Candles	2.6 kg		
Lamp oil	2.6 L		
Fuel	5.0 M BTU[a]		
Total		1,946	86

Note:
a. Millions of BTUs.

1, that is, Indian workers could barely purchase the subsistence basket. England had opened up a large lead over India in living standards, and it increased during the nineteenth century.

What were English workers buying? They spent much of their extra income on food *quality* (Allen et al. 2005). Calories and protein are only two aspects of food. Everyone probably tries to get enough calories to avoid feeling hungry. If incomes rise above that, some money may be spent on more calories or even nonfood goods, but much of the increase is devoted to improving the quality of the food. In Europe this meant meat, cheese, bread, and alcohol. English laborers had the purchasing power to do that; Indian laborers, by and large, did not. The command over high-quality food is a measure of Europe's lead over Asia.

Superlative Indices and Real Income Comparisons

Welfare ratios (with culturally adjusted food baskets) are a common method of comparing living standards in the preindustrial world. They have revealed the importance of food quality as an indicator of well-being. Welfare ratios force us to focus on the different culinary practices of Europe and Asia. Another methodology requiring the same regard are conventional real wage calculations using superlative price indices as the deflators. This methodology turns out to give similar conclusions as the welfare ratios.

The real wage approach to comparing living standards involves dividing the ratio of European to Asian nominal wages (actually, annual earnings) by the ratio of European to Asian prices. The latter ratio is measured as an index number of European prices relative to Asian. Here I use a Fisher Ideal Index. This index is the geometric average of two component indices. The first looks at the world from a European perspective: The cost of a European basket of goods is computed with European and with Asian prices, and the European cost is divided by the Asian cost. The constituents of this approach were already developed when the cost of the European consumption basket in table 1.2 was computed in both Britain and India.

The second component index in the Fisher Ideal looks at the world from an Asian perspective. The cost of an Asian basket of goods is computed with both European and Asian prices, and the ratio of costs is obtained. I develop two versions: one for east and south India and the second for north and west India. This approach is based on the rice and millet subsistence budgets in table 1.3. While I have already computed their cost in India, their cost in English prices must now be determined. From 1659 onward, the cost of rice in London is available (Beveridge 1939, 432–433), so the cost of the rice diet can be computed. The millet diet is more difficult because millet was not sold in Britain. I use the price of oats, the inferior grain, as a proxy for the price of millet.

Figure 1.5 shows real annual earnings of laborers in London and in Oxford relative to their counterparts in east and north India. (There is little difference between these results and comparisons with south and west India.) The comparisons between England and north India span the whole period. In the seventeenth century, average real earnings in London were slightly above the north Indian level, and earnings in Oxford were slightly below. This finding corroborates the earlier conclusions based on welfare ratios. Figure 1.5 shows that England pulled ahead of India in the eighteenth century, and the lead was extended in the nineteenth. Calculations for Bengal in the eighteenth century confirm the generality of this pattern. Analyzing the wage data in the framework of superlative price indices gives historical results that are similar to those supported by welfare ratios.

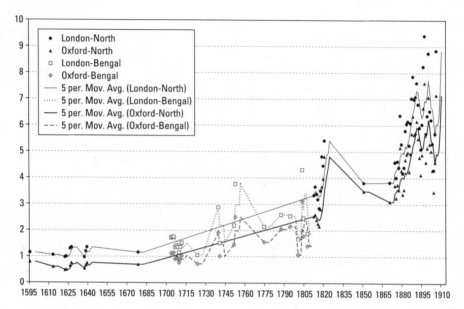

Figure 1.5
Real wage comparisons, fisher ideal price index, 1595–1913.

Conclusion

This chapter supports a more dynamic view of relative living standards in Europe and Asia than either the traditionalists or the revisionists maintain. The revisionist view is sustained for the seventeenth century because real annual earnings look similar in India and England in the period. If this result proves robust, it calls into question the grand classical theories of the great divergence. Malthus's contention that England and India had different demographic systems that equilibrated at different incomes is beside the point if the income levels were the same. Similarly, Marx's ideas about the hydraulic state and the static village are undermined by similar economic outcomes in Europe and Asia. Similarity in income in the early modern period points to less fundamental causes of the great divergence.

It is not all smooth sailing for the revisionists, however. Parity in income was not maintained in the eighteenth century, for the standard of living fell in India. By 1800, England had a big lead in living standards, much as the classical economists maintained. The great divergence began earlier than revisionist historians contend. The collapse of the Mogul Empire and the extension of British hegemony are obviously potential explanations for the fall in Indian income, and world empire may have played a role in the rise of English income, as the revisionists maintain. The income comparisons of this chapter suggest that economic success and failure owed more to policy than to fundamentals. Policy explanations are intrinsically contingent: History could easily have turned out otherwise. These explanations raise a dark possibility: Maybe the rise of the West was fundamentally an accident.

Notes

I would like to thank Roman Studer for excellent research assistance and Jan Luiten van Zanden for data on cotton prices in Gujarat.

1. The Indian wages and prices used here were collected from the following sources: *Accompaniements Nos. 1 to 9* (1864); Arasaratnam (1980; 1986); Brenning (1975); Broadberry and Gupta (2006); S. Chaudhuri (1975); Divekar, Indukar, and Vilangekar (1989); Dutt (1906); Gupta (1937); Haider (2004); Hariharan (2002); Hassan and Gupta (1967); Hossein (1988); Hussain (1976); Kinloch (1852); Mitra (1978); Mizushima (1986); Montgomery (1849); Mukerjee (1939); Parthasarathi (1998; 2001); Prakash (1985); *Prices and Wages in India 1893–1910* (1920); Raju (1941); Raychaudhuri and Habib (1982); Shattacharya (1954); Siddiqi (1981); *Statistical Abstract Relating to British India, 1867–1922*; Van Santen (1953).

2. See Allen (2001), who also details the sources of the data used for the European side of the comparison.

References

Accompaniements Nos. 1 to 9 to the Letter from the Bombay Government to the Government of India, No. 1184, dated 8th July, 1864.

Allen, R. C. 2001. The Great Divergence in European Wages and Prices from the Middle Ages to the First World War. *Explorations in Economic History* 38: 411–447.

———. 2003. Poverty and Progress in Early Modern Europe. *Economic History Review* 56 (3): 403–443.

———. 2005. Real Wages in Europe and Asia: A First Look at the Long-Term Patterns. In *Living Standards in the Past: New Perspectives on Well-Being in Asia and Europe*, ed. R. C. Allen, T. Bengtsson, and M. Dribe. Oxford: Oxford University Press.

Allen, R. C., J.-P. Bassino, D. Ma, C. Moll-Murata, and J. L. van Zanden. 2005. Wages, Prices, and Living Standards in China, Japan, and Europe, 1738–1925. GPIH (Global Price and Income History Group) Working Paper 1, University of California, Davis. ⟨http://gpih.ucdavis.edu/Papers.htm gpih.ucdavis.edu/⟩.

Allen, R. C., T. Bengtsson, and M. Dribe. 2005a. Introduction. In *Living Standards in the Past: New Perspectives on Well-Being in Asia and Europe*, ed. R. C. Allen, T. Bengtsson, and M. Dribe. Oxford: Oxford University Press.

———, eds. 2005b. *Living Standards in the Past: New Perspectives on Well-Being in Asia and Europe*. Oxford: Oxford University Press.

Arasaratnam, S. 1980. The Handloom Industry in Southeastern India, 1750–1790. *Indian Economic and Social History Review* 17 (3): 257–281.

———. 1986. *Merchants, Companies, and Commerce on the Coromandel Coast, 1650–1740*. Delhi: Oxford University Press.

Bassino, J.-P., and D. Ma. 2004. Japanese Wages and Living Standards in 1720–1913: An International Comparison. In *Proceedings of the International Institute of Social History Conference, Utrecht.*

Bayly, C. A. 1989. *Imperial Meridian: The British Empire and the World, 1780–1830.* London: Longman.

Beveridge, Sir W. 1939. *Prices and Wages in England from the Twelfth to the Nineteenth Century.* London: Longmans, Green.

Blaut, J. M. 1993. *The Colonizer's Model of the World: Geographical Diffusionism and Eurocentric History.* New York: Guilford.

Brenning, J. J. 1975. The Textile Trade of Seventeenth Century Northern Coromandel. Ph.D. diss., University of Wisconsin, Madison.

Broadberry, S., and B. Gupta. 2006. The Early Modern Great Divergence: Prices, Wages, and Economic Development in Europe and Asia, 1500–1800. *Economic History Review* 59: 2–31.

Chaudhuri, K. N. 1978. *The Trading World of Asia and the English East India Company.* Cambridge: Cambridge University Press.

———. 1985. *Trade and Civilisation in the Indian Ocean: From the Rise of Islam to 1750.* Cambridge: Cambridge University Press.

Chaudhuri, S. 1975. *Trade and Commercial Organization in Bengal, 1650–1720: With Special Reference to the English East India Company.* Calcutta: K.L. Mukhopadhyay.

Clingingsmith, D., and J. G. Williamson. 2005. Mughal Decline, Climate Change, and Britain's Industrial Ascent: An Integrated Perspective on India's 18th and 19th Century Deindustrialization. NBER (National Bureau of Economic Research) Working Paper 11730. ⟨http://www.nber.org/papers/W11730⟩.

Deane, P., and W. A. Cole. 1969. *British Economic Growth, 1688–1959: Trends and Structure.* 2d ed. Cambridge: Cambridge University Press.

Dermigne, L. 1964. *Le commerce à Canton au xviiie siècle, 1719–1833.* Paris: SEVPEN.

Diewert, W. E. 1976. Exact and Superlative Index Numbers. *Journal of Econometrics* 4: 115–145.

Divekar, V. D., S. V. Indukar, and A. Vilangekar. 1989. *Hundred Years of Commodity Prices in Pune Market.* Pune, India.

Dutt, R. 1906. *The Economic History of India under Early British Rule.* 2d ed. London: Routledge and Kegan Paul.

Frank, A. G. 1998. *ReOrient: Global Economy in the Asian Age.* Berkeley: University of California Press.

Gupta, R. B. 1937. *Agricultural Prices in the United Provinces.* Allahabad, India.

Haider, N. 2004. Prices and Wages in India, 1200–1800: Source Material, Historiography and New Directions. In *Proceedings of the International Institute of Social History Conference, Utrecht.*

Hamilton, A. 1744. *A New Account of the East Indies.* London.

Hariharan, S. 2002. *Cotton Textiles and Corporate Buyers in Cottonpolis: A Study of Purchases and Prices in Gujarat, 1600–1800.* Delhi: Manak Publications.

Hassan, S. N., and S. P. Gupta. 1967. *Price of Food Grains in the Territory of Amberö.* Patiala, India: PIHC.

Horrell, S., and J. Humphries. 1992. Old Questions, New Data, and Alternative Perspectives: Families' Living Standards in the Industrial Revolution." *Journal of Economic History* 52: 849–880.

Hossein, H. 1988. *Company Weavers of Bengal: The East India Company and the Organization of Production in Bengal, 1750–1813.* Delhi: Oxford University Press.

Hussain, A. 1976. A Quantitative Study of Price Movements in Bengal during Eighteenth and Nineteenth Centuries. Ph.D. diss., University of London.

Jones, E. L. 1981. *The European Miracle: Environments, Economies, and Geopolitics in the History of Europe and Asia.* Cambridge: Cambridge University Press.

Keller, W., and C. H. Shiue. 2004a. Market Integration and Economic Development: A Long-Run Comparison. NBER (National Bureau of Economic Research) Working Paper 10300. ⟨http://www.nber.org/papers/W10300⟩.

———. 2004b. Markets in China and Europe on the Eve of the Industrial Revolution. NBER (National Bureau of Economic Research) Working Paper 10778. ⟨http://www.nber .org/papers/W10778⟩.

Kinloch, C. W. 1852. *Statistical Report of the District of Futtehpore.* Calcutta.

Landes, D. S. 1998. *The Wealth and Poverty of Nations: Why Some Are So Rich and Some So Poor.* New York: W.W. Norton.

Laveley, W., and R. B. Wong. 1998. Revising the Malthusian Narrative: The Comparative Study of Population Dynamics in Late Imperial China. *Journal of Asian Studies* 57: 714–748.

Lee, J., C. Campbell, and G. Tan. 1992. Infanticide and Family Planning in Late Imperial China: The Price and Population History of Rural Liaoning, 1774–1873. In *Chinese History in Economic Perspective*, ed. T. G. Rawski and L. Li. Berkeley: University of California Press.

Lee, J., and F. Wang. 1999. *One Quarter of Humanity: Malthusian Mythology and Chinese Realities, 1700–2000*, Cambridge, Mass.: Harvard University Press.

Lockyer, C. 1711. *An Account of the Trade in India.* London.

Malthus, T. R. 1803. *An Essay on the Principle of Population.* 2d ed. The 6th ed., with introduction by T. H. Hollingsworth, published London: J.M. Dent, 1973.

Marx, K. 1853. "The British Rule in India" and "The Future Results of British Rule in India." In *The Portable Karl Marx*, ed. E. Kamenka, 329–341. New York: Penguin, 1983.

Mitra, D. 1978. *The Cotton Weavers of Bengal, 1757–1833.* Calcutta: KLM.

Mizushima, T. 1986. *Nattar and the Socio-economic Change in South India in the 18th–19th Centuries.* Tokyo.

Morse, H. B. 1926–1929. *The Chronicles of the East India Company Trading to China, 1635–1834.* Oxford: Clarendon Press.

Montgomery, Sir R. 1849. *Statistical Report of the District of Cawnpoor.* Calcutta.

Morgan, S. L. 1998. Biological Indicators of Change in the Standard of Living in China during the 20th Century. In *The Biological Standard of Living in Comparative Perspective*, ed. J. Komlos and J. Baten, 7–34. Stuttgart: Franz Steiner.

Mukerjee, R. 1939. *The Economic History of India, 1600–1800.* London: Longmans, Green.

Parthasarathi, P. 1998. Rethinking Wages and Competitiveness in the Eighteenth Century: Britain and South India. *Past & Present* 158: 79–109.

———. 2001. *The Transition to a Colonial Economy: Weavers, Merchants, and Kings in South India, 1720–1800.* Cambridge: Cambridge University Press.

Pomeranz, K. 2000. *The Great Divergence: China, Europe, and the Making of the Modern World.* Princeton: Princeton University Press.

Prakash, O. 1985. *The Dutch East India Company and the Economy of Bengal, 1630–1720.* Princeton: Princeton University Press.

———. 1998. *European Commercial Enterprise in Pre-Colonial India.* Cambridge: Cambridge University Press.

Prices and Wages in India, 1893–1910. 1920. Calcutta.

Raju, A. S. 1941. Economic Conditions in the Madras Presidency, 1800–1850. Ph.D. diss., University of Madras, India.

Raychaudhuri, T., and I. Habib, eds. 1982. *The Cambridge Economic History of India.* Vol. 1, *c. 1200–c. 1750.* Cambridge: Cambridge University Press.

Sandberg, L. G., and R. H. Steckel. 1980. "Soldier, Soldier, What Made You Grow So Tall?" *Economy and History* 23: 91–105.

Shattacharya, S. 1954. *East India Company and the Economy of Bengal.* London: Luzac.

Siddiqi, A. 1981. Money and Prices in the Early Stages of Empire: India and Britain, 1760–1840. *Indian Economic and Social History Review* 18: 231–262.

Smith, A. 1776. *An Inquiry into the Nature and Causes of the Wealth of Nations,* ed. E. Cannan. New York: Modern Library, 1937.

Statistical Abstract Relating to British India, 1867–1922. London: HM Stationery Office.

Van Santen, H. W. 1953. De Vereinigde Oost-Indische Compagnie in Gujarat en Hindustan. Ph.D. diss., University of Leiden.

Wittfogel, K. A. 1957. *Oriental Despotism: A Comparative Study of Total Power.* New Haven, Conn.: Yale University Press.

Wong, R. B. 1997. *China Transformed: Historical Change and the Limits of European Experience.* Ithaca, N.Y.: Cornell University Press.

2 What Made Britannia Great? How Much of the Rise of Britain to World Dominance by 1850 Does the Industrial Revolution Explain?

Gregory Clark

By 1850, at the apogee of its power, Britain had 1.8 percent of world population. The area of the British Isles is less than 0.2 percent of the world land mass. Yet Britain then strode as a colossus on the world political, military, and economic stages. It had extensive colonial possessions, including Ireland, much of modern India, Pakistan, Bangladesh, and Sri Lanka, Canada, Australia, New Zealand, the Cape Colony in South Africa, Belize, Jamaica, Trinidad, and Guyana. Its navy was the largest in the world, by design larger than the next two largest navies combined. In 1842 it humiliated the proud Chinese empire, forcing it to cede Hong Kong and to allow the British to ship opium into China. By 1860 the British and French had captured Beijing and forced even more degrading terms on the empire.[1]

Even where it did not exert formal control, Britain considerably influenced the economic policy of many states, as in the Indian subcontinent. Britain was so confident of its manufacturing prowess that it pursued both within its formal empire and beyond a policy of free trade, even though many of its trading partners had far lower wages. Thus Britain supported Brazilian independence from Portugal in return for preferential trade privileges, and used the threat of force in both Egypt and Persia in 1841 to persuade these states to grant it free trade.[2]

The ascendance of this minor country on the northwest corner of Europe, which in 1700 had a population about one-third that of France, and about 4 percent that of both China and India, to the position of power it occupied by 1850 is often seen as being largely the result of the Industrial Revolution, which occurred in Britain after 1760. Thus Kennedy (1983, 150–151) wrote,

[The Industrial Revolution] was to provide the foundation for the country's continuing and increasing growth, making it in to a new sort of state—the only real world power at the time. Industrialization not only furthered the British supremacy in commerce and finance and shipping, it also underpinned its own naval supremacy with a previously unheard-of economic potential.

He states even more bluntly, "Britain enjoyed effortless naval supremacy in the years following 1815" in part because its competitors "possessed an industrial strength that was infantile by comparison" (157). The eventual decline of Britain's political and military position is similarly traced to the decline of its economic position. "Whether historians date the beginnings of imperial decline from about 1870 or after 1914, they associate it almost exclusively with the steady erosion of Britain's industrial supremacy" (Cain and Hopkins 1986, 502).

However, Britain in the years 1760–1860 experienced two completely different, and independent, revolutionary changes. The first, of course, was the famous Industrial Revolution based on technological advance in industry. But the second was a population explosion that has been dubbed by some the Demographic Revolution. This growth in population occurred all across the English economy with equal force, from the centers of the new revolutionized industry to the remotest rural backwater.[3] It began just before the discoveries in cotton textiles that date the beginnings of the Industrial Revolution in the late 1760s. But there is no direct link between population growth and the unusual technological growth of England in this era.

Here I argue that for most of the ways in which the Industrial Revolution mattered for the British position in the world—relative living standards compared to Britain's competitors, relative economic output, relative military capacity—the technological gains of the Industrial Revolution were irrelevant. Suppose efficiency (TFP) in both industry and agriculture in the 1860s had stayed exactly as it had been in the 1730s. This would have significantly reduced living standards in England by the 1860s compared to their actual level. But it would have little affected Britain's *relative* position in the world economy, its income relative to its competitors such as France or the Netherlands. The size of the industrial sector would have been nearly as large, and the degree of urbanization nearly as great. Britain would have still shifted in the late eighteenth century from near autarky toward great reliance on raw material imports paid for by manufactured exports. That shift would in turn have given the political impetus for formal and informal imperialism, and the desire to maintain a strong navy to protect vital shipping routes.

If, however, England's population had stayed at its 1730s level, then even with significant technological advance, most of the features of the

Industrial Revolution era would not be replicated. With a population size in 1815 of closer to 6 than to 12 million, the defeat of Napoleon would have been more difficult, even with the classic productivity growth of the Industrial Revolution. A Britain with smaller population in 1860 would have been much more agricultural, more rural, less urbanized. Crucially it would have engaged in much less international trade. Thus one of the great driving forces for nineteenth-century imperialism, the need to assure markets for Britain's great manufacturing exports, and to assure raw material supplies for the British economy, would have been absent. The supply of officials, police, and soldiers to govern Britain's colonial possessions would similarly have been reduced, as would the supply of convict labor to people Australia.[4] Even with the same rate of TFP advance in each industry, the overall rate of productivity growth for the economy would have slowed significantly had a population boom not accompanied the Industrial Revolution.

This chapter is not the first to consider such counterfactuals. Mokyr (1999, 114–115) considered what income per person would have been in England in 1830 absent technological advance. His conclusion, however, was that technological change was likely more important to income levels than is suggested by the model developed here. More recently Crafts and Harley (2004) carried out a related counterfactual exercise, for the shorter period 1770–1841, which focused just on what most importantly caused the shift of the labor force in Britain out of agriculture in the Industrial Revolution: population growth, unbalanced technological progress in industry, or labor-releasing institutional change in agriculture. Their conclusion, contrary to the one here, is that population growth played a very minor role in reducing the share employed in agriculture by 1841. Instead, they conclude, in line with O'Brien (1996), that it was the (alleged) switch in Industrial Revolution England from peasant to capitalist agriculture, which substantially increased labor productivity in agriculture, that accounted for most of the structural shift. I show that this conclusion stems from their assumption that absent population growth, nonfarm prices would have risen significantly relative to farm prices. I also explain why the assumption made here, that the relative prices observed in the 1860s would be the same at a smaller British population, is the right one.

English Economic History, 1730s–1860s

Table 2.1 shows the basic facts of the English economy from the 1730s to the 1860s, as constructed from new data on prices, wages, land rents, and

Table 2.1
The Basics of Growth, England, 1730s, 1860s

Variable	1730–1739	1860–1869
Population (millions)	5.8	21.1
Farm[a] efficiency	100	121
Nonfarm[a] efficiency	100	160
p_{NF}/p_F	1.00	0.716
Farm share of employment	0.55	0.24
Land rent/GDP (%)	20.6	6.9
GDP	100	548
GDP per person	100	149
Efficiency (TFP)	100	145
Farm share output	0.50	0.20
Farm output	100	176
Farm output per person	100	48
Nonfarm output	100	980
Nonfarm output per person	100	269
Farm imports/GDP	0.0	0.22
Farm consumption per person	100	102
Nonfarm consumption per person	100	297
Farm share of consumption	0.50	0.42
Real income/N	100	141
Urban share (%)	15	62

Sources: Nominal output is estimated as a combination of the estimates of Clark (1998; 1999; 2001; 2002a; 2002b; 2002c; 2005; 2007) and Clark and Jacks (2007) on farmland, property, wage, and capital incomes. Real outputs are estimated from the prices from Clark (2004) and Clark and Jacks (2007) for farm and coal, and unpublished series for other prices. Efficiencies are estimated as the ratio of costs to prices in each sector and nationally. Population is from Wrigley et al. (1997).
Note:
a. Farm includes the coal industry. Nonfarm is the economy minus farm and coal.

returns to capital.[5] Total nominal income is calculated for the economy as a whole and for the farm sector. This income was deflated by various different price indices, calculated as detailed in appendix B, to calculate the growth of GDP, farm output, nonfarm output, and income.[6]

England moved from an agrarian autarkic economy in the 1730s to a largely industrialized open economy in the 1860s. From the 1730s to 1860s population increased to more than 3.5 times its level in the 1730s, mainly from the increased birth rate. Yet agricultural output increased by

Table 2.2
Farm Consumption per Person in England, 1700s, 1860s

	1700–1709	1860–1869
Population (millions)	5.51	21.15
English farm net output (£ millions)	63.1	107.2
Net food imports (£ millions)	2.2	75.2
Net raw material imports (£ millions)	−1.3	62.7
Domestic coal consumption (£ millions) (at pithead price)	1.7	17.5
Total food, energy, and raw material consumption (£ millions)	65.7	262.6
Consumption per person (£)	11.9	12.4
Imports as a share of consumption (%)	1	53

Sources: Farm output, Clark (2002c); coal, Flinn and Stoker (1984, 26), Church (1986, 19, 53, 85–97). Pithead prices, Clark and Jacks (2007). Trade 1860–1869, Parliamentary Papers (1870), Mitchell (1988, 221–222); trade 1700–1709, Schumpeter (1960, tables 7, 9, 10, 12, 13, 15, 17).
Note: Cotton, wool, flax, and silk retained for home consumption are estimated by subtracting the raw material content of textile exports, estimated using figures given in Deane and Cole (1967). The import figures are for the United Kingdom, but it is assumed that on net these all went to England (Ireland was supplying food imports to England, which I assume equaled its share of food and raw material imports).

only 54 percent. Thus farm output per person in England in the 1860s was only 42 percent of its level in the 1730s.[7] This domestic farm output was supplemented by two main sources of the goods traditionally produced by the farm sector. First were imports of food and raw materials. Second was English coal output. Thus by the 1860s England depended heavily on food and raw material imports, and on locally mined coal, to supply the food, raw materials, and energy its population required. Table 2.2 shows the food, energy, and raw materials account for the 1700s, where the situation would be very similar to the 1730s, and the 1860s. In the 1700s the economy had few net raw material imports (sugar and spices were being imported, but wool in woolen goods exported). These had swollen to 22 percent of income by the 1860s.

Since coal was a close substitute for wood energy produced in the farm sector in what follows, and in table 2.1, I amalgamate domestic coal production with farming output (coal production in this period was very similar to farming, involving a lot of digging and human hauling of materials, except done underground). Valuing coal output at pithead prices increases farm output per person in the 1860s to 48 percent of the level of the 1730s, as compared to 42 percent. This is the number reported in table 2.1.

England paid for imported food and raw materials mainly through exporting manufactures. As Temin (1997) noted, these included not just

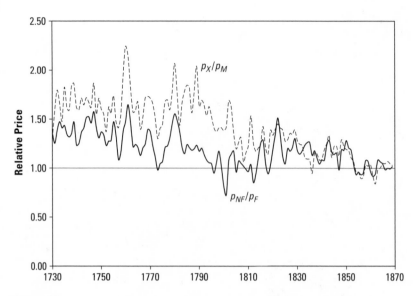

Figure 2.1
Terms of trade between farm and nonfarm output, England, 1730s–1860s. Farm prices from
Clark (2004), Clark and Jacks (2007). Nonfarm prices, import prices, and export prices are
unpublished calculations of the author from the sources listed in Clark (2005).

the classic textiles and iron and steel of the new Industrial Revolution
industries, but a host of products from industries that are not believed to
have experienced significant technological advances. Together other manufactures were about 22 percent of all exports. With this rise in exports
nonfarm output rose nearly tenfold between the 1730s and 1860s. England truly became the workshop of the world.

Relative prices changed in England over these years, as relative produc-
tivities in different sectors of the economy changed. The price of nonfarm
output relative to farm output fell to 72 percent of its earlier level. Figure
2.1 shows the price of English-produced nonfarm items relative to the
price of farm output, and the price of English exports relative to imports.
Export prices declined even more relative to import prices.

Importantly for what follows the decline in the relative price of nonfarm to farm goods closely echoed the observed changes in relative pro-
ductivities across the two sectors. Thus in a competitive market for each
product, i, the price will be

$$p_i = \frac{r_i^{a_i} w_i^{b_i} s_i^{c_i}}{A_i}$$

where r is the return on capital, w the wage, s land rents, A the TFP of the sector, and a, b, and c the shares of each input in costs. The relative price of nonfarm versus farm products will thus be

$$\frac{p_{NF}}{p_F} = \frac{A_F}{A_{NF}} \frac{r_{NF}^{a_{NF}} w_{NF}^{b_{NF}} s_{NF}^{c_{NF}}}{r_F^{a_F} w_F^{b_F} s_F^{c_F}}$$

Over the Industrial Revolution era agricultural efficiency increased by only 21 percent, and coal mining efficiency growth was also modest (Clark 2002c; Clark and Jacks 2007). Efficiency growth was concentrated in the nonfarm, nonmining sector, where it is estimated at 60 percent. Thus the relative prices of nonfarm goods fell only slightly more than their relative productivity within England. The reason that relative price movements in the Industrial Revolution were largely predictable from relative TFP levels is that capital rents, wages, and land rents moved in similar ways over the years 1730–1870. Thus the different shares of these factors in the farm and nonfarm sectors made little difference to relative prices.

These relative price movements also imply that the productivity gains of the Industrial Revolution mainly went to consumers rather than to entrepreneurs in the revolutionized sectors. Importantly these consumers lived abroad as well as at home.

We can portray this transformation of England between the 1730s and 1860s, summarized in table 2.1, using production possibilities frontiers (PPFs). Figure 2.2 shows outputs and consumption in each period, and the associated relative price lines.

British History, 1730s–1860s, A Simple Model

What would Britain have looked like in the 1860s without the Industrial Revolution? To consider this counterfactual I employ the simple model detailed in appendix A. There are just two goods, farm (including coal) and nonfarm, and only two inputs, land and labor.[8] Farm, but not nonfarm, output requires land. Britain in the 1730s is assumed self-sufficient with no net imports of farm products. I am not, however, assuming that the economy in the 1730s was closed to international trade. The assumption is just that the relative more equal land endowments of England and the other European states as of the 1730s, as portrayed in table 2.3, limited the possibilities of trade.

The six parameters of the model—α, β, A_F, A_{NF}, θ, and H—are chosen so that the crucial features of the 1730s economy are reproduced: the

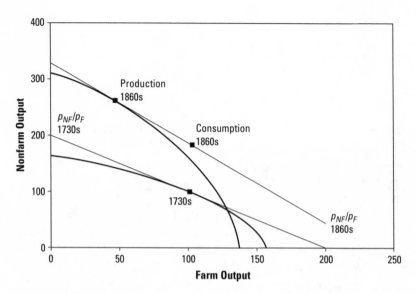

Figure 2.2
The change in the English economy, 1730s–1860s.

share of land rents in total output, the share of employment in each sector, the share of output from each sector, the absence of significant farm imports, and the income elasticity of farm output demand.

Fitting the model to these data for the 1730s requires setting all six parameters, leaving no degrees of freedom to adjust the results for the 1860s. Thus the model cannot precisely fit the actual situation in the 1860s. Once population, A_F, A_{NF}, and the labor share in agriculture were set for the 1860s, all the other variables were constrained. Thus, as will be seen by comparing the last column of table 2.1 with the second column of table 2.4, the model only approximates the key parameters in the 1860s. In particular, the price of nonfarm output relative to farm is 0.674 as opposed to the correct value of 0.716. However the fit with these parameters derived from the 1730s, as well as these efficiency changes, is still very good for the 1860s.[9]

The shift from the 1730s to the 1860s as estimated from this simple model looks just like figure 2.2. Thus this very simple model, parameterized for the 1730s economy, fits the gross outlines of the Industrial Revolution reasonably well. In the following sections I employ this model to ask what history would have looked like absent either the Demographic Revolution or the Industrial Revolution.

Table 2.3
Farmland and Population in England relative to Europe and the United States, 1730s, 1800s

	1730s	1800s	1860s
England			
Population (millions)	5.5	9.2	21
Farm area (million acres)	26	26	26
Acres/N	4.7	2.8	1.2
Western Europe[a]			
Population (millions)	83[b]	103	152
Farm area (million acres)[c]	317	317	317
Acres/N	3.8	3.1	2.1
Russia			
Population (millions)	42[b]	53	74
Farm area (million acres)[c]	702	702	702
Acres/N	16.7	13.2	9.5
U.S.			
Population (millions)	≈1	6.2	35
Farm area (million acres)	—	—	407
Acres/N	—	—	11.6

Sources: Food and Agriculture Organization of the United Nations (FAO) statistics database; Mitchell (1998).
Notes:
a. Western Europe includes Austria, Belgium, Denmark, Finland, France, Germany, Ireland, Italy, Netherlands, Norway, Portugal, Spain, Sweden, and Switzerland.
b. Estimated to be equal to the 1760s populations.
c. Based on modern areas from the FAO.

England in the 1860s without Productivity Growth

Suppose we abolished all the productivity growth of the Industrial Revolution era. What would England look like in the 1860s? To answer this we need to crucially answer what would be the relative price of industrial as opposed to farm goods in that case in the 1860s.

I assume that this would stay as in the 1730s. The justification for this is that the English price relativity in the 1730s seems to have been close to the European price ratio. Indeed, food prices were low enough in England that in some years in the early eighteenth century there were grain exports. And English demand and supply of food and raw materials was a small share of European and North American demand. Table 2.3, for example, gives data illustrating the smallness of England relative to just Europe and North America in terms of farm area and population in these

Table 2.4
England in the 1860s under Two Alternative Counterfactuals

Variable	Baseline	No Industrial Revolution	No Population Growth
Population (millions)	21.1	21.1	5.8
Farm efficiency	121	100	121
Nonfarm efficiency	160	100	160
p_{NF}/p_F	0.674	1.00	0.674
Farm share of employment	0.24	0.30	0.48
Land rent/GDP (%)	8.7	10.7	17.7
GDP	528	329	152
GDP per person	145	90	152
Efficiency (TFP)	145	100	139
Farm share output	0.21	0.26	0.43
Farm output	171	167	110
Farm output per person	47	46	110
Nonfarm output	982	477	214
Nonfarm output per person	270	131	214
Farm imports/GDP	0.26	0.35	0.02
Farm consumption per person	107	94	114
Nonfarm consumption per person	181	83	207
Farm share of consumption	0.47	0.53	0.45
Real income/N	135	94	144

years. It also shows the enormous addition of farmland and woodland in the United States to the effective European land stock in the late eighteenth and early nineteenth centuries. The farm area of England by the 1860s was less than one-tenth that of the rest of Western Europe, and only about 2 percent of the combined area of all areas shipping food to England.

Thus without an Industrial Revolution there is no reason to expect farm prices to have become higher relative to nonfarm prices in England by the 1860s compared to the 1730s. Instead the addition of the farm areas of North America would, if anything, have increased nonfarm prices in England relative to farm, leading to even greater industrialization than predicted here.

With the assumption of an unchanged price ratio, figure 2.3 shows the predicted outcome for the economy with no Industrial Revolution. What

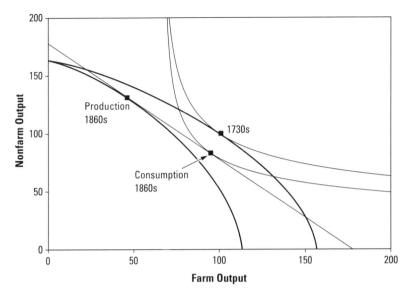

Figure 2.3
England in the 1860s without the Industrial Revolution.

is remarkable is that apart from the lower level of industrial output per person, England looks just the same in the 1860s without an Industrial Revolution than it did with it. Table 2.4 shows the detailed predicted values of various features of the economy. The share employed in farming (including coal) is predicted to have fallen sharply from 55 percent to 30 percent, compared to the actual fall to 24 percent. Land rents fall from 21 percent of income to 11 percent, creating exactly the decline in the economic position of the traditional landed ruling classes as was actually witnessed.

Imports supply as large or larger a share of farm consumption by the 1860s, at 57 percent. Industrial production rises sharply to pay for these food, raw material, and energy imports, so that total industrial output is nearly five times its level of the 1730s, despite the absence of productivity advances. This shift to industrial production would have produced the rise in towns and cities in England that was witnessed in the Industrial Revolution era. The need to pay for food and raw materials with exports of manufactured product would have supplied the same impetus as before, given the protectionist tendencies of independent states such as the United States to use military power to ensure access to markets through a process of formal and informal imperialism.

Incomes per person would, of course, have been significantly lower in this case than they were in practice in the 1860s, and indeed about 6 percent lower than they were in the 1730s. But in terms of Britain's position relative to its competitors—France in particular—the absence of the Industrial Revolution would make modest differences. For the competitive nature of product and labor markets, and the very poor protection of property rights in new techniques in the Industrial Revolution era, meant that there was little extra gain to those areas and people who devised more effective production techniques in the cases where the outputs were tradable. The main gainers from the improved techniques of the Industrial Revolution were the consumers of the products, and it did not matter whether these consumers were in England, in Ireland, or in the Netherlands or France.

This can be illustrated in several ways. First consider what happened to real wages in the Industrial Revolution period in the north versus the south of England. Figure 2.4 shows that these two regions had very different productivity growth rates in these years. The north, with its heavy em-

Figure 2.4
Efficiency growth rates in north and south England, 1770–1869. The north is Cumberland, Northumberland, Westmorland, Lancashire, Durham, Yorkshire, and Cheshire. The aggregate productivity growth of England was split into the contribution from north and south by attributing all productivity growth in cotton and wool textiles to the north and correspondingly reallocating farm productivity growth. Same sources as for table 2.1.

phasis on the revolutionized sectors of cotton, linen and wool textiles, saw rapid productivity growth. The south, which was much more heavily involved in agriculture, in government, and in services, witnessed very little productivity growth at all. In many ways the south of England had the same relationship to the Industrial Revolution as France or the Netherlands. It was a bystander. Corresponding to this difference in productivity growth was a difference in population growth as labor migrated south to north, and from Ireland to the north. Thus from 1801 to 1841 the north had a 103 percent gain in population, but the south only a 71 percent gain.

But despite the huge difference in productivity growth rates, and the evidence of labor migration, wages in the north rose little relative to those in the south. Figure 2.5 shows the relative wage in the north versus the south for building workers and farm workers from the 1760s to 1860s. Wages in the north increased relative to those in the south by only 11 percent in the mainly urban building industry and 25 percent in agriculture. The great majority of the Industrial Revolution productivity gains in the north went to consumers all across England, and indeed across the world, in the form of lower prices. There was a relatively elastic supply of labor and capital from traditional industries, from agriculture, and from non-revolutionized regions into the flagship industries of the Industrial Revolution. Consequently the efficiency advances went to consumers.

Evidence of this can be found in the movement of real wages in Ireland compared to England in these years. Ireland had few of the high

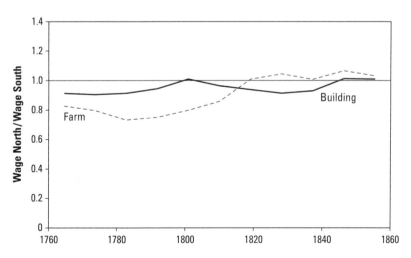

Figure 2.5
Wages in the north vs. the south in the Industrial Revolution. From Clark (2001; 2005a).

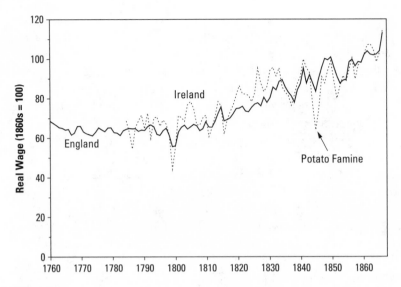

Figure 2.6
Real wages in England and Ireland, 1760s–1860s. From Clark (2005a, 1324–1325), Geary and Stark (2004).

productivity growth industries of the Industrial Revolution, except for linens. By the nineteenth century its main exports were agricultural products sent to England in exchange for industrial goods: clothing, housewares, machinery. Its labor market, as measured by the much lower wage in Ireland than in England, was less integrated with that of the high productivity growth region of northern England than was the rest of England. Yet, as figure 2.6 shows, real wages, as measured for building workers in Ireland, grew just as fast as those in England, even in the years before the famine of 1845 when Ireland's population was growing fast.

Finally, we can do a very rough comparison on income per person from 1600 on for England and the Netherlands. Figure 2.7 shows that comparison, using both my estimates of English real income per person and the GDP estimates of Crafts and Harley (1992) for 1700–1831 and Deane and Cole (1967) for 1831–1871. Any gains in English income compared to the Netherlands would show up in the decades after the 1780s, since there was no significant TFP advance in England as a result of the Industrial Revolution until the 1790s. Yet between the decade of the 1780s and the 1860s, in an interval when income per person in England rose 53 percent as a result of the Industrial Revolution, income per person in the Netherlands relative to England fell by only 12 percent. Income per cap-

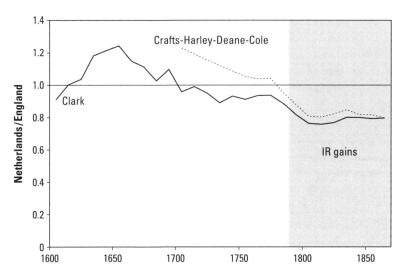

Figure 2.7
Income per person, the Netherlands versus England, 1600–1869. Income per person in England: same sources as for table 2.1; Crafts-Harley-Deane-Cole from Crafts and Harley (1992); Deane and Cole (1967). Smits, Horlings, and van Zanden (1999) estimated Dutch GDP from 1807 to 1913. De Vries (2000) tentatively carries these estimates back to 1600. Dutch GDP per capita in 1913 is assumed to be 79 percent that of England, based on Prados de la Escosura (2000).

ita in the Netherlands rose 39 percent as a result of the Industrial Revolution, almost as much as in England. Britain gained little compared to either Ireland or the Netherlands as a result of the technological advances of the Industrial Revolution, and I suspect the same may be true of other countries such as France. So the loss in England's comparative position in Europe—in terms of total output relative to its competitors—from the absence of an Industrial Revolution would be small. The gains of the Industrial Revolution were being exported to England's competitors, either in the form of more favorable terms of trade for English industrial goods or in the form of the use of the knowledge itself for production in these countries.

Thus Britain in the nineteenth century, absent the technologies of the Industrial Revolution, would not have been significantly poorer compared to its European competitors.

But could it have achieved the same domination outside Europe with a GDP that was one-third lower in the 1860s, without steam power, and without cheap iron and steel for European weapons? Here it is important to emphasize that naval power remained based on sailing ships until surprisingly late in the Industrial Revolution. The first steam-powered ocean-going warship, the French *Le Napoléon*, did not enter service until 1852. This was still a wooden ship. The modern iron-hulled armored battleship came only with the British *Warrior*, which entered service in 1861. So until 1850 naval ships would have looked very similar with no Industrial Revolution.

Similarly the triumph of the British Navy in the Napoleonic War era was achieved not mainly by technological advantages that the Industrial Revolution conferred on British ships, but by the greater sailing abilities of the British, and their ability to deliver a much higher rate of fire from their guns (Kennedy 1983, 123–128; Baugh 2004). In part these abilities came from the large numbers of British merchant seamen the Royal Navy could draw on from their normal employment in coastal and foreign shipping. But the switch to an industrial economy created by population growth even absent the Industrial Revolution would have created similar increases in the volume of British merchant shipping after 1760.

English History, 1760–1860, without the Demographic Revolution

Alternatively, what would have happened if the Industrial Revolution had occurred in an England that maintained after 1740 the population stability that had characterized it for the hundred years before 1740? To consider this counterfactual, I fix population in the 1860s in the model detailed in appendix A to its value in the 1730s. I assume productivity advance by sector was the same as in the actual Industrial Revolution, as were relative farm and nonfarm prices.

The prices are kept at those of the actual 1860s prices on the basis of the preceding discussion that relative price movements in the Industrial Revolution era seem to have depended mainly on relative productivity movements. A smaller population in England by the 1860s would have reduced farm product demands for the European and North American suppliers of England. But given the population sizes of Britain versus its trading partners, shown in table 2.3, the effect would have been minimal.

The results are shown in figure 2.8 and detailed in the last column of table 2.4. Now farm production within England is close to farm consumption, so that there is little net export of industrial goods or net import of farm produce. The share of the labor force in the farm sector at 48 percent is close to the share in the 1730s. England in these respects looks much as it did in the 1730s.[10]

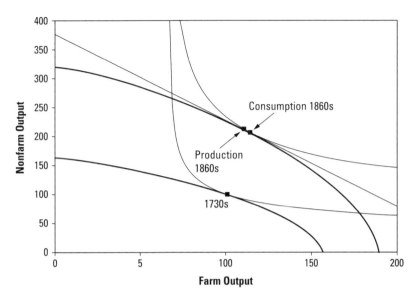

Figure 2.8
England in the 1860s without population growth.

Real income would increase somewhat more than it did with this model when population growth accompanied the Industrial Revolution (44 percent versus 35 percent) because of the greater amount of land per person. But GDP increases by only 52 percent overall, compared to 229 percent under the alternative counterfactual of not productivity gains but substantial population growth. Similarly, total industrial production increases more from population growth than from the productivity advances of the Industrial Revolution per se.

The economywide growth of TFP would have been lower without population growth, even though the growth rates in each sector were the same. This is because the national TFP growth rate is

$$g_{TFP} = \sum_i \eta_i g_{TFP_i}$$

where i indexes subsectors of the economy, and η_i their share in value added in the economy. In the model economy TFP grows 21 percent in farming and 60 percent in industry. But the increase in the relative size of the farming sector without population growth reduces overall TFP growth from 45 percent to 39 percent. Thus though there was no direct connection between population growth and the TFP advance of the Industrial Revolution, indirectly population growth contributed more to TFP advance in Britain in the Industrial Revolution than did most of the innovators celebrated in the conventional histories of the period. Population growth alone increased national productivity advance by more than 15 percent.

In this connection we also see that another factor leading to greater measured rates of TFP advance in England in the Industrial Revolution era that appears in this model is the low share of the population in England already, by the 1730s, engaged in farm production. At 55 percent this was low by the conventional standards for preindustrial economies, where we typically find 70 percent to 80 percent of the population engaged in farming. English incomes in the 1730s were high for a preindustrial economy because England in the years 1600–1740 followed a strong version of the European Marriage Pattern, which significantly limited fertility (see Wrigley et al. 1997). In the Malthusian world before 1800, England was unusually wealthy, and consequently the farm share in consumption was low.

Even with the sectoral productivity growth rates of the Industrial Revolution, without the demographic changes England in the 1860s would have had much less trade with the rest of the world, and hence much less incentive to maintain and defend bases on these trade routes and to secure access for its manufactures to markets across the world. Thus Britain's outward orientation in the nineteenth century, its engagement with the rest of the world, can be attributed much more to unusual population growth than to unusual development of technology.

Conclusion

Britain by 1850 was the envy of nations. It had high living standards, extensive colonies, extensive informal political influence, and the biggest navy in the world. There is a tendency to think that the explanation of the relative economic and political success of Britain by 1850 must lie with the technological advances of the Industrial Revolution.

Here I have argued to the contrary that very little of the position of Britain in 1850 is directly explained by such things as innovations in textiles. High British incomes relative to its competitors were probably mainly achieved before the Industrial Revolution. Insofar as economic forces influenced the political and military successes of Britain, the one that mattered more in the competition with the other European states was population growth, not technological advance. Further, the transformation of Britain from the 1730s to the 1860s from a heavily agrarian economy dominated politically by the landed classes to the urban, industrialized economy of the 1860s again depended almost entirely on population advances. Finally, the outward orientation of the economy, with huge volumes of imports and exports, and a substantial merchant navy, with the political and military consequences that entailed, again was created by population growth, not technological advance.

Thus it seems that Britain's rise to world dominance was a product more of the bedroom labors of British workers than of their factory toil.

Appendix A: The Model

Production

There are two sectors in the model economy, farm and nonfarm. The production functions for these, per capita, are

$$q_{NF} = A_{NF} n_{NF}^a$$

$$q_F = \frac{A_F n_F^b}{N^{1-b}}$$

where n_{NF} is the share of labor in the nonfarm sector, n_F the share in the primary sector (including coal). N is total population. Industry has no land constraint, but agriculture does. Since I assume that there is a perfectly elastic supply of capital at a constant real rate of return, r, capital in the industrial sector will be employed in fixed proportion to labor. That is why capital is not shown explicitly.

This implies that the production possibilities frontier (PPF) for England, measured in terms of outputs per person is

$$q_{NF} = A_{NF} \left[1 - \left(\frac{q_F}{A_F}\right)^{1/b} N^{(1/b)-1} \right]^a$$

The marginal rate of transformation (MRT) from farm into nonfarm output, the slope of the PPF at any level of q_F, is

$$\frac{dq_{NF}}{dq_F} = -\frac{p_F}{p_{NF}} = -\frac{a}{b} A_{NF} A_F^{-(1/b)} (Nq_F)^{(1/b)-1} \left[1 - \left(\frac{q_F}{A_F}\right)^{1/b} N^{(1-b)/b} \right]^a$$

The curvature of the MRT is determined by a and b. The larger these are, the less curvature. In the simulations b is taken as 0.750 on the basis of studies of English agriculture (Clark 2002c). To fit the empirical data in the 1730s with this simple model we also need to have $a = 0.614$. This is because the share of agriculture in the value of output, s_F, is

$$s_F = \frac{an_F}{an_F + bn_{NF}}$$

Since in the 1730s, $n_F = 0.55$, and $s_F = 0.50$, that in turn implies that $a = 0.614$.

The price of nonfarm relative to farm goods is

$$\frac{p_{NF}}{p_F} = \left(\frac{1 - s_F}{s_F}\right)\frac{q_F}{q_{NF}}$$

Consumption

The utility function of the representative consumer is

$$U(q_F, q_{NF}) = (q_F - H)^\theta q_{NF}^{1-\theta}$$

Taking agricultural output as the numeraire, the budget constraint is

$$y = q_F + p_{NF}q_{NF}$$

Maximizing utility subject to this constraint gives

$$q_F = \theta y + (1 - \theta)H, \qquad y \geq H$$

$$q_{NF} = \frac{(1 - \theta)}{p_{NF}}(y - H)$$

Thus the consumer is assumed to consume a minimum subsistence food amount H, then a constant share, θ, of income above H as food. At income $y = H$, only food is consumed. As income rises, the food share falls. θ was taken as 0.25 in the simulations.

With this specification the income elasticity of demand for farm and nonfarm outputs are

$$\eta_F = \frac{dq_F}{dy} \cdot \frac{y}{q_F} = \frac{\theta y}{\theta y + (1 - \theta)H} < 1$$

$$\eta_{NF} = \frac{dq_{NF}}{dy} \cdot \frac{y}{q_{NF}} = \frac{y}{y - H} > 1$$

At very high levels of income both income elasticities approach 1. At close to the subsistence level of food consumption, H, the income elasticity for food approaches θ, and that for industrial products approaches infinity. θ and H were chosen to make the income elasticity of demand for food in the simulation be about 0.5, in line with empirical estimates (Clark, Huberman, and Lindert 1995).

The price elasticities of demand are

$$\varepsilon_F = \frac{dq_F}{dp_F} \cdot \frac{p_F}{q_F} = -\frac{\theta}{s_F} > -1$$

$$\varepsilon_{NF} = \frac{dq_{NF}}{dp_{NF}} \cdot \frac{p_{NF}}{q_{NF}} = -\frac{(1-\theta)(y-H)}{s_{NF}} > -1$$

Again, as y gets very large, both price elasticities approach -1. At close to the subsistence level of food consumption H, the price elasticity for food is lower and approaches -0.25.

Appendix B: Price Indices for England, 1730–1869

Define the following price indices:

p_{FO} = price of final outputs of the English economy (retail prices)

p_{GDP} = price of gross domestic output

p_M = price of imports (wholesale prices)

p_X = price of exports

p_{DC} = price of domestic consumption (including investment)

p_F = price of domestic farm output (including coal)

p_{NF} = price of domestic nonfarm output

The price indices are calculated as geometric indices:

$$p_M = \prod_i p_i^{a_i}, \qquad p_{FO} = \prod_i p_i^{b_i}$$

where a_i and b_i are the shares, respectively, in import and export costs of each good, and $\sum_i a_i = \sum_i b_i = 1$.

For each price the annual rate of change is defined as

$$\pi = \frac{\dot{p}}{p}$$

Define θ as the ratio of the value of imports to GDP. Then

$$\pi_{\text{FO}} = \left(\frac{1}{1+\theta}\right)\pi_{\text{GDP}} + \left(\frac{\theta}{1+\theta}\right)\pi_{\text{M}}$$

$$\Rightarrow \quad \left(\frac{\dot{p}}{p}\right)_{\text{GDP}} = (1+\theta)\left(\frac{\dot{p}}{p}\right)_{\text{FO}} - \theta\left(\frac{\dot{p}}{p}\right)_{\text{M}}$$

$$\Rightarrow \quad \ln(p_{\text{GDP}}) = (1+\theta)\ln(p_{\text{FO}}) - \theta\ln(p_{\text{M}})$$

With this specification the GDP price index will be of the form

$$p_{\text{GDP}} = \prod_i p_i^{c_i}$$

where $\sum_i c_i = 1$, but the individual weights can be positive or negative. Negative weights will correspond to imported commodities.

Both the final output and import prices are measured as including all taxes and fees. By similar reasoning we can also establish that, where ϕ is the ratio of the value of imports to domestic consumption,

$$\pi_{\text{FO}} = \left(\frac{1}{1+\theta}\right)\pi_{\text{GDP}} + \left(\frac{\theta}{1+\theta}\right)\pi_{\text{M}} = \left(\frac{1}{1+\phi}\right)\pi_{\text{DC}} + \left(\frac{\phi}{1+\phi}\right)\pi_{\text{X}}$$

$$\Rightarrow \quad \pi_{\text{GDP}} = \left(\frac{1+\theta}{1+\phi}\right)\pi_{\text{DC}} + \left(\frac{\phi(1+\theta)}{1+\phi}\right)\pi_{\text{X}} - \theta\pi_{\text{M}}$$

$$\Rightarrow \quad \ln(p_{\text{GDP}}) = \left(\frac{1+\theta}{1+\phi}\right)\ln(p_{\text{DC}}) + \left(\frac{\phi(1+\theta)}{1+\phi}\right)\ln(p_{\text{X}}) - \theta\ln(p_{\text{M}})$$

If trade is in balance, so that the value of imports equals that of exports ($\theta = \phi$), then this simplifies to

$$\Rightarrow \quad \ln(p_{\text{GDP}}) = \ln(p_{\text{DC}}) + \theta\ln\left(\frac{p_{\text{X}}}{p_{\text{M}}}\right)$$

To calculate real GDP we thus just deflate total nominal incomes in the economy by the GDP deflator. To calculate real income we deflate by the Domestic Consumption deflator.

Farm versus Nonfarm

The rate of increase of the price of GDP can also be decomposed into the rate of increase of the price of domestic farm output and domestic nonfarm output, using the share of GDP that was domestic farm output. Thus,

$$\pi_{\text{GDP}} = \mu\pi_{\text{F}} + (1 - \mu)\pi_{\text{NF}}$$

I use this expression to calculate the movement of nonfarm prices from the movement of GDP prices, and that of farm output.

Notes

The data underlying this paper were compiled with the aid of National Science Foundation grants SES 91-22191 and SES 02-41376. I thank Tim Hatton, Kevin O'Rourke, and Alan Taylor for helpful editorial comments.

1. It is claimed that by 1855 Chinese tariff policy was firmly under British control, the only restraint on the British being the fear of toppling the current regime by pushing it too far.

2. The British and French similarly in 1845 intervened in Uruguay in support of a liberal regime that favored freer trade. Cain and Hopkins (1980, 479–481).

3. Wrigley et al. (1997, 182–194) show for their sample group of 26 reconstituted parishes that fertility increases were as great in those classified as rural as in those that were engaged in trade or industry.

4. Convicts were transported to Australia between 1788 and 1852. By 1840, Britain had shipped 111,000 convicts.

5. This data construction is still in part a work in progress, but the series are near enough to their final form to serve as a good preliminary basis for the following discussion.

6. These data differ in a number of ways from the well-known series of Crafts and Harley (1992) on output growth in Industrial Revolution England. In particular, there is less growth of farm output than Harley (1993) assumes in these years on the basis of CGE modeling of the Industrial Revolution (neither Crafts and Harley 1992 nor Harley 1993 has direct observations on farm output).

7. This claim, based on Clark (2002a) and Clark (2004), is controversial. Allen (1994), for example, suggests much more output growth. But it is founded on very strong estimates of the factor incomes and prices in agriculture in these years.

8. This is because capital is assumed supplied elastically at a fixed rate of return, so that with the production functions used, capital per worker in each sector remains the same.

9. Land rents as a share of income may seem low in the 1730s compared to the measured share of land rents, but the rent here is the pure site value of the land, and that in England was much less than the rent paid per acre, which included rents for housing, roads, fences, and other land improvements.

10. In contrast, Crafts and Harley (2004) in a CGE exercise conclude that population growth explains only a modest part of the structural change in the British economy in the years 1770–1841. This conclusion follows mainly from the assumption that, absent British population growth, the British terms of trade would have shifted 44 percent toward industrial products. Without such a shift the absence of population growth in their model raises the farm share in employment in 1841 from the observed 22 percent to approximately 39 percent. This is similar to the results in table 2.4.

11. I have discussed why assuming that relative industrial prices would be substantially higher at the end of the Industrial Revolution without British population growth seems unwarranted.

References

Allen, R. C. 1994. Agriculture during the Industrial Revolution, 1700–1850. In *The Economic History of Britain Since 1700*. 2d ed. Vol. 1. Ed. R. Floud and D. N. McCloskey. Cambridge: Cambridge University Press.

Baugh, D. A. 2004. Naval Power: What Gave the British Navy Superiority? In *Exceptionalism and Industrialization: Britain and Its European Rivals, 1688–1815*, ed. L. Prados de la Escosura, 235–260. Cambridge: Cambridge University Press.

Cain, P. J., and A. G. Hopkins. 1980. The Political Economy of British Overseas Expansion, 1750–1914. *Economic History Review* 33 (4): 463–490.

———. 1986. Gentlemanly Capitalism and British Expansion Overseas I. The Old Colonial System, 1688–1850. *Economic History Review* 39 (4): 501–525.

Church, R. 1986. *The History of the British Coal Industry*. Vol. 3, *1830–1913*. Oxford: Clarendon Press.

Clark, G. 1998. Land Hunger: Land as a Commodity and as a Status Good in England, 1500–1910. *Explorations in Economic History* 35 (1): 59–82.

———. 1999. Too Much Revolution: Agriculture and the Industrial Revolution, 1700–1860. In *The British Industrial Revolution: An Economic Assessment*. 2d ed., ed. J. Mokyr, 206–240. Boulder, Colo.: Westview Press.

———. 2001. Farm Wages and Living Standards in the Industrial Revolution: England, 1670–1870. *Economic History Review* 54 (3): 477–505.

———. 2002a. The Agricultural Revolution and the Industrial Revolution: England, 1500–1912. ⟨http://www.iga.ucdavis.edu/clarkpapers.html⟩.

———. 2002b. Farmland Rental Values and Agrarian History: England, 1500–1912. *European Review of Economic History* 6 (3): 281–309.

———. 2002c. Shelter from the Storm: Housing and the Industrial Revolution, 1550–1912. *Journal of Economic History* 62 (2): 489–511.

———. 2004. The Price History of English Agriculture, 1209–1914. *Research in Economic History* 22: 41–124.

———. 2005. The Condition of the Working-Class in England, 1209–2004. *Journal of Political Economy* 113 (6): 1307–1340.

Clark, G. 2007. The Long March of History: Farm Wages, Population, and Economic Growth, England 1209–1869. *Economic History Review* 60 (1): 97–136.

Clark, G., M. Huberman, and P. Lindert. 1995. A British Food Puzzle, 1770–1850. *Economic History Review* 48: 215–237.

Clark, G., and D. S. Jacks. 2007. Coal and the Industrial Revolution, 1700–1869. *European Review of Economic History* 11 (1): 39–72.

Crafts, N.F.R., and C. K. Harley. 1992. Output Growth and the Industrial Revolution: A Restatement of the Crafts-Harley View. *Economic History Review* 45: 703–730.

———. 2004. Precocious British Industrialization: A General Equilibrium Perspective. In *Exceptionalism and Industrialization: Britain and Its European Rivals, 1688–1815*, ed. L. Prados de la Escosura. Cambridge: Cambridge University Press.

Deane, P., and W. A. Cole. 1967. *British Economic Growth, 1688–1959*. 2d ed. Cambridge: Cambridge University Press.

de Vries, J. 2000. Dutch Economic Growth in Comparative Historical Perspective, 1500–2000. *De Economist* 148 (4): 443–467.

Flinn, M. W., and D. Stoker. 1984. *The History of the British Coal Industry*. Vol. 2, *1700–1830*. Oxford: Clarendon Press.

Geary, F., and T. Stark. 2004. Trends in Real Wages during the Industrial Revolution: A View from across the Irish Sea. *Economic History Review* 57: 362–395.

Harley, C. K. 1993. Reassessing the Industrial Revolution: A Macro View. In *The British Industrial Revolution: An Economic Assessment*, ed. J. Mokyr, 227–266. Boulder, Colo.: Westview Press.

Kennedy, P. 1983. *The Rise and Fall of British Naval Mastery*. London: Macmillan.

Mitchell, B. R. 1988. *British Historical Statistics*. Cambridge: Cambridge University Press.

————. 1998. *International Historical Statistics: Europe, 1750–1993*. London: Macmillan.

Mokyr, J. 1999. Editor's Introduction: The New Economic History and the Industrial Revolution. In *The British Industrial Revolution: An Economic Perspective*, ed. J. Mokyr, 1–127. Boulder, Colo.: Westview Press.

O'Brien, P. 1996. Path Dependency, or Why Britain Became an Industrialized and Urbanized Economy Long Before France. *Economic History Review* 49: 213–249.

Parliamentary Papers. 1870. *Statistical Abstract of the United Kingdom, 1855–1869*. Vol. 68: 85.

Prados de la Escosura, L. 2000. International Comparisons of Real Product, 1820–1990: An Alternative Data Set. *Explorations in Economic History* 37: 1–41.

Schumpeter, E. 1960. *English Overseas Trade Statistics, 1697–1808*. Oxford: Oxford University Press.

Smits, J.-P., E. Horlings, and J. L. van Zanden. 1999. *Dutch GNP and Its Components, 1800–1913*. Monograph Series 5, Groningen Growth and Development Center, University of Groningen, Netherlands.

Temin, P. 1997. Two Views of the British Industrial Revolution. *Journal of Economic History* 57 (1): 63–82.

Wrigley, E. A., R. S. Davies, J. E. Oeppen, and R. S. Schofield. 1997. *English Population History from Family Reconstitution, 1580–1837*. Cambridge: Cambridge University Press.

3 Did European Commodity Prices Converge during 1500–1800?

Süleyman Özmucur and Şevket Pamuk

Until recently, the dominant view of the European economy during the early modern era was that it was unable to generate long-term economic growth. This interpretation, as articulated by Wilhelm Abel, Michael Postan, Emmanuel Leroy Ladurie, and others, was based, at least in part, on the available evidence for stagnating land productivity and urban real wages. It was also consistent with the prevailing interpretations of the Industrial Revolution. During the last two decades, however, this picture of the stagnant economy that supposedly preceded the Industrial Revolution began to change. The new and downwardly revised estimates of per capita income increases for the eighteenth and early nineteenth centuries implied higher levels of per capita income for the earlier period. In addition, economic historians of the early modern period began to point out that the industrialization of the late eighteenth and early nineteenth centuries was made possible by structural changes that had taken place earlier. The volume of European trade increased steadily in the centuries leading up to the Industrial Revolution. Increases in agricultural productivity, urbanization, national patterns of specialization, the emergence and development of regional, national, and international trade networks have been cited among the important changes that facilitated the rises in income or so-called Smithian growth in the early modern era, or at the very least, made faster growth possible during the era of the Industrial Revolution (de Vries 1994; Persson 1988; van Zanden 1999; 2002).

This recent literature and the findings on the early modern era point to market integration as one of the key processes inducing structural change in early modern Europe. Since the contribution of technological innovation remained limited, according to this view, improvements in productivity were generated by the development of trade between previously distinct markets and the requirements of an interregional and increasingly international division of labor. In short, various types of market integration have been considered one of the key characteristics of Europe before the Industrial Revolution.

Although maritime trade and overseas discoveries have often loomed large in explanations of European ascendancy and economic growth in the early modern era, the extent to which long-distance markets inside Europe were integrated remains to be explored. As Federico and Persson emphasize in chapter 4, examining market integration and its consequences in a variety of contexts has been a central theme in Jeffrey G. Williamson's lifelong research agenda. Following his lead, we explore in this study the extent to which one may speak of integration between selected long-distance markets across Europe during the early modern era. We utilize annual price data for identical commodities from Istanbul in the Ottoman Empire, Modeno in Italy, Madrid and Barcelona in Spain, western Holland, southern England, Paris, Vienna, and Sopron in Hungary to examine whether there was price convergence between long-distance markets in the Mediterranean and central and northwestern Europe for the period 1500–1800. Our list of commodities includes wheat, which has been studied in relation to this question for other periods and regions, and other commodities such as olive oil, rice, honey, sugar, soap, meat, and butter. There is no question that these markets were linked during the early modern era, and trade did take place among them though not always on a regular basis. This inquiry should help us learn more about the extent and the limits of market integration in early modern Europe.

Market Integration in Early Modern Europe, 1500–1800

Market integration can be defined as the opening and development of trade between previously autonomous markets and their integration into a single operative entity or a single division of labor. The concept carries with it important implications for structural change as the fabric of each economy is tailored to the requirements of an interregional and increasingly international division of labor. Improvements in productivity are thus generated by the territorial expansion of the division of labor and a reallocation of resources within regions or national economies. For market integration to have an independent influence on an economy, two conditions must be fulfilled: (1) trade-creating forces must change domestic commodity prices; and (2) changes in domestic commodity prices must induce a reshuffling of resources. While price convergence is not a sufficient reason for market integration, and it is possible to think about causes of price convergence without market integration, such as large-scale climatic changes, without the tendency for prices to converge it is clear that the process of market integration loses much of its force (Jacks 2000).

Sources of Market Integration

The causes of market integration and price convergence can be grouped under two headings. One important cause is technological change, bringing about decline in transportation costs and related costs associated with storage and spoilage. The decline in freight costs is usually seen as the most important cause of trade growth and price convergence in international and intercontinental markets during the nineteenth century, for example. A similar case can be made for the importance of railroads in bringing about price convergence in overland transportation. If the growth in trade in the early modern era had a techological source, it was the introduction, in the latter part of the fifteenth century, of the three-masted, larger trading vessel, which lowered costs of transportation and allowed trading over greater distances. Such technological changes remained limited after the fifteenth century, however (Rosenberg and Birdzell 1986, 71–96).

In fact, while some economic historians emphasize the importance of market integration and price convergence, others point out that little or no market integration took place and price differentials persisted throughout the early modern era. These authors argue that the admittedly fragmentary evidence on freight rates within Europe during the early modern era does not point to significant decreases in transportation costs. Freight rates in Europe appear to have moved together with commodity prices from the fourteenth century until the end of the eighteenth. Freight charges in the mid-eighteenth century were only slightly lower than their levels in the best years of the high Middle Ages in both nominal and real terms. On the basis of the available data on freight rates, then, one cannot make a case for a premodern European transport revolution led by technical innovations. Productivity gains rooted in better techniques appear to have played only a minor role in the growth of trade in these centuries (Unger 1983; Allen and Unger 1990; Menard 1991).

The literature on market integration may have paid too much attention to transportation costs and not enough to other factors. Even for the nineteenth century, for which there is strong evidence of declining transportation costs, that evidence can explain only part of the observed decline in price differentials (North 1958; Harley 1988; Mohammed and

Willliamson 2003; Jacks 2004; Persson 2004). The second set of causes for market integration and price convergence is the removal or lowering of a wide range of institutional and other barriers. The presence of national borders, or more generally of different jurisdictions, was often an important barrier or the source of a variety of barriers. Not only tariffs and other policy instruments but payments mechanisms, monetary regimes, and interstate conflict need to be included under this heading.

In an important recent study Epstein (2000, 38–72) emphasizes that in late medieval and early modern Europe, market structures that determined regional growth paths depended upon the complex social, economic, and political struggles between sovereigns, feudal lords, cities, and rural communities, and could differ significantly between regions. In grains, for example, jurisdictional fragmentation was the main cause of price volatility. The decline of predatory states and political centralization increased domestic stability and reduced coordination failures between markets. Epstein cites empirical evidence from different parts of western Europe for 1300–1650 indicating that even though transportation costs did not decline significantly, market integration as measured by price dispersion did take place. Innovations that reduce transaction costs by increasing mobility of capital, lowering information costs (e.g., bills of exchange or manuals), or spreading risk (e.g., marine insurance) can also be included under this heading. Epstein concludes that premodern Smithian growth, which was a function of market integration, depended ultimately on the progress of political integration and institutional change rather than on technical change in the period from the Black Death to the Industrial Revolution.[1]

Long-Distance vs. Regional and National Markets

A large part of the institutional changes that Epstein observes for early modern Europe concern regional or short- and medium-range trade. In fact, it is not clear whether the political and institutional changes he emphasizes would apply to long-distance and international trade around Europe and beyond before the nineteenth century. For example, trade inside the Mediterranean was often combined with raiding and freebooting during the early modern era. Moreover, these activities could not have been carried out in isolation. Knowledge of these activities, contributions to their conduct, and profits from their success must have been widely shared, directly or indirectly. Maritime trade was thus at once a major field of economic growth and a field resistant to political control (Rosenberg and Birdzell 1986, 92–96). It may be useful to make a distiction between short- and medium-range trade, on the one hand, and long-distance trade, on the other, when discussing market integration and Smithian growth in early modern Europe. Maritime trade and overseas discoveries have often loomed large in explanations of the late medieval recovery and European ascendancy, and there is often a temptation in the literature to exaggerate the importance of overseas trade in the early modern era. In fact, there were other, much less dramatic sources of market growth that tend to be neglected, such as rise in population, rise in incomes, urbanization, and growth in interurban trade.

For this reason, it is not clear whether foreign markets grew faster than domestic markets during the early modern era. In fact, until the nineteenth century domestic trade was much more important than international trade for most European countries. The volumes of long-distance maritime trade and international long-distance trade were still small in comparison to domestic trade and overland trade, and they were all sharply lower than the levels reached at the end of the long nineteenth century.

Regional Differentiation within Europe?

One may take a more nuanced perspective, of course. While it is clear that most of Europe did not become engrossed in a complete and over-arching system of markets, some regions within the continent were becoming more integrated within themselves and perhaps among one another during the early modern era. Not all regions of Europe were influenced in the same manner or to the same extent by the institutional changes. With respect to long-distance trade as well as domestic trade, the experience of northern and northwestern Europe was very different than that of southern and eastern Europe (de Vries 1976, 160–164). For example, there is evidence that the wheat markets in the Baltic–North Sea region showed a tendency toward greater integration, especially during the first half of these three centuries until 1650, and these gains were not reversed after 1650 (Jacks 2000). Similarly, Granger and Elliot (1967) have argued that England began to constitute a national market in wheat by the early eighteenth century. On the other hand, raiding and freebooting inhibited Mediterranean trade as late as the eighteenth century.

Evidence from European Intercontinental Trade

Another reason for the recent rise in interest in the history of market integration is the current wave of globalization and the studies by economists and economic historians of earlier episodes of globalization. Some historians have argued that the discovery of the Americas and the oceanic route to Asia integrated the continental markets and ushered in a new and global era beginning around 1500. O'Rourke and Williamson (2002a; 2002b) have explored whether there occurred an earlier episode of globalization after the voyages by Columbus and Vasco da Gama. O'Rourke and Williamson define globalization as commodity market integration and emphasize that because an increase in trade volume may be due to shifts in demand or supply curves, the best way to gauge that process is to measure the extent to which prices of the same commodities converged over time worldwide. After studying a large set of prices of commodites subject to intercontinental trade, however, they find no price convergence in intercontinental markets in the three centuries before 1800. In the absence of any decline in transportation costs or in human-made barriers to trade such as tariffs or trade monopolies, they conclude that the increases in European incomes was the most important cause of the intercontinental trade boom during the early modern era.

It is interesting that O'Rourke and Williamson observe no price convergence during a period for which Epstein observes significant reductions in price dispersion. It is worth noting, however, that spatially speaking, these studies are examining market integration at different ends of the spectrum. While Epstein focuses on regional, short- to medium-range trade, O'Rourke and Williamson examine intercontinental trade.

There is no doubt that the concept of market integration remains highly useful for understanding long-term change in early modern Europe. Determining the extent and limits of market integration is very important for further understanding the economic changes in early modern Europe. At the same time, however, this review of the literature suggests that a more nuanced, more disaggregated view of market integration is necessary for making better sense of these trends. In what follows, we do not focus on European intercontinental trade or domestic trade but explore the extent to which market integration applied to long-distance and international trade within Europe.

Statistical Tests and Results

In its simplest form, the theory of market integration is distilled into the so-called law of one price (LOOP). As intermarket trade commences, any observed differentials in the prices of goods will tend to decline and eventually disappear subject to transportation and institutional costs. Since demand or supply curves may be shifting in the meantime, the only irrefutable evidence that market integration is taking place is not the rise in trade volumes but a decline in price differentials or in the dispersion of prices, or what might be called commodity price convergence. The simplicity of the theory of market integration, however, conceals the difficulties in empirical measurement. In the literature on historical and contemporary commodity markets, there have been numerous proposals for the correct measure of market integration.

The traditional approach to market efficiency looks at the correlation of prices or the speed of adjustments to an equilibrium price differential between markets in bilateral trade. The latter approach makes the determination of equilibrium differentials quite easy: price differences shall not exceed transport and transaction costs (including tariffs), and prices must adjust to that equilibrium. However, arbitrage in the world economy is normally multilateral, and therefore bilateral LOOP might not hold for markets when they do not trade with each other. Nonetheless, they can still be integrated by trading with a common third market, although the speed of adjustment may depend on whether they trade directly with another market or indirectly through a common third market.

We are now in a position to directly test for market integration in long-distance markets across Europe in the early modern period. We utilize annual price data for identical commodities from Istanbul in the Ottoman Empire, Modeno in Italy, Madrid and Barcelona in Spain, western Holland, southern England, Paris, Vienna, and Sopron in Hungary for the period 1500–1800. These annual series were obtained from a variety of sources.[2] These cities or regions were all linked to each other by maritime trade during the early modern era. Our commodities include wheat, olive oil, rice, honey, sugar, soap, meat, and butter (figure 3.1). Six of these eight commodities were subject to long-distance maritime trade in the early modern era, although there was less trade in the last two, meat and butter, during the early modern era. Nonetheless, we chose to include them in our study.

Most if not all studies of early modern intra-European market integration have looked at wheat.[3] We are able to examine market integration in seven additional commodities. Clearly, there must have been some correlation between wheat and other commodities as transportation costs, trade policies, and more generally the institutional environment changed together in a given location. At the same time, however, there are many reasons for variations in market integration across commodities because of variations in transportation technology and trade policies. Thus, studying other commodities as well as wheat may allow us new insights.

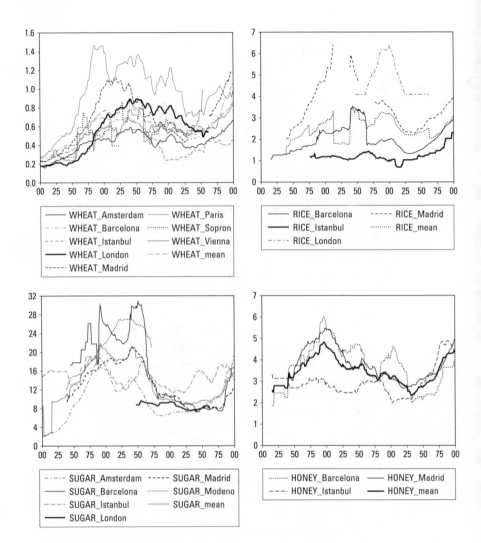

Figure 3.1
Commodity prices, 1500–1800.

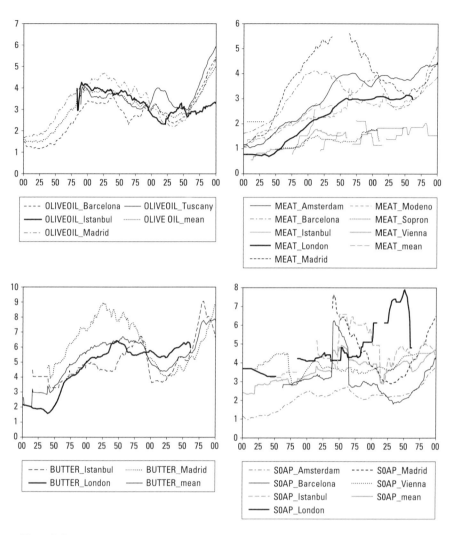

Figure 3.1
(continued)

Standard weight and monetary units are adopted by converting all prices to grams of silver per metric unit. In addition, 25-year moving averages are used in the analysis, for two reasons. First, there are large fluctuations in agricultural prices owing to weather-related crop failures. The procedure of taking moving averages of available data gives a relatively smooth series. Since the ultimate goal is to study long-term tendencies rather than annual changes, averaging would be an appropriate method. Second, a large number of observations are missing in some of the price series. Taking moving averages helps to create a relatively continuous series comparable to others (figure 3.1). In most cases, prices move rather closely, with a positive trend and some spikes. However, this does not really mean there is convergence of prices.

Coefficient of Variation

One frequently used measure of convergence in prices is the decrease in the coefficient of variation of prices.[4] If relative prices stay the same, the coefficient of variation stays the same. On the other hand, if prices converge, both the standard deviation and the coefficient of variation decrease. A statistical test for this decrease may be performed by testing for a unit root.

Figure 3.2 provides the coefficient of variation for each of the eight commodities. For wheat we were able to use data for all eight cities, namely Amsterdam (A), Barcelona (B), Istanbul (I), London (L), Madrid (M), Paris (P), Sopron (S), and Vienna (V) (see figure 3.1). On the other hand, annual price data were available for four cities for rice, six cities for sugar, three cities for honey, four cities for olive oil, eight cities for meat, three cities for butter, and five cities for soap. The coefficient of variation for each commodity is based on the number of cities for which data are available. There is also the problem of missing annual observations, which may create difficulties in interpreting results. The coefficients of variation are actually calculated with data from fewer cities for some years because of this problem. We have added a ninth, combined, commodity to this panel by weighting the coefficient of variation of each commodity by the number of cities for which data were available, namely, the coefficient of variation of wheat by eight, rice by four, and so on.

Is there a negative trend in the coefficient of variation, or is it relatively stable over the period under study? Rather than simply follow the value of this coefficient (increase or decrease) over time, we prefer to answer this question formally, with the help of unit root tests, which look for a stochastic trend in a series. These tests are more restrictive than following the value of the cofficient of variation over time because they look for a permanent trend. In testing for the presence of a unit root (nonstationary) in the coefficient of variation, it is a good idea to use more than one method because unit root tests are asymptotic tests. Accordingly, we have used the augmented Dickey-Fuller (1979) ADF, Phillips-Perron (1988) PP, and Kwiatkowski et al. (1992) KPSS tests. The last test differs from the other two in that the series is assumed to be trend-stationary under the null.[5]

Summary results of the three tests on the coefficient of variation are presented in table 3.1. In the case of wheat, according to the ADF test, the coefficient of variation is a stationary series at the 10 percent significance level. The null hypothesis of a nonstationary series can be rejected at the 10 percent level. Therefore, the coefficient of variation is statistically steady, indicating no convergence in prices in eight cities. A similar result is obtained using the PP test: the null hypothesis of a nonstationary series can be rejected at the 10 percent level, indicating no convergence in prices in eight cities. In the KPSS test, the null hypothesis is "stationary" and the rejection of the null would indicate that there is convergence. Our coefficient of variation of wheat prices in eight cities is stationary at the 10 percent significance level. The null hypothesis cannot be rejected at the 10 percent level. Therefore, there is no convergence in prices. In other words, in the case of wheat all three tests indicate no convergence at the 10 percent significance level.[6]

As summarized in table 3.1, all three tests indicate convergence in rice, olive oil, meat, and soap prices but no convergence in prices of honey at the 10 percent level. On the other hand, conflicting results are obtained in the tests on prices of sugar and butter. According to the ADF and PP tests, sugar prices are stationary at the 1 percent level, indicating no convergence. Yet the KPSS test rejects the hypothesis that sugar prices are stationary at the 5 percent level, indicating convergence. The price of butter is nonstationary at the 10 percent level according to the ADF test, indicating convergence. This series is stationary at the 10 percent level according to the PP test, indicating no convergence. It is nonstationary, indicating convergence, according to the KPSS, indeed a very strong rejection of the null.[7]

The case of sugar may deserve additional attention. The sharp decline in the coefficient of variation of sugar during the sixteenth century (figure 3.2) suggests a story similar to that of O'Rourke and Williamson (2005)

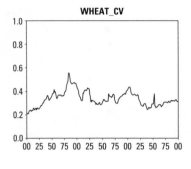

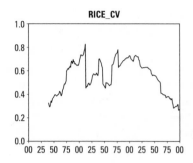

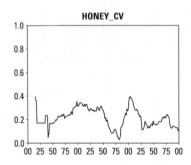

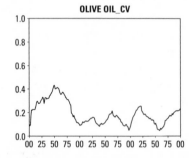

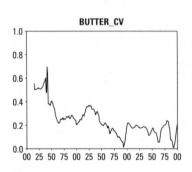

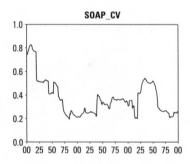

Figure 3.2
Coefficient of variation of prices, 1500–1800.

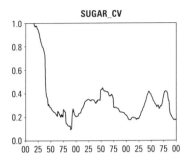

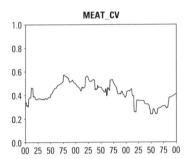

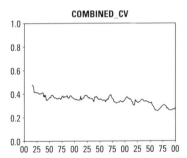

Figure 3.2
(continued)

Table 3.1
Unit Root Tests for Coefficient of Variation

CV	ADF	Test Result	Implied Conclusion with 90% Level of Confidence
Wheat	−2.59	nonstationary rejected at the 10 percent level	no convergence
Rice	−1.69	nonstationary cannot be rejected at the 10 percent level	convergence
Sugar	−3.40	nonstationary rejected at the 1 percent level	no convergence
Honey	−2.80	nonstationary rejected at the 10 percent level	no convergence
Olive oil	−1.67	nonstationary cannot be rejected at the 10 percent level	convergence
Meat	−2.05	nonstationary cannot be rejected at the 10 percent level	convergence
Butter	−2.37	nonstationary cannot be rejected at the 10 percent level	convergence
Soap	−2.40	nonstationary cannot be rejected at the 10 percent level	convergence
Combined CV	−2.85	nonstationary rejected at the 10 percent level	no convergence
CV	**PP**		
Wheat	−2.58	nonstationary rejected at the 10 percent level	no convergence
Rice	−1.70	nonstationary cannot be rejected at the 10 percent level	convergence
Sugar	−3.45	nonstationary rejected at the 1 percent level	no convergence
Honey	−2.99	nonstationary rejected at the 5 percent level	no convergence
Olive oil	−1.83	nonstationary cannot be rejected at the 10 percent level	convergence
Meat	−2.11	nonstationary cannot be rejected at the 10 percent level	convergence
Butter	−2.62	nonstationary rejected at the 10 percent level	no convergence
Soap	−2.50	nonstationary cannot be rejected at the 10 percent level	convergence
Combined CV	−2.92	nonstationary rejected at the 5 percent level	no convergence

Table 3.1
(continued)

CV		KPSS	
Wheat	0.28	stationary cannot be rejected at the 10 percent level	no convergence
Rice	0.36	stationary rejected at the 10 percent level	convergence
Sugar	0.48	stationary rejected at the 5 percent level	convergence
Honey	0.27	stationary cannot be rejected at the 10 percent level	no convergence
Olive oil	0.80	stationary rejected at the 1 percent level	convergence
Meat	0.80	stationary rejected at the 1 percent level	convergence
Butter	1.37	stationary rejected at the 1 percent level	convergence
Soap	0.52	stationary rejected at the 5 percent level	convergence
Combined CV	1.65	stationary rejected at the 1 percent level	convergence

on the impact of Vasco da Gama's voyage on European pepper markets. As was the case with pepper, this was a one-time event, however. European sugar prices did not show any further convergence after the sixteenth century. For this reason, we cannot accept the convergence hypothesis for the early modern era as a whole. Two of the three tests indicate no convergence.

Finally, the combined coefficient of variation, which is a weighted average of coefficient of variations of individual commodity prices with number of cities as weights, can perhaps be taken as an indicator of the aggregate trend in the sample. Two out of three of the tests indicate no convergence for this combined coefficient. According to the ADF and PP tests, a unit root in the combined coefficient of variation is rejected at the 5 percent level, indicating no convergence.[8] On the other hand, the KPSS test rejects stationarity at the 1 percent level, indicating convergence. These are very strong but contradictory results. It is also interesting that the combined coefficient of variation does not show large fluctuations over time. On the basis of the combined coefficient of variation in figure 3.2, it is not possible to identify subperiods when the tendency for convergence was stronger and subperiods when the tendency was in the opposite direction.

In short, the results based on coefficient of variation are mixed. There is convergence in prices of rice, olive oil, meat, and soap, and no convergence in prices of wheat and honey. There are conflicting results on prices of sugar and butter, leaning toward convergence (two out of three tests) in prices of butter and no convergence in prices of sugar. The combined coefficient of variation of prices also indicates no-convergence in two out of three tests.

Cointegration of Prices

Recently, there has been a resurgence of the study of convergence largely because of the issues related to the European Economic and Monetary Union (EMU), where member and candidate countries are expected to satisfy certain criteria associated with targets such as inflation, interest rates, budget deficits and debt. A number of methods have been introduced to tackle this problem. As the convergence in EMU is an ongoing process, it necessitates the use of several related concepts such as long-term convergence, catching up, and common trend (Bernard and Durlauf 1995; 1996; Oxley and Greasley 1995; Greasley and Oxley 1997; Camarero, Esteve, and Tamarit 2000). However, since we are dealing here with a process that has been completed, the problems are not as complicated as the ones faced by those studying the EMU.

Bernard and Durlauf (1995; 1996) define long-run convergence between two countries if the long-term forecasts of the prices are equal sometime in the future given the information at present.[9] This definition is satisfied if the difference in prices is a stationary process with mean zero (Camarero, Esteve, Tamarit 2000). It is possible to use the Engle and Granger (1987) cointegration methodology to see if two prices move toward a long-run equilibrium.[10] The test is applied to residuals from a regression of price in the first city on the price in the other city, with the unit coefficient. The Dickey-Fuller unit root test may then be used.[11]

Tests for cointegration of prices are conducted using two price series at a time. As summarized in table 3.2, in the case of wheat we begin with a regression of wheat prices in Amsterdam on wheat prices in Barcelona with a restriction on the slope coefficient (equaling 1). The Dickey-Fuller unit root test is then applied to residuals from this regression. In this case, the null hypothesis of a nonstationary series cannot be rejected at the 10 percent level.[12] We therefore conclude that wheat prices in Amsterdam and wheat prices in Barcelona are not cointegrated. They do not have a long-run equilibrium, hence indicating no-convergence. In fact, among the wheat pairs, only Amsterdam and Vienna are cointegrated, indicating convergence at the 5 percent level. There is no convergence in the prices of other pairs of cities in the wheat sample.

Similarly, based on the Engle and Granger (1987) methodology, we find no convergence among any pairs of cities in prices of rice, honey, olive oil, meat, and butter. On the other hand, there is convergence in sugar

Table 3.2
Tests for Cointegration of Prices

Wheat	Wheat Barcelona	Wheat Istanbul	Wheat London	Wheat Madrid	Wheat Paris	Wheat Sopron	Wheat Vienna
Wheat Amsterdam	-0.85	-1.36	-1.05	-0.87	-2.03	-1.68	-2.96[a]
Wheat Barcelona	n	0.38	-1.31	-1.49	-1.61	-1.23	-2.11
Wheat Istanbul	n		-0.199	0.97	-1.65	-0.03	-1.05
Wheat London	n			-0.58	-1.93	-0.46	-1.56
Wheat Madrid	n				-1.15	-0.34	-1.51
Wheat Paris	n					-0.64	-2.06
Wheat Sopron	n						-2.54

Rice	Rice Istanbul	Rice London	Rice Madrid
Rice Barcelona	-1.81	-2.11	1.56
Rice Istanbul		-1.14	0.20
Rice London			-1.22

Sugar	Sugar Barcelona	Sugar Istanbul	Sugar London	Sugar Madrid	Sugar Modeno
Sugar Amsterdam	-1.13	-0.39	-1.82	-0.11	-1.28
Sugar Barcelona		-1.57	-4.44[b]	-2.06	-1.67
Sugar Istanbul			-1.12	-1.21	-1.30
Sugar London				-3.66[a]	3.13[c]
Sugar Madrid					-1.38

Table 3.2
(continued)

Honey	Honey Istanbul	Honey Madrid
Honey Barcelona	-1.52	-1.57
Honey Istanbul		-1.20

Olive Oil	Olive Oil Istanbul	Olive Oil Madrid	Olive Oil Tuscany
Olive oil Barcelona	1.47	-0.83	-2.60
Olive oil Istanbul		0.17	-0.07
Olive oil Madrid			-0.79

Meat	Meat Barcelona	Meat Istanbul	Meat London	Meat Madrid	Meat Modeno	Meat Sopron	Meat Vienna
Meat Amsterdam	-1.23	1.14	-2.05	-0.76	2.55	-0.51	-1.49
Meat Barcelona		-1.03	-0.99	-2.51	-0.81	-1.46	-0.82
Meat Istanbul			0.72	-1.55	0.49	-1.47	-1.92
Meat London				-0.98	1.45	0.01	-1.02
Meat Madrid					0.15	-1.21	-1.32
Meat Modeno						-2.68	-1.77
Meat Sopron							-1.11

Butter	Butter London	Butter Madrid
Butter Istanbul	-2.20	-1.24
Butter London		-1.15

Soap	Soap Barcelona	Soap Istanbul	Soap London	Soap Madrid	Soap Vienna
Soap Amsterdam	−2.21	−2.07	−1.32	−5.31[b]	−1.63
Soap Barcelona		−2.23	−1.33	−1.55	−2.07
Soap Istanbul			−1.72	−2.73	−2.37
Soap London				−2.25	−0.70
Soap Madrid					−4.01[b]

Notes:
a. Significant at the 5 percent level.
b. Significant at the 1 percent level.
c. Significant at the 10 percent level.

Table 3.3
Number of Cointegrating Equations according to the Johansen Test

	Trace Statistic	Max-Eigen Statistic	No. of Observations	No. of Cities
Wheat	3	3	86	8
Rice	1	0	87	4
Sugar	4	3	24	6
Honey	1	0	256	3
Olive oil	1	1	210	4
Meat	5	2	52	8
Butter	0	0 .	218	3
Soap	2	2	109	6

and soap prices in some cities. For example, sugar prices in Barcelona and London (at the 1 percent significance level), London and Madrid (at the 5 percent level), and London and Modeno (at the 10 percent level) are cointegrated, indicating convergence. Soap prices in Amsterdam and Madrid, and in Madrid and Vienna, are cointegrated at the 1 percent level, indicating convergence. It is clear from these results that based on the cointegration methodology strong support for convergence of prices does not exist in the sample of eight cities.

We also used the Johansen methodology to test for convergence. The technique introduced by Johansen (1988) allows for multivariate systems and is more general than the Engle-Granger (1987) single equation and two-step methodology. This technique is used to determine the number of cointegrating equations—the number of long-run equilibrium relations.[13] Since the method requires data for all cities for the same period, total number of observations available is not 301 but much less in many cases. According to the Johansen technique, there is no convergence in prices of rice, butter, and honey (table 3.3). On the other hand, there is a possible long-run equilibrium (convergence) for prices of wheat, olive oil, soap, sugar, and meat. However, findings on meat and sugar are based on a small number of observations (52 and 24, respectively) and therefore not sufficiently reliable.

We end this section with an overview of the results of our tests. The coefficient-of-variation methodology yielded mixed results. The three tests agree that there is convergence in four commodities and no convergence in two. They also yield contradictory results in two commodities and in the combined coefficient of variation. The Engle-Granger cointegration methodology, on the other hand, indicates no convergence in most of the cases with the exception of just one pair of cities in wheat (Amsterdam and Vienna), three pairs in sugar (Barcelona and London, London and Madrid, and London and Modeno), and two pairs in soap (Amsterdam and Madrid, and Madrid and Vienna). Finally, according to the multivariate cointegration technique of Johansen, there is no convergence in prices of rice, butter, and honey, and there is convergence in prices of wheat, olive oil, and soap.

The differences in the test results require some elaboration. Since the Engle-Granger cointegration methodology involves two cities at a time, it is probably less affected by data issues. In contrast, the coefficient of variation is calculated using data on all cities. There may be missing data, with the exception of wheat prices, that can affect these calculations. For example, a city with a high price may have missing values toward the end of the period. This will give a misleading impression that prices are converging. On the other hand, Engle-Granger cointegration tests, as implemented here, have the restriction that prices be equal at equilibrium. This may be quite restrictive, if compared to the method using the coefficient of variation. These differences may have led to the differences in the test results.

While there are differences in the results based on alternative methodologies, including the panel unit root tests conducted in an earlier version of the chapter, we should emphasize that the tests offer only weak support for the convergence hypothesis. None of the eight commodities and none of the more than two dozen city pairs yielded the result of convergence in all tests. In fact, the results provide greater support for the no-convergence hypothesis. Most of the tests indicate no convergence in prices of rice, sugar, honey, and butter, and convergence in prices of soap, the only nonfood item in the sample. There is only partial support for some convergence in wheat and olive oil prices.

Conclusion

There is some evidence that parts of Europe were becoming more integrated within themselves and with other parts of the continent during the early modern era. Even though transportation costs did not decline significantly, market integration as measured by price dispersion did take place in different parts of western Europe during this period. It has been argued that such market integration during the early modern era was due to the the removal or lowering of a wide range of institutional and other barriers, and to increasing political centralization that increased domestic stability and reduced coordination failures between markets.

We utilized annual price series for wheat, which is often used in these studies, and for seven additional commodities from eight cities around the Mediterranean and in northern and central Europe to study the integration of these long-distance and mostly international markets as measured by price convergence. We employed a number of additional methodologies as well as the frequently used coefficient of variation. Admittedly, our statistical tests for convergence were more demanding than simply looking at the coefficient of variation over time. The results do not provide support for the hypothesis that price convergence occurred as a permanent trend between these markets during the early modern centuries. While there are differences in the results based on alternative methodologies, the tests provide greater support for the no-convergence hypothesis. The differences in the results from alternative techniques also suggest that drawing inferences from data about price convergence is not a methodologically simple enterprise.

It would have been interesting to explore the extent to which regional variations in patterns of market integration might have existed in early modern Europe. Unfortunately, since very few of the pairs of cities actually indicate convergence in the cointegration tests, a regional pattern is not immediately obvious. At this point, we also should note that the Mediterranean is strongly represented in our data. If long-distance markets around the Mediterranean experienced less market integration than other regions of Europe during the early modern era, it is possible that the data is biased in this respect. Hopefully, larger and geographically more representative data sets will allow for more nuanced answers to this and other questions in the future.

Although maritime trade and overseas discoveries have often loomed large in explanations of the late medieval recovery and European ascendancy, the body of evidence we have gathered cannot sustain a blanket conclusion that the integration of long-distance markets across Europe was a significant trend during the early modern era. Our results suggest, instead, not only that transportation costs did not decline but that, despite some exceptions, political and institutional changes did not have a significant effect on long-distance and international trade before the nineteenth century. In the absence of any decline in transportation costs or institutional barriers such as tariffs or national borders, the increases in the volume of long-distance trade during the early modern era must have been due to shifts in demand or supply, and to increases in incomes.

The absence of price convergence and market integration in long-distance and international trade should not mean the end of the concept of market integration, however. We would argue for a distinction between long-distance trade, on the one hand, and short- and medium-range trade, on the other. Trade in Europe, and for that matter around the globe, was still mostly regional and domestic before and even well into the nineteenth century. For most countries, the volume of long-distance trade was still small in comparison to domestic or regional trade before 1800. Our results suggest strongly that market integration did not apply to long-distance trade during this period. Price convergence and market integration may have occurred in some short- and medium-range trade thanks to institutional changes in parts of Europe. In other words, market integration and Smithian growth need to be considered mostly in connection with short- and medium-range domestic or regional trade in early modern Europe.

Notes

1. Persson (1999, 98–100) also provides evidence of increased regional integration of wheat markets during the sixteenth and seventeenth centuries in Tuscany, and between Tuscany and southern France, but not inside France.

2. The price data for Istanbul were obtained from Şevket Pamuk, ⟨http://www.iisg.nl/hpw/data.php#ottoman⟩. Data for Modeno, Paris, Vienna, and Sopron are from the Global Price and Income History Group data set, ⟨http//gpih.ucdavis.edu/⟩. Data for Madrid and Barcelona were originally gathered by Earl Hamilton; they have since been updated by Feliu and Montfort. Data for western Netherlands were obtained from Jan Luiten van Zanden, ⟨http://www.iisg.nl/hpw/data.php⟩, and data for southern England from Bob Allen. We are pleased to acknowledge the support of these groups and individuals.

3. O'Rourke and Williamson (2002a; 2002b) are a significant exception.

4. The convergence literature relies heavily on the income convergence concept introduced by Baumol (1986), and Barro and Sala-i-Martin (1992; 1995). Using cross-country data, researchers of the economics of growth indicated that growth in the ratio of incomes in two countries is negatively related to the ratio of incomes at the base period. As a result of this finding, they concluded that the difference between per capita incomes is expected to diminish in time. This is called beta convergence. However, researchers do not solely rely on beta convergence. Sigma convergence, which is defined as the standard deviation of incomes at a given period, is also utilized. Variation of incomes among various countries, measured as the standard deviation, should also decrease in time to conclude that there is convergence of incomes. There are many critics of the method, and almost as many alternatives or variants, for example, Quah (1993; 1996), Linden (2002), Johnson (2000), and Rassekh, Panik, and Kolluri (2001).

5. There are two practical issues in performing a unit root test: first, the choice of including a constant, a constant and a linear time trend, or neither, in the test regression; and second, the specification of the number of lagged difference terms to be added to the test regression. A constant is used in the test regression. The number of lags is determined using Akaike and Schwartz criteria. MacKinnon (1991) critical value calculations are used in performing ADF and PP tests. *Eviews* software by Quantitative Micro Software QMS (2005) is used in our calculations.

6. It should be noted that the null hypothesis of a nonstationary series cannot be rejected at the 5 percent level of significance, according to the ADF and PP tests. The probability significance associated with -2.59 in the ADF is .095, and .098 for -2.58 in the PP, very close to .10 for the rejection of the null nonstationary but far from the probability of .05. In other words, one can argue that the conclusion at the 5 percent level of significance is failure to reject the null, therefore nonstationary, indicating convergence. At the 5 percent level of significance, the conclusion based on these two tests is that there is convergence in prices. The critical levels for the KPSS test are 0.347 for the 10 percent level of significance, 0.463 for the 5 percent level of significance, and 0.739 for the 1 percent level of significance. The calculated 0.28 is far below these and not large enough to reject the null, in this test, stationary. Therefore, the KPSS test is closer to the no-convergence conclusion than the other two.

7. With a test statistic of 1.37.

8. Very close in the ADF test, with a significance level of .0533.

9. Also Carlino and Mills (1993), Ewing and Harter (2000), Haldane and Hall (1991), Hall, Robertson, and Wickens (1997), St. Aubyn (1999), and Trivez (2001).

10. For an earlier version of the study presented at the Harvard conference, we had conducted unit root tests for the ratios of prices, which is almost equivalent to testing for cointegration of prices with a coefficient of 1. Results obtained in the two versions are similar. Moreover, multiple unit root tests, panel tests, that were conducted in the earlier version also indicated no convergence in prices. Panel-based unit root tests, which may have higher power, differ in the assumption regarding the persistence parameters. Im, Pesaran, and Shin (2003), Fisher-ADF, and Fisher-PP tests allow the persistence parameters to vary freely across cross-sections. The latter two are based on the idea that a test statistic may be derived from an individual test, suggested by Fisher (1932) and proposed by Maddala and Wu (1999) and Choi (2001). On the other hand, Levin, Lin, and Chu (2002), Breitung (2000), and Hadri (2000) assume a parameter common across cross-sections. The Hadri test is similar to the KPSS test for a single series.

11. Critical values provided by Davidson and MacKinnon (1993, 772) need to be used in this case because the test is not applied to an original time series but to a series of residuals that is estimated from a regression. For tests with a constant, these critical values are 1 percent, -3.90; 5 percent, -3.34; and 10 percent, -3.04.

12. In this case, critical values from Davidson and MacKinnon are used rather than the critical values for the D-F test. The calculated value of -0.85 is smaller in absolute value than the critical value of -3.4.

13. The test can be conducted using the maximum eigenvalue or trace statistics. Both statistics were developed by Johansen (1988). *Eviews* software by Quantitative Micro Software QMS (2005), which is used here, provides critical values published by MacKinnon, Haug, and Michelis (1999).

References

Allen, R. C. 2001. The Great Divergence in European Wages and Prices from the Middle Ages to the First World War. *Explorations in Economic History* 38: 411–447.

Allen, R. C., and R. W. Unger. 1990. The Depth and Breadth of the Market for Polish Grain, 1500–1800. In *Baltic Affairs: Relations between the Netherlands and North-Eastern Europe, 1500–1800*, ed. J.P.S. Lemmink and J.S.A.M. van Koningsbrugge. Nijmegen, Netherlands: Instituut voor Noord-en Oost-europese Studies (INOS).

Barro, R. J., and X. Sala-i-Martin. 1992. Convergence. *Journal of Political Economy* 100: 223–251.

———. 1995. *Economic Growth*. New York: McGraw-Hill.

Baumol, W. 1986. Productivity Growth, Convergence, and Welfare: What the Long-Run Data Show. *American Economic Review* 76: 1072–1085.

Bernard, A. B., and S. N. Durlauf. 1995. Convergence in International Output. *Journal of Applied Econometrics* 10: 97–108.

———. 1996. Interpreting Tests of the Convergence Hypothesis. *Journal of Econometrics* 71: 161–173.

Breitung, J. 2000. The Local Power of Some Unit Root Tests for Panel Data. In *Advances in Econometrics.* Vol. 15, *Nonstationary Panels, Panel Cointegration, and Dynamic Panels,* ed. B. Baltagi, 161–178. Amsterdam: JAI Press.

Camarero, M., V. Esteve, and C. Tamarit. 2000. Price Convergence of Peripheral European Countries on the Way to the EMU: A Time Series Approach. *Empirical Economics* 25: 149–168.

Carlino, G. A., and L. O. Mills. 1993. Are U.S. Regional Incomes Converging? A Time Series Analysis. *Journal of Monetary Economics* 32: 335–346.

Choi, I. 2001. Unit Root Tests for Panel Data. *Journal of International Money and Finance* 20: 249–272.

Davidson, R., and J. G. MacKinnon. 1993. *Estimation and Inference in Econometrics.* New York: Oxford University Press.

de Vries, J. 1976. *The Economy of Europe in an Age of Crisis, 1600–1750.* Cambridge: Cambridge University Press.

———. 1994. The Industrial Revolution and the Industrious Revolution. *Journal of Economic History* 54: 249–270.

Dickey, D. A., and W. A. Fuller. 1979. Distribution of the Estimators for Autoregressive Time Series with a Unit Root. *Journal of the American Statistical Association* 74: 427–431.

Engle, R. F., and C.W.J. Granger. 1987. Cointegration and Error Correction: Representation, Estimation, and Testing. *Econometrica* 55: 251–276.

Epstein, S. R. 2000. *Freedom and Growth: The Rise of States and Markets in Europe, 1300–1750.* Vol. 17. London: Routledge.

Ewing, B. T., and C. L. Harter. 2000. Co-movements of Alaska North Slope and UK Brendt Crude Oil Prices. *Applied Economics Letters* 7: 553–558.

Fisher, F. A. 1932. *Statistical Methods for Research Workers.* 4th ed. Edinburgh: Oliver and Boyd.

Granger, C.W.J., and C. M. Elliot. 1967. A Fresh Look at Wheat Prices and Markets in the Eighteenth Century. *Economic History Review* 20: 257–265.

Greasley, D., and L. Oxley. 1997. Time Series Based Tests of the Convergence Hypothesis: Some Positive Results. *Economics Letters* 56: 143–147.

Hadri, K. 2000. Testing for Stationary in Heterogeneous Panel Data. *Econometric Journal* 3: 148–161.

Haldane, A. G., and S. G. Hall. 1991. Sterling's Relationship with the Dollar and the Deutschemark, 1976–1989. *Economic Journal* 101 (406): 436–443.

Hall, S. G., D. Robertson, and M. R. Wickens. 1997. Measuring Economic Convergence. *International Journal of Finance and Economics* 2: 131–143.

Harley, C. K. 1988. Ocean Freight Rates and Productivity, 1740–1913: The Primacy of Mechanical Invention Reaffirmed. *Journal of Economic History* 48: 851–875.

Im, K. S., M. H. Pesaran, and Y. Shin. 2003. Testing for Unit Roots in Heterogeneous Panels. *Journal of Econometrics* 115: 53–74.

Jacks, D. S. 2000. Market Integration in the North and Baltic Seas, 1500–1800. Working Paper 55, Economic History Series, London School of Economics and Political Science.

———. 2004. What Drove Nineteenth Century Commodity Market Integration? In *Proceedings of the International Institute of Social History Conference, Utrecht.*

Johansen, S. 1988. Statistical Analysis of Cointegration Vectors. *Journal of Economic Dynamics and Control* 12: 231–254.

Johnson, P. A. 2000. A Non-parametric Analysis of Income Convergence across the U.S. *Economics Letters* 69: 219–223.

Kwiatkowski, D., P.C.B. Phillips, P. Schmidt, and Y. Shin. 1992. Testing the Null Hypothesis of Stationarity against the Alternative of a Unit Root. *Journal of Econometrics* 54: 159–178.

Levin, A., C. F. Lin, and C. Chu. 2002. Unit Root Tests in Panel Data: Asymptotic and Finite-Sample Properties. *Journal of Econometrics* 108: 1–24.

Linden, M. 2002. Trend Model Testing of Growth Convergence in 15 OECD Countries, 1946–1997. *Applied Economics* 34: 133–142.

MacKinnon, J. G. 1991. Critical Values for Co-integration Tests. In *Long-Run Economic Relationships*, ed. R. Engle and C. W. Granger. Oxford: Oxford University Press.

MacKinnon, J. G., A. A. Haug, and L. Michelis. 1999. Numerical Distribution Functions of Likelihood Ratio Tests for Cointegration. *Journal of Applied Econometrics* 14: 563–577.

Maddala, G. S., and S. Wu. 1999. A Comparative Study of Unit Root Tests with Panel Data and a New Simple Test. *Oxford Bulletin of Economics and Statistics* 61: 631–652.

Menard, R. R. 1991. Transport Costs and Long-Range Trade, 1300–1800: Was There a European "Transport Revolution" in the Early Modern Era? In *The Political Economy of Merchant Empires*, ed. J. D. Tracy, 228–275. Cambridge: Cambridge University Press.

Mohammed, S.I.S., and J. G. Williamson. 2003. Freight Rates and Productivity Gains in British Tramp Shipping, 1869–1950. NBER (National Bureau of Economic Research) Working Paper 9531. ⟨http://www.nber.org/papers/W9531⟩.

North, D. C. 1958. Ocean Freight Rates and Economic Development, 1750–1913. *Journal of Economic History* 18: 537–555.

O'Rourke, K. H., and J. G. Williamson. 2002a. After Columbus: Explaining Europe's Overseas Trade Boom, 1500–1800. *Journal of Economic History* 62: 417–456.

———. 2002b. When Did Globalization Begin? *European Review of Economc History* 6: 23–50.

———. 2005. Did Vasco da Gama Matter for European Markets? Testing Frederick Lane's Hypothesis Fifty Years Later. NBER (National Bureau of Economic Research) Working Paper 11884. ⟨http://www.nber.org/papers/W11884⟩.

Oxley, L., and D. Greasley. 1995. A Time-Series Perspective on Convergence: Australia, UK, and USA Since 1870. *Economic Record* 71: 259–270.

Pamuk, Ş. 2001. *500 Years of Prices and Wages in Istanbul and Other Cities, 1469–1914.* Ankara: State Institute of Statistics. ⟨http://www.ata.boun.edu.tr/Faculty/Sevket%20Pamuk/curriculum_vitae/publications.htm⟩.

Persson, K. G. 1988. *Pre-industrial Economic Growth, Social Organization and Technological Progress in Europe.* Oxford: Blackwell.

———. 1999. *Grain Markets in Europe, 1500–1900: Integration and Deregulation.* Cambridge: Cambridge University Press.

———. 2004. Mind the Gap! Transport Costs and Price Convergence in the Nineteenth Century Atlantic Economy. *European Review of Economic History* 6: 125–147.

Phillips, P.C.B., and P. Perron. 1988. Testing for a Unit Root in Time Series Regressions. *Biometrica* 75: 335–346.

Quah, D. 1993. Empirical Cross-Section Dynamics in Economic Growth. *European Economic Review* 37: 426–434.

———. 1996. Empirics for Economic Growth and Convergence. *European Economic Review* 40: 1353–1375.

Quantitative Micro Software QMS. 2005. *Eviews 5.1.* Riverside, California.

Rassekh, F., M. J. Panik, and B. R. Kolluri. 2001. A Test of the Convergence Hypothesis: The OECD Experience, 1950–1990. *International Review of Economics and Finance* 10: 147–157.

Rosenberg, N., and L. E. Birdzell, Jr. 1986. *How the West Grew Rich.* New York: Basic Books.

St. Aubyn, M. 1999. Convergence across Industrialized Countries, 1890–1989: New Results Using Time Series Methods. *Empirical Economics* 24: 23–44.

Trivez, F. J. 2001. Analysis of the Long-Term Relationships of the Underlying Rates of Inflation in the EMU Member States. *Applied Economics* 33: 2001–2007.

Unger, R. W. 1983. Integration of Baltic and Low Countries Grain Markets, 1400–1800. In *The Interactions of Amsterdam and Antwerp with the Baltic Region, 1400–1800,* ed. J. M. van Winter, 1–10. Leiden: Martinus Nijhoff.

van Zanden, J. L. 1999. Wages and Standards of Living in Europe, 1500–1800. *European Review of Economic History* 2: 175–197.

———. 2002. The "Revolt of the Early Modernists" and the "First Modern Economy": An Assessment. *Economic History Review* 55: 619–641.

4 Market Integration and Convergence in the World Wheat Market, 1800–2000

Giovanni Federico and Karl Gunnar Persson

Market integration has been one of the major issues in Williamson's research since his pioneering book on *Late Nineteenth-Century American Development* (1974). His more recent work, notably *Globalization and History* (1999), with O'Rourke, has deeply shaped the conventional wisdom about globalization well beyond the charmed circle of economic historians (World Bank 2002). His overall research agenda can be summed up in four (sets of) questions:

· What happened? Did prices converge or diverge? How fast was the process, if any?

· Why did it happen? What was the contribution of the fall in transportation costs, increased market efficiency, and policy decisions?

· What consequences did market integration have on welfare, income distribution, and long-term economic growth?

· How did these consequences shape the political agenda and foster the adoption of restrictive policies?

Apparently, scholars have been busy tackling the first two questions. Indeed, integration of commodity markets is a hot topic in economic history; in the last year alone, the four major journals in the discipline have published six papers on this issue (Jacks 2005; 2006; Dobado and Marrera 2005; Trenkler and Wolf 2005; Shuie 2005; Klovland 2005), and a lot of other work is in progress. Yet, Williamson's agenda is still largely unexplored (O'Rourke 2002). In fact, most of the current research aims at testing, with increasingly sophisticated econometrics, whether the markets violated the law of one price, that is, whether they were efficient in the Fama (1970) definition. This is a different though related issue. In fact, a degree of efficiency is a precondition for integration, but it is unlikely that inefficiency was so substantial as to prevent integration altogether. We believe that this is the really important story and that Williamson's research agenda deserves to be put back on center stage. In this chapter we focus on the market for wheat and consider the process of integration (or lack of it) from the early nineteenth century to the present. The next section deals with price convergence between the United States and the United Kingdom, the archetypal producer and consumer countries. Subsequent sections explore the patterns of integration in a wider range of countries (Williamson's Atlantic economy); domestic versus international convergence; and the causes of integration.

Price Convergence between the United States and the United Kingdom

As a starting point, figure 4.1 compares ratios of wheat prices in the United Kingdom with prices in New York (1800–1900) and Chicago (1840–present). Both series fluctuate widely in the short run, so the figure reports also the results of a kernel fitting.[1]

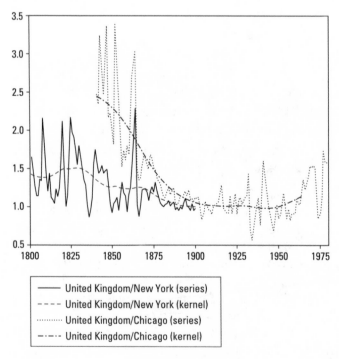

Figure 4.1
Price ratio, United States to United Kingdom, 1800–2000.

The long-term U.K.–New York trend is unambiguously downward from the 1830s to the end of the century. However, the process was not particularly fast: price gap declined at a yearly rate of −0.57 percent p.a. from 1841 to 1900, that is, by about one-third over the whole period. The convergence was much faster between the United Kingdom and Chicago: in the same years, the ratio fell by two-thirds (rate of change −1.78 percent). The price differential remained roughly constant in the first half of the twentieth century, but after 1950 it increased noticeably, at the yearly rate of 1.34 percent. This trend was insufficient to reverse the previous globalization: by 1985 the U.K.–Chicago price differential was only about half its level in the 1840s.

This simple comparison highlights the contribution of trends in the domestic U.S. market to price convergence. Indeed the Chicago–New York price differential halved in the same period. Interestingly, the contribution of short-range integration seems quite small, if not negligible: the ratio of farm-gate prices in Wisconsin and Iowa and market prices in Chicago, or of farm-gate prices in upstate New York and market prices in New York are essentially trendless, with cumulated variation around or below 10 percent.[2]

The importance of domestic integration is somewhat neglected in the current debate, but these results tally fairly well with the conventional wisdom. However, they are subject to two important caveats.

First, both the U.K. price (the well-known Gazette series) and the U.S. series refer to a mix of different qualities of wheat, changing over time. This may be a problem because prices could differ substantially between qualities.[3] Therefore, the measured price gaps might be spurious, and their movement might reflect quality changes instead of genuine integration. Market integration should be measured with prices of the same quality in both markets. Unfortunately, these data are quite difficult to find, but the available information suggests that quality did matter. The adjustment for quality reduces the extent of convergence in the nineteenth century by about one-fifth between New York and Chicago and by half between New York and London.[4] In fact, U.S. wheat improved relative to British domestic production (Ejrnæs, Persson, and Rich 2004). Quality-adjusted price differentials remained constant in the years between the wars and increased very slowly in the 1980s and 1990s.[5] Unfortunately, these data are not directly comparable with the unadjusted differentials quoted previously because they refer to different pairs of markets (London-Winnipeg and Gulf port–Rotterdam versus London-Chicago) and, in the

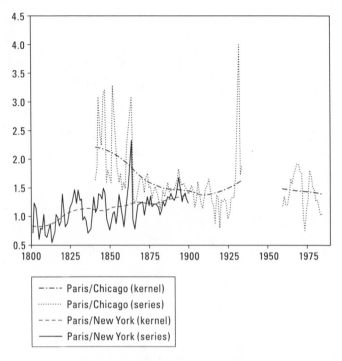

Figure 4.2
Price ratio, France to United States, 1800–2000.

latter case, also to a different period (the adjusted series starts in 1985, exactly when the unadjusted one stops).

Second, the United Kingdom and the United States are not necessarily
representative of the whole Atlantic economy. To illustrate this fairly
obvious (but sometimes overlooked) point, one can consider the case of
France. Figure 4.2 reports data for (unadjusted) price differentials between Paris and the same two U.S. cities, New York and Chicago. The
Paris-Chicago price differential declined from the 1840s to the 1920s.
Price convergence was, however, slower than between United Kingdom
and Chicago (the rate is only −0.94 percent from 1840 to 1900) and,
above all, it was accounted for entirely by the integration of the
domestic U.S. market. In fact, the Paris–New York differential increased
almost continuously throughout the whole nineteenth century. Until the
1840s wheat prices were lower in Paris than in New York, so prices converged from below. This trend must reflect independent developments
in the two countries, as France did not export wheat to New York. But

the price ratio went on growing also later: for instance, in 1870–1900 it increased by 20 percent, whereas the United Kingdom–New York ratio in the same years decreased by about the same amount. The (straightforward) explanation of these trends is given later. It is sufficient to emphasize here the difference with the British experience.

Price Convergence in the Atlantic Economy

The graphical analysis of the previous section is too cumbersome to be replicated for a number of markets/countries large enough to be representative of the whole Atlantic economy. A much simpler measure of market integration is the coefficient of variation, a decrease corresponding to σ-convergence. One can resort to two sources, the impressive database collected by Jacks (2005) for the period 1830–1913, and the journal *Wheat Studies* for the interwar years, from 1923 to 1939. The former consists of 107 series of prices in as many cities in ten countries (Austria-Hungary, Belgium, France, Germany, Norway, Italy, Spain, Russia, United Kingdom, and United States), but gaps in series force us to focus the analysis on a core group of about 40 series in six countries from 1830 to 1907.[6] *Wheat Studies* reports data for eight markets, one each for the four major exporting countries (United States, Canada, Australia, and Argentina) and for the four major European importers (United Kingdom, France, Germany, and Italy). Thus clearly it cannot consider domestic integration. Both samples cover about 70–80 percent of the Atlantic economy.[7] Thus they are fairly representative, provided that the markets selected (out of necessity) are representative. Unfortunately, these prices are not adjusted for quality, and thus results are noisier than one would like.

Quite surprisingly, there is no evidence of a trend toward integration in the long nineteenth century (figure 4.3). Prices converged until the late 1870s and diverged quite fast in the 1880s and early 1890s (the backlash), while dispersion remained roughly constant in the last 15 years of the period. On the eve of World War I, the coefficient of variation of prices in core countries was slightly *higher* than in the early 1830s.[8]

World War I brought about a dramatic change: in the early 1920s the coefficient of variation was less than one-half its prewar level (figure 4.4). This difference is not accounted for by differences in the sample; the gap would be even greater if the coefficient of variation were computed for the same (small) group of markets.[9] This interlude of high integration was,

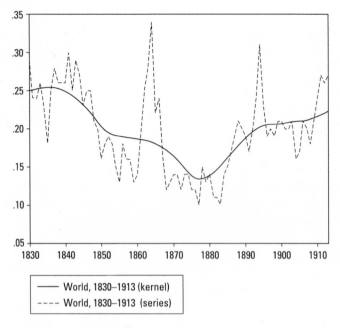

Figure 4.3
Coefficient of variation, "world" 1830–1913.

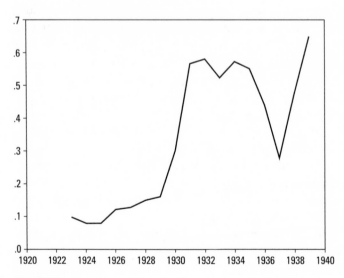

Figure 4.4
Coefficient of variation, "world" 1923–1939.

however, very short-lived. From 1929 to 1931, the coefficient of variation tripled, reaching an all-time peak, about double the previous levels.

Domestic versus International Integration

Movements in the "world" coefficient of variation are the outcome of widely different trends within and across countries. Table 4.1 focuses on the process of domestic integration for 11 countries (adding Sweden to Jacks's sample). For each of them, it reports the coefficient of variation of wheat prices at the starting date and in 1911–1913, and the rates of change over the whole period.

As expected, prices converged in all countries but two, Norway and Sweden. The integration was faster the higher the initial level of dispersion. It can be estimated that a 10 percent higher initial coefficient of variation augmented the absolute rate of change by 15 points. Unfortunately, about half of the series (lower part of table 4.1) are useless for a long-term comparison, as they cover only a part of the period. The comparable series (upper part of table 4.1) show that price convergence accelerated throughout the century. However, in four out of six cases (Austria-Hungary, France, United Kingdom, and United States), half or more of the total fall in price dispersion had been achieved by 1870. The importance of domestic integration in the first half of the century is confirmed by other research. Slaughter (1995) finds evidence of a strong process of convergence in the ante-bellum United States for a wide range of goods (omitting wheat but including flour). Ejrnæs and Persson (2000) argue that a French national market for wheat was already well developed by the mid-nineteenth century. Federico (2005b) shows that wheat prices in Italy converged in two distinct phases, the 1840s and 1850s, and the 1870s and early 1880s. Metzler (1974) speculates, admittedly on the basis of very limited evidence, that integration in Tsarist Russia had started well before 1893.

If domestic integration went on throughout the century, the sharp increase in worldwide dispersion must have been caused by divergence among countries. This was indeed the case, but, as table 4.2 shows, only for some countries.

Both the anti-integration backlash of the years 1870–1890 and the stagnation of the years to World War I can be attributed solely to the divergence among protectionist countries.[10] Price convergence among free-trade countries went on and even accelerated relative to the pre-1870 years.

Table 4.1
Domestic σ-Convergence, 1800–1913

| | Coefficient of Variation | | Rates of σ-Convergence | | | |
	Initial Date[a]	Final Date[b]	1800–1870	1830–1890	1870–1913	Full Period
Austria-Hungary A	0.264	0.046	−0.81[c]	−1.98[c]	−3.05[c]	−1.90[c]
Belgium	0.077	0.013	−0.45	−1.58[d]	−3.07[c]	−1.13[c]
France	0.226	0.072	−1.13[c]	−1.26[c]	−0.73[c]	−1.00[c]
Spain	0.229	0.064	−1.30[c]	−0.96[c]	−1.83	−1.21[c]
Sweden	0.090	0.057	0.51[c]	0.00	−0.82[c]	−0.06
United Kingdom	0.074	0.019	−1.09[c]	−0.50[c]	−1.55[c]	−0.73[c]
United States A	0.268	0.024	−1.01	−2.34[c]	−2.59[c]	−2.29[c]
Austria-Hungary B	0.085	0.053			−2.28[c]	−2.39[c]
Germany	0.091	0.076			−1.01[d]	−1.01[d]
Italy	0.219	0.072		−2.19[c]		−2.09[c]
Norway	0.017	0.053		2.67[c]	0.26	2.00[c]
Russia	0.125	0.076			−1.61[d]	−1.61[d]
United States B	0.208	0.045		−2.85[c]	−2.45[c]	−2.71[c]
United States C	0.076	0.053			−2.98[e]	−2.98[e]

Sources: Italy, Federico (2005b); Sweden, Jorberg (1972); all other data, Jacks (2005).
Notes:
a. Austria-Hungary A, Belgium, Sweden, and United Kingdom 1800–1803; France 1806–1809; Spain 1814–1816; United States A 1816–1818; Italy 1826–1829; Norway 1830–1833; United States B 1841–1843; United States C and Germany 1899–1902.
b. All countries 1911–1913 except Italy 1888–1890 and Spain 1905–1907.
c. Significant at the 10 percent level.
d. Significant at the 1 percent level.
e. Significant at the 5 percent level.

Table 4.2
International σ-Convergence, 1830–1913

	1830–1913	1830–1870	1870–1890	1890–1913
Free-trade Europe	−1.80[a]	−3.17[a]	−2.04[b]	−2.82[c]
Protectionist Europe	−0.49[b]	−1.36[b]	2.14[a]	0.85[c]
Europe	0.27	−0.82	3.43[a]	0.14
Free-trade "world"	−2.26[a]	−1.24	−4.11[a]	−3.77[a]
"World"	0.12	−0.83[c]	3.17[a]	0.90

Source: Jacks (2005).
Notes:
a. Significant at 1 percent level.
b. Significant at 5 percent level.
c. Significant at 10 percent level.

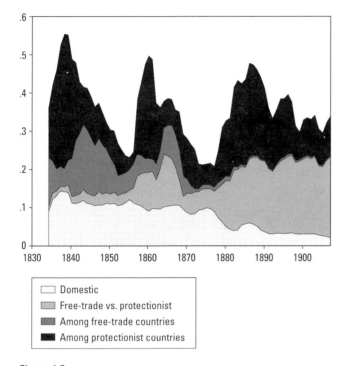

Figure 4.5
Decomposition of "world" price variance, 1830–1913.

So far, each component of total change has been considered in isolation. It is possible to estimate their contribution to integration (or disintegration) of the "world" market with a simple variance analysis (figure 4.5). Total variance is decomposed into (1) domestic (within-country) variance, (2) variance between protectionist countries and free-trade countries, (3) variance among free-trade countries, and (4) variance among protectionist countries.[11]

Domestic integration was a fairly steady process: the within-country variance decreased by three-quarters in the whole period. Two-thirds of this decrease is accounted for by integration in Spain (especially in the 1870s and 1880s) and France. Other countries contributed much less, mainly because by 1830 price dispersion was comparatively low.[12] Without any contribution from international integration, domestic integration would have reduced world price dispersion by about one-sixth. Although not negligible, this improvement is overshadowed by the convergence within free-trade countries, which accounted for most of the reduction in price dispersion in the first stage. From the 1830s to the 1870s, it would have reduced total variance by 15 points, more than 90 percent of the total decline in that period. Afterwards, price differentials among free-trade countries remained negligible, accounting for no more than 2–3 percent of "world" variance. As implicit in table 4.2, the backlash is to be attributed to the increase in the variance between free-trade and protectionist "world" and that among protectionist countries. From the late 1870s to the mid-1890s, both increased by five times, accounting for about 40 percent each of the rise in total "world" variance. However, in the long run, trends in these two components differed substantially. The variance among protectionist countries decreased both before the 1870s and from the mid-1890s to World War I, so its effect in the long run was fairly small (a 10 percent increase in total variance). In contrast, prices of the free-trade and protectionist "world" diverged in all three periods. This component alone accounts for more than half the total increase in variance. Had this price gap remained constant throughout the whole period, total price dispersion on the eve of World War I would have been half its initial level.

Domestic integration cannot be considered for the interwar years because *Wheat Studies* covers only one market per country. This omission is less devastating than it seems. In fact, before the war, all countries in the sample had attained quite a high level of integration, and it seems very unlikely that the wartime destruction changed this situation. It is nevertheless possible that political changes, such as the dissolution of Austria-Hungary, disrupted integration. However, the case of Poland shows how resilient market integration was: a national market for wheat flour was organized a few years after the birth of the new nation (Trenkler and Wolf 2005). Therefore, total variance in the interwar period is decomposed into (1) variance between free-trade countries (United Kingdom and overseas producers) and protectionist countries (France, Germany, and Italy), (2) variance among protectionist countries, and (3) variance among free-trade countries (figure 4.6).

The results of the decomposition are quite clear. The increase in total dispersion in the 1930s reflects the divergence between prices in free-trade and protectionist countries. It caused total variance to increase by 40 times from 1923 to 1939. In comparison to this rise, the contribution from the two other sources disappears, although in absolute terms it is far from negligible (total variance would have tripled even if the price gap between free-trade and protectionist countries had remained constant).

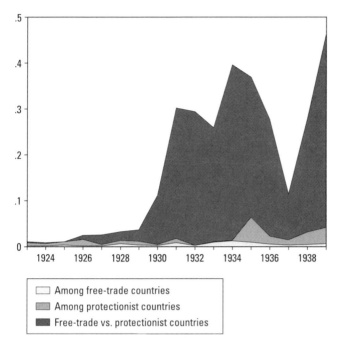

Figure 4.6
Decomposition of "world" price variance, 1923–1939.

These results are not wholly unexpected. However, three points deserve emphasis. First, domestic integration mattered, and its timing differed sharply from that of international integration. Second, most of the action, both within and across countries, predates 1870, the conventional starting point of the first globalization. Third, the integration of the "world" wheat market peaked in the early 1920s, when, according to the conventional wisdom, antiglobalizing forces were already gaining the upper hand. These stylized facts suggest that the level of market integration depended more on policy-determined barriers to trade than on changes in transaction costs.

The Causes of Convergence

In theory, in a perfectly efficient market, the (quality-adjusted) price gap between two markets is equivalent to total transaction costs, which include transportation costs, barriers to trade (if any), and other costs, such as insurance charges, commissions, and minor costs (short-term storage, porter charges, and so on). The difference between these costs and the actual price gap measures the risk premium and inefficiency, that is, the violations of the law of one price. In theory, if complete and accurate data on all costs were available, one could measure the contribution to changes in transaction costs to price convergence (or divergence). The residual, if any, would measure changes in risk premium and/or efficiency of the market. Let us consider, for instance, the quality-adjusted price gap between Chicago and London. From 1857–1865 to 1890–1900, it fell from 75 percent to 26 percent of the Chicago price, while transport costs declined only from 46 percent to 15 percent of the price. In other words, the measured residual decreased from 30 percent of the Chicago price to only 11 percent in the 1890s. These figures seem too high to be accounted for by other costs, even taking into account the small duty levied on imports to the United Kingdom until 1869. In fact, transaction costs were unlikely to exceed 5–8 percent, possibly 10 percent of wheat price, and the two main items, commissions and insurance fees, were proportional to price. Therefore, the fall in the residual must reflect an improvement in pure market efficiency or a sharp decrease in the risk premium (itself evidence of improvement in the market), plus measurement errors, which should, however, be unbiased. It is impossible to be more precise or a fortiori to replicate this analysis for all the pairs of market for the whole period. However, some insights can be obtained by considering separately the changes in two main items of costs: transportation and barriers to trade.

The best measure of long-term change of transportation costs is the so-called freight factor, that is, the ratio of nominal freight to the price of wheat from the place of origin. This method of deflation corresponds to the "iceberg" approach to transaction costs in trade models.

Figure 4.7 reports separate indexes for freight factors for transportation of U.S. wheat from Chicago to New York and from New York to London. The difference is striking, especially in the first period. The domestic factor declined from about 25 percent in the late 1850s to slightly less than 10 percent in the late 1870s, drifting gently downward until War World I and then remaining stable.[13] In contrast, the international freight factor remained constant in the very long run, although with huge fluctuations.[14] It declined fast in the 20 years before World War I and also from 1950 to 1990, and it increased in the years between the wars and, above all, between the late 1930s and the 1950s (it almost tripled from 1936–1938 to the all-time peak of 1957–1959). Actually, one would not expect a big fall because by the late 1850s transatlantic transportation was fairly cheap: the nominal freights accounted for about 7 percent of

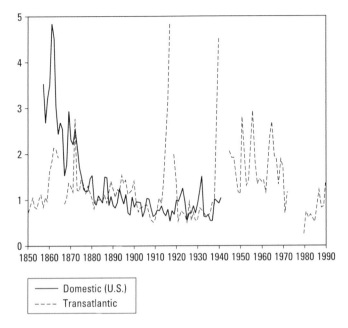

Figure 4.7
Freight factors, 1850–1990 (1884 = 1).

the New York price. The cost of transportation by sea must have declined earlier, in the first half of the century. Indeed, the Odessa-London freight, in nominal terms, halved from the early 1820s to the late 1860s (Harley 1989, table 9). Unfortunately, it is impossible to compute the freight factor because prices in Odessa are not available before 1893. One has to use other price series, and the choice matters. From 1820–1822 to 1849–1851, the freight factor declined by 44.4 percent if computed with New York prices; by 28 percent if computed with Paris prices; and only by 18 percent if computed with London prices. Although the exact measure of decline is uncertain, freights did decrease substantially in the first half of the nineteenth century.

One would be tempted to attribute the difference between domestic and transatlantic freight factors to the direct competition of railways. One must resist this temptation. In fact, transportation from Chicago to New York remained cheaper by water (lake and canal) than by rail until World War I and afterwards.[15] But the cost of domestic transportation fell much more than transatlantic freight: in 1857–1859 it cost 6.71 cents to ship a bushel of grain from Chicago to New York and 3.57 cents to forward it to the United Kingdom. In 1881–1883 the transatlantic freight had declined by 12 percent to 3.17 cents, while the cost of internal transport had plunged by 60 percent to 2.87 cents. It seems implausible that such a big difference was caused only by differential technological change in shipping between the Great Lakes and the Atlantic. It might reflect change in market organization, such as a growing competition among domestic shippers (while transatlantic shipping was more competitive from the start). Or it might reflect the indirect effect of the building of railways: their rates set the upper bound for water-borne transportation costs, which was slower and less reliable. As Williamson (1974) pointed out, one should compute the gains from railways by comparing rail rates not with the actual (post-railways) cost of water transportation but with the counterfactual cost in the absence of railways. Metzler (1974) attributes to railways a major role in fostering integration in Russia, but his inference is based mainly on the coincidence in time between their construction and the process of integration. In contrast, the construction of railways did not contribute much to market integration in nineteenth-century Italy (Federico 2005b). Prices did converge, but mainly because the fall in maritime freight rates fostered Italy's integration with the "world" (i.e., pan-European) market.

The barriers to trade were not so important in the first half of the nineteenth century; many European countries, including France and Prussia, were net exporters of wheat, and thus their duties were irrelevant in practice. The only exception were the British Corn Laws, which, however, accounted for a minor proportion of "world" variance before the repeal.[16] After the abolition of the Corn Laws, wheat trade was practically free all over the continent until the protectionist backlash of the 1880s (O'Rourke 1997). The extent of this can be observed in figure 4.8.[17]

The duties of the three main continental countries in the mid-1890s exceeded 60 percent of the Chicago price, and all other transaction costs did not amount to 20–25 percent. The paramount importance of trade policy in determining integration is confirmed by the results of a paper by Jacks (2006).

All European countries abolished their duties with the outbreak of World War I, and freedom to import accounts for the very high level of integration in the early 1920s. As the figure shows, duties were imposed again from the mid-1920s, but the real watershed was the Great Depression. Importing countries dramatically increased their duties, and resorted to new instruments, such as forcing millers to process a minimum share of

Figure 4.8
Duties on wheat in Europe, 1860–1929. Data on duties from Bacon and Schloemer (1940), appendix 2.

national wheat (usually in excess of 95 percent), setting quotas, and managing the whole wheat trade (Tracy 1989; Federico 2005a). Also the traditionally free-trade United Kingdom followed this path for a couple of years before letting imports from Commonwealth countries free after the Ottawa agreement of 1932 and subsidizing farmers directly (Rooth 1992, 89–94, 212–231). In the United States, the Agricultural Adjustment Act, one of the first measures of the New Deal, set a minimum price for agricultural products after 1933 (Libecap 1998, 186–196).[18] Many of these policies were maintained well after the end of the emergency, until the 1990s. Indeed, the price differential between Gulf States and Rotterdam, inclusive of duty, was quite different from the series without duty (figure 4.9). The latter remained constant at around 1.2, and the former started around 2.5 in the mid-1980s and fell very quickly to about 1.30 after 1992, after the McSharry reform of the Common Agricultural Policy. Just for comparison, the London–New York price ratio exceeded 2 only three times before the repeal of Corn Laws, in 1808, 1820, and 1825. The

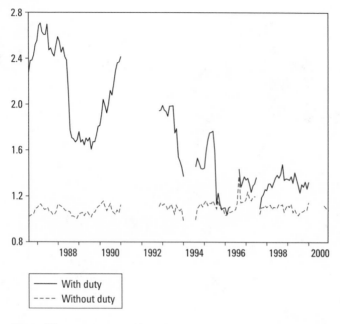

Figure 4.9
The impact of the Common Agricultural Policy.

world market for wheat was less integrated in the 1980s than at the beginning of the nineteenth century.

Conclusion

This chapter makes four points:

• Although unadjusted prices are better than no price, one should be careful when drawing inferences from them. Quality mattered, even for a relatively homogeneous commodity such as wheat. Integration of markets created incentives for standardization and quality improvement in exporting markets, so unadjusted data could bias the extent of integration upward.

• The story of market integration is long and complex, and focusing only on one specific period, such as 1870–1913, might yield a biased picture. Arguably, prices converged even faster before 1870, and the 1920s stand out as a short interlude of high integration.

• Price convergence (and divergence) has been a far-reaching process, involving both domestic and international markets and, to a different degree, all the countries in the Atlantic economy. But trends differed, and thus focusing only on transatlantic integration between the United Kingdom and United States is not enough and might even be misleading.

• The emphasis on transatlantic freight as a cause of convergence might be misplaced. Domestic transportation costs also mattered, and, above all, prices were largely determined by trade policies.

These statements refer to wheat and possibly to other cereals. Do they hold true for other commodities? It is not easy to answer because few studies deal with them (Froot, Kim, and Rogoff 1995; O'Rourke and Williamson 1994; Slaughter 1995; Klovland 2005; Bukenya and Labys 2005; Federico 2005b). It is impossible to draw any inference from their results, but it is possible to make some educated guesses on the basis of information about commodity-specific transaction costs. Freight rates for all primary commodities moved in parallel from the 1860s to World War I (Mohammed and Williamson 2004).[19] It is also likely that all commodities benefited from improvements in the circulation of information and in overall efficiency. However, one cannot rule out that the effect differed across commodities. For instance, the grading system was much less developed for other primary commodities than for wheat, and the quality problem was, if anything, greater.[20] But trade policy differed quite markedly. Raw materials remained largely exempt from duties, and thus, *ceteris paribus*, integration must have been easier in the market for cotton or coal than in the market for grain. This inference is not necessarily true for manufactured goods, which were hit by protection. Given these contrasting influences, the least bad guess suggests that wheat may be fairly, although not fully, representative. However, this hypothesis, and all the conclusions of this chapter, should be buttressed by further research. Williamson's research agenda still remains exciting and full of promise for our understanding of modern economic growth.

Appendix A: The Variance Decomposition

1830–1913
Total world variance is decomposed as

World = Free vs Protectionist + U.S. vs Free Europe + Within Free Europe + Within Protectionist Europe + Within Austria-Hungary + Within France + Within Norway + Within Spain + Within United Kingdom + Within United States

We define

P = price in a market

μ = average price

n = number of markets in each area

and subscripts

W = world

FC = free-trade countries (United States, Belgium, United Kingdom)

P = protectionist countries (Austria-Hungary, France, Norway, Spain)

FE = free-trade European countries

PE = protectionist European countries

AH = Austria-Hungary

B = Belgium

F = France

N = Norway

S = Spain

UK = United Kingdom

US = United States

Then

$$\text{World} = \sum (P_i - \mu_W)^2$$

$$\text{Free vs Protectionist} = (\mu_{FC} - \mu_W)^2 n_{FC} + (\mu_{PC} - \mu_W)^2 n_{PC}$$

$$\text{US vs Free Europe} = (\mu_{US} - \mu_{FC})^2 n_{US} + (\mu_{FE} - \mu_{FC})^2 n_{FC}$$

$$\text{Within Free Europe} = (\mu_B - \mu_{FE})^2 n_B + (\mu_{UK} - \mu_{FE})^2 n_{UK}$$

$$\text{Within Protectionist Europe} = (\mu_{AH} - \mu_{PE})^2 n_{AH} + (\mu_F - \mu_{PE})^2 n_F$$
$$+ (\mu_N - \mu_{PE})^2 n_N + (\mu_S - \mu_{PE})^2 n_S$$

$$\text{Within Austria-Hungary} = \sum (P_{AH} - \mu_{AH})^2$$

Within France $= \sum (P_{\mathrm{F}} - \mu_{\mathrm{F}})^2$

Within Norway $= \sum (P_{\mathrm{N}} - \mu_{\mathrm{N}})^2$

Within Spain $= \sum (P_{\mathrm{S}} - \mu_{\mathrm{S}})^2$

Within United Kingdom $= \sum (P_{\mathrm{UK}} - \mu_{\mathrm{UK}})^2$

Within United States $= \sum (P_{\mathrm{US}} - \mu_{\mathrm{US}})^2$

$$\frac{\sum (P_i - \mu_{\mathrm{W}})^2}{\mu_{\mathrm{W}} n_{\mathrm{W}}}$$

$$= \frac{(\mu_{\mathrm{FC}} - \mu_{\mathrm{W}})^2 n_{\mathrm{FC}} + (\mu_{\mathrm{PC}} - \mu_{\mathrm{W}})^2 n_{\mathrm{PC}}}{\mu_{\mathrm{W}} n_{\mathrm{W}}}$$

$$+ \frac{(\mu_{\mathrm{US}} - \mu_{\mathrm{FC}})^2 n_{\mathrm{US}} + (\mu_{\mathrm{FE}} - \mu_{\mathrm{FC}})^2 n_{\mathrm{FC}}}{\mu_{\mathrm{W}} n_{\mathrm{W}}}$$

$$+ \frac{(\mu_{\mathrm{B}} - \mu_{\mathrm{FE}})^2 n_{\mathrm{B}} + (\mu_{\mathrm{UK}} - \mu_{\mathrm{FE}})^2 n_{\mathrm{UK}}}{\mu_{\mathrm{W}} n_{\mathrm{W}}}$$

$$+ \frac{(\mu_{\mathrm{AH}} - \mu_{\mathrm{PE}})^2 n_{\mathrm{AH}} + (\mu_{\mathrm{F}} - \mu_{\mathrm{PE}})^2 n_{\mathrm{F}} + (\mu_{\mathrm{N}} - \mu_{\mathrm{PE}})^2 n_{\mathrm{N}} + (\mu_{\mathrm{S}} - \mu_{\mathrm{PE}})^2 n_{\mathrm{S}}}{\mu_{\mathrm{W}} n_{\mathrm{W}}}$$

$$+ \frac{\sum (P_{\mathrm{AH}} - \mu_{\mathrm{AH}})^2 + \sum (P_{\mathrm{F}} - \mu_{\mathrm{F}})^2 + \sum (P_{\mathrm{N}} - \mu_{\mathrm{N}})^2 + \sum (P_{\mathrm{S}} - \mu_{\mathrm{S}})^2 + \sum (P_{\mathrm{UK}} - \mu_{\mathrm{UK}})^2 + \sum (P_{\mathrm{US}} - \mu_{\mathrm{US}})^2}{\mu_{\mathrm{W}} n_{\mathrm{W}}}$$

1923–1939

Total variance is decomposed as

World = Free vs Protectionist + Within Free Countries + Within Protectionist Europe

In this case the free-trade countries are United States (US), Canada (C), Australia (AU), Argentina (AR), and United Kingdom (UK), and the protectionist ones are France (F), Germany (G), and Italy (I). Therefore, the formula is

$$\frac{\sum (P_i - \mu_W)^2}{\mu_W n_W}$$

$$= \frac{(\mu_{FC} - \mu_W)^2 n_{FC} + (\mu_{PC} - \mu_W)^2 n_{PC}}{\mu_W n_W}$$

$$+ \frac{(\mu_{US} - \mu_{FE})^2 n_{US} + (\mu_{UK} - \mu_{FE})^2 n_{UK} + (\mu_{AU} - \mu_{FE})^2 n_{AU} + (\mu_C - \mu_{FE})^2 n_C + (\mu_{AR} - \mu_{FE})^2 n_{AR}}{\mu_W n_W}$$

$$+ \frac{(\mu_G - \mu_{PE})^2 n_G + (\mu_F - \mu_{PE})^2 n_F + (\mu_I - \mu_{PE})^2 n_I}{\mu_W n_W}$$

It is possible to compute two alternative counterfactual measures of variance at time t—under the assumptions that: (1) one single component remained constant at the initial level, e.g., for domestic integration,

$$\frac{\sum (P_i^t - \mu_W^t)^2}{\mu_W^t n_W}$$

$$= \frac{(\mu_{FC}^t - \mu_W^t)^2 n_{FC} + (\mu_{PC}^t - \mu_W^t)^2 n_{PC}}{\mu_W^t n_W}$$

$$+ \frac{(\mu_{US}^t - \mu_{FC}^t)^2 n_{US} + (\mu_{FE}^t - \mu_{FC}^t)^2 n_{FC}}{\mu_W^t n_W}$$

$$+ \frac{(\mu_B^t - \mu_{FE}^t)^2 n_B + (\mu_{UK}^t - \mu_{FE}^t)^2 n_{UK}}{\mu_W^t n_W}$$

$$+ \frac{(\mu_{AH}^t - \mu_{PE}^t)^2 n_{AH} + (\mu_F^t - \mu_{PE}^t)^2 n_F + (\mu_N^t - \mu_{PE}^t)^2 n_N + (\mu_S^t - \mu_{PE}^t)^2 n_S}{\mu_W^t n_W}$$

$$+ \frac{\sum (P_{AH}^0 - \mu_{AH}^0)^2 + \sum (P_F^0 - \mu_F^0)^2 + \sum (P_N^0 - \mu_N^0)^2 + \sum (P_S^0 - \mu_S^0)^2 + \sum (P_{UK}^0 - \mu_{UK}^0)^2 + \sum (P_{US}^0 - \mu_{US}^0)^2}{\mu_W^0 n_W};$$

or (2) all but one single component remained constant at the initial level, e.g., for free-trade vs protectionist countries,

$$\frac{\sum (P_i^t - \mu_W^t)^2}{\mu_W^t n_W}$$

$$= \frac{(\mu_{FC}^t - \mu_W^t)^2 n_{FC} + (\mu_{PC}^t - \mu_W^t)^2 n_{PC}}{\mu_W^t n_W}$$

$$+ \frac{(\mu^0_{US} - \mu^0_{FC})^2 n_{US} + (\mu^0_{FE} - \mu^0_{FC})^2 n_{FC}}{\mu^0_W n_W}$$

$$+ \frac{(\mu^0_B - \mu^0_{FE})^2 n_B + (\mu^0_{UK} - \mu^0_{FE})^2 n_{UK}}{\mu^0_W n_W}$$

$$+ \frac{(\mu^0_{AH} - \mu^0_{PE})^2 n_{AH} + (\mu^0_F - \mu^0_{PE})^2 n_F + (\mu^0_N - \mu^0_{PE})^2 n_N + (\mu^0_S - \mu^0_{PE})^2 n_S}{\mu^0_W n_W}$$

$$+ \frac{\sum(P^0_{AH} - \mu^0_{AH})^2 + \sum(P^0_F - \mu^0_F)^2 + \sum(P^0_N - \mu^0_N)^2 + \sum(P^0_S - \mu^0_S)^2 + \sum(P^0_{UK} - \mu^0_{UK})^2 + \sum(P^0_{US} - \mu^0_{US})^2}{\mu^0_W n_W}$$

This approach was used to estimate the contribution of each component for figures 4.5 and 4.6.

Appendix B: Sources for Prices

United Kingdom and France

To 1903 British Board of Trade (1904). Gazette average for United Kingdom; quality not specified for France.

1904–1934 National Bureau of Economic Research (NBER) Historical Database, ⟨http://www.nber.org/databases/macrohistory/contents/⟩. Grades not specified.

1960–1985 Economic Research Service, U.S. Department of Agriculture.

United States (New York)
A British bushel is assumed to be 1.0321 times an American one.

1800–1849 Cole (1938). *Grades:* New York, 1800–1836, North River; 1837, Genesee; 1838–1840, North River; 1841–1845, Genesee; 1846–1848, North River; 1849, Genesee.

1850–1900 Persson (2004). Main sources were *New York Times* and *Beerbohm's Evening Corn Trade List. Grades:* 1850–1854, White Genesee; 1855–1877, Red Western/Red and Amber; 1878–1900, Red Winter No. 2.

United States (Chicago)

1840–1995 National Bureau of Economic Research (NBER) Historical Database; Harley (1980); Cole (1938), 1800–1849; Persson (2004), 1850–1900. *Grades:* 1841–1849, Spring Wheat (NBER); 1850–1859, Spring No. 2 (Harley); 1860–1863, Spring No. 2 (NBER); 1864–1865, Spring No. 1 (NBER); 1866–1878, Spring No. 2 (*New York Times*); 1879–1897, Spring No. 2 (NBER); 1898–1904, "Regular Wheat"; 1905–1918, Red Winter No. 2; 1919–1920, Northern No. 2; 1921–1922, Red Northern No. 2.

United States (Other)

Iowa—Williamson (1974, table A.5); Wisconsin—Mortenson et al. (1933); Upstate New York—Ronk (1935).

Sources for Transatlantic Freight Factor

1850–1868 Persson (2004).

1869–1950 Mohammed and Williamson (2003, table A.3D).

1950–1974 FAO (1967; 1975).

1980–2004 *World Grain Statistics*, published annually by International Grains Council, London.

Notes

1. Each point is obtained by fitting a polynomial and weighting the observations with an Epanechnikov kernel. All the rates of change quoted in this chapter are computed with linear interpolation, adding an AR(1) term when necessary.

2. The rates of change are Chicago-Iowa (1870–1910), −0.18 percent p.a. (cumulated 7 percent decrease); Chicago-Wisconsin (1844–1900), 0.21 percent (cumulated change +14 percent), and (1845–1932), 0.04 percent (+4 percent); and New York–Upstate New York (1842–1900), −0.11 percent (−6.5 percent).

3. For instance, the allowed spread between the best and the worst deliverable quality at the Chicago futures markets in the early 1920s was about 7.5 percent of the reference price (Prices of Cash and Wheat Futures 1934). This spread in all likelihood underestimates the true range, as low-quality wheat was not deliverable. If two qualities were perfectly substitutable, their price differentials would reflect only their intrinsic qualities, e.g., in the maximum milling ratio, and thus would be constant over time. However, it is unclear to what extent different qualities of wheat were perfect substitutes. For instance, it is well known, at least in Italy, that good pasta can be made only with hard wheat. In this case, movements in price gaps might reflect also changes in demand and supply of different varieties.

4. The London–New York ratio does refer to the same quality (the U.S. Red Western, later Red Winter No. 2), but there are no data for the same quality in London and Chicago. It is nevertheless possible to estimate the implicit price of Red Western in Chicago as the price of Spring No. 2 times the ratio between Red Winter and Spring No. 2 in New York. The rate of change for the quality-adjusted price ratio between Chicago and New York (1859–1900) is −0.65 percent versus −0.80 percent for the unadjusted series in the same period. Adding a dummy for 1865, the rate drops to −0.51 percent. The rate of change for the London–New York ratio is 0.54, and 0.40 percent with a dummy for 1864; neither coefficient is significant even at 10 percent. The first figure can be compared with the −0.99 percent decline in the unadjusted United Kingdom–New York series.

5. The interwar data refer to Canadian wheat (Manitoba No. 1 or 3) in Winnipeg and London. The rate of change (1923–1939), 0.65 percent, drops to 0.38 with a 1931–1932 dummy. The price gap for the Dark Northern Spring No. 2 between Gulf ports and in Rotterdam increased by 0.3 percent p.a. from 1985 to 2005.

6. This core group includes four markets in Austria-Hungary, three in Belgium, twelve in France, two or three (depending on the years) in Norway, twelve in the United Kingdom, and four to seven (depending on the year) in the United States. A further eight markets can be added, including Spain, but these series stop in 1907. The results are very similar. In two cases, Austria-Hungary and the United States, it is possible to extract different samples of cities (Austria-Hungary A and B, United States A, B, and C). The data are available at ⟨http://www.sfu.ca/~djacks/⟩.

7. The Atlantic economy consists of the whole Europe, including Russia (until 1913), Serbia, Bulgaria, and Romania, and its Western offshoots (North America, Oceania, and Argentina). Population from Maddison (2003), wheat production from Mitchell (1998a; 1998b; 1998c). The countries of the core sample accounted for only 44.5 percent of production and 44 percent of the population of the Atlantic economy before 1913. However, a chi-square test fails to reject the hypothesis that the country distributions of population and wheat production are equal in the sample and in the universe.

8. The long-term rate of change is 0.12, both in 1830–1907 (including Spain) and in 1830–1913 (omitting Spain), but neither coefficient is significant.

9. The sample includes five cities: London, Paris, St. Louis, Berlin, and Milan; the prewar data are collected from *Il Sole*, the leading Italian trade newspaper. The coefficient of variation was 0.22 in 1911–1913 (versus 0.21 in the core Jacks sample), 0.09 in 1923–1925, and 0.14 in 1929. The difference with the prewar dispersion is not accounted for, nor is the omission of domestic variance. In fact, the coefficient of variation among country averages was 0.26 in 1905–1907 (including Spain) and 0.20 in 1911–1913 (excluding Spain).

10. "Protectionist" Europe includes Austria, France, Norway (belonging to Sweden until 1905), and Spain, and "free-market" Europe includes the United Kingdom (despite the Corn Laws) and Belgium. The row "free world" includes the United States and "free-market" European countries. All countries are considered a single market.

11. The computation proceeds from the local to the general (see appendix A). At each stage, all markets of the previous stage are treated as one, with a price equal to the corresponding average. For example, "protectionist" Europe consists of Austria, France, Norway, and Spain, and its variance is computed as if all markets in these countries had the same price. The variance is standardized by dividing by the world price times the number of markets in the relevant area. This method keeps symmetry in summations, but the results are not strictly comparable with the coefficients of variation, which are standardized with national prices. Total within-country variance is the sum of variances of individual countries. All series are computed as five-year moving averages.

12. Price dispersion was unusually low in the United States in 1831: the coefficient of variation in that year, 0.09, was half the average of the other years of the decade.

13. The yearly rates of change are −4.90 percent (1858–1880), −1.20 percent (1880–1913), +0.41 percent (1913–1941) (not significant), and −1.41 percent for the whole period.

14. The yearly rates of change for the whole period (1851–1990) is 0.12, and it reduces to 0.08 if one adds dummies for the Civil War years. The rate is −0.37 for the period 1850–1890, but it comes out positive (0.38) by adding the Civil War dummies. None of these rates is significant. The rates of change are −2.84 (1890–1913), 2.18 (1920–1938) (not significant), and −2.32 (1950–1990).

15. By 1912 the lake and canal route cost 5.37 cents/bushel versus 6.54 for lake and rail, and 9.73 for all-rail (Chicago Board of Trade 1912). By 1929 the lake and rail route for exported grain cost 10.42 cents/bushel versus 12.37 for all-rail.

16. The variance between United Kingdom and Belgium accounted for about 10 percent of the total in 1839–1841 and fell to about 2 percent in 1843–1845. Had it remained constant at its 1841 level, by 1843–1845 the "world" variance would have decreased by 9 percent instead of by 16 percent.

17. When duties changed within a year, they were computed by averaging the rates before and after the change, weighted with the proportion of months under each regime. This method yields unbiased figures if imports are evenly distributed across the year.

18. The ratio of the U.S. price to the average of the three other free-trade countries jumped from 1.12 in March 1932–February 1933 to 1.57 from April 1933.

19. The rates of change in nominal freights from 1869 to 1913 are −2.12 percent for wheat from the Black Sea, −2.98 percent for coal to Genoa, and −2.68 percent for cotton from Alexandria (all significant at 1 percent). The cumulated decrease amounts to 60 percent for wheat, 69 percent for coal, and 73 percent for cotton (Mohammed and Williamson 2004).

20. For instance, there were 15 basic qualities of silk according to provenance and method of production, and the price range doubles (Federico 1997). Many of them were further subdivided: the best qualities, such as the Italian, Japanese, and Shanghai legislatures, were classified according to title *and* quality.

References

Anderson, J., and E. van Wincoop. 2004. Trade Costs. *Journal of Economic Literature* 42: 691–751.

Bacon, L. B., and F. C. Schloemer. 1940. *World Trade in Agricultural Products: Its Growth, Its Crisis, and the New Trade Policies.* Rome: International Institute of Agriculture.

Balker, N. S., and R. J. Gordon. 1989. The Estimation of Prewar GNP: Methodology and New Evidence. *Journal of Political Economy* 97: 38–92.

Bradford, S., and R. Z. Lawrence. 2004. *Has Globalization Gone Far Enough? The Costs of Fragmented Markets.* Washington: Institute for International Economics.

British Board of Trade. 1904. British Parliamentary Papers. Second Series of Memoranda, Statistical Tables, and Charts: Prepared in the Board of Trade with Reference to Various Matters Bearing on British and Foreign Trade and Industrial Conditions. London.

Bukenya, J. O., and W. C. Labys. 2005. Price Convergence on World Commodity Markets: Fact or Fiction? *International Regional Science Review* 28 (3): 302–329.

Chicago Board of Trade. 1912. *Annual Report.*

Cole, A. H. 1938. *Wholesale Commodity Prices in the United States, 1700–1861.* Cambridge, Mass.: Harvard University Press, 1969.

Dobado, R., and G. A. Marrero. 2005. Corn Market Integration in Porfirian Mexico. *Journal of Economic History* 65: 103–128.

Ejrnæs, M., and K. G. Persson. 2000. Market Integration and Transport Costs in France, 1825–1903: A Threshold Error Correction Approach to the Law of One Price. *Explorations in Economic History* 37: 149–173.

———. 2005. The Nature and Cost of Disequilibrium Trade: The Case of Nineteenth Century Transatlantic Grain Trade. Discussion Paper 2. Department of Economics, University of Copenhagen.

Ejrnæs, M., K. G. Persson, and S. Rich. 2004. Feeding the British: Convergence and Market Efficiency in Nineteenth Century Grain Trade. Discussion Paper. Department of Economics, University of Copenhagen.

Engel, C., and J. H. Rogers. 1996. How Wide Is the Border? *American Economic Review* 86: 1112–1125.

Fackler, P. L., and B. K. Goodwin. 2001. Spatial Price Analysis. In *Handbook of Agricultural Economics*, ed. B. Gardner and G. Rausser. Vol. 1B, *Marketing, Distribution, and Consumers*, 971–1024. Amsterdam: Elsevier.

Falkus, M. E. 1968. Russia's National Income, 1913: A Revaluation. *Economica* 35: 52–73.

Fama, E. 1970. Efficient Capital Markets: A Review of Theory and Empirical Work. *Journal of Finance* 25: 383–417.

FAO (Food and Agriculture Organization of the United Nations). 1967. *Production Yearbook*.

———. 1975. *Production Yearbook*.

Federico, G. 1997. *An Economic History of the Silk Industry*. Cambridge: Cambridge University Press.

———. 2004. The Growth of World Agricultural Production, 1800–1938. *Research in Economic History* 22: 125–182.

———. 2005a. *Feeding the World*. Princeton: Princeton University Press.

———. 2005b. Market Integration and Market Efficiency: The Case of Nineteenth Century Italy. ⟨www.iue.it/HEC/People/Faculty/Profiles/federico/gfederico-market-integration.pdf⟩. Forthcoming, *Explorations in Economic History*.

———. 2005c. A Theory of Market Integration. Mimeo.

Federico, G., and K. H. O'Rourke. 2000. Much Ado about Nothing? The Italian Trade Policy in the Nineteenth Century. In *The Mediterranean Response to Globalisation before 1950*, ed. J. G. Williamson and S. Pamuk, 269–296. London: Routledge.

Feinstein, C. H. 1972. *National Income, Expenditure, and Output of the United Kingdom, 1855–1965*. Cambridge: Cambridge University Press.

Findlay, R., and K. H. O'Rourke. 2003. Commodity Market Integration. In *Globalization in Historical Perspective*, ed. M. D. Bordo, A. M. Taylor, and J. G. Williamson, 13–64. Chicago: University of Chicago Press.

Froot, K. A., M. Kim, and K. Rogoff. 1995. The Law of One Price over 700 Years. NBER (National Bureau of Economic Research) Working Paper 5132. ⟨http://www.nber.org/papers/W5132⟩.

Gregory, P. 1982. *Russian National Income 1885–1913*. Cambridge: Cambridge University Press.

Harley, C. K. 1980. Transportation, the World Wheat Trade, and the Kuznets Cycle, 1850–1913. *Explorations in Economic History* 17: 218–250.

———. 1986. Late Nineteenth Century Transportation, Trade, and Settlement. In *The Emergence of a World Economy, 1500–1914, Part 2: 1850–1914*, ed. W. Fischer, R. M. McInnis, and J. Schneider, 593–617. Wiesbaden: F. Steiner.

———. 1989. Coal Export and British Shipping, 1850–1913. *Explorations in Economic History* 26: 311–338.

Harrison, C. A. 1938. *Wholesale Commodity Prices in the United States, 1700–1861*. Cambridge, Mass.: Harvard University Press.

Headrick, D. 1988. *The Tentacles of Progress: Technology Transfer in the Age of Imperialism, 1850–1940*. Oxford: Oxford University Press.

Hufbauer, G., E. Wada, and T. Warren. 2002. *The Benefits of Price Convergence: Speculative Computations.* Washington: Institute for International Economics.

Imbs, J., H. Mumtaz, M. Ravn, and H. Rey. 2005. PPP Strikes Back: Aggregation and the Real Exchange Rate. *Quarterly Journal of Economics* 120: 1–43.

Isard, P. 1977. How Far Can We Push the Law of "One Price"? *American Economic Review* 67: 942–948.

Jacks, D. S. 2005. Intra- and International Commodity Market Integration in the Atlantic Economy. *Explorations in Economic History* 42: 381–413.

———. 2006. What Drove Nineteenth Century Commodity Market Integration? *Explorations in Economic History* 43: 383–412.

Jörberg, L. 1972. *A History of Prices in Sweden, 1732–1914.* Lund, Sweden: CWK Gleerup.

Klovland, J. T. 2005. Commodity Market Integration, 1850–1913: Evidence from Britain and Germany. *European Review of Economic History* 9 (2): 163–197.

Libecap, G. D. 1998. The Great Depression and the Regulating State: Federal Government Regulation of Agriculture, 1884–1970. In *The Defining Moment: The Great Depression and the American Economy in the Twentieth Century,* ed. M. Bordo, C. Goldin, and E. N. White, 181–224. Chicago: University of Chicago Press.

Maddison, A. 2003. *The World Economy: Historical Statistics.* Paris: OECD.

McCallum, J. 1995. National Borders Matter: Canada-U.S. Regional Trade Patterns. *American Economic Review* 85: 614–623.

Metzler, J. 1974. Railroad Development and Market Integration: The Case of Tsarist Russia. *Journal of Economic History* 34: 529–549.

Mitchell, B. R. 1998a. *International Historical Statistics: The Americas, 1750–1993.* 4th ed. London: Macmillan.

———. 1998b. *International Historical Statistics: Europe, 1750–1993.* 4th ed. London: Macmillan.

———. 1998c. *International Historical Statistics: Africa, Asia, Oceania, 1750–1993.* 3d ed. London: Macmillan.

Mohammed, S.I.S., and J. G. Williamson. 2003. Freight Rates and Productivity Gains in British Tramp Shipping, 1869–1950. NBER (National Bureau of Economic Research) Working Paper 9531. ⟨http://www.nber.org/papers/W9531⟩.

———. 2004. Freight Rates and Productivity Gains in British Tramp Shipping, 1869–1950. *Explorations in Economic History* 41: 174–203.

Morgenstern, O. 1959. *International Financial Transactions and Business Cycles.* Princeton, N.J.: Princeton University Press.

Mortenson, W. P., H. H. Erdman, and J. H. Draxler. 1933. *Wisconsin Farm Prices, 1841–1933.* Research Bulletin 119. Madison: University of Wisconsin Agricultural Experiment Station.

Ojala, E. M. 1952. *Agriculture and Economic Progress.* Oxford: Oxford University Press.

O'Rourke, K. H. 1997. The European Grain Invasion. *Journal of Economic History* 57: 775–801.

———. 2002. Europe and the Causes of Globalization, 1790 to 2000. In *Europe and Globalization,* ed. H. Kierzowski, 64–85. London: Macmillan.

O'Rourke, K. H., and J. G. Williamson. 1994. Late Nineteenth Century Anglo-American Factor Price Convergence: Were Heckscher and Ohlin Right? *Journal of Economic History* 54: 892–916.

———. 1999. *Globalization and History: The Evolution of the Nineteenth Century Atlantic Economy.* Cambridge, Mass.: MIT Press.

Persson, K. G. 2004. Mind the Gap! Transport Cost and Price Convergence in the Nineteenth Century Atlantic Economy. *European Review of Economic History* 8: 127–147.

Prest, A. R., and A. A. Adams. 1954. *Consumers' Expenditure in the United Kingdom, 1900–1919.* Cambridge: Cambridge University Press.

Prices of Cash Wheat and Futures at Chicago since 1933. *Wheat Studies,* 1934.

Rogoff, K. 1996. The Purchasing Parity Puzzle. *Journal of Economic Literature* 34: 647–668.

Ronk, S. E. 1935. *Prices of Farm Products in New York State, 1841–1935.* Ithaca, N.Y.: Cornell University Agricultural Experiment Station.

Rooth, T. 1992. *British Protectionism and the International Economy,* Cambridge: Cambridge University Press.

Shuie, C. 2005. From Political Fragmentation Towards a Custom Union: Border Effects of the German Zollverein, 1815–1855. *European Review of Economic History* 9 (2): 129–162.

Slaughter, M. J. 1995. The Antebellum Transportation Revolution and Factor-Price Convergence. NBER (National Bureau of Economic Research) Working Paper 5303. ⟨http://www.nber.org/papers/W5303⟩.

Strauss, F., and L. H. Bean. 1940. Gross Farm Income and Indices of Farm Production and Prices in the United States, 1869–1937. United States Department of Agriculture Technical Bulletin 703. Washington: Government Printing Office.

Toutain, J.-C. 1961a. Le produit de l'agriculture française de 1700 à 1958: 1. Estimation du produit au XVIIIe siècle. No. 1 Série AF. Paris: Institut des Sciences Mathématiques et Economiques Appliquées (ISMEA).

———. 1961b. Le produit de l'agriculture française de 1700 à 1958: 2. La croissance. No. 2 Série AF. Paris: Institut des Sciences Mathématiques et Economiques Appliquées (ISMEA).

Tracy, M. 1989. *Government and Agriculture in Western Europe, 1880–1988.* 3d ed. New York: New York University Press.

Trenkler, C., and N. Wolf. 2005. Economic Integration across Borders: The Polish Interwar Economy. *European Review of Economic History* 9: 199–231.

U.S. Bureau of the Census. 1975. *Historical Statistics of the United States: Colonial Times to 1975.* Washington: Government Printing Office.

Williamson, J. G. 1974. *Late Nineteenth-Century American Development: A General Equilibrium History.* Cambridge: Cambridge University Press.

———. 1980. Greasing the Wheels of Sputtering Export Engines: Midwestern Grains and American Growth. *Explorations in Economic History* 17: 189–217.

———. 2004. The Tariff Response to World Market Integration in the Periphery before the Modern Era. Paper presented at the Market Integration Workshop, European University Institute, Fiesole, Italy. ⟨post.economics.harvard.edu/faculty/jwilliam/papers/Fiesole04-text.pdf⟩.

World Bank. 2002. *Globalization, Growth, and Poverty: Building an Inclusive World Economy.* Oxford: Oxford University Press.

Yates, P. L. 1959. *Forty Years of Foreign Trade.* London: Allen and Unwin.

5 Biological Globalization: The Other Grain Invasion

Alan L. Olmstead and Paul W. Rhode

Jeffrey Williamson has inspired a fruitful collaborative investigation into the causes and consequences of the great globalization wave that transformed the world economy over the long nineteenth century. Surging flows of goods and factors of production signaled a significant increase in the international division of labor that greased the skids of economic growth. In Williamson's analysis, innovations in transportation technologies and more efficient institutional structures propelled the globalization process by driving down the costs of moving goods over long distances. In this chapter we argue that in addition to transport innovations, the development and spread of new biological technologies were crucial for the emergence of the new global economy. We concentrate on world wheat production, but many of the same lessons apply to most other major crops and livestock products.

Studies of more recent globalization experiences suggest that our focus on past biological innovations may pay dividends. As an example, the economic development literature highlights the contribution of research and development to agricultural productivity growth and trade. The Green Revolution and the Genetic Revolution are part and parcel of the modern globalization debates. The role of research institutes such as the International Maize and Wheat Improvement Center (CIMMYT) in advancing agricultural technologies takes center stage. We argue that the nineteenth century also witnessed biological innovations that fundamentally changed economic opportunities around the world. This was not just a haphazard process because well before CIMMYT existed, institutional structures and networks developed to convey these innovations across the planet. The opportunities to increase productivity were immense because it is unlikely that all the miraculous achievements of the recent Green Revolution exceed the importance of the Columbian Exchange when biological technologies were transferred between the Old and New Worlds (Crosby 1972). This involved nothing less than learning how to adapt alien crops to whole continents. The unlocking of the productive potential of the vast expanses of virgin land that would make cheap grain exports possible involved much more than laying railroad tracks. Agricultural innovations were especially important because of the relative size of the agricultural sector. In the nineteenth century agricultural products dominated international trade, and global labor and capital flows were closely linked to agricultural development. Thus, innovations that affected agricultural productivity and helped transplant agricultural production across a wide range of geoclimatic zones deserve attention.

The insights of endogenous growth theory suggest another reason to pay heed to biological innovations of the past. In the models of Grossman and Helpman (1991), the flow of ideas across international borders reduces the fixed cost of product development. We argue that international spillovers in the agricultural sector were important in explaining the process and consequences of globalization in the pre–World War I period. Biological innovations in past centuries were generally not subject to patenting as were mechanical innovations, and thus we must look elsewhere for what Paul Krugman has termed a "paper trail of ideas." The paper trail exists in the records of farmers and scientists. This collective record shows that not only were the technological advances nonexclusive but inventors preferred it this way. Much like CIMMYT created and promoted the diffusion of new germplasm, nineteenth- and early twentieth-century plant breeders made spectacular advances and freely exchanged both their methodologies and their creations. The new technologies often spread rapidly. Moreover, unlike primary products, which mostly flowed from the periphery to the center, the flow of ideas and biological technologies moved in every direction. The Great European Grain Invasion of the late nineteenth century was itself the product of the earlier invasion of the Americas and Oceania by Eurasian plants that were essentially invasive species in their new homes.

Biologists who catalog invasive species usually include wild oats but not wheat. Why? Both are non-native plants, imported to many of the areas where they are now grown. The difference in billing is likely because wild oats are weeds, hardy but worthless, whereas wheat is of economic value but does not thrive without the sweat of our brows. If the invasive species are defined as non-native organisms that "completely take over and entirely change whole established ecosystems," then wheat grasses, aided by their human cultivators, clearly fit the bill.[1] Vast tracts of forest and grass lands were cleared and broken in the Americas and Australia to allow for the cultivation of wheat. O'Rourke (1997) has called attention to the effects of cheap grain from the periphery on factor prices in Europe and on pressures for protectionism. This chapter highlights the advances in knowledge behind the earlier biological invasion that made cheap grain exports from the periphery possible.

Of Williamson and Wheat

The grain trade has figured prominently in Williamson's work, including his first book, *American Growth and the Balance of Payments, 1820–1913* (1964). His classic application of general equilibrium modeling to history asked whether Midwestern grain lubricated the U.S. export engine of growth (Williamson 1974). The grain trade remains central to his more recent analysis as, for example, in *Globalization and History* (O'Rourke and Williamson 1999). Narrowing price gaps for wheat between the Chicago (or Odessa) and the Liverpool markets frequently serve as the key indicator of falling transport costs and increasing globalization (O'Rourke and Williamson 1999, 43, 53; Persson 2004). The repeal of the Corn Laws in Britain was the key event signaling the beginning of an era of freer trade. And "the invasion of cheap New World and Ukrainian grain, which threatened to reduce agricultural incomes" in Europe was the "major event" initiating the political backlash against the nineteenth-century globalization wave (O'Rourke and Williamson 1999, 93). Indeed, the backlash is introduced with language ringing with the themes of this chapter:

The impact of the railroad and the steamship was reinforced by political develop-ments after 1860 as European economies moved rapidly toward free trade. The world was becoming a much smaller place, and to an observer in 1875, it must have seemed as if it was going to get a lot smaller. Yet nothing is inevitable. His-tory shows that globalization can plant the seeds of its own destruction.

O'Rourke and Williamson (1999, 53) argue that falling transportation costs undermined the "tyranny of distance" and encouraged the growth of wheat production across the world's periphery. Our earlier work docu-mented the dramatic geographic shift of U.S. grain production. Based on county-level agricultural output data, we showed that the mean geographic center of U.S. grain production was near Wheeling, West Vir-ginia, in 1839 but moved roughly 1,260 kilometers northwest to the re-gion around Omaha, Nebraska, by 1919 (Olmstead and Rhode 2002;

2003). To give context to these movements, we can combine our production data with the local 1910–1914 farm-gate prices reported in Zapoleon (1918). The differentials in these prices are typically interpreted as reflecting transport costs.[2] These data indicate that under the 1839 distribution, wheat producers were roughly 10 cents (that is, 13 percent of the average farm-gate price) closer to the consumer markets than under the 1909 distribution. An important implication of the change in the locus of production is that the reduction in transportation costs between two fixed locations (e.g., Chicago and Liverpool) overstates the cost decline to marginal producers who were pushing the frontier out from Chicago.

The Changing Locus of World Wheat Production

How far from the consumption centers of Western Europe did wheat production spread during the great globalization wave, and how did the new areas of production compare to the old? Given the scope of the task required to answer these questions, we rely on aggregate national-level data. As discussed in the chapter appendix, we used Food Research Institute (FRI) data to compile a comprehensive production series for the 1885–1930 period, which we linked to the available production and export data for 18 nations over the 1866–1899 period. Our calculations required measuring distance from each country—the convention in gravity model literature is to use the national capitals—to a single global center, for which we used London. The appendix discusses our reservations with this approach, but we note that the movements of the wheat belts to the interiors of the leading new producing countries suggest that the capital-to-capital measures generally understate the increase in distance.

Figure 5.1 shows the changing average distance of wheat production between 1866 and 1930. The distance from London almost doubled, climbing from 2,377 km in 1866–1870 to 4,725 km in 1920–1925. The most rapid change occurred between 1866 and 1880, when the average distance grew 2.5 percent p.a., or about 1,000 km. Growth slowed thereafter, but almost 600 km were added by the First World War. There was another rapid rise and then retreat in the aftermath of this conflict.

What geographic shifts explain these changes? Figure 5.2 charts wheat production statistics by major country from 1885 to 1930. The fluctuating distance over WWI and its aftermath was due to the Bolshevik Revolution. Russia's share (2,130 km from London) of world production fell from 25 percent in 1913 to 8 percent in 1922 and then rebounded to 21 percent by 1930. The rise in the shares of world production of Australia

Figure 5.1
Average distance of world wheat production from London, 1866–1930.

(16,956 km), Argentina (11,052 km), and Canada (5,401 km) largely explains the increasing distance from 1885 to 1914. The combined share of these three exporters rose from less than 4 percent in 1885 to over 10 percent in 1913 and then to 19 percent in 1930. Their growth accounted for four-fifths of the measured increase in distance between 1885 and 1930. Over this period, the output share of European countries excluding Russia fell from just over one-half of world production to less than one-third. India's share (6,747 km) declined by a similar percent, whereas the U.S. share (5,932 km) was roughly equal at the beginning and end of the period. These data obviously cannot explain the rapid growth of distance before 1885. But it is clear that the United States was driving that change. It was the major country experiencing a rapidly growing share of world production (almost a doubling) that was also located further than the average distance of producers from London.

The global shift of wheat cultivation had dramatic effects on typical growing conditions, with a movement onto drier and colder lands. Table 5.1 documents these changes.[3] World production in 1926–1930 was distributed to lands that, on average, were 3.2°C colder and received 10.8

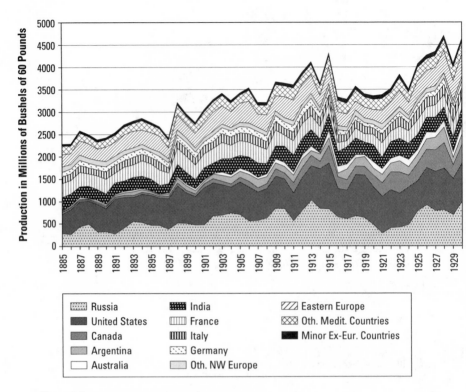

Figure 5.2
World wheat production, 1885–1930.

Table 5.1
Changing Climatic Conditions of Wheat Production

	Annual Temperature (degrees C)	Pre-Harvest Temperature (degrees C)	Annual Precipitation (cm)	Yield (M tons/ hectare)
1866–1870	14.4	20.1	72.8	1.01
1886–1890	12.7	18.6	68.1	0.94
1910–1914	11.7	18.3	63.9	0.91
1926–1930	11.2	18.0	62.0	0.90

Note: The series was derived from fixed national climate and yield values reflecting typical 1920–1934 conditions and changing national shares in global wheat production. The 1866–1870 data were derived from splicing the 1866–1899 series for the 18 countries to the 1885–1930 series calculated for the full FRI sample.

fewer centimeters of precipitation than the areas where wheat had been cultivated in 1866–1870. Given large and expanding production in Europe, the changes in the conditions facing farmers near the frontier were significantly greater than the changes displayed in table 5.1. The 1926–1930 land base was also associated with lower average yields per planted hectare. Had the acreage been distributed as it was in 1866–1870, yields would have been about 12 percent higher. Clearly, global wheat cultivation was shifting to poorer lands, making the growth of world yields over this period all the more impressive. Actual world yields rose 17 percent between 1886–1890 and 1926–1930 in spite of a geographic redistribution of production that should have led to a 4 percent decline.

These changes in average climatic conditions were not exogenous to the globalization process. Rather, they were the predictable consequences of lower transportation costs opening the continental interiors to profitable production. As the FRI researchers noted, there was a tendency

for yields of wheat to decline from east and west toward the interior regions of each of the principal land masses, North America and Eurasia. The central regions of such large continents not only suffer from generally light precipitation, but are also characterized by extreme variations in precipitation and temperature.... These climatic characteristics are generally unfavorable for wheat yields. (Bennett and Farnsworth 1937, 283)

Globalization had induced a shift of wheat cultivation from maritime areas with temperate climates to interior regions with harsher continental climates.[4]

These findings are in keeping with our earlier results for the United States, where grain production moved from the humid East to the dry and harsh Great Plains. Accounting for such internal shifts would increase the measured global changes.

In the United States pushing wheat production onto the new lands required new technologies—the development and diffusion of new types of wheat and new cultural methods. If western farmers had persisted in planting old varieties, the boom in wheat production that fueled the global economy simply would not have been forthcoming. All the transportation improvements imaginable could not have induced English wheats to thrive in North Dakota. Success in the United States and Canada also depended on innovations that mitigated the destructive forces of ever-evolving pest and disease environments.

The biological transformation in the United States was part of a worldwide process. The farmers who extended the wheat frontier in Canada, Australia, Argentina, and Russia faced similar challenges of producing in new and harsh environments. In all these areas the first attempts to grow wheat failed. Success depended on biological innovation. Farmers and plant breeders from all these countries scoured the globe for varieties that might meet local needs. They selected and increased the seeds from particularly promising plants, and by the end of the nineteenth century a number of scientists were creating hybrids that combined the favorable traits of varieties drawn from around the world. This was a purposeful and sophisticated process led by people whom plant scientists today still revere as the pioneering giants of their discipline. Advances were accelerated by a loose but effective international network of plant scientists that facilitated the exchange of ideas, methods, and varieties. These exchanges highlight the importance of international technological spillovers in the globalization process.

The technological changes based on plant selection and breeding flowed in every direction. At first, they flowed from the center to the periphery. But the wheat varieties that made the expansion of the extensive margin possible for the most part did not come from the old center, but from the old periphery. Poland, Ukraine, Russia, India, and Africa supplied much of the germplasm underpinning the Grain Invasion. The international flow of technology was even more complex because new varieties developed in the New World were sent back to the old center, where breeders selectively combined their strengths (earliness, rust resistance, tolerance for drought and cold, and high gluten content and baking quality) with the best of northern European varieties (typically high-yielding). By the early twentieth century the new generations of successful European wheats—distinct varieties tailored for the United Kingdom, France, Germany, or Italy—often contained germplasm introduced from North America and Australia (as well as directly from other regions of the old periphery, including Russia, Ukraine, India, and Japan). A similar exchange linked the different lands of the New World; varieties developed in North America were a crucial factor in the expansion of the Australian wheat frontier, and Australian varieties proved valuable to producers in California and the Pacific Northwest. A brief account of the biological dynamics that accompanied the global expansion of wheat production will illustrate these general points.

The Development of Wheat Breeding in Britain and the Core

During Britain's age of industrialization, there were many key advances in cereal production. British farmers had long experimented with new wheats from across the Channel (Walton 1999, 34). Largely through

chance discoveries and "selections from a single particularly fine or productive individual," agricultural improvers developed several new wheats
by 1840, and in the process invented the method of pure-line selection.[5]
John Le Couteur of Jersey discovered "Bellevue de Talavera"; Banham
selected Browick from a field of Scotch Annat in Norfolk; and Patrick
Shirreff, the Scottish agriculturalist, discovered Mungoswell in Hadding-
tonshire, Scotland, in 1819 and found the basis for the Hopetoun line in a
single ear in a field near Sussex in 1832.[6] The efforts of Shirreff and Le
Couteur received lengthy notice in Charles Darwin's *Variation of Animals
and Plants Under Domestication* (1868).[7]

Over the 1840–1870 period, "more organized attempts were set up
to find superior specimens" (Brassley 2000, 525). Building on British
attempts to hybridize wheat dating to the 1790s, Hallett began extensive
trials near Brighton in the late 1840s, employing a variety of red and
white wheats from England and Australia, the latter "which were fixed
upon on account of their quality alone" (Hallett 1861). The leading new
variety was Squarehead, which "offered a new combination of high yield
and strong straw which was to have a profound influence on wheat breeding throughout north and central Europe, extending to Scandinavia, Germany, and even to Poland" (Lupton 1987, 51, 64–65). Squarehead was
purportedly discovered in 1868; Mr. Scholey of Yorkshire increased and
sold the seed of the new variety beginning in 1870. After 1870 the pace of
improvement picked up with "a spate of selections, introductions and
hybridizations" that would come to dominate the market by 1914. In
1873, Shirreff published his classic memoir, *Improvement of the Cereals*,
detailing his selection and hybridization efforts (Shirreff 1873; Roberts
1929, 110–117). Among the important introductions was Japhet (mar-
keted in England as Red Marvel), developed by Henri Vilmorin of Paris
in the 1890s. The leading new hybrid wheat was Squareheads Master,
derived from a cross between Scholey's Squarehead and Golden Drop in
1880. The new varieties had important consequences in the battle against
diseases.

The most serious rust problems in humid Britain were stripe rust and
leaf rust. Angus (2001, 111–112) indicates that Squareheads Master was
developing problems with stripe rust. But periodically, stem rust—the
type that bedeviled growers in the arid lands of the United States, Canada, and Australia—also struck. In Britain this fungal disease was known
as wheat mildew. During a serious outbreak, as in 1892, stem rust could
have locally devastating consequences, inducing a frantic search for less
susceptible varieties.[8] Once a strain of rust adapted to attack a specific
variety, that variety remained vulnerable.

At the turn of the century the rediscovery of Mendel's laws of inheritance opened up new possibilities. The most innovative work was done by Cambridge University's Rowland H. Biffen, who initiated a hybridization program in 1901. In addition to advancing basic science, Biffen made practical innovations such as Little Joss (1908), a cross between Squareheads Master and the rust-resistant Russian spring wheat, Ghirka (Brassley 2000, 525). The ability of Little Joss to withstand stripe rust made it popular with farmers following its release in 1910. Breeding research in the United Kingdom became more institutionalized in 1912 with the creation of the government-supported Plant Breeding Institute at Cambridge (Angus 2001, 111–113; Lupton 1987, 64–65). Another key advance came in 1916 with the release of Yeoman. This cross between Browick and the Canadian variety, Red Fife, offered superior milling and baking qualities and high yields. By this time, British breeders were transforming the wheat varieties grown in the United Kingdom by combining germplasm drawn from western Europe, North America, Australia, and Russia.

A similar process was at work on the continent. Before 1850 in France and Belgium, a number of wheat varieties had been adapted for specific regions. For example, the wheat grown in eastern France was more tolerant of cold than that grown in the west. However, in any region there was little variation from farm to farm, resulting in "slow evolution over the centuries from the effect of natural selection due to the environment and the mass selection done by man selecting the best filled grains." After 1850 new varieties imported from Odessa gained importance in southern France, and English varieties such as Squarehead became popular in the north. These introductions were followed by a succession of new varieties developed by pioneering breeders. Most prominent was Henri Vilmorin, who began experimenting with wheat hybridization in 1873. By the mid-1880s, Vilmorin had successfully crossed wheats from Aquitaine (which were themselves recent imports from the Ukraine) with the high-yielding Squarehead. Although French breeders made important strides in the nineteenth century, it was not until 1921 that the government established a formal breeding program with the founding of the Institut de Recherches Agronomiques (Bonjean, Doussinault, and Stragliati 2001; Lupton 1987, 53–56).

From the Center to the Periphery

The histories of other land-abundant, labor-scarce economies such as Canada, Australia, and Argentina support our emphasis on the importance of biological learning in the long nineteenth century. The Canadian literature emphasizes the crucial role that new rapid fruiting and drought and cold-tolerant varieties played in western settlement, and in particular credits Charles Saunders's path-breaking achievement in creating Marquis. In a similar fashion, the Australian literature emphasizes the work of William Farrer in developing drought-hardy and rust-resistant varieties. Mechanization plays a prominent role in the histories of both nations, but there is a clear recognition that biological innovation was essential for the expansion of the wheat belts in both countries.

Canada

Wheat cultivation was introduced to Canada in 1605 at the first French settlement at Port Royal in what is now Nova Scotia. Cultivation in eastern Canada expanded over the coming centuries but generally suffered from diseases, insects, and the propensity of the soft white winter wheat to die from winterkill. Farmers tried a "succession of types or landraces," including Red Chaff, White Flint, Kentucky White Bearded, and Genesee White Flint, "in search of ones that would overcome some of the impediments to successful wheat production" (White 1995, 6; DePauw, Boughton, and Knott 1995; DePauw and Hunt 2001). The key breakthrough came with the development of Red Fife by David and Jane Fife of Peterborough, Ontario. The Fifes selected and increased the grainstock from a single wheat plant grown on their farm in 1842. The original seed came from a Scottish source out of a cargo of winter wheat shipped from Danzig to Glasgow (the grain itself likely originated in Ukraine). Mrs. Fife, who was the daughter of a farmer and seedsman, evidently saved the precious seed stock from foraging cattle. Red Fife proved to be the first successful hard spring wheat grown in North America, and it became the basis for the westward and northern spread of the wheat frontier. It also provided much of the parental stock for later wheat innovations (Buller 1919; Symko 1999).

Wheat cultivation in the region west of the Great Shield experienced an even more troubled development. The first sustained attempt to grow wheat was made in the 1810s by members of the ill-fated Selkirk settlement on the Red River near Lake Winnipeg. Winter wheat, first tried in 1811–1812, proved a failure. The fields were resown with spring wheat, which died due to drought. In 1813–1814 the settlers obtained a small amount of spring wheat from Fort Alexander, which produced sufficient grain for the colony to continue cultivation. But in 1818 grasshoppers devoured most of what had been a promising crop. In 1819 another grasshopper attack devastated the colony's wheat crop, leaving it without seed.

In the dead of winter, a band of the desperate settlers traveled over 1,060 km to Prairie du Chien on the upper Mississippi River to secure replacement seed. This spring wheat performed well, but it was not until 1824 that the settlers had their first truly successful wheat crop. Over the next several decades, the region's farmers experimented with varieties from England, Ireland, and Ukraine.

Mennonites, who settled in southern Manitoba in 1874–1875, are generally credited as the first Europeans to cultivate wheat on Canada's open prairie. These migrants planted a seed, White Russian, which they brought with them from Europe. But the future wheat of Manitoba, indeed the entire west, was Red Fife. According to one account, immigrants from Ontario first introduced Fife to the region around 1857.[9] An alternative account suggests Fife came in only after the devastating grasshopper attack that "destroyed every vestige of the crop in 1868."[10] The success of the hard red wheat was due in part to the efforts of Minnesota millers to import Hungarian techniques in the mid-1870s. With the application of the steel roller mill, flour made from Red Fife acquired a reputation of unparalleled quality. Fife wheats became the dominant cultivars on the Canadian prairies as they opened to greater settlement after 1885. These wheats also played a role in Sir John A. Macdonald's national policy of incorporating the west into Canada. To encourage the more rapid development of the prairies, the Canadian government and the Canadian Pacific Railway gave new settlers free Red Fife seed (DePauw, Boughton, and Knott 1995, 6–14).

But the role of state intervention was far greater. In 1886, Parliament created the Canadian federal experiment station system, with the Central Experimental Farm established in Ottawa and additional stations subsequently opened across the country. William Saunders began breeding work at Central Farm shortly after its inception. One of Saunders's early (if only partial) successes was the introduction of the Ladoga cultivar from northern (60° N) Russia in 1887. This wheat matured earlier than Red Fife but yielded poorer-quality flour. The value of earliness was reinforced by the virtual destruction of the western crop in 1888 by a very early autumn frost. William Saunders's more lasting contribution resulted from a systematic program of hybridizing early-maturing cultivars with high-quality cultivars. In 1903 his son, Charles Saunders, took over the work. The most valuable result of their combined research efforts was Marquis, a cross between Red Fife and Red Calcutta, a very early wheat from India.[11] Released in 1909, this cultivar matured about ten days earlier than Red Fife and was more resistant to disease. These qualities led to its rapid adoption. By 1918, Marquis accounted for over 80 percent of western Canada's wheat (Buller 1919, 254).

Ward (1994) has convincingly linked the famed Canadian wheat boom to these biological developments. His estimates show that between 1885 and 1910 the ripening period of wheat at four Canadian experiment stations fell on average by 12 days—days that meant the difference between success and failure in many years. His regression estimates capture other effects besides the switch to Marquis. He notes, for example, that the time of ripening of Red Fife declined over the period because of changes in cultural techniques such as the use of grain drills. Kenneth Norrie's quantitative study of the settlement of the Canadian prairies between 1870 and 1911 found that pushing the wheat frontier further north and west required the adoption of dry farming technologies and the development of drought-resistant and early-ripening wheat varieties suitable for the region. Midway through the period, by the 1890s, Canadian farmers were pushing the commercial wheat belt above 55° latitude.[12]

As wheat culture spread onto the prairies, it was increasingly subject to attacks of leaf and stem rusts. Rust was first noted in western Canada in 1891 and some damage was reported in 1892 and 1896 (Johnson 1961). Much more serious outbreaks occurred in 1902, 1904, 1911, 1916, 1927, and 1935. Eastern Saskatchewan and all of Manitoba proved especially prone to rust problems. In response to the severe 1916 epidemic, when 100 million bushels were destroyed, the Dominion Rust Research Laboratory was established in 1924 at the University of Manitoba. Its plant breeders, working closely with plant pathologists, developed a line of wheats possessing enhanced resistance to the rust diseases. These varieties, including Apex, Renown, Regent, and Redman, together with Thatcher from Minnesota rapidly replaced Marquis after it succumbed to the rust in the devastating 1935 attacks.

Argentina

In *Frontier Development*, Adelman (1994) makes a classic comparison between the expansion of wheat cultivation in Canada and Argentina. No Argentine figure emerges to play the starring role as prominently as did the Saunderses in Canada. The Spanish introduced wheat into Argentina in the sixteenth century, but the crop did not emerge as an important export commodity until the mid-1880s (Scobie 1964, 70). In the first half of the 1920s, Argentina ranked fourth in the world in wheat production and third in exports, behind only the United States and Canada (Canada 1925).

Much less is known about nineteenth-century breeding activities in Argentina than in the other major New World producers. Scobie is downright disdainful of the farming methods generally employed. He maintains that Argentine wheat growers "knew or cared little about seed selection" and often sold their best seed for consumption and kept poorer-quality seed for planting.[13] Even if his critical assessment captures the attitudes and behavior of the vast majority of farmers, it is likely there was still considerable progress. By the turn of the century an important new Italian wheat variety, Barletta, had gained widespread favor, indicating that at least some farmers were making improvements.[14] Barletta was well suited to a wide range of Argentine conditions because of a tolerance for drought, the ability to survive relatively extreme temperatures, and rust resistance. In addition, it had high gluten content and was prized by European millers (Scobie 1964, 87). The names of some of the other popular varieties in the early twentieth century, including Ruso, Hungaro, Rieti, Japones, Costa De Bari, Frances Blanco, and Frances Colorado, suggest that the globalization of germplasm had not bypassed the Southern Cone (Bicknell 1904, 51–54; Nisi and Antonelli 2001, 535).

A major step was taken in 1912 when the Minister of Agriculture hired William O. Backhouse, who initiated the country's first formal wheat-breeding program. Backhouse, a Cambridge graduate who studied under Biffen, tested foreign varieties at diverse locations to establish their suitability for Argentine conditions. In 1913 he began crossing the best local varieties with the imports to fight leaf rust. Barletta was becoming increasingly vulnerable to rust, which destroyed roughly one-fifth of the nation's crop in 1916. Backhouse's endeavor was a global undertaking as he imported varieties from India, North America, Europe, and China. One by one Backhouse narrowed his search. The Indian wheat varieties, obtained through A. C. Howard, director of economic botany at Pusa, adapted very well to the new environment but showed no resistance to leaf rust. The North American imports showed almost complete resistance to leaf rust but did not mature at the same time as their potential breeding partner, Barletta. Further experiments were conducted with Rieti (from Italy, containing English, Dutch, Italian, Japanese, and likely Ukrainian germplasm) and Chino. Chino, a native of Szechuan, possessed immunity to leaf rust. In 1925 the Backhouse team released a Chino-Barletta cross, wheat cultivar 38 M.A., which rapidly gained popularity over a wide region. Until the mid-1940s this variety accounted for roughly 20 percent of Argentine production (Backhouse 1917; Backhouse and Brunini 1925; Nisi and Antonelli 2001, 535–536; Guitierrez 1985, 13).

The Argentine program benefited from similar developments underway in Uruguay. In 1912–1913 two German scientists, Alberto Boerger and Enrique Klein, began breeding programs at the National Nursery of Toledo near Montevideo and at the Agronomic Station of Cerro Largo in northeastern Uruguay. In 1919, Klein moved to Argentina, where he founded the privately owned Argentine Plant Breeding Company (Nisi and Antonelli 2001, 519, 535–541). Backhouse, Boerger, and Klein were part of a growing cadre of plant scientists trained at European universities who brought their expertise to the far-flung periphery, including Kenya and India.

Australia

As in Canada, wheat breeding plays a prominent role in Australia's historiography. William Farrer, the nation's most famous wheat scientist, is regarded as Australia's "Great Benefactor" with his likeness adorning the two-dollar bill. In his authoritative account, Davidson tells us that the first attempt to grow wheat near Sydney failed:

The original seed brought from Britain by Phillip failed to germinate. This was probably fortunate as these were the English winter wheats which are sown [in Britain] in the autumn and ripen in the shortening days of the following autumn. As they are light-sensitive they will not ripen when the days are lengthening. What was required in Australia was wheat which could be sown in autumn, grown through the winter and spring and ripen in the lengthening days of late spring before the summer drought sets in. By good fortune the next wheat seeds were obtained from Rio de Janeiro and were of the early flowering Mediterranean types which, because they are insensitive to light will ripen in a period when the hours of daylight are increasing.[15]

Other accounts confirm these difficulties: "The early colonists found themselves attempting to grow wheat under conditions that were completely different from anything that they had known, in a new country, in a new hemisphere" (O'Brien et al. 2001, 611). But there is disagreement about what types of wheat the early settlers planted. Many assert that the first successful varieties were winter wheats from England (Red and White Lammas), while others speculate that they were spring wheats (Macindoe and Walkden-Brown 1968, 2, 147, 152; Dunsdorfs 1956, 16, 73, 101).

An intriguing study by Aitken (1966) suggests an answer to this puzzle. She argues that "the first wheats must have been early types, and it is likely that they were unwittingly introduced from Mediterranean stocks via Rio de Janeiro" following the failure of the English and South

African seed sown in 1788. Aitken's evidence is impressive. Drawing on contemporary testimony, she first reconstructs the dates of sowing, flowering, and harvesting for the years 1789 to 1805 showing that the crops were mostly planted in June and harvested in November or early December. Aitken then conducted field experiments with several early and late flowering wheats, including Red Lammas. The results showed that the late varieties did not ripen until January, whereas the early varieties ripened in time for an early December harvest. The puzzle of the early years appears resolved—the first successful wheats grown in Australia most likely did not come from England.[16]

Starting with the first pioneers, there was an ongoing effort to discover varieties more suitable for Australian conditions. In 1822 the Agricultural Society of New South Wales initiated a program to introduce and test new wheat varieties, but with little success. Although scores of varieties were introduced, the first significant breakthrough occurred around 1860 in South Australia with the selection of the Purple Straw variety.[17] This variety ripened earlier than previous varieties, providing some rust protection and helping extend the wheat-sheep frontier. At about the same time, Dr. Richard Schomburgh, director of Botanic Gardens in Adelaide, introduced Du Toit from South Africa. Du Toit was distributed "widely in South Australia, where it became popular because of its early maturity and moderate resistance to stem rust" (Macindoe and Walkden-Brown 1968, 2). Over the next several decades, astute farmers and plant breeders selected varieties, including Ward's Prolific, Steinwedel, and Gluyas, that were more suitable for the drier areas of South Australia. Another important variety, Early Baart, was introduced from South Africa in 1884 by Professor Custance of the Roseworthy Agricultural College (Macindoe and Walkden-Brown 1968, 2; Wrigley and Rathjen 1981, 99–103; Dunsdorfs 1956, 189–190). These new varieties provided the genetic material for many subsequent varieties developed by deliberate hybridization.

By the 1880s successful programs to artificially outcross wheat were underway in England, the United States, Germany, France, Australia, and Austria-Hungary, among others. The first Australian efforts to hybridize wheat date to the work of A. B. Robin (also of Roseworthy), who evidently was experimenting with F1 hybrids by 1887. But the most prominent plant breeder of this era was William Farrer.

Farrer belongs to a small group of scientists who fundamentally changed the agricultural prospects of a nation. Farrer became interested in rust after witnessing the enormous damage it caused in 1882. Drawing on both his reading of Darwin and his knowledge that European and U.S. breeders were developing disease resistance in other crops, Farrer reasoned that creating rust-resistant wheat varieties might be possible. Without conducting any experiments, he published his plans for "making" high-quality rust-resistant wheats. This bold pronouncement earned him considerable scorn, as befitting of an unknown dilettante with no formal training in plant sciences.[18]

Farrer would have the last laugh. He began his experimental work in 1885 at the age of 41, and in 1889 he commenced work on hybridization. His objectives were to breed for rust resistance, to increase the gluten content and lower the starch content, to develop wheat to meet Australian conditions, and finally to increase yields in a farming regime characterized by low inputs. He would succeed on all fronts (Evans 1980, 3–13; Farrer Memorial Trust). Farrer's most important creation was Federation. In 1894 he discovered a particularly early maturing plant with purple straw (probably a pure Purple Straw) growing in a row of Improved Fife. In 1895, Farrer crossed this purple straw with Yandilla, a variety that he had previously created by crossing Improved Fife (obtained from Canada) with Etawah (from India). In 1901, Farrer released the new variety, Federation, and by 1910 it had become the most popular variety on the continent, proving remarkably productive over a diverse range of growing conditions (Macindoe and Walkden-Brown 1968, 110–111). Within a decade Federation became an important variety on the West Coast of the United States. It was early-maturing, rust-resistant, of excellent quality, and because of its Purple Straw lineage, relatively high-yielding. It possessed short, strong straw suitable for stripper harvesting as practiced in Australia. Before Farrer, wheat growing had been largely limited to the cooler table lands where later maturing varieties could survive. Federation, along with new varieties (based on drought-resistant introductions from South Africa and India), allowed farmers to push wheat cultivation into drier, hotter regions, less susceptible to rust. The early maturation of Farrer's wheats gave them added rust protection because there was less time for the spores to multiply. In New South Wales alone wheat acreage increased from 1 to 4 million acres largely because of Farrer's accomplishments.

In the course of his work he would experiment with varieties from all over the world. Many of these varieties were sent by other breeders. Farrer returned the favor. Evans (1980, 13) captures the essence of these transactions: "In 1894 he [Farrer] wrote, 'I have been sending wheats to Europe and America, and intend to send some to India and France. I hope also to soon be able to start a correspondence with people in different parts of the world....' He was, in fact, a one-man international agricultural research centre." In addition to exchanging seeds, Farrer discussed experimental procedures and myriad details of his research with some of the leading breeders of the day, including Henri Vilmorin in France, A. E. Blount, B. T. Galloway, and Mark A. Carleton in the United States, Charles Saunders of Canada, and Rowland H. Biffen in England (Evans 1980, 5, 10; Farrer Memorial Trust). The international exchange of ideas and germplasm represents an important way that the world was getting smaller.[19]

Aitken's (1966) agronomic studies highlight the importance of the new varieties. In the late 1950s she conducted experiments on the physical development of a number of modern and obsolete wheat varieties. The out-of-date varieties included the winter wheats Purple Straw, Red Lammas, and Little Joss and the spring wheat Federation. Under a variety of geo-climatic conditions the winter wheats suffered damage to their root structures because of high soil temperature, and they were later to mature, thus exposing them to environmental risks. The root damage was far more serious than generally thought, lowering yields and in some instances preventing fruiting. Of special interest, she found that when it was winter-sown, Federation wheat flowered five weeks earlier than Lammas and developed leaf structures more suitable to hot climates.[20]

Although wheat producers in Canada and Australia confronted dramatically different environments, major concerns being frigid weather in Canada and hot weather in Australia, there were also striking similarities in conditions and in the responses. In both countries, farmers pushed wheat production into arid regions unlike anything experienced in the old northern European center. Moreover, the challenge created by both cold and heat called for spring wheat varieties with relatively short growing seasons. A variety that did not ripen early was in danger of being damaged or killed by frost in Canada and by heat in Australia. Thus both Charles Saunders and William Farrer followed a common path by cross-breeding Red Fife (originating in the Ukraine, shipped to Poland, forwarded to Scotland, reshipped to Canada, and later sent to Australia) with Indian wheats noted for early ripening and drought tolerance. Such were the international pedigrees of the two wheat varieties, Marquis and Federation, credited with making possible the opening of millions of acres of new wheat lands.

Conclusion

The long nineteenth century saw substantial changes in the loci of wheat production. Between the late 1860s and the late 1920s, the average distance of world wheat production from London almost doubled, as measured in our capital-to-capital calculations. This change in average distance occurred in spite of a large increase in production in western Europe. Allowing for internal shifts *within* the United States, Canada, and other producing countries on the periphery would add further to the economically meaningful change in distance. Relative to the 1860s, wheat cultivation in the 1920s was distributed to lower-yielding lands that were typically both colder and drier. The geoclimatic differences between the old center and the frontiers of wheat production were so great that few varieties grown in western Europe were of value in the new lands. These shifts in production would not have been possible without a sustained and highly successful research and development effort to find wheat varieties that would prosper in the more hostile conditions. This was truly an international endeavor that depended on identifying, transferring, selecting, and genetically recombining varieties from both the center and distant locales on the periphery.

Wheat breeding in many ways reflected the character of the nation where it was conducted. In Britain the work was performed by heroic improvers such as Shirreff, Le Couteur, and Biffen. In the United States improvement efforts were more decentralized at the state agricultural experiment stations, with federal officials like Mark A. Carleton concentrating on discovering and testing appropriate varieties from around the globe. Efforts were more organized in Canada, resulting in the early creation of Marquis, which crossed eastern European and Indian wheats. Australia followed a similar course. In Argentina the first varieties were imported by migrants, with wheats from Italy, Hungary, and Russia gaining popularity. Later breeding involved scientists from Britain and Germany who were well connected to the scientific institutions of Europe. Although the breeding efforts in different countries evolved in ways reflecting their individual national character and environmental conditions, by the end of the nineteenth century, breeding had become a global enterprise with the exchange of ideas, scientists, and germstock between every continent. These exchanges were facilitated by the research and extension programs that flourished in every major wheat-producing nation (and within the United States in every important wheat-producing state). The scientific community functioned more efficiently as personal contacts, informal networks, and professional journals united researchers into a closely knit community.

Wherever wheat was grown commercially in the nineteenth and early twentieth centuries, it was constantly being reformulated to fit local conditions, conditions that were constantly evolving because of changing disease and pest environments. Even more than the immigrants who populated the new lands, the grains they grew were the product of "melting pots," with their "ancestors" coming from areas across Europe, Asia, and many of the periphery countries of recent settlement.[21] Advances in basic science and the international exchange of ideas and biological material constituted the "other grain invasion" that was a necessary condition for and an integral part of the globalization story popularized by Williamson and others.

Appendix

Wheat Production

Comprehensive data on world wheat production from 1885 to 1930 are available in the Food Research Institute's *Wheat Studies*. The data cover 43 wheat-producing countries spread across every continent (except, of course, Antarctica).[22] The FRI data exclude "large wheat-producing areas in China and southwestern Asia, and also numerous insignificant producing areas," but this is not too worrisome because little wheat from these areas was exported to European markets. What is more important is that the series, assembled by leading authorities, contain reasonably consistent data for every major player in world grain markets.

Production data before 1885 are more problematic. Our approach was to assemble annual series, where available, for the period between 1866 and 1896. We relied heavily on Mitchell's *International Historical Statistics*. Reasonably consistent production data exist for many European countries (Austria, France, Denmark, Great Britain, Germany, Hungary, Italy, the Netherlands, Romania, and Sweden) as well as Algeria, Australia, Canada, and the United States.[23] We thank Albert Carreras for providing his unpublished production series for Spain. Long annual series exist for exports (though not total production) from Argentina, Russia, and British India. Unfortunately, we located annual production series for only a few of the small producing countries in Europe, Asia, and Africa. Given that the consistent data available for Russia before 1885 cover only exports (which represent less than one-third of the total crop during the brief 1870–1877 period when both series are reported), the series from the early period understates the average distance of production from London. In the 1885–1896 period, when the comprehensive FRI-based series and our 18-nation series overlap, the ratio between the two distances averages 1.142. For purposes of comparison, we raised the 1866 distance from 2,081 km to 2,377 km, and so on, to form the adjusted series.

Distance

It is conventional in the international trade literature investigating gravity models to measure distance between countries based on the locations of their capitals.[24] Using London as the center of the world wheat market is not too problematic. Liverpool might be a better choice, but the differences are small. Taking Buenos Aires and Canberra as the centers of production in Argentina and Australia, respectively, will likely raise concerns among some scholars. But each of these capitals is located near its nation's main grain-producing belt. We have far stronger reservations about using Washington, D.C., as the center for U.S. wheat production and Ottawa as Canada's center. For example, based on our earlier work, we know that the geographic center of U.S. wheat production circa 1839 was well north and west of the nation's capital and moving further westward over time. Whereas London was always 5,932 kilometers from Washington, D.C., it was 6,136 km from the 1839 center and 6,989 km from the 1919 center. The difference in the distances measured from London is less than the distance between the two centers because the three locations form a triangle rather than lying on a straight line. The 1919 centroid was also closer to London in latitude (though further in longitude) than the 1839 centroid.

An examination of maps for Canada showing the spread of wheat production from Ontario to Manitoba, Saskatchewan, and Alberta, indicates a similar process was at work. But to abide by the conventions of the gravity literature, we retained Washington, D.C., and Ottawa as the measuring points for the United States and Canada, respectively. The North American examples do suggest that our calculations likely understate the increase in distance during the great globalization wave. We know that between 1885 and 1904 the Russian wheat belt moved about one-half a degree in longitude to the east. And we suspect similar results would hold for other expanding producers on the periphery.[25]

Climate Data

The climate data were constructed from data in Bennett and Farnsworth (1937, appendix, 303–308). This source presents a highly detailed survey of the geographic distribution of wheat acreage, yields, and climates covering 223 subunits. As an example of the detail, the province of Saskatchewan is divided into nine subregions. For each of the subunits, the FRI reports the acreage (planted), yields, and average precipitation and temperature that were typical during the 1920–1934 period. From these data, we can form national aggregates, reflecting average conditions prevailing in the wheat-producing areas, that can be combined by using weights derived from the production data investigated before to derive series showing the changing conditions under which wheat was grown. Note that the national aggregate captures conditions prevailing at the end of the period, and to the extent that there were shifts in the location of production within the United States, Canada, Russia, and other countries that pushed wheat production into harsher environments, our series likely understate the overall changes in climatic conditions.

Notes

We thank Julian Alston, Liam Brunt, Albert Carreras, Dana Dalrymple, Robert C. Feenstra, Jeffrey Graham, Shelagh Mackay, and Pablo Reynolds for providing comments, research materials, and assistance to make this chapter better. Work on this chapter was facilitated by a fellowship granted by the International Centre for Economic Research (ICER).

1. The definition of invasive species is at ⟨http://www.eco-pros.com/invasive_non-native_species.htm⟩. Weeds are typically defined as plants that grow where they are not wanted, plants that are hardy, aggressive, and prone to spread quickly.

2. Williamson was well aware of the importance of measuring the difference between farm prices (as opposed to Chicago prices) and urban markets, and in *Late Nineteenth-Century Economic Development* (1974, 257–262) he calculated that between 1870–1875 and 1905–1910 the gap fell by about 55 percent between Iowa and New York City, and Wisconsin and New York City. But this calculation fails to capture the effect of the moving wheat frontier over that period.

3. The construction of the data, which is discussed in the appendix, involves aggregating regional FRI statistics on acreages, yields, and climates (Bennett and Farnsworth 1937).

4. The calendar of the world wheat harvest also filled out, dampening seasonal fluctuations in supplies and prices. Formerly the harvest relevant for the center countries occurred almost exclusively in June, July, and August. By the 1920s about one-quarter of the harvest took place in the Northern Hemisphere's nonsummer months. Australia and South America gathered their wheat crops in December and January; India, Iran, Turkey, and Mexico, in March, April, and May (*Wheat and Rye Statistics* 1926, 23; *Monthly Crop Reporter*, July 1920, 71).

5. Brassley (2000, 522–532); Angus (2001, 111–113). For a comprehensive examination of the general forces (other than breeding activities) determining yields, see Brunt (2004).

6. de Vries (1907, 29–90) includes an extensive discussion of the ideas and work of Le Couteur and Shirreff.

7. See volume 2, chapter 9, "Cultivated Plants: Cereal and Culinary Plants." An alternative to the Le Couteur and Shirreff approach, which stressed initial selection and then multiplication of the self-pollinating wheat, was offered by F. Hallett, who attempted to improve the seed by growing the plants under favorable conditions and continuing selection. Hallett developed and sold a series of pedigreed wheats under this name (Carleton 1916, 192–195).

8. British Board of Agriculture (1894). We thank Liam Brunt for this reference.

9. Murray (1967, 37); Pritchett (1942, 113, 228). Fife had the decided advantage of maturing about ten days earlier than the variety from Prairie du Chien.

10. DePauw, Boughton, and Knott (1995, 6). These native insects had also injured the crops in 1857, 1858, 1864, and 1867. For a general treatment, see Lockwood (2004).

11. The actual cross leading to Marquis was probably made in 1892. William Saunders led the effort, and his sons Arthur and Charles assisted (Pomeroy 1956, 48–52; Clark and Bayles 1935, 69; de Kruif 1928, 42; Morrison 1960).

12. Ward (1994). Buller (1919, 175–176) credits Marquis with giving adopters about one extra week between harvest and freeze-up, thus giving farmers a significant advantage in preparing their land for the next season (de Kruif 1928, 41).

13. Scobie (1964, 77). This account draws heavily on Bicknell (1904, 38–39).

14. Presumably many other varieties were tried and rejected. As an example, Bicknell (1904, 54) reports that in 1902–1903 the USDA sent leading Argentine farmers a number of varieties for local testing, including Pelissier from Algeria, and Crimean and Kubanka from Russia.

15. Davidson (1981, 49). The early settlers also obtained an unknown variety in Cape Town, but this too failed (Macindoe and Walkden-Brown 1968, 1; Wrigley and Rathjen 1981, 96–98; Campbell 1937).

16. The blanket assertion that winter wheat could not be grown is undermined by an 1868 survey of wheat varieties. But we still have little idea why farmers adopted late varieties such as Red Lammas. Such varieties evidently would ripen, albeit dangerously late, in the relatively favorable wheat-growing areas of New South Wales, Victoria, and South Australia, which composed the early Australian wheat belt. They would be totally unacceptable for what would eventually become the new areas of production in the more arid inland regions. For regional production data, see Dunsdorfs (1956, 206, 531–533).

17. Macindoe and Walkden-Brown (1968) and many others attribute Purple Straw to a selection made by a now anonymous farmer in the Adelaide area ca. 1860, but based on an 1862 Adelaide newspaper account, Wrigley and Rathjen (1981, 100) attribute the creation to John Fraine, whom they credit with employing relatively sophisticated pure-line breeding methods to develop Purple Straw. Also see Dunsdorfs (1956, 148).

18. Evans (1980, 3–5); Wrigley and Rathjen (1981, 105). Farrer attended Pembroke College, Cambridge, where he studied mathematics. He worked as a surveyor from 1875 to 1886 before becoming one of the world's leading plant scientists.

19. The exchange, even very early in his career, was a two-way street. Evans (1980, 6) notes that Farrer's mention of using cross-breeding to improve wheat quality was an innovative proposition and that Farrer put the idea into practice a decade before Biffen's successes in England.

20. Federation also outperformed Red Fife, which was the latest of the spring wheats tested.

21. Some of the flows of wheat germplasm may be interpreted as a variant of the South-South migration that Hatton and Williamson highlighted in their studies on nineteenth-century labor flows. Hatton and Williamson (2002) observe that the causes and consequences of the migration of 50 million Europeans before 1914 have attracted intense scholarly attention, whereas the 50 million people who left their homes in China and India for jobs elsewhere in the periphery have largely escaped notice.

22. Bennett (1933). The FRI series do make adjustments for the United States and Russia that create differences from standard series. For a critical evaluation of these data, see Malenbaum (1953, 54–62).

23. In a handful of cases we extrapolate and interpolate the series for smaller producers to extend and fill in their series over small stretches. It would be possible to add series for Finland and Norway using this procedure, but wheat production is negligible in those countries.

24. Another convention is that distance is measured as zero in the home country and in all countries sharing a land border. Further, the calculations use great arc distance between the capitals. One might well object that, at least before the advent of aircraft, great arc distances poorly reflect the number of kilometers that shipments would actually travel. To take an extreme example, San Francisco and Liverpool are 8,362 km apart by great arc distance, but wheat shipped from the California port to the English had to travel 25,006 km around the Straights of Magellan, or 14,492 km after the Panama Canal became available.

25. The exception might be Australia, where production moved westward as well as inland. We will make one important concession to the actual geography of production for Russia by using the Ukrainian capital, Kiev, in place of Moscow. Kiev is 2,130 km from London and is located proximate to (if somewhat west of) the nation's wheat-producing region, whereas Moscow (2,512 km away from London) is far outside the wheat belt.

References

Adelman, J. 1994. *Frontier Development: Land, Labour, and Capital on the Wheatlands of Argentina and Canada, 1890–1914*. Oxford: Clarendon Press.

Aitken, Y. 1966. Flower Initiation in Relation to Maturity in Crop Plants: The Flowering Response of Early and Late Cereal Varieties to Australian Environments. *Australian Journal of Agriculture Research* 17: 1–15.

Angus, W. J. 2001. United Kingdom Wheat Pool. In *The World Wheat Book: A History of Wheat Breeding*, ed. A. P. Bonjean and W. J. Angus, 103–126. Paris: Intercept.

Backhouse, W. 1917. *Mejoramiento de Trigos: Orientación General, Primeros Resultados*. Talleres Gráficos del Ministerio de Agricultura de la Nación.

Backhouse, W., and V. Brunini. 1925. *Genética del Trigo: Observaciones Generales sobre su Cultivo: Conclusiones Extraidas de los Trabajos de Mejoramiento de la Semilla*. Talleres Gráficos del Ministerio de Agricultura de la Nación.

Bennett, M. K. 1933. World Wheat Crops, 1885–1932. *Wheat Studies* 9 (7): 239–274.

Bennett, M. K., and H. C. Farnsworth. 1937. World Wheat Acreage, Yields, and Climates. *Wheat Studies* 13 (6): 265–308.

Bicknell, F. W. 1904. *Wheat Production and Farm Life in Argentina*. USDA Bureau of Statistics Bulletin 27.

Bonjean, A. P., G. Doussinault, and J. Stragliati. 2001. French Wheat Pool. In *The World Wheat Book: A History of Wheat Breeding*, ed. A. P. Bonjean and W. J. Angus, 140–149. Paris: Intercept.

Brassley, P. 2000. Crop Varieties. In *The Agrarian History of England and Wales*, ed. E.J.T. Collins. Vol. 7, *1850–1914*, 522–532. Cambridge: Cambridge University Press.

British Board of Agriculture. 1894. Report of the Intelligence Department on Rust or Mildew on Wheat Plants, 1893–1894. *British Parliamentary Papers* 23.

Brunt, L. 2004. Nature or Nurture? Explaining English Wheat Yields in the Industrial Revolution, c. 1770. *Journal of Economic History* 64 (1): 193–225.

Buller, A.H.R. 1919. *Essays on Wheat*. New York: Macmillan.

Campbell, W. S. 1937. Wheats in New South Wales from the Foundation of the Colony. *Royal Australian Historical Society Journal and Proceedings* 22: 406–433.

Canada as a Producer and Exporter of Wheat. 1925. *Wheat Studies* 1 (8): 218.

Carleton, M. A. 1916. *The Small Grains*. New York: Macmillan.

Clark, J. A., and B. B. Bayles. 1935. *The Classification of Wheat Varieties Grown in the United States*. USDA Technical Bulletin 459.

Crosby, A. 1972. *The Columbian Exchange: Biological and Cultural Consequences of 1492*. Westport, Conn.: Greenwood.

Davidson, B. R. 1981. *European Farming in Australia: An Economic History of Australian Farming*. Amsterdam: Elsevier.

de Kruif, P. 1928. *Hunger Fighters*. New York: Harcourt, Brace and World.

de Vries, H. 1907. *Plant-Breeding: Comments on the Experiments of Nilsson and Burbank*. Chicago: Open Court.

DePauw, R. M., G. R. Boughton, and D. R. Knott. 1995. Hard Red Spring Wheat. In *Harvest of Gold: The History of Field Crop Breeding in Canada*, ed. A. E. Slinkard and D. R. Knott, ch. 2. Saskatoon, Canada: University Extension Press, University of Saskatchewan.

DePauw, R. M., and T. Hunt. 2001. Canadian Wheat Pool. In *The World Wheat Book: A History of Wheat Breeding*, ed. A. P. Bonjean and W. J. Angus, 479–515. Paris: Intercept.

Dunsdorfs, E. 1956. *The Australian Wheat-Growing Industry: 1788–1948*. Melbourne: Melbourne University Press.

Evans, L. T. 1980. Response to Challenge: William Farrer and the Making of Wheats: Farrer Memorial Oration, 1979. *Journal of the Australian Institute of Agricultural Science* 46.

Farrer Memorial Trust. William James Farrer Papers, February 1885–May 1906. CGS 55. ⟨http://www.records.nsw.gov.au/cguide/ab/agric.htm⟩.

Grossman, G. M., and E. Helpman. 1991. *Innovation and Growth in the Global Economy*. Cambridge, Mass.: MIT Press.

Guitierrez, M. 1985. *El Origen de las Semillas Mejoradas de Trigo y Maiz en la Argentina: La Dinámica de las Creatión y las Modalidades de Investigación Publica y Privada*. Buenos Aires: Centro de Investigaciones Sociales sobre el Estado y la Administración.

Hallett, F. F. 1861. On "Pedigree" in Wheat as a Means of Increasing the Crop. *Journal of the Royal Agricultural Society of England* 22: 371–381.

Hatton, T. J., and J. G. Williamson. 2002. What Fundamentals Drive Mass Migration? NBER (National Bureau of Economic Research) Working Paper 9159. ⟨http://www.nber.org/papers/W9159⟩.

Johnson, T. 1961. *Rust Research in Canada and Related Plant-Disease Investigation*. Agriculture Canada Publication 1098.

Lockwood, J. A. 2004. *Locust: The Devastating Rise and Mysterious Disappearance of the Insect That Shaped the American Frontier*. New York: Basic Books.

Lupton, F. G. H. 1987. History of Wheat Breeding. In *Wheat Breeding: Its Scientific Basis*, ed. F. G. H. Lupton, 51–70. London: Chapman and Hall.

Macindoe, S. L., and D. C. Walkden-Brown. 1968. *Wheat Breeding and Varieties in Australia*. 3d ed. Sydney: New South Wales Department of Agriculture.

Malenbaum, W. 1953. *The World Wheat Economy: 1885–1939*. Cambridge, Mass.: Harvard University Press.

Morrison, J. W. 1960. Marquis Wheat: A Triumph of Scientific Endeavor. *Agricultural History* 34 (4): 182–188.

Murray, S. N. 1967. *The Valley Comes of Age: A History of Agriculture in the Valley of the Red River of the North, 1812–1920*. Fargo, N.D.: Institute for Regional Studies.

Nisi, J. E., and E. F. Antonelli. 2001. Argentine Wheat Pool. In *The World Wheat Book: A History of Wheat Breeding*, ed. A. P. Bonjean and W. J. Angus, 519–547. Paris: Intercept.

O'Brien, L., M. Morrel, C. W. Wrigley, and R. Appels. 2001. Genetic Pool of Australian Wheats. In *The World Wheat Book: A History of Wheat Breeding*, ed. A. P. Bonjean and W. J. Angus, ch. 23. Paris: Intercept.

Olmstead, A. L., and P. W. Rhode. 2002. The Red Queen and the Hard Reds: Productivity Growth in American Wheat, 1800–1940. *Journal of Economic History* 62 (4): 929–966.

————. 2003. Biological Innovation in American Wheat Production: Science, Policy, and Environmental Adaptation. In *Industrializing Organisms: Introducing Evolutionary History*, ed. S. Schrepfer and P. Scranton, 43–83. New York: Routledge.

O'Rourke, K. H. 1997. The European Grain Invasion, 1870–1913. *Journal of Economic History* 57 (4): 775–801.

O'Rourke, K. H., and J. G. Williamson. 1999. *Globalization and History: The Evolution of the Nineteenth Century Atlantic Economy*. Cambridge, Mass.: MIT Press.

Persson, K. G. 2004. Mind the Gap! Transport Cost and Price Convergence in the Nineteenth Century Atlantic Economy. *European Review of Economic History* 8: 127–147.

Pomeroy, E. M. 1956. *William Saunders and His Five Sons: The Story of the Marquis Wheat Family*. Toronto: Ryerson Press.

Pritchett, J. P. 1942. *The Red River Valley, 1811–1849: A Regional Study*. New Haven, Conn.: Yale University Press.

Roberts, H. F. 1929. *Plant Hybridization before Mendel*. Princeton, N.J.: Princeton University Press.

Scobie, J. R. 1964. *Revolution on the Pampas: A Social History of Argentine Wheat, 1860–1910*. Austin: Texas University Press.

Shirreff, P. 1873. *Improvement of the Cereals and an Essay on the Wheat-Fly*. London: Blackwood.

Symko, S. 1999. From a Single Seed: Tracing the Marquis Wheat Success Story in Canada to Its Roots in the Ukraine. ⟨http://res2.agr.gc.ca/publications/marquis/index_e.htm⟩.

Walton, J. R. 1999. Varietal Innovation and the Competitiveness of the British Cereals, 1760–1930. *Agricultural History Review* 47: 29–57.

Ward, T. 1994. The Origins of the Canadian Wheat Boom, 1880–1910. *Canadian Journal of Economics* 27 (4): 864–883.

Wheat and Rye Statistics. 1926. USDA Statistical Bulletin 12.

White, W. J. 1995. Plant Breeding in Canada's Formative Years. In *Harvest of Gold: The History of Field Crop Breeding in Canada*, ed. A. E. Slinkard and D. R. Knott, ch. 1. Saskatoon, Canada: University Extension Press, University of Saskatchewan.

Williamson, J. G. 1964. *American Growth and the Balance of Payments, 1820–1913: A Study of the Long Swing*. Chapel Hill: University of North Carolina Press.

————. 1974. *Late Nineteenth-Century American Development: A General Equilibrium History*. Cambridge: Cambridge University Press.

Wrigley, C. W., and A. Rathjen. 1981. Wheat Breeding in Australia. In *Plants and Man in Australia*, ed. D. J. Carr and S. G. M. Carr, 96–135. Sydney: Academic Press.

Zapoleon, L. H. 1918. *Geography of Wheat Prices: Summary of Conditions Affecting Farm Prices of Wheat in Different Parts of the United States*. USDA Bulletin 594.

6 Other People's Money: The Evolution of Bank Capital in the Industrialized World

Richard S. Grossman

Jeffrey G. Williamson and like-minded practitioners of the New Comparative Economic History focus on analyses of historical events, highlighting issues of contemporary importance. Because of its long-run comparative framework, the New Comparative Economic History can provide insights into current-day policy issues that research based on shorter time series and narrower geographic scope cannot. In the spirit of Williamson's work, this chapter takes a long-run comparative approach to the evolution of bank capital in Europe, the United States, Canada, Australia, and Japan from the nineteenth century through the Second World War.

From the enactment of the first commercial banking codes in Britain (1844) and Sweden (1846), through the establishment of the Basel (1988) and Basel II (2004) capital accords, policymakers have argued that capital promotes bank "soundness and stability" (Basel Committee 1988; 2004). Even in the absence of explicit government regulation of capital, the investing and depositing public has an interest in bank capital levels, what Berger, Herring, and Szegö (1995) refer to as "market capital requirements." The goal of this chapter is to present data on the evolution of bank capital-to-asset ratios across countries and U.S. states, and to assess the relative importance of market capital requirements, government capital regulation, and other factors in that evolution.

Briefly, I find that capital-to-asset ratios declined consistently across countries from the mid-nineteenth century through the end of World War I. The findings from the interwar period are less clear-cut. I find an important role for market capital requirements: banking crises and other indicators of increased risk are associated with higher capital-to-asset ratios. The effects of government policies, such as deposit insurance and other aspects of the bank safety net, are more ambiguous, although these policies are notoriously difficult to measure accurately. Interestingly, higher government-mandated capital requirements do not appear to have been systematically associated with increases in capital-to-asset ratios and may have been, if anything, associated with lower capital-to-asset ratios.

The next section discusses the importance of bank capital. Subsequent sections present capital-to-asset ratio data for a number of countries from the mid-nineteenth century through World War II and a statistical analysis of those data, and attempt to explain the variation of capital-to-asset ratios by looking across U.S. states during the period 1890–1930.

Bank Capital

Broadly speaking, banks—and other firms—have two sources of funds with which to conduct operations: debt and equity.[1] According to Modigliani and Miller (1958), in a world with efficient capital markets, no tax distortions, and no bankruptcy costs, firm value will be invariant to the mix of debt and equity, so managers and shareholders will be indifferent to the relative levels of debt and equity financing. Since a primary business of banks is to take deposits, it would seem that banks could operate with virtually no capital; managers could simply make loans and buy securities with borrowed funds. If the returns on the loans and investments were greater than the interest paid to depositors, it would be in owners' interest to finance as much of the bank's operation with borrowed money as possible; the less dispersed the ownership, the fewer shareholders with whom to share the profits. And, in fact, banks are among the most highly leveraged firms. The average debt-to-equity ratio in U.S. agriculture today is about 1; the average in manufacturing is close to 2; the average in banking is over 9 (Troy 2004).

Of course, exclusive reliance on debt has a downside. While dividend payments to equity holders can be postponed or canceled without an existential threat to the firm, obligations owing from debt must be met. Since a large fraction of deposits are payable on demand, this concern is especially relevant to banks.

Bank capital, then, serves several roles. First, it provides a buffer against a shortfall in cash flow. Dividends can be suspended without catastrophic consequences, freeing up money to pay depositors and other creditors. Second, if a bank is forced to close, capital serves as a reserve that can be drawn upon to liquidate unpaid debts. Third, higher holdings of capital can encourage banks to undertake less risk. Because capital is at risk in case of failure, banks have an incentive not to take risks that might put them out of business.[2] Fourth, because banks know more about their operations than their investors (information asymmetry), the decision to hold more capital, that is, to subject owners to a greater loss in case of failure, can signal to depositors and investors that the bank will undertake less risk than it otherwise might. Finally, banks hold capital because government regulations force them to do so. Such government regulation is typically justified on the grounds that it promotes soundness and stability in the banking sector, that is, for all the reasons cited previously.

Although government-mandated capital requirements are common today, they were far from universal in the late nineteenth and early twentieth centuries. A number of industrial countries had no specific commercial banking regulations before the twentieth century (e.g., France, Germany, Italy, the Netherlands). Consequently, in some countries there were no official minimum capital requirements. Still, even in the absence of government-mandated capital requirements, for the reasons noted, banks will hold more than token amounts of capital. Berger, Herring and Szegö (1995) term the amount of capital that banks hold to maximize the value of their institutions "market capital requirements."

How does the market capital requirement evolve as a country's financial system matures? It should fall, for two reasons. First, as information about financial institutions becomes more widely available, through, for example, the publication of balance sheets, and as reputations become better known, depositors and shareholders will require banks, on average, to hold less capital. In other words, since banks hold capital in part to mitigate the information asymmetry, as information flows improve, less capital should be necessary. Second, since the role of capital is largely tied to reducing the likelihood of bank failure and mitigating the effects of bank failures once they happen, as the risk of bank failure declines, market capital requirements should fall.[3]

Why does the risk of failure decline with economic development? First, as money markets develop, banks are able to hold some fraction of their assets in liquid securities rather than choosing between liquid cash and illiquid loans. This allows banks to hold lower levels of nonearning assets, boosting cash flow, while maintaining protection against sudden deposit withdrawals, which can lead to failure. Second, as banking systems grow, and individual banks increase in size and geographic spread, their ability to diversify increases and the risk of failure falls.[4] Third, as financial systems prosper, the stakes for managers, shareholders, depositors, and the public rise. These actors therefore have a greater incentive to develop mechanisms to reduce the risk of bank

failure. These mechanisms might include the emergence of bankers' associations, which, among other things, could promote increased standardization and the development of conventional (conservative) banking
practices.[5] Such failure-reducing mechanisms might also take the form of
a bank safety net, encompassing formal government programs, such as
bank inspection, double liability,[6] deposit insurance, and lender of last resort facilities, as well as unofficial elements, such as clearing houses.[7]

Data

Figure 6.1 presents capital-to-asset ratio data for 12 countries.[8] To the extent possible, the data represent the ratio of paid-up capital to total assets
for all commercial banks within each country. Central banks, savings
banks, savings and loans, and credit cooperatives are excluded. Because
state-level regulations varied widely, the U.S. data analyzed in this section include only national banks. The series for Japan represents the ratio

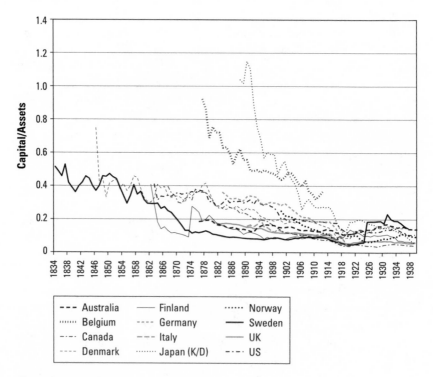

Figure 6.1
Capital-to-asset ratios, 1834–1939.

of capital to total deposits and is not used in any of the statistical calculations presented in the next section.

It should be remembered that data collection efforts by national authorities, the contemporary financial press, and secondary sources vary substantially in the completeness and accuracy of their coverage. Additionally, since the early years of each series may well include only a few banks, it is possible that sharp fluctuations may be due to the entry of new banks. In Finland, for example, the capital-to-asset ratio dropped dramatically in the second and third years of the sample, from over 40 percent in 1862 to less than 20 percent in 1864, and fell consistently thereafter until 1873–1874, when it tripled, from slightly over 9 percent to nearly 28 percent. This can be explained by the fact that there was only one commercial bank in Finland between 1862 and 1873; when a new bank with a substantially higher capital-to-asset ratio entered in 1874, the aggregate ratio rose substantially as well before the preexisting downward trend resumed.

Despite the cluttered nature and volatility of the series, the data presented in figure 6.1 clearly illustrate a downward trend in capital-to-asset ratios throughout in the nineteenth and early twentieth centuries.[9] This trend slowed and, for some countries, reversed around the end of World War I. There was no discernible trend during the 1920s and 1930s. By 1937 aggregate capital-to-asset ratios were higher than they had been in 1918 in about half the sample and lower in about half. The downward trend accords well with the predictions of the previous section: as economies matured during the second half of the nineteenth century, aggregate capital-to-asset ratios fell. The trend breaks down right around World War I. We can speculate that the instability of the interwar period led to the end of the nineteenth-century trend in capital-to-asset ratios.

Did government regulation lead to higher capital-to-asset ratios? A cursory examination of the data suggest it did not. Figure 6.2 presents average capital-to-asset ratios for countries with and without capital requirements.[10] Before the end of World War I, banks in countries without specific capital requirements held *higher* capital-to-asset ratios than countries in which there were capital requirements; the averages converge during World War I and are not appreciably different during the interwar period.[11] There are at least two possible explanations for this result.

First, if government regulation was more likely to be established in countries that were perceived by market participants as having more stable banking systems, the market might not have required banks to hold as high a proportion of their assets in capital as they would have in a

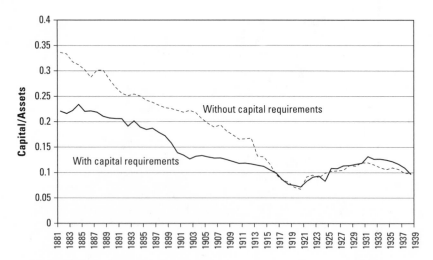

Figure 6.2
Capital-to-asset ratios, 1881–1939, countries with and without capital requirements.

country perceived as being more susceptible to crisis. Second, nineteenth-century banking laws typically regulated minimum capital levels, not capital ratios. If smaller banks held higher capital-to-asset ratios than larger banks—perhaps because the market viewed smaller banks as more susceptible to failure—countries with particularly high capital requirements and populated with relatively large banks might well have lower capital-to-asset ratios than countries populated by smaller but better capitalized banks.[12] It is therefore possible that although high minimum capital requirements did not lead to higher capital-to-asset ratios, they may have discouraged entry into banking, leading to a banking system characterized by fewer and larger, if less well-capitalized, banks.[13]

In order to take a closer look at the possible consequences of the imposition or alteration of capital requirements, figures 6.3 and 6.4 present capital-to-asset ratio data for five countries that experienced such changes. Figure 6.3 presents data for three countries (Canada, Sweden, and the United States) that established or altered capital requirements during the nineteenth century. Figure 6.4 focuses on two countries (Denmark and Norway) that established capital requirements anew during the interwar period.

Sweden's first banking code was enacted in 1846; it established a minimum capital requirement of SKr 1,000,000. A decree of 1824 had permitted the establishment of banks. However, that law only provided

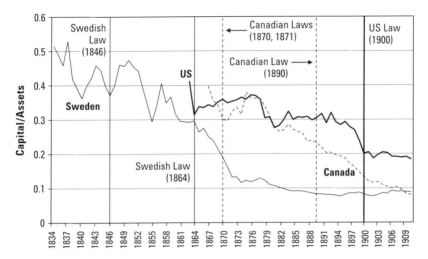

Figure 6.3
Capital-to-asset ratios, 1834–1910, Canada, Sweden, and the United States.

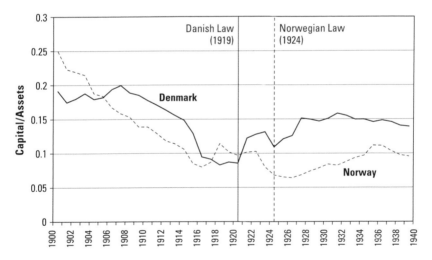

Figure 6.4
Capital-to-asset ratios, 1900–1939, Denmark and Norway.

that the bank's articles of association, including the amount of capital, had to be approved by the Crown; it did not specify a minimum capital requirement. According to Flux (1910, 37), the SKr 1,000,000 capital requirement was notable because, of the six banks that had been established under the 1824 decree, four had started with less—and one still had less—than SKr 1,000,000 in capital. Not surprisingly, the aggregate capital-to-asset ratio rose during the next two years. A subsequent law, passed in 1864, did not change the minimum capital requirement but did shorten the period within which the capital had to be paid. Unlike the 1846 law, this law was followed by a ten-year period of rapidly declining aggregate capital-to-asset ratios.

The Canadian experience was not dissimilar: minimum capital requirements were established by laws enacted in 1870 and 1871, and the banking system's aggregate capital-to-asset ratio rose for the next five years. An 1890 law did not change the minimum capital level but did reduce the time in which capital had to be paid. This law was enacted during a period in which aggregate capital-to-asset ratios were declining; the trend appears to have continued unabated.

Capital requirements for national banks in the United States had been established under the National Banking Acts (1863–1864). Because state bank note issues were taxed out of existence at the time, the national banking system grew quickly while state-chartered banks declined in numbers and assets. The growth of deposit taking as an alternative source of funds, combined with lower capital requirements, led to a resurgence in state banking; by 1894 state banks once again outnumbered their federally chartered counterparts. In recognition of the competition between the two systems, Congress lowered the capital requirements for banks in cities with populations below 3,000 in the Gold Standard Act of 1900. This legislation coincided with a slowdown in, but not an end to, the decline in aggregate national bank capital-to-asset ratios.

Unlike the Swedish, Canadian, and U.S. requirements, the post–World War I laws in both Denmark (1919) and Norway (1924) specified minimum absolute levels of capital as well as minimum capital-to-liabilities ratios. The 1919 banking law in Denmark, the country's first commercial banking law, coincides with the post–World War I turnaround in capital-to-asset ratio. Denmark's aggregate capital-to-asset ratio in 1918 was at its lowest point of the entire 1854–1939 period.[14] Norway's banking law was enacted following two years of sharp declines in the capital-to-asset ratio and was followed by two more years of relatively slowly declining ratios before the start of a decade-long increase.

Because figures 6.3 and 6.4 show only aggregate ratios and dates of capital legislation, and omit many other variables that might affect capital-to-asset ratios, they should be interpreted with extreme caution. The upturns following the enactment of the Swedish 1846 and Canadian 1870–1871 laws are dramatic. Without more specific microdata, it is impossible to say conclusively that the establishment of minimum capital requirements led to the increase in aggregate capital-to-asset ratios, although the correspondence is suggestive. The later Canadian and Swedish laws, both of which shortened the amount of time banks had to pay up capital, coincided with—and appear not to have interrupted—long-run declines in capital-to-asset ratios. The U.S. law of 1900, enacted so national banks could remain competitive with state banks, came in the midst of a downward trend in national bank capital-to-asset ratios. As one would expect, the general trend continued after the law's enactment.

The Danish and Norwegian patterns are more difficult to interpret. Both countries endured substantial post–World War I recessions, which could have led to an increase in market capital requirements due to the increased risk of bank failure, although Norway's legislation (1924) followed a banking crisis (1922–1923), and Denmark's 1919 law preceded a crisis in 1922. Hence, it is not clear whether market forces, government regulation, government regulation reacting to (or anticipating) market forces, or some other factor was responsible for the turnaround in these countries.

Cross-Country Estimation

In theory, each of the capital-to-asset ratios presented in figure 6.1 could be analyzed individually by inspection, in the manner of figures 6.3 and 6.4. As should be clear from the preceding section, there are enough complicating factors to make such an analysis problematic. We can approach the analysis more systematically by pooling the observations and seeking empirical regularities across countries and time.

Which factors were responsible for the change in capital-to-asset ratios? The two main forces I have identified are government capital requirements and market capital requirements. Of the two, government capital requirements are more easily recognizable. Despite the difficulties in interpreting government-mandated capital requirements, they can be identified as having been enacted at a particular time.

I attempt to capture changes in government regulation with four separate dummy variables. One variable takes on the value of 1 in a year in which capital requirements are established or raised, and 0 in all other years. This is intended to capture short-term consequences of changes in capital requirements. A second dummy variable, intended to capture longer-term consequences of capital regulation, takes on the value of 1 in the year in which capital requirements are raised and in each subsequent year. A third dummy variable takes on the value 1 in any year that any government regulatory requirements (not just capital requirements) are made more stringent, and 0 otherwise (capturing short-term effects of greater regulatory stringency), and a fourth takes on the value of 1 in the year in which regulatory requirements are made more stringent and in all subsequent years (capturing longer-term effects).[15]

Market capital requirements, reflecting increasing information and reduced risk of bank failure, are harder to measure. One way of measuring the soundness and stability of a banking system is to consider ex post banking stability. We would expect that banking crises would raise the specter of further banking instability and hence cause aggregate capital-to-asset ratios to rise. Ideally, banking instability would be measured in terms of the percentage of banks, or the percentage of assets in banks, that fail in a given year. Since these measures are not available for most countries, I use a dummy variable to indicate a banking crisis.[16]

Another factor that might strengthen banking stability, and therefore lower capital-to-asset ratios, is the development of government and private mechanisms for lowering the likelihood and reducing the cost of banking failures, that is, the development of the financial safety net. Important elements of the safety net would include deposit insurance and the emergence of a lender of last resort. Additionally, government or private-sector bailouts of a troubled institution, whether or not part of a systematic mechanism for promoting financial stability, could also indicate a turning point in the development of the financial safety net. Once the government, central bank, or some other entity has found a way to rescue a troubled institution, the market at large may well view such assistance as being available to other troubled banks and therefore demand that banks hold less capital (Flannery and Rangan 2002).

For purposes of this chapter, I take the financial safety net to include the enactment of deposit insurance, the emergence of a lender of last resort, or a government or private-sector bailout of an individual financial institution. The financial safety net is measured in two ways, first as a variable that takes on the value of 1 in the first year that a country's financial safety net becomes evident (through the enactment of deposit insurance, a lender of last resort action, or a bailout) and in all subsequent years. The theory behind this measure is that, having been used once, market participants view the financial safety net as operational and permanent.[17] Alternatively, one could argue that markets have relatively short-term memories and that a safety net far enough in the past will be discounted by market participants. In order to allow for that possibility, a second safety net dummy variable takes on the value of 1 if a country's safety net was active at any time during the past ten years, and 0 otherwise.

Finally, I use the long-term government bond interest rate as an imperfect proxy for overall economic risk. As the risk of economic and financial disturbance declines, one would expect interest rates to decline as well.[18] Of course, long-term interest rates are driven by a number of factors, including expected inflation (and currency depreciation) and changes in the government's fiscal position, in addition to the risk of economic or financial disturbance.[19] The sample includes a substantial period when countries were on the international gold standard. One would expect bond rates to be a better measure of pure economic risk (rather than exchange rate risk) during the years that countries adhered to the gold standard.

The results of OLS panel regressions with country fixed-effects are presented in tables 6.1 and 6.2.[20] Results presented in table 6.1 include regressions run over all available observations. For reasons noted, results presented in table 6.2 include only country-year combinations in which the country in question was on the gold standard.[21]

The results in table 6.1 show highly significant estimated coefficients on the lagged dependent variable and the time trend. The estimated coefficients on the lagged dependent variable are positive and significantly less than 1. The estimated coefficients on the time trend are negative, as we would expect, given the sustained decline in capital-to-asset rates. It is tempting to interpret this coefficient as reflecting a long-run trend increase in financial efficiency and information flows, although there is no evidence in the data available to suggest that financial efficiency increased at a steady rate.

The coefficients on the crisis variable are positive and statistically significant, indicating that capital-to-asset ratios rose with banking crises. Whether this effect was due to crisis-induced shedding of assets (with relatively stable capital levels) or to bank efforts to increase capital in the aftermath of a crisis, the result that crises coincide with higher capital-to-asset ratios is as expected.[22]

Few of the other estimated coefficients are significantly different from zero. The estimated coefficients on the bond rate are positive, while those

Table 6.1
Dependent Variable Is Capital-to-Asset Ratio, Entire Sample

	1	2	3	4	5	6	7	8
Constant	1.069[a]	1.064[a]	1.075[a]	1.073[a]	0.622[a]	0.620[a]	0.011[a]	0.008[a]
	0.153	0.153	0.154	0.153	0.137	0.136	0.004	0.002
Capital-to-asset ratio ($t-1$)	0.8[a]	0.817[a]	0.816[a]	0.817[a]	0.857[a]	0.857[a]	0.941[a]	0.943[a]
	0.018	0.018	0.018	0.018	0.016	0.016	0.009	0.009
Year	−0.00054[a]	−0.001[a]	−0.001[a]	−0.001[a]	−0.00031[a]	−0.00031[a]		
	0.00008	0.000	0.000	0.000	0.00007	0.00007		
Tighter legislation		−0.004						
		0.005						
Capital-raising legislation			−0.005					
			0.007					
Crisis				0.011[a]		0.012[a]		
				0.004		0.003		
Bond rate					0.0013	0.00099		
					0.0010	0.00098		
Safety net (in last 10 years)							−0.0037	
							0.0031	
Safety net (ever)								−0.0016
								0.0026
Country dummies?	Yes	Yes	Yes	Yes	Yes	Yes	No	No
N	700	700	700	700	610	610	623	623
Adjusted R-squared	0.954	0.954	0.954	0.954	0.971	0.972	0.954	0.953
D-W	1.707	1.711	1.709	1.712	1.767	1.778	1.929	1.929
Log likelihood	1516.6	1517.0	1516.8	1519.7	1477.5	1483.1	1321.9	1321.9

Notes: Estimated with OLS. Standard errors are shown below coefficients.
a. Significant at the 2.5 percent level.

Table 6.2
Dependent Variable Is Capital-to-Asset Ratio, pre-1914 Gold Standard Countries

	1	2	3	4	5	6	7	8	9
Constant	1.140[a]	1.146[a]	1.155[a]	1.100[a]	1.193[a]	0.001	0.002	0.004	0.006[a]
	0.267	0.268	0.267	0.264	0.300	0.009	0.009	0.003	0.002
Capital-to-asset ratio $(t-1)$	0.841[a]	0.842[a]	0.842[a]	0.842[a]	0.833[a]	0.899[a]	0.900[a]	0.952[a]	0.950[a]
	0.022	0.022	0.022	0.022	0.023	0.017	0.016	0.007	0.008
Year	−0.0006[a]	−0.0006[a]	−0.00059[a]	−0.000562[a]	−0.000615[a]				
	0.0001	0.0001	0.000139	0.000137	0.000155				
Tighter legislation		−0.0043							
		0.0052							
Capital-raising legislation			−0.00983						
			0.007423						
Crisis				0.0126[a]			0.0130[a]	0.0147[a]	0.0155[a]
				0.0037			0.0041	0.0040	0.0040
Bond rate					0.0034	0.0063[b]	0.0054[c]		
					0.0029	0.0029	0.0029		
Safety net (in last 10 years)									−0.0040
									0.0026
Safety net (ever)								0.0013	
								0.0024	
Country dummies?	Yes	Yes	Yes	Yes	Yes	Yes	Yes	No	No
N	352	352	352	318	318	318	318	315	315
Adjusted R-squared	0.98	0.98	0.98	0.98	0.98	0.98	0.98	0.98	0.98
D-W	2.17	2.17	2.17	2.21	2.21	2.24	2.27	2.27	2.29
Log likelihood	926.6	926.9	927.5	831.3	831.3	823.2	828.3	812.2	812.2

Notes: Estimated with OLS. Standard errors are shown below coefficients.
a. Significant at the 2.5 percent level.
b. Significant at the 5 percent level.
c. Significant at the 10 percent level.

on the safety net variables are mixed, although none of the coefficients are significant at standard levels. Of the four estimated coefficients on regulatory tightening and increase in capital requirements, the short-run estimated coefficients are negative and the long-run estimated coefficients are positive, although only the long-run coefficient on regulatory tightening is significant.

The estimated coefficients on the lagged dependent variable, time trend, and crisis dummy presented in table 6.2 are similar in sign and significance to the results presented in table 6.1, and all are significant at standard levels. The estimated coefficients on the regulatory dummies are not significantly different from zero, although a safety net action within the past ten years has a significantly negative coefficient, as predicted.

A change from the regressions presented in table 6.1 is that the sample is restricted to country-years prior to World War I in which the country adhered to the gold standard. Given that the gold standard implies a commitment to price and exchange rate stability, we would expect the bond rate to better represent economy-wide risk than in times when exchange rates were not fixed. The estimated coefficients on the bond rate are again positive and, in two out of three specifications, they are significantly different from zero. This result suggests that declines in economy-wide risk were translated into lower bank capital-to-asset ratios.

The cross-country results presented in this section have several implications. First, capital-to-asset ratios clearly declined over time. We can speculate that this decline reflected gradually growing banking efficiency and increased information flows. Second, the crisis variable is clearly important; crises led to higher capital-to-asset ratios, as predicted. The result is statistically significant and quantitatively large. If the mean capital-to-asset ratio is around 20 percent, this suggests that a banking crisis increased it by about 1.5 percent, about 20 times the trend rate of decline. Third, evidence from the gold standard period suggests that increased risk, as proxied for by the long-term government bond rate, led to increased capital-to-asset ratios.

Several factors that we would expect to affect both government-mandated and market capital requirements yielded more ambiguous results. First, changes in government regulation do not appear to have systematically affected aggregate capital-to-asset ratios. The coefficient on higher capital requirements and tighter overall regulation are more often negative than positive. One possible explanation for this ambiguity is that regulatory changes were temporally close to financial crises, so that the effects of regulation are difficult to separate from the effects of crises.

Another plausible explanation is that tightening regulatory requirements in general—and specifically increasing minimum capital requirements—increased barriers to entry and led to a banking system characterized by fewer, larger banks. If larger banks are viewed as being less susceptible to failure, then higher capital requirements and tighter regulations may, in fact, have led to lower market capital requirements. The net result might well be ambiguity in the observed effects of higher capital requirements.

Second, the signs and significance on the safety net are not consistent. A safety net action within the past ten years had a negative and significant effect upon capital-to-asset ratios in the pre–World War I period. However, other measures and different time horizons yield results that are not significant. The weakness of this result might be because the safety net is imprecisely measured. It is entirely plausible that the emergence of the safety net was far more gradual than can be captured by the measures employed here, and hence is being picked up by the negative and significant estimated coefficient on the time trend variable.

Regulatory Variety: The United States

The results presented in the previous section do not find any consistent evidence of the effects of government capital requirements or the development of the financial safety net on aggregate capital-to-asset ratios. That is not to say that these factors did not play a role in the long-run decline of capital-to-asset ratios, but the cross-national evidence presented in the last section does not support such a claim.

This absence of a systematic relationship may lie, in part, with the nature of data. In the previous section financial instability was coded as a relatively crude dichotomous variable: country-years in which banking crises occurred took on the value 1 and in all other years took on the value 0. This coding leaves no role for banking instability short of a full-blown crisis to affect capital-to-asset ratios. Additionally, since regulatory changes frequently coincided with banking crises, it may be that the crisis variable, which yielded positive and significant coefficients, in fact reflected the consequences of regulation or crisis-induced regulation. Similarly, the regulatory variables employed in the previous section were all dichotomous: either a capital-raising or regulatory-tightening reform took place or it did not. The measures of the financial safety net employed are also less than precise.

The importance of government versus market capital requirements can be assessed using data on state-chartered banks in the United States from the late nineteenth and early twentieth centuries. Prior to the establishment of the national banking system in 1863–1864 the only federally chartered banks were the protocentral First (1791–1811) and Second (1816–1836) Banks of the United States. Aside from these institutions, all commercial banks in the United States operated under charters granted under state law. From the establishment of the national banking system, then, there was a "dual banking system" in the country—parallel sets of state- and federally chartered and regulated banks.

In this section I use data on state-chartered banks to assess the effects of government and market capital regulation.[23] State-level data offer a number of advantages over cross-country data. First, each state set the capital requirements for the banks under its jurisdiction, and changed capital requirements relatively frequently (about 60 times) during the course of the sample period (1891–1930). By contrast, in the cross-country sample capital requirements were established or changed only about a dozen times. Additionally, state capital requirements should be easier to compare across jurisdictions because they are all denominated in dollars. Second, rather than relying upon dichotomous bank crisis variables, we can employ the percentage of state-chartered banks that failed, as well as the percentage of state-chartered bank assets in failed banks, in any given year as a more nuanced measure of banking instability. Third, states enacted a variety of reforms (e.g., deposit insurance, permissibility of branching, double liability), including safety net reforms, which might have had an effect on banking system risk and capital-to-asset ratios. Thus, an analysis of banking data across U.S. states makes it possible to develop a richer analysis of both capital and noncapital regulation.

Regression results on state-level aggregates are presented in table 6.3. The dependent variable in each regression is the aggregate capital-to-asset ratio of all state-chartered banks within the given state in a given year. As in the cross-country regressions, lagged values of the capital-to-asset ratio are positive and significant and significantly below 1, while the estimated coefficients on the time trend are negative and significant. The downward trend in capital-to-asset ratios, found in the cross-country data, is also present among U.S. state banks.

Two measures of state-level banking risk are included: the rate of state bank failures (the number of state bank failures divided by the total number of state banks) and the asset failure rate of state banks (assets of failed state banks divided by the total assets of state banks). The estimated coefficients on these variables are uniformly positive and almost always statistically significant.[24] This confirms the earlier finding that banking crises

Table 6.3
Panel OLS Results: State Bank Aggregates, United States, 1891–1932 (fixed effects)

	1	2	3	4	5	6
Constant	1.014[a]	0.990[a]	0.837[a]	0.902[a]	0.384[b]	0.394[a]
	0.251	0.247	0.251	0.254	0.172	0.172
Capital-to-asset ratio ($t-1$)	0.837[a]	0.834[a]	0.826[a]	0.825[a]	0.901[a]	0.895[a]
	0.020	0.020	0.022	0.022	0.013	0.013
Year	−0.00052[a]	−0.00051[a]	−0.00043[a]	−0.00046[a]	−0.00020[b]	−0.00020[a]
	0.00013	0.00013	0.00013	0.00013	0.00009	0.00009
State bank failure rate	0.107[a]		0.059		0.090[a]	
	0.037		0.036		0.034	
State bank asset failure rate		0.163[a]		0.155[a]		0.119[a]
		0.058		0.058		0.052
Change in minimum capital requirements			−4.07E-08	−6.39E-08		
			2.11E-07	2.12E-07		
State deposit insurance system					−0.00125	−0.00105
					0.001773	0.001713
N	546	537	443	435	546	537
Years	1891–1930	1892–1930	1891–1930	1892–1930	1891–1930	1892–1930
States included	34	34	27	27	34	34
Adjusted R-squared	0.94	0.94	0.93	0.93	0.94	0.94
Log likelihood	1577.9	1570.8	1318.0	1296.2	1561.1	1554.2
D-W	1.75	1.87	1.80	1.83	1.76	1.86

Notes: Estimated with OLS. Standard errors are shown below coefficients.
a. Significant at the 2.5 percent level.
b. Significant at the 5 percent level.

led to increases in the capital-to-asset ratio.[25] Finally, two other measures of government intervention are included: the change in the minimum capital requirement, that is, the capital requirement for banks in the smallest locations,[26] and a dummy variable for every year in which a state had a deposit insurance system.

The presence of a state deposit insurance system yields negative estimated coefficients, which we would expect from a measure that strengthens the financial safety net; however, they are not significantly different from zero. The estimated coefficients on changes in the minimum capital requirement have negative signs, that is, increases in the minimum capital requirement led to lower capital-to-asset ratios, although these coefficients are not significant at standard levels. This may suggest that higher capital requirements led to larger, less well-capitalized banks, although the results are not statistically significant.

Other variables, including the legality of branching (which might increase diversification and reduce risk), double liability (which reduced risk taking),[27] and changes in the maximum population of cities in the smallest capital category, did not yield statistically significant coefficients. The absence of any effect from any of these measures, which should, and in the case of double liability did, reduce risk, is puzzling and requires further investigation.

Can we discern any other consequences of increased capital requirements? Is it possible that increased capital requirements caused smaller banks to exit and discouraged the entry of new banks? Although I do not have data on new entrants, I can use the percentage change in the number of state banks as a proxy: reduced entry and greater voluntary exit will have a negative effect upon this measure. Table 6.4 presents panel regressions testing the effects of changes in capital requirements upon net bank growth. The dependent variable is the percentage change in the number of state banks in a given state in a given year. Independent variables include the percentage increase in the number of national banks, the state bank failure rate, the change in the minimum capital requirement, and a time trend. The percentage increase in national banks is included to capture the effects of economic conditions. Other things being equal, the forces that would lead to an increase (decrease) in the number of national banks should exert a similarly positive (negative) impact upon the number of state banks. The state bank failure rate is included because state banks were typically more volatile and had higher failure rates than national banks; hence, the change in the number of national banks may understate the effect on state banks.[28] The estimated coefficient on the

Table 6.4
Fixed Effects Panel Regressions: Dependent Variable Is Percent Change in Number of State Banks

	1	2
Constant	8.27[a]	7.84[a]
	1.60	1.67
Year	−0.00429[a]	−0.00407[a]
	0.00084	0.00088
Percent change in number of national banks	0.33[a]	0.42[a]
	0.10	0.10
State bank failure rate	−0.75[a]	
	0.28	
State bank asset failure rate		−0.49
		0.30
Change in minimum capital requirement	−8.72E-06[a]	−8.68E-06[a]
	2.79E-06	2.80E-06
Number of cross-sections	29	29
N	909	884
Years	1891–1930	1892–1930
Adjusted R-squared	0.070	0.0720
Log likelihood	−55.14	−54.24
D-W	2.30	2.33

Notes: Estimated with OLS. Standard errors are shown below coefficients.
a. Significant at the 2.5 percent level.

change in the minimum capital requirement is negative and significant. This suggests that tighter capital regulation may have slowed the net increase of state banks, leading to fewer, larger, less well-capitalized banks. If larger banks held smaller capital-to-asset ratios than smaller banks, increasing barriers to entry in banking may have led to lower aggregate capital-to-asset ratios.

The results based on state panel data are consistent with those on cross-country data. Market capital requirements appear to have been an important determinant of capital-to-asset ratios. We still cannot discern the impact of declining levels of risk on capital-to-asset ratios, beyond noting the negative and significant coefficient on the time trend. A perhaps more surprising result is the absence of any detectable effect of government-mandated capital requirements or a government-sponsored safety net upon capital-to-asset ratios. Neither changes in minimum capital requirements nor the presence of a deposit insurance system brought about higher capital-to-asset ratios (or slowed the decline of those ratios). Additional tests on branching and double liability (not reported) similarly yield nonsignificant coefficients.

Although I do not find a statistically significant effect of changes in government capital requirements upon aggregate capital-to-asset ratios, the evidence suggests that increased government capital requirements may have affected the banking system by slowing the growth of the state-chartered banking system, either by encouraging exit or discouraging entry.

Conclusion and Extensions

What explains the behavior of commercial bank capital-to-asset ratios during the later nineteenth and early twentieth centuries? The cross-country and cross-state analyses presented here find persuasive evidence that market capital requirements played an important role. Banking instability, whether measured as a dichotomous banking crisis variable or as a bank failure rate, increased capital-to-asset ratios. Given that bank capital typically adjusts slowly, and the absence of a long-term impact of financial instability on capitalization, it appears that the crisis-induced decline in capital-to-asset ratios was brought about via asset shedding. Similarly, the decline in economic risk, as measured by government bond rates during the gold standard period, also appears to have had a negative effect on capital-to asset ratios.

Surprisingly, it is difficult to find a systematic effect of government capital regulation on bank capital-to-asset ratios. Analysis of U.S. state-level data suggests that increased capital requirements did have a statistically significant impact upon banking sector growth: it may be that tightening regulatory restrictions, whether or not they involved capital requirements, led to a banking sector composed of fewer, larger, and less well-capitalized banks, although direct tests of the influence of capital requirements on capital-to-asset ratios did not yield statistically significant results. Similarly, safety net variables, such as the presence of bailouts or lender of last resort (in the cross-country data) and the introduction of deposit insurance (in the U.S. data) did not yield consistently statistically significant coefficients. The results accord with Flannery and Rangan's (2002) conclusion that market forces, rather than government regulation, may be the binding constraint on bank leverage.

A third finding is that, after controlling for other variables, there was a statistically significant downward trend in capital-to-asset ratios, both in the cross-country data and in the U.S. data. The estimated coefficient on the trend suggests several possibilities. First, it may be that the data here do not accurately capture economy-wide risk, banking instability, or the evolution of the government safety net, and so the trend captures these variables. Additionally, the trend may capture a gradual increase in banking efficiency and improved information flows.

The results suggest an agenda for further research. First, given the ambiguous nature of the consequences of government regulation, it will be important to focus on the political debates over regulation. To what extent was more stringent regulation brought about by bankers in order to discourage entry and reduce competition? This question can be addressed with more systematic historical research on the policy debates of the time. Second, the results highlight the need for an analysis of bank-level microdata in order to determine the effects of regulation upon entry, exit, size distribution, and intensity of competition among banks. Bank-level data can also be used to examine the effects of changes in requirements upon capital-constrained banks.

More history, more data, and many more questions—just the prescription that Jeff Williamson would give.

Notes

I thank Masami Imai, David Selover, Kevin Stiroh, and the editors of this volume for helpful comments and discussions, and Sandy Cass, Kosin Chantikul, Joon-Young Choi, Tak Wai Chung, John Dolfin, Amit Doshi, Bryan Kim, Gregory Ramkhelawan, Janet Rosenbaum, Nhi Ha Truong, Pierce Woodward, and Jielun Zhu for research assistance. The research was supported by the National Science Foundation and the German Marshall Fund of the United States.

1. Retained earnings may also be available. This section draws heavily on Berger, Herring, and Szegö (1995).

2. This presupposes that the incentives of bank managers shareholders are aligned (i.e., assuming no principal-agent problem) (Glassman and Rhoades 1980). The incentive effect can be even more powerful when shareholder liability is not limited (Grossman 2001).

3. Berger, Herring, and Szegö (1995, 402) document the decline in bank capital-to-asset ratios in the United States.

4. Demsetz and Strahan (1997) find a link between bank holding company size and diversification, but not between bank size and risk.

5. See Kennedy (1987) and Collins (1989) on the increasing conservatism of British bankers in the later nineteenth century. Bankers' associations founded at this time include Chartered Institute of Bankers in Scotland (1875), Chartered Institute of Bankers in Great Britain (1879), American Bankers Association (1875), Canadian Bankers Association (1891), the German Zentralverband des Deutschen Bank- und Bankiergewerbes (1901), and Finnish Suomen Pankkiyhdistys (1914). A Bankers Library (Keizai Bunko) was established in Tokyo in 1897.

6. In the nineteenth-century United States, economically more developed states were more likely to enact stability-promoting double liability than less developed states (Grossman 2001).

7. See, for example, Cannon (1910), Gorton (1985), Gorton and Mullineaux (1987), and Timberlake (1984) on the operations of private bank clearinghouses in the United States during nineteenth- and early twentieth-century banking panics.

8. Aggregate capital-to-asset ratios come from various national annual or retrospective publications, most often produced by governments or central banks. Belgian data come from the financial press.

9. One could argue that this convergence in capital-to-asset ratios occurs in response to greater global competition. However, banks in many countries conducted primarily local business and were often insulated from foreign competition.

10. Countries without capital requirements (and years for which data are available): Australia (1876–1939), Belgium (1877–1912), Denmark (1876–1918), Germany (1883–1920), Italy (1890–1920), Norway (1900–1923), and the United Kingdom (1881–1939). Countries with capital requirements: Canada (1876–1939), Denmark (1919–1939), Norway (1924–1939), Sweden (1876–1937), and the United States (1876–1939).

11. The difference in means is significant at the 10 percent level for four years around the turn of the century.

12. The early banking codes in Sweden, Britain, and Canada each fixed minimum absolute levels of capital. In Japan and the United States minimum capital requirements were determined by the population of the city within which the bank was located.

13. Yet another possibility is that in countries where parallel sets of institutions had different regulatory requirements (e.g., state and national banks in the United States; banks and savings banks; private and chartered banks in many other countries), capital-to-asset ratios may merely reflect the presence or absence of alternative regulatory regimes.

14. The number of commercial banks continued to rise, albeit at a reduced rate, for two years following the imposition of the new law.

15. Regulatory tightening includes higher capital requirements and other measures that imposed stricter regulation on banks (e.g., more frequent or detailed reporting to regulatory authorities; greater power to regulatory authorities to intervene in bank business). I code capital and other regulatory requirements based on my reading of the secondary literature.

16. Bordo et al. (2001) present a catalog of banking crises. My catalog of crises is qualitatively similar.

17. An obvious shortcoming of this method is that bailouts, where assistance is given to firms on a discretionary basis, may depend crucially upon the identity of the institution to be rescued: institutions with stronger political connections may be rescued, while those less well connected may be allowed to fail. Lender of last resort assistance, by contrast, is available to any bank with good collateral.

18. Rates on government bonds (as close to ten-year maturity as possible) are taken from *Global Financial Data*, ⟨http://www.globalfinancialdata.com/index.php3⟩.

19. Bordo and Rockoff (1996) use long-term bond rates as an indicator of the government's commitment to the gold standard.

20. About half the capital-to-asset ratios are nonstationary. Lagged dependent variables are included in all regressions. The presence of a lagged dependent variable in a fixed-effect panel regression can lead to bias that varies inversely with the length of the time series. Since the time series used here are relatively long, I do not resort to the GMM estimator. See Arellano and Bond (1991).

21. Because of the turbulence in financial markets during the interwar gold standard period, I restrict the sample of observations to country-years prior to 1914 where the gold standard prevailed.

22. Estimated coefficients on lagged crises are typically not significantly different from zero, suggesting that the crisis effect is short-lived.

23. Data on state and national bank balance sheets are taken from the Annual Report of the Comptroller of the Currency. Data on regulations are taken from state statutes.

24. Equation 3 of table 6.3, where the *p* value is 10.5 percent, is an exception.

25. Failure rates also yield positive and significant when lagged two years, although not when lagged one year.

26. Because state banking statutes frequently specified several minimum capital requirements based on the population of the city in which the bank was located, no single number can completely summarize a state's capital requirement. I use the minimum capital require-

ment established for banks in the smallest localities as an indicator of the state's capital requirements.

27. Double liability means that shareholders of failing banks might be called upon to pay twice the amount they initially invested in the bank in the event of failure. Grossman (2001) demonstrates that in times of relative financial calm double liability in fact reduced bank risk taking.

28. If the state bank failure rate is omitted, the significance of the change in the minimum capital requirement remains negative but is no longer significant.

References

Arellano, M., and S. Bond. 1991. Some Tests of Specification for Panel Data: Monte Carlo Evidence and an Application to Employment Equations. *Review of Economic Studies* 58 (2): 277–297.

Basel Committee on Banking Supervision. 1988. *International Convergence of Capital Measurement and Capital Standards.* Basel.

———. 2004. *Basel II: International Convergence of Capital Measurement and Capital Standards: A Revised Framework.* Basel.

Berger, A. N., R. J. Herring, and G. Szegö. 1995. The Role of Capital in Financial Institutions. *Journal of Banking and Finance* 19 (3–4): 393–430.

Bordo, M., B. Eichengreen, D. Klingebiel, and M. S. Martinez-Peria. 2001. Is the Crisis Problem Growing More Severe? *Economic Policy* 32: 53–82.

Bordo, M., and H. Rockoff. 1996. The Gold Standard as a "Good Housekeeping Seal of Approval." *Journal of Economic History* 56 (2): 389–428.

Cannon, J. G. 1910. *Clearing Houses.* Washington: Government Printing Office.

Collins, M. 1989. The Banking Crisis of 1878. *Economic History Review* 42 (4): 504–527.

Demsetz, R. S., and P. E. Strahan. 1997. Diversification, Size, and Risk at Bank Holding Companies. *Journal of Money, Credit, and Banking* 29 (3): 300–313.

Flannery, M. J., and K. P. Rangan. 2002. Market Forces at Work in the Banking Industry: Evidence from the Capital Buildup of the 1990s. Mimeo.

Flux, A. W. 1910. *The Swedish Banking System.* Washington: Government Printing Office.

Glassman, C. A., and S. A. Rhoades. 1980. Owner vs. Manager Control Effects on Bank Performance. *Review of Economics and Statistics* 53: 263–270.

Gorton, G. 1985. Clearinghouses and the Origin of Central Banking in the United States. *Journal of Economic History* 45 (2): 277–283.

Gorton, G., and D. J. Mullineaux. 1987. The Joint Production of Confidence: Endogenous Regulation and Nineteenth Century Commercial-Bank Clearinghouses. *Journal of Money, Credit, and Banking* 19 (4): 457–468.

Grossman, R. S. 2001. Double Liability and Bank Risk Taking. *Journal of Money, Credit, and Banking* 33 (2): 143–159.

Kennedy, W. 1987. *Industrial Structure, Capital Markets, and the Origins of British Economic Decline.* Cambridge: Cambridge University Press.

Modigliani, F., and M. Miller. 1958. The Cost of Capital, Corporation Finance, and the Theory of Investment. *American Economic Review* 48 (3): 261–297.

Timberlake, R. H. 1984. The Central Banking Role of Clearinghouse Associations. *Journal of Money, Credit, and Banking* 16 (1): 1–15.

Troy, L. 2004. *Almanac of Business and Industrial Financial Ratios.* Englewood Cliffs, N.J.: Prentice-Hall.

7   Education, Migration, and Regional Wage Convergence in U.S. History

William J. Collins

The comparative perspective in the New Comparative Economic History often entails looking across countries to discern how differences in factor endowments and changes in factor and commodity market integration have influenced long-run economic phenomena (Williamson 1996). But the logic and force of the approach are every bit as compelling when comparing regions within a country, especially when the regions are as diverse as those in the United States (Williamson 1965; 1980). In that spirit, this chapter describes the twentieth-century economic ascendance of the American South with a focus on convergence between the South and the rest of the country in terms of workers' formal education and earnings.[1]

Before the Civil War, Southerners made comparatively small investments in formal education, even among white children. For white children, the economic shock and social dislocation associated with the war appear to have further reduced educational attainment compared to any reasonable no-war counterfactual. For slaves (who had been forbidden to learn to read) and their offspring, the Civil War obviously had different implications; from an extremely low base, African-Americans rapidly increased their literacy rate. But even 35 years after the war, the North-South gap in educational attainment and institutions was still very large. The median Southern child (aged 7–17) attended school for five months less than the median non-Southern child in 1900.

Woodward, in his landmark history, *Origins of the New South* (1951), writes, "The public schools of the South at the opening of the new century were for the most part miserably supported, poorly attended, wretchedly taught, and wholly inadequate for the education of the people. Far behind the rest of the country in nearly all respects, Southern education suffered from a greater lag than any other public institution in the region" (398). Nevertheless, by the end of the twentieth century, the regional gap in educational attainment had nearly disappeared.

After documenting regional trends in educational attainment and children's school attendance with microlevel census data, this chapter pursues two main questions. First, how can one account for Southern workers' twentieth-century educational catch-up? The rate of educational improvement did not slow down outside the South; rather, the Southern labor force accumulated schooling at a consistently faster rate than the rest of the country from at least 1940 onward. I find that part of the regional convergence was driven by migration flows. On net, migrants to the South had relatively high levels of human capital, whereas migrants to the rest of the country (including the foreign-born) had relatively low levels of human capital. However, the bulk of the regional convergence in workers' education is accounted for by local investment in regional natives. The educational gains of each new cohort of Southern-born African-American workers are significant in this regard.

Second, how much did convergence in average educational attainment contribute to convergence in average earnings? To gauge the direct contribution, I estimate counterfactual interregional income gaps for each census year from 1950 to 2000, supposing that there had been no educational convergence in the preceding decade. From this perspective, which yields conservative estimates, it appears that education's direct contributions were economically significant, accounting for (on average) roughly 40 percent of the income convergence that occurred in each decade from 1950 to 2000.

This chapter does not directly address the civil rights movement, but many connections between Southern educational history and the civil rights movement are manifest here. To wit, civil rights leaders and many of the rank and file stepped forward from a growing well-educated segment of the Southern black population. In this sense, blacks' pre-1950 educational gains set the stage for the civil rights movement, even if such gains were not a sufficient condition for the movement's success. Civil rights organizations, in turn, pursued litigation that motivated improvements in black schools long before the U.S. Supreme Court's *Brown v. Board of Education* ruling in 1954 (Tushnet 1987; Margo 1990). And in the 1960s, changes in federal policy directly targeted discrimination in the South, improved labor market opportunities for black workers (Donohue and Heckman 1991), and may have boosted incentives for young blacks to acquire more and better schooling. The success of the civil rights movement lowered the likelihood of out-migration by well-educated blacks and made the region more attractive for well-educated native-born and foreign-born migrants. Thus, although the South's educational convergence on the North began some time before the civil rights movement's most famous events, the histories of schooling, race, and income in the South are at all times intertwined.

Regional Divergence and Convergence in Education, 1850–2000

Regional convergence in educational attainment is clearly evident in the second half of the twentieth century, but the nineteenth- and early twentieth-century evidence is much more mixed. Analysis of individual-level data from IPUMS, the Integrated Public Use Microdata Series (Ruggles et al. 2004), reveals that in the decade before the Civil War, the South/non-South gaps in school attendance among white children (aged 7–17) and in literacy rates among young white adults (aged 20–25) narrowed slightly.[2] The attendance gap fell from 22 to 20 percentage points between 1850 and 1860, and the literacy rate gap fell from 10 to 7 percentage points. There are indications, however, that Southern whites' school attendance and literacy deteriorated around the time of the Civil War and Reconstruction in both absolute terms and relative to the rest of the country. Southern white school attendance fell from 52 to 38 percent from 1860 to 1870, and literacy among young Southern white adults fell from 89 to 81 percent from 1860 to 1880. The regional gap in school attendance (for whites) jumped to 33 percentage points in 1870, and the literacy rate gap jumped to 14 percentage points in 1880 (20- to 25-year-olds in 1880 would have been of school age during the Civil War and Reconstruction). This represents a remarkable educational setback for a generation of Southern white children.

Despite this setback, and although Woodward (1951) dates the "great educational awakening" in the South to the turn of the century, Southern children of both race categories sharply increased their rates of school attendance after 1870. Between 1870 and 1900 the proportion of Southern children (aged 7–17) who attended school for at least part of the year jumped from 28 to 58 percent (from 9 to 44 percent for black children, and from 38 to 65 percent for white children). Comparable figures for all non-Southern children are 70 percent in 1870 and 72 percent in 1900.

The Census's school attendance question set a very low bar for an affirmative answer. Typically, the question asked whether the child attended school at all in the previous school year or calendar year. To infer the real educational implications of rising attendance rates, it helps to examine measures of outcomes such as literacy and highest grade of attainment. Prior to 1940, unfortunately, literacy is the only gauge of

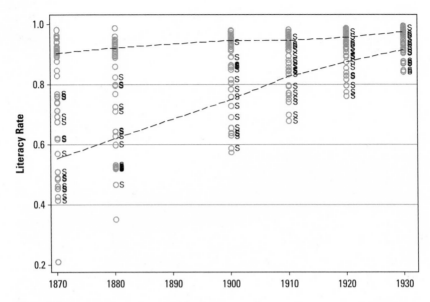

Figure 7.1a
Literacy rates for adults, 1870–1930. Calculated using IPUMS microdata (Ruggles et al. 2004). Dashed lines connect the Southern and non-Southern averages from year to year. Each open circle marks a state average in a particular year. "S" is noted next to Southern states. Washington, D.C., is not plotted but is included in the Southern average. Samples include everyone aged 18–64; respondents are counted as literate if they can read and write. The low outliers for 1870 and 1880 represent New Mexico.

educational attainment available in nationally representative samples. Figure 7.1a plots state-level literacy rates from 1870 to 1930 calculated using samples of 18–64-year-olds from all race categories and the foreign-born. The overall Southern literacy rate was just 55 percent in 1870 compared to the non-Southern rate of 90 percent.[3]

The South's enormous deficit in literacy in the late nineteenth century is largely, but not solely, attributable to slavery and its preclusion of African-Americans' educational opportunities. In the antebellum South, it was illegal to teach slaves to read because it was thought that educated slaves were more likely to run away or lead insurrections (for instance, literacy makes it easier to forge passes, write letters, and follow complex directions). Although some slaves did learn to read and write (Anderson 1988; Williams 2004), as far as one can tell from the Census data, there was little or no upward trend in literacy among slaves prior to the Civil War (Margo and Collins 2006). The overwhelming majority of black workers had little or no formal schooling in 1870. Only 12 percent of black workers were literate, and they comprised 42 percent of the South-

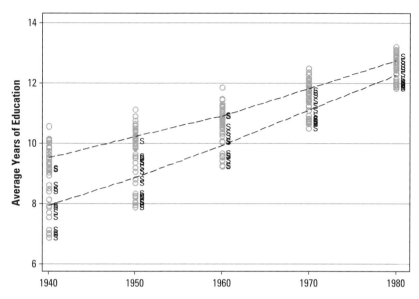

Figure 7.1b
Average years of education, 1940–1980. Calculated using IPUMS microdata (Ruggles et al. 2004). State averages are calculated using person weights. Dashed lines connect the Southern and non-Southern averages from year to year. Each open circle marks a state average in a particular year. "S" is noted next to Southern states. Washington, D.C., is not plotted but is included in the Southern average. Samples include only those in the labor force, ages 18–64; averages are based on respondents' highest grade of completion in 1940 and highest grade of attendance in other years.

ern labor force. Southern white workers continued to lag behind non-Southerners, too, but the interregional gap among whites was much smaller (about 10 percentage points in 1870).

By 1930, when the Census last inquired about literacy, there had been considerable interstate convergence in literacy rates (figure 7.1a). But literacy, as defined by the Census, was an extremely low educational threshold, typically achieved after approximately two years of schooling (Margo 1990). Therefore, the figure might mask divergence in more finely tuned measures of educational attainment. The "high school movement," which accelerated outside the South nearly a full generation before it did in the South (Goldin 1998), is a central concern in this regard.

As noted, the 1940 Census was the first to inquire about highest grade of attainment. Measurement issues associated with ungraded schools and regional differences in school quality will tend to overstate the level of Southern educational attainment in 1940 relative to non-Southern attainment, and the degree of bias should lessen over time.[4] Therefore, the educational convergence documented here, which does not attempt to adjust for quality differences, is a conservative description of the true magnitude of change.[5] In the 1940 IPUMS sample, individuals who were born in the South between 1880 and 1920 averaged about two grades less education than non-Southern-born natives. Thus, in contrast to the literacy-based perspective in figure 7.1a, there is little or no evidence of convergence in average highest grade of attainment among natives who entered the labor force in the early twentieth century.

From the 1920 birth cohort onward, however, educational convergence was significant, and as the new cohorts entered the labor force (and as the old cohorts departed), the interregional gap in workers' human capital narrowed (figure 7.1b). The regional gap in workers' average years of education was large in 1940. Among Southern workers, the average was only 7.9 years, compared to the non-Southern workers' average of 9.5. Again, the African-American educational deficit is a significant factor in the interregional gap. In 1940 Southern black workers averaged only 5.4 years of education, compared to 8.8 years for Southern white workers. After 1940 the regional gap in average educational attainment fell from 1.6 years to less than 0.50 years by 1980 and to less than 0.25 years by 2000.

Figure 7.2 summarizes the post-1940 pattern of convergence in educational attainment for each state by graphing changes in average educational attainment among workers from 1940 to 1980 against initial (1940) values. Southern states are clearly grouped in the upper left corner of the graph; they had low initial values and high growth rates. Workers in the deep South (Alabama, Mississippi, Louisiana, Georgia, and South Carolina) had extremely rapid gains between 1940 and 1980, adding about five grades to a 1940 base of only seventh-grade attainment.

The Roots of the Southern Schooling Deficit

History, Political Economy, and Southern Public Schooling
The historical literature on the relatively low level of Southern investment in public goods and public education in particular describes an evolving balance of power in the region's political economy. At the risk of oversimplification, both before and after the Civil War the economic interests of wealthy white landowners (planters) were a roadblock to the expansion of the Southern public education system, especially in rural areas and for blacks (Woodward 1951; Nicholls 1960; Tindall 1967; Wright 1986; Anderson 1988; Margo 1990). Anderson (1988, 26) writes,

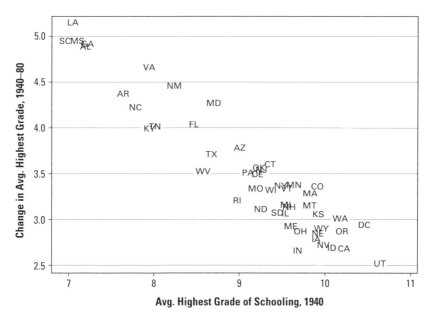

Figure 7.2
Convergence in workers' educational attainment, 1940–1980. Calculated using IPUMS microdata (Ruggles et al. 2004). Averages are based on respondents' highest grade of completion in 1940 and highest grade of attendance in 1980.

Before the war poor [white] children were unable to afford private schooling and only rarely had the opportunity to attend charity institutions. In the immediate postwar years the region's poor whites, in general, were still too closely tied to the planters' interests and ideology to pursue a different conception of education and society.... The South's white middle classes, unorganized and subservient to planter interests throughout the nineteenth century, did not begin their campaign for universal education until the dawn of the twentieth century.

The problem with public education, from the planters' perspective, was fourfold: (1) it required tax revenue; (2) educated workers were more likely to leave agriculture (and the South);[6] (3) children of school age provided a nontrivial amount of farm labor, especially at periods of peak demand; and (4) in the context of post-Reconstruction disenfranchisement, education had the potential to shift political power toward poor whites and blacks (Anderson 1988; 98). With the exception of the Reconstruction period, planters held disproportionate political influence in the South, and a relatively low level of support for public schooling ensued.[7]

During Reconstruction, however, Southern states adopted new constitutions that included substantial provisions for tax-supported public education for all children, including blacks. This set a foundation for public school systems throughout the region, but after 1877 (the end of Reconstruction) the Southern commitment to public schooling faltered. Southern planters reestablished their political dominance, and critics linked public schools with "carpetbaggers" of the Reconstruction era. Woodward (1951) explains, "Redemption governments, often describing themselves as the 'rule of the taxpayer,' frankly constituted themselves champions of the property owner against the propertyless and allegedly untaxed masses" (59). In addition, for decades thereafter, Alston and Ferrie (1999) claim, appeals to race issues "enabled politicians to cater to the economic interests of the white upper class while maintaining the support of whites in general" (39). Because wage laborers and sharecroppers valued schools for their children and would move to take advantage of educational opportunities, an incentive to support schools remained even where blacks and poor whites were politically disenfranchised (Margo 1990).[8] But the average level of quality was low, as emphasized by Woodward and as is evident in records of expenditures per pupil, teachers per pupil, and length of school year.

The idea that public schooling was socially desirable, especially for white children, slowly gained political momentum in the South. By the end of the nineteenth century, many Southern whites, including small farmers, professional educators, and advocates of Southern industrialization, were fighting vigorously to expand educational opportunities for Southern children (Nicholls 1960). In addition, black parents and northern philanthropists stepped in to improve the meager educational facilities available to black children (Donohue, Heckman, and Todd 2002). As noted, Woodward (1951) dates the "great educational awakening" (400) in the South to the turn of the century, but at all times it was an uphill run to catch up to the rest of the country, where educational standards and attainment were constantly increasing. In Goldin's (1998) description of the takeoff of America's high school movement in the early 1900s, the South was left, literally but temporarily, in the dust.[9]

A Closer Look at School Attendance at the Turn of the Twentieth Century

The 1900 Census is especially useful for characterizing the size and nature of the regional schooling gap because it recorded the number of months that children attended school in the previous year, whereas other censuses simply asked whether the child had attended school at all in the past year (or in past several months).[10] In 1900 nearly half of Southern children (aged 7–17) attended school for less than one month compared to about

30 percent of non-Southern children. Less than one-tenth of Southern children attended school for nine months or more compared to nearly 40 percent of non-Southern children.[11] By 1960 racial and regional disparities in children's school attendance had essentially disappeared for those aged 7–15, although regional gaps remained at both ends of the school-age distribution.[12]

Do regional gaps in economic characteristics, such as income and urbanization, easily account for the large regional gaps in investment in children's education circa 1900? Or was the South distinctly below the regression line in its investment in children's schooling? To explore these questions, I estimated regressions of the following basic form for samples of children (aged 7–17) using the 1900 IPUMS data:

$$\text{Months}_{ijr} = \alpha + \gamma_{\text{age}} + \beta_1 \, \text{South}_r + \beta_2 \, \text{Urban}_{ijr}$$

$$+ \, \beta_4 \, \text{State income}_j + \beta_4 \, \text{Parent income}_{ijr} + e_{ijr}$$

Months is the number of months the child attended school, γ is a vector of age dummy variables, *South* is a region of residence dummy variable, log *State income* per capita is from Mitchener and McLean (1999), and log *Parent income* is an estimate based on the race-gender-region-occupation category of the household head.[13]

The inclusion of age dummies implies that the coefficient on *South* is identified from within age-cohort differences in months of schooling across regions, conditional on the other variables. Such a regression cannot truly explain the South's attendance deficit, but it can quantify the residual significance of "Southernness" that extends beyond regional differences in income and urban residence. The unadjusted regional gap in average months of schooling in 1900 was approximately 2.8 months; the median gap was 5 months. An OLS regression that conditions on these variables yields a coefficient on *South* of -0.91, whereas a quantile regression (at medians) yields a coefficient of -1.5.[14] In this sense, about two-thirds of the total interregional gap in months of school attendance in 1900 can be accounted for by fundamental economic variables, but the residual regional gap is still economically and statistically significant.[15]

The *South* coefficient is nearly identical if a dummy for race (black = 1) is included in the OLS regression (the *Race* coefficient is -0.203, standard error = 0.096). Alternatively, if only white children are included in the sample, the *South* coefficient is only slightly smaller in magnitude than originally $(\beta_1 = -0.819)$. Finally, replacing the "months of school" dependent variable with a binary variable for school attendance $(= 1$

if attended at all) yields a Southern coefficient of -0.092 (standard error $= 0.037$), implying that Southern students were about 9 percentage points less likely to be enrolled in school than non-Southern students, conditional on the other independent variables. Again, the estimate is only slightly affected by adding a control variable for race to the specification.

Thus, at the beginning of the twentieth century, the South lagged the North in educating its children by a wide margin, and only part of that disparity is attributable to regional differences in income, urban residence, and racial composition. Conditional on a basic set of economic characteristics, Southern children attended school for fewer months than non-Southern children. How, then, did the South catch up?

Convergence in Educational Attainment: The Roles of Migration and Local Investment

It has often been noted that higher levels of education facilitated black migration out of the South, particularly before World War II (e.g., Margo 1990; Vigdor 2002). Scholars have paid much less attention to the selective nature of migration *into* the South (Fein 1965; Suval and Hamilton 1965; Wright 1986). In 1940 non-Southern-born (but U.S. native) workers residing in the South had an average of 10.6 years of education compared to the Southern-born residents' average of 7.8 years and the Northern-born "stayer" average of 10.0.[16]

Tables 7.1a and 7.1b account for regional differences and changes in all workers' average educational attainment. At a point in time, the average education level in a region can be expressed as a weighted average of the attainment of those who were born in the region and continue to reside there ("stayers") and those who were born elsewhere but moved into the region either from elsewhere in the United States or from another country (migrants). Columns 1–4 of table 7.1a decompose the average years of schooling for each year from 1940 to 2000 for the South and non-South.

Three key points emerge. First, migrants to the South have always been better educated (on average) than regional native workers ("stayers"), but migrants to the non-South (many of whom were foreign-born) have always been less educated than non-Southern regional native workers. Second, while the non-South maintained a roughly constant proportion of migrant workers (column 4; again, a combination of interregional and foreign-born migrants) at around 20 percent, the South steadily increased its share of migrants, from one-tenth of its labor force in 1940 to one-third in 2000. This is one way of viewing the breakdown of regional isolation emphasized by Wright (1986). Third, over time, both the regional natives and the migrants in the Southern labor force came to resemble workers elsewhere in the country (table 7.1a, panel C, columns 2 and 3), but nontrivial differences remained. "Locally produced" non-Southern workers are still better educated than "locally produced" Southern workers on average, and the migrants to the South are still better educated than the migrants to the non-South.

Columns 1–4 of table 7.1a could be misleading characterizations of the role of net migration in changing the skill mix of the Southern labor force. For example, if the out-migration of highly educated Southerners had been large relative to the in-migration of highly educated workers from elsewhere, then one would *not* want to conclude that interregional migration had a net positive influence on Southern workers' average educational attainment. Columns 5–8 help address this concern. Southern-born emigrants were, in fact, better educated than Southern-born "stayers" in every census sample, although the difference in 1960, 1970, and 1980 is much smaller than in 1940. This is consistent with the idea that Southern emigration was more selective on education before World War II than afterward (Vigdor 2002).[17] But the South's loss of relatively well-educated emigrants (compared to Southern "stayers") was more than offset by the inflow of well-educated workers in determining the overall average educational attainment of Southern workers. The net migration effect, reported in column 8 of table 7.1a, is simply the difference between the average educational attainment of workers born in the South and of those residing in the South. The net effect for the South is positive up to 2000, and is especially strong in the 1960–1980 samples.

The net effect of migration for the non-South is even larger in magnitude, but it is negative (table 7.1a, panel B, column 8). The combined implications for regional convergence are reported in table 7.1a, panel C, column 8. The regional gap in worker education was about 0.5 years less than it would have been on the basis of place of birth, assuming that each individual's educational attainment is fixed.[18]

Table 7.1b decomposes changes over time in average educational attainment for workers residing in each region using the identity

$$\Delta S = \alpha_1(S_{N1} - S_{N0}) + (1 - \alpha_1)(S_{M1} - S_{M0}) + (\alpha_1 - \alpha_0)(S_{N0} - S_{M0})$$

where S is the average schooling level in a region's labor force, α is the proportion of workers who were born in the region (natives), S_N and S_M refer to the regional native average schooling level and migrant schooling

Table 7.1a
Accounting for the Regional Differences in Workers' Education, 1940–2000

	(1)	(2)	(3)	(4)
	Av. for Residents	Av. for "Stayers"	Av. for In-Migrants	In-Migrant Weight
Panel A: South				
1940	7.94	7.77	9.68	0.093
1950	8.86	8.60	10.83	0.116
1960	9.92	9.63	11.75	0.137
1970	11.10	10.80	12.59	0.169
1980	12.25	11.98	13.17	0.227
1990	13.05	12.87	13.51	0.287
2000	13.43	13.35	13.60	0.336
Panel B: Non-South				
1940	9.51	10.01	7.76	0.223
1950	10.22	10.63	8.61	0.201
1960	10.90	11.22	9.55	0.193
1970	11.81	12.02	10.83	0.177
1980	12.73	12.92	11.86	0.180
1990	13.38	13.60	12.46	0.195
2000	13.67	13.90	12.86	0.219
Panel C: Difference, South – Non-South				
1940	−1.54	−2.24	1.92	−0.130
1950	−1.36	−2.03	2.22	−0.085
1960	−0.98	−1.59	2.20	−0.056
1970	−0.71	−1.22	1.76	−0.008
1980	−0.47	−0.93	1.31	0.047
1990	−0.32	−0.73	1.05	0.092
2000	−0.24	−0.56	0.74	0.118

Source: Calculated using IPUMS microdata (Ruggles et al. 2004).
Notes: Samples include workers between 18 and 64 years of age who are in the labor force. The "average for residents" is a weighted average of education for "stayers" and in-migrants. "Stayers" are those who reside in the region in which they were born. In-migrants include both foreign-born workers and migrants from other U.S. regions. The "average for born in region" is a weighted average for "stayers" and out-migrants. Out-migrants are those born in one region but residing in the other; workers who left the United States would

	(5) Av. for Born in Region	(6) Av. for Out-Migrants	(7) Out- Migrant Weight	(8) Net Migration Effect $(1 - 5)$
Panel A: South				
1940	7.91	8.72	0.151	0.03
1950	8.72	9.20	0.203	0.14
1960	9.68	9.86	0.231	0.24
1970	10.85	11.05	0.220	0.25
1980	12.04	12.26	0.201	0.21
1990	12.94	13.31	0.175	0.11
2000	13.44	13.93	0.153	−0.01
Panel B: Non-South				
1940	10.03	10.63	0.035	−0.52
1950	10.67	11.47	0.047	−0.45
1960	11.28	12.21	0.057	−0.38
1970	12.08	12.90	0.070	−0.27
1980	12.97	13.48	0.097	−0.24
1990	13.65	14.00	0.120	−0.27
2000	13.95	14.28	0.132	−0.28
Panel C: Difference, South − Non-South				
1940	−2.12	−1.91	0.116	0.55
1950	−1.95	−2.27	0.156	0.59
1960	−1.60	−2.35	0.174	0.62
1970	−1.23	−1.85	0.150	0.52
1980	−0.93	−1.22	0.104	0.45
1990	−0.71	−0.69	0.055	0.38
2000	−0.51	−0.35	0.021	0.27

exit the sample altogether. Migrant status is determined by place of birth compared with place of residence; it is impossible to identify those who moved as children (and therefore might have been educated in a region other than their birth region). Educational attainment codes changed in 1990. For comparison with earlier years, I assigned midpoint values for workers with low levels of education (e.g., first to fourth grade code is assigned a value of 2.5); "some college" and associate degree holders are assigned two years of college (value of 14); bachelor's degree, 16; master's degree, 18; professional degree, 19; and doctorate, 21.

Table 7.1b
Accounting for the Regional Convergence in Workers' Education, by Region of Residence, 1940–2000

	Total Change	Contribution of Native Education	Contribution of Migrant Education	Contribution of Migrant Share
Panel A: South				
1940–1950	0.915	0.736	0.133	0.046
1950–1960	1.061	0.890	0.126	0.045
1960–1970	1.182	0.971	0.142	0.069
1970–1980	1.151	0.915	0.132	0.104
1980–1990	0.799	0.630	0.099	0.071
1990–2000	0.379	0.317	0.030	0.032
1940–1980	*4.309*	*3.512*	*0.533*	*0.264*
1940–2000	*5.487*	*4.460*	*0.661*	*0.367*
Panel B: Non-South				
1940–1950	0.715	0.495	0.171	0.048
1950–1960	0.680	0.482	0.182	0.017
1960–1970	0.910	0.656	0.226	0.027
1970–1980	0.915	0.734	0.185	−0.005
1980–1990	0.649	0.547	0.118	−0.016
1990–2000	0.300	0.239	0.087	−0.027
1940–1980	*3.220*	*2.368*	*0.764*	*0.088*
1940–2000	*4.169*	*3.154*	*0.969*	*0.046*
Panel C: Difference, South − Non-South				
1940–1950	0.200	0.241	−0.037	−0.003
1950–1960	0.381	0.408	−0.056	0.028
1960–1970	0.272	0.315	−0.084	0.042
1970–1980	0.236	0.181	−0.053	0.108
1980–1990	0.150	0.083	−0.019	0.087
1990–2000	0.079	0.078	−0.058	0.059
1940–1980	*1.089*	*1.144*	*−0.231*	*0.176*
1940–2000	*1.318*	*1.305*	*−0.308*	*0.321*

Source: Calculated using IPUMS microdata (Ruggles et al. 2004).
Notes: The columns report the components of the decomposition described in the text and in the equation for ΔS. Migrants to each region include both foreign-born workers and in-migrants from other U.S. regions.

level, respectively, and 0 or 1 denotes the beginning or end year of a decade. So, the overall change in a region's stock of educational attainment (among workers) can be partitioned into a weighted *change* in natives' average attainment, a weighted *change* in migrants' average attainment, and the *change* in native/migrant mix in the labor force weighted by the difference in their average attainment.

Within each regional grouping, the lion's share of rising educational attainment is accounted for by investments in human capital by native-born workers. This is not surprising because regional natives comprise a large portion of the labor force (around 80 percent on average) and educational attainment among natives (both South and non-South) was rising quickly. The more interesting result is the influence of the changing native/ migrant mix in each region's labor force. The South received relatively well-educated migrants, and these migrants increased their share of the Southern labor force over time. The non-South received relatively poorly educated migrants, and the migrant share of workers fell from 1940 to 1970 (a positive influence on average attainment) before rising again to 2000 (a negative influence on average attainment). The combined implications of the changing native/migrant mix are reported in table 7.1b, panel C, rightmost column. In the 1940s, 1950s, and 1960s the changing mix of migrants made little difference to the overall pace of educational convergence. However, in the 1970s, 1980s, and 1990s the shifting native/ migrant composition of the labor force accounts for about half (or more in the 1990s) of the interregional educational convergence, although the overall pace of convergence was slower than in earlier decades.

Why did the South attract relatively high human capital workers (on average), while the non-South attracted relatively low human capital workers? For the period prior to 1940 it is not possible to compare average wages across education groups by region with great certainty. It appears, however, that wages in skilled occupations in the South (especially the South Central subregion) were nearly on par with those in the Northeast and Midwest, whereas wages for Southern unskilled labor were comparatively low, implying a relatively high skill premium in the South. This pattern is evident at least as far back as 1890 (Coelho and Shepherd 1979; Sundstrom and Rosenbloom 1993), and Margo (2004) has shown that it existed even in the antebellum period.

Using the 1950 IPUMS sample, I calculated median weekly earnings, by education level, for workers who worked at least 40 weeks in 1949, including adjustments to account for state-level differences in the cost of living (from Williamson and Lindert 1980). Again, Southern regions offered nearly the same (pretax) earnings as non-Southern regions for male workers who had 12 years or more of formal education (e.g., $81 per week in Mid-Atlantic compared to $76 in the South Atlantic, in 1949 dollars) and much lower wages than non-Southern regions for workers with less than 12 years of education (e.g., $59 in Mid-Atlantic compared to $39 in South Atlantic). This is not merely a reflection of the racial composition of the South; essentially the same story can be told when looking at separate samples for white and black men.[19] A similar regional pattern is evident for income in 1979 income, but by that time Southern workers with more than 12 years of education earned slightly *more* in the South than elsewhere, and the regional wage gap for workers with less than 12 years was much smaller (in percentage terms) than in 1949.[20] Thus, throughout the second half of the twentieth century, real weekly earnings (pretax) in the South were as high as those elsewhere in the country for workers with some college education, but earnings were lower in the South than elsewhere for poorly educated workers.

The long-standing regional differences in wage structure have been interpreted as evidence of regional labor market isolation, especially before 1940 (Wright 1986; Rosenbloom 2002). Whatever the extent of Southern labor market isolation in the early twentieth century, several factors contributed to its erosion: labor demand booms in Northern industrial centers during World Wars I and II; the interruption of the supply of unskilled European immigrants; new agricultural policies and technologies that weakened Southern agriculture's hold on unskilled labor; vast improvements in transportation and communication into and out of the South; economic incentives and federal government decisions to locate more industrial, military, and research capacity in the South; and the success of the civil rights movement in revolutionizing Southern race relations.[21] The consequent increase in the regional exchange of workers complemented the South's rising investments in its own children in driving the regional convergence in workers' productive characteristics.

Implications for Income Convergence after 1940

The thorough education of all classes of people is the most efficacious means for promoting the prosperity of the South.

—Robert E. Lee, 1867.[22]

The historical evidence from the late nineteenth century indicates that local policymakers in the postbellum South did not embrace Robert E.

Lee's advice regarding educational investment. Indeed, the South's low level of investment in human capital has been cited in numerous studies of the region's economic shortcomings (Nicholls 1960; Colberg 1965; Wright 1986). What, then, were the implications of regional convergence in workers' education for regional convergence in average earnings? Did Southern prosperity move in lockstep with educational gains?

Two recent contributions highlight the role of human capital accumulation in understanding regional income convergence. Caselli and Coleman (2001) argue that the convergence of agricultural on nonagricultural wages and the movement of workers from agricultural to nonagricultural activities (which they group together as "structural transformation") account for most of interregional wage convergence between 1880 and 1990. A key aspect of their explanation is that the cost of acquiring "nonagricultural skills" declined over time, primarily because of declining costs of attending school (though not documented directly), and that this led to a labor supply shift away from the agricultural sector. Connolly (2004) argues that human capital accumulation increased the South's relative income both directly, through workers' productivity, and indirectly, by facilitating technological diffusion from more advanced places.

In this section, I take a methodological approach that is closer in spirit to the wage analyses that are common in labor economics than to the macroeconomic approaches described previously. For each decade, I calculate the change in average educational attainment among workers in each region between the census dates (ΔED). Then, using estimated returns to education for each region (β_{ED}), I calculate a counterfactual average log wage level by subtracting $\beta_{ED} \times \Delta$ED from the actual average log wage. I estimate the average returns to education using separate Mincerian regressions for workers in the South and non-South, controlling for state fixed effects, so that the returns to education are measured based on within-state variation in attainment. For simplicity, the regressions assume a linear relationship between log income and years of education, and the estimates are made conditional on a quartic in age, and dummy variables for gender, race, foreign birth, and weeks of work (the IPUMS "wkswork2" variable). The basic idea is to take, say, the 1949 wage structure in each region as given and to reset the average education level to its 1940 position to predict a counterfactual level of mean earnings for 1949.

This approach might lead to understatement of education's contribution. For example, the incremental increase in educational attainment might lead to faster technological transfer or region-specific innovation

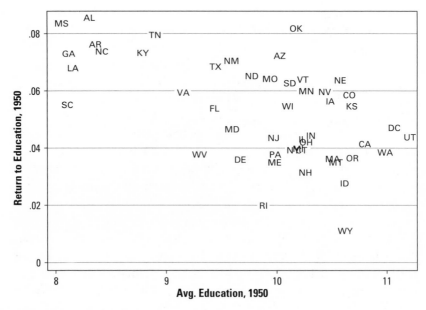

Figure 7.3
Returns to education and average education of workers, 1950. Calculated using IPUMS microdata (Ruggles et al. 2004). Returns to education are estimated from separate regressions for each state in which log total annual income is regressed on highest grade of attendance and several other worker characteristics (age, sex, race, foreign birth, and weeks worked).

that makes all workers more productive; if so, the subtracted-off portion of wages ($\beta_{ED} \times \Delta ED$) misses an important component of education's contribution, and the counterfactual wage level is set too high. Even so, the calculations provide a conservative basis for sizing up the extent to which incremental improvements in workers' education directly influenced earnings.

To illustrate the factors that drive the subsequent calculations, figure 7.3 graphs estimated returns to education at a more disaggregated level than just South and non-South. From a set of separate regressions for each state in 1949, the figure plots returns to education against average educational attainment in the state.[23] The Southern states typically had significantly higher returns to human capital and significantly lower initial levels of education. Additional analysis (not shown) reveals that states with high returns to education in 1949 experienced rapid improvements in the average education level of their workers. We know from the previous section that this was accomplished primarily through investments in regional natives and that interregional migration also boosted the rate of educational convergence.

The combination of high returns and rapid educational gains suggests potentially large effects on interstate income convergence. Over time, one would expect the returns to education in the South to fall relative to those elsewhere as the South accumulated more human capital (and they did), but in the meantime educational convergence had an amplified impact on wage convergence because of the interstate differences in returns to education.

Table 7.2 reports South versus non-South comparisons for each census year from 1940 to 2000. The first column reports the change in average educational attainment for workers with positive earnings and a full set of reported characteristics for the wage regressions. The second column reports the estimated returns to education in the later census year. Two important points are evident: first, as suggested in figure 7.3, the returns are higher in the South than elsewhere throughout the second half of the century; second, the estimated returns converge strongly, and by 2000 there was virtually no difference between South and non-South. The third column is the product of the first two and measures (with the caveats noted) the contribution of education to average wage growth. These values are always larger in the South than in the non-South and therefore help drive income convergence.

In 1960, for example, the actual gap between the South and the rest of the country in average log wages was 0.357, but the counterfactual gap is 0.397 (in the absence of the South's educational catch-up during previous ten years). Overall, there was very little regional convergence in actual wages during the 1950s; the gap was 0.371 in 1950 and 0.357 in 1960. In the absence of the influence of educational convergence (0.040), the calculations suggest that the regional income gap would have actually widened. During the 1960s there was strong interregional convergence in the average log wage (from 0.357 to 0.212), and 0.030 log points of that convergence is attributable directly to educational convergence. Changes of similar magnitudes occurred in the 1970s. After 1980 the pace of interregional convergence in both income and education slowed considerably. Summed over the second half of the twentieth century (1950–2000), earnings in the South converged on those elsewhere by 0.286 log points, of which 0.120 can be directly attributed to convergence in workers' educational attainment at prevailing rates of return.

This view of Southern convergence emphasizes *changes* in the level of workers' education leading to *changes* in the level of workers' income.

Table 7.2
Educational Convergence and Regional Income, 1940–2000

	ΔED $t_1 - t_0$	β_{ED} t_1	ΔED $\times \beta_{ED}$	Counter-factual Mean Log Income, t_1	Actual Mean Log Income, t_1	Total Convergence $(NS - S)_1 -$ $(NS - S)_0$
1940–1950						
South (S)	0.960	0.070	0.068	7.256	7.323	
Non-South (NS)	0.709	0.045	0.032	7.662	7.694	
Difference, NS − S	−0.251	−0.026	−0.036	0.407	0.371	
1950–1960						
South	1.045	0.075	0.079	7.729	7.808	
Non-South	0.689	0.057	0.039	8.126	8.165	
Difference, NS − S	−0.356	−0.018	−0.040	0.397	0.357	−0.013
1960–1970						
South	1.180	0.075	0.088	8.291	8.380	
Non-South	0.910	0.064	0.059	8.533	8.591	
Difference, NS − S	−0.270	−0.010	−0.030	0.241	0.212	−0.146
1970–1980						
South	1.183	0.067	0.079	9.022	9.101	
Non-South	0.942	0.057	0.053	9.156	9.210	
Difference, NS − S	−0.241	−0.010	−0.026	0.135	0.109	−0.103
1980–1990						
South	0.807	0.085	0.069	9.559	9.627	
Non-South	0.660	0.077	0.051	9.695	9.746	
Difference, NS − S	−0.147	−0.007	−0.017	0.136	0.119	0.010
1990–2000						
South	0.383	0.091	0.035	10.001	10.036	
Non-South	0.309	0.089	0.028	10.093	10.120	
Difference, NS − S	−0.075	−0.002	−0.007	0.092	0.085	−0.034

Source: Calculated using IPUMS microdata (Ruggles et al. 2004).
Notes: The counterfactual average equals the actual average minus ($\Delta ED \times \beta_{ED}$). In 1940 only wage and salary income is reported, so convergence in income in the 1940s cannot be calculated on the basis of total income (as the 1950 to 2000 figures are). Samples include workers from 18 to 64 who are in the labor force, report positive income, and positive weeks worked. Top-coded income figures are multiplied by 1.4. The coefficient on highest grade of attainment is from regressions in which log income is regressed on a quartic in age, state fixed effects, a series of dummies for weeks worked, and sex, race, and foreign-birth dummies.

In this regard, it is important to note that in standard macroeconomic convergence regressions I find no sign of an "impoverished sophisticate" theme to U.S. convergence after 1940.[24] Conditional on log initial income per worker, states with fast per worker income growth between 1940 and 1980 were *not* those with initially high levels of educational attainment: the 1940 education coefficient is negative, small, and statistically insignificant ($\beta = -0.028$; standard error $= 0.022$). However, replacing the level of educational attainment with the change in educational attainment reveals a positive, sizable, and statistically significant relation ($\beta = 0.049$; standard error $= 0.025$).[25] Instrumenting for the change in average educational attainment between 1940 and 1980 with the change in the average number of days schools were open between 1910 and 1950 yields a larger coefficient estimate ($\beta = 0.199$, standard error $= 0.116$).[26] This instrumental variable is not ideal, but it may sidestep the problem of reverse causality running from post-1940 income gains to educational investments. The OLS and IV results are consistent with the argument that educational gains were a key factor in driving Southern income gains relative to the rest of the country.

Conclusion

In the context of educational convergence between blacks and whites, Margo and Collins (2006) emphasize that intergenerational factors have always moderated the pace of convergence. Historically, children whose parents had low levels of education tended to acquire significantly less education than other children, all else being equal. In the context of regional education gaps, the same considerations are likely to be important. Even if all else had been equal, the erosion of the large regional gap in educational attainment would have taken decades. But, in fact, all else was far from equal. After the Civil War, the South had a relatively low level of average income, a predominantly agricultural economy, and a high degree of inequality. Income and urbanization alone can account for a significant part, but not all, of Southern children's lag in school attendance in 1900. There was long-standing opposition to public school expenditures by politically influential Southerners who benefited from the vast supply of unskilled labor and who did not wish to foot the bill for universal public education. Finally, blatant racial discrimination in Southern schooling slowed blacks' educational gains.[27]

Nonetheless, after the first three decades of the twentieth century, measures of school quality, school attendance, and educational attainment did converge between the South and non-South. Because of data imperfections, the exact timing is difficult to pinpoint, but the convergence appears to be especially strong after 1940, as the post-1920 birth cohorts entered the labor force and as interregional migration rates increased. Over time, the opposition to Southern public schooling eroded with the emergence of the political and economic forces (both internal and external) that shaped the New South. Early in the twentieth century, philanthropic efforts helped boost educational opportunities for black students, and later the civil rights movement ended blatant racial discrimination by state and local governments in the provision of public schooling. Rising urbanization and transportation improvements also facilitated increased schooling in the South.

I began by posing two main questions: one about the sources of Southern educational convergence, and a second about the contributions of educational convergence to income convergence. Analysis of microlevel census data reveals that most of the South's relative gains were driven by increasing "local investment" in Southern-born children, but there was also a significant net flow of outside talent to the South. While the South was absorbing relatively high human capital in-migrants, the rest of the country was absorbing relatively low human capital in-migrants (some Southern-born, many foreign-born).

The data also suggest that the timing and pace of Southern workers' educational improvements strongly influenced the magnitude of interregional income convergence. Education was only one mechanism contributing to regional income convergence, but it appears to have been an economically important channel even when gauged in a conservative fashion (by private labor market returns to education). Additionally, improvements in the educational attainment of the Southern work force might have facilitated technology transfers, capital transfers, and relative health improvements.

By 2000 the gaps in average educational attainment, income, and returns to education between Southern and non-Southern workers were small by historical standards. The massive racial disparities of the late nineteenth century also narrowed markedly by the late twentieth century, although racial convergence has stalled in recent decades.[28] The U.S. story echoes a major theme of the New Comparative Economic History —that economic integration can lead to factor price and income convergence through factor mobility, accumulation, and trade. But even with no internal political barriers to trade or labor mobility and with relatively strong private incentives for the accumulation of human capital in the South, more than a century passed after the Civil War before regional levels of human capital and earnings approached equality.[29] The history of the long struggle to raise Southern educational standards and especially to improve educational opportunities for African-Americans cautions against interpreting regional convergence in educational attainment as merely an automatic response to high returns. History and politics, both local and national, mattered in this story, and they often worked against the forces that economists stress in theoretical descriptions of the convergence phenomenon. Thus, the U.S. story also underscores how long it can take for regions to converge, how the process can be derailed by politics, and how deeply rooted institutional, legal, and social arrangements may resist the economics of convergence.

Notes

Martha J. Bailey, Leah Platt Boustan, Robert Driskill, Stanley Engerman, Timothy Hatton, Robert A. Margo, Jacob Vigdor, and Gavin Wright provided helpful suggestions. Emily Boleman supplied excellent research assistance. National Science Foundation support is gratefully acknowledged (SES 0095943).

1. Throughout the chapter, "South" refers to the U.S. Census definition of the region, including Alabama, Arkansas, Delaware, District of Columbia, Florida, Georgia, Kentucky, Louisiana, Maryland, Mississippi, North Carolina, Oklahoma, South Carolina, Tennessee, Texas, Virginia, and West Virginia.

2. Accurate measures of literacy and schooling for African-Americans prior to 1870 are not available, as the U.S. Census did not inquire about slave literacy. The low level of literacy among African-Americans in 1870 indicates that very few blacks learned to read and write under slavery. Approximately 19 percent of all 20- to 25-year-old blacks in 1870 could read and write. See Margo and Collins (2006) for more exploration of the "treatment effect" of the Civil War on literacy among blacks.

3. The outlier in figure 7.1a, New Mexico, had a literacy rate of only 22 percent.

4. See Margo (1986), Margo (1990), or Margo and Collins (2006) for more detailed discussions of the accuracy of the years of education data.

5. Rough measures of school quality, such as length of the school term, students per teacher, and expenditures per student, show clear evidence of regional convergence, reinforcing the quantity convergence that is conveyed in the highest-grade-of-attainment measures. See Card and Krueger (1992) and Ashenfelter, Collins, and Yoon (2006) on the labor market implications of racial disparities in school quality within the South.

6. Wright (1986, 79) cites an Arkansas planter in 1900: "My experience has been that when one of the younger class gets so he can read and write and cipher, he wants to go to town. It is rare to find one who can read and write and cipher in the field at work."

7. The low level of support for public education in the South may be interpreted in light of the more general link between ethnic heterogeneity and low public goods provision described by Alesina, Baqir, and Easterly (1999).

8. With respect to blacks, Margo (1990, 49) quotes a report by J. W. Joyner in 1910, superintendent of North Carolina's schools: "There is no surer way to drive the best of them from the state than by keeping up this continual agitation about withdrawing from them the meager educational opportunities that they now have. Their emigration in large numbers would result in a complication of the labor problem. Some of our Southern farms would be compelled to lie untenanted and untilled."

9. Lleras-Muney (2002) finds that compulsory schooling laws passed in the early 1900s had positive but small effects on educational attainment in both the South and North. The scope for contributing to interregional convergence in average attainment appears to be small.

10. The published volumes of the 1890 Census also have months of schooling information, but there is no microdata sample for that year.

11. As bleak as that characterization is, the situation was especially poor for black children. Southern states maintained separate school systems for white and black children, and the state boards of education produced regular reports that describe basic characteristics of the schools (Margo 1990; Card and Krueger 1992; and Donohue, Heckman, and Todd 2002). Around 1910 black school sessions were more than 30 days shorter than white school sessions in the South (on average), and black schools had many more students per teacher than white schools (Margo 1990).

12. In 1960 non-Southern five- and six-year-olds were about 25 percentage points more likely to attend school than Southern children of the same age. See Cascio (2004) on the late expansion of kindergarten programs in the South. Nontrivial interregional attendance gaps open up from ages 15 to 17 (on the order of 5 to 8 percentage points) before narrowing for 18- to 21-year-olds to about 3 percentage points. Direct federal involvement in primary and secondary education was minimal until the passage of the Elementary and Secondary School Act of 1965.

13. I thank Mitchener and McLean for sharing the state-level figures. The income estimates for the household heads are based on earnings of workers in the same race-gender-region-occupation category in the 1960 Census.

14. OLS results are as follows, with standard errors clustered by state in parentheses: $\beta_1 = -0.907\ (0.249)$; $\beta_2 = 0.867\ (0.207)$; $\beta_3 = 0.682\ (0.136)$; $\beta_4 = 1.250\ (0.062)$.

15. See Wright (1986, 80) and Goldin and Katz (1997, table 3) on this point. Goldin and Katz find that Southern states had lower high school graduation rates in 1910 and 1928 than can be accounted for by differences in basic economic and demographic characteristics; the same is true for the change in the graduation rate between 1910 and 1928.

16. This pattern is consistent with a Roy model of migration in which skilled workers in the area with relatively low returns to education (North) tend to seek employment in places with higher returns (South). See Borjas (1987) for a description of how the Roy model (1951) relates to migration into the United States. Estimates of regional differences in returns to education are discussed later in the chapter.

17. Based on the Roy model, one might expect migrant selection from the South to be negative, that is, most attractive to the least educated. Indeed, evidence discussed later indicates that the regional real wage gap was much larger for unskilled than for skilled workers. The higher level of emigration by the educated might reflect greater ease in finding information about distant opportunities, financing for the move, and jobs on arrival.

18. This is not a trivial assumption. For example, Southern-born out-migrants who left as children would have been educated in the non-South before joining the labor force, and this might have had a positive influence on their educational attainment. This would perhaps work in the opposite direction for children moving into the South. A second consideration is that Southern-born children might have invested more in education than they would otherwise to facilitate interregional migration.

19. Although the Southern wage was low for blacks of all education levels, the interregional gap was far larger for workers with low levels of education. But even with a relatively small gap, more educated blacks could have found it easier to finance migration, to learn about distant employment opportunities, and to get hired for any given job.

20. For the 1980 calculations, I used a cost-of-living index for each state from Berry, Fording, and Hanson (2000).

21. Emphasizing the 1940s as a turning point, Parker (1980, 1046) writes, "What a Civil War, populist agitation and limited progressivist good will, New South industrialists, New

York capital, self-help and cooperatives could not do over nearly a century, was accomplished at last. The back of the Southern institutional peculiarity was broken, and its energies and resources released to be merged with the national society."

22. This is cited in Nicholls (1960, 109). Subsequent investigation revealed that the quote is from a letter written by Lee in 1867 to John Brown Gordon.

23. The choice to start with estimated returns to education in the 1950 Census is influenced by data constraints in the 1940 Census, which reports only wage and salary income rather than total income. The neglect of self-employment income in 1940 is a significant problem because a large portion of Southerners were still working in agriculture.

24. The "impoverished sophisticate" reference is to Sandberg (1979), who argues that Sweden's late nineteenth-century growth spurt is in large part attributable to its relatively high preexisting level of education (given its low level of initial income). See O'Rourke and Williamson (1997) for further discussion of Scandinavian growth and education. See Barro and Sala-i-Martin (1992) for a study of income convergence within the United States since 1880.

25. These results are based on simple conditional convergence regressions using state-level data on income per worker (price adjusted) from Mitchener and McLean (1999). The average dependent variable (ln (income1980/income1940)) value is 2.68. The states are not weighted.

26. The rationale for the instrument is that a state's length-of-school-year policy change influences the change in the workers' average educational attainment (F-stat in first stage is 7.1). Because the policy change largely preceded the post-1940 change in income per worker, the approach lowers the likelihood of finding a spurious correlation between contemporary education and income gains due to reverse causality. However, conditional on 1940 income, if states undertook other policy changes that were correlated with the length-of-school-year changes and that had long delayed effects on income growth, then the instrument is not valid.

27. Although not discussed here, the interaction of children's health, cognitive skills, life expectancy, and educational attainment might have influenced the regional gap in human capital.

28. Neal (2006), however, cites evidence of racial divergence among students after 1980.

29. See Margo (2000, 45) for wage differences by occupation and region in 1850. See Margo and Collins (2006) for estimated returns to literacy by race and region from 1870 to 1930. See Coelho and Shepherd (1979, 76) for wages by occupation and region in 1890 based on the Aldrich Report. Sundstrom and Rosenbloom (1993) also report occupation-based regional wage figures for cities in the late nineteenth century.

References

Alesina, A., R. Baqir, and W. Easterly. 1999. Public Goods and Ethnic Divisions. *Quarterly Journal of Economics* 114: 1243–1284.

Alston, L. J., and J. P. Ferrie. 1999. *Southern Paternalism and the American Welfare State: Economics, Politics, and Institutions in the South, 1865–1965*. New York: Cambridge University Press.

Anderson, J. D. 1988. *The Education of Blacks in the South, 1860–1935*. Chapel Hill: University of North Carolina Press.

Ashenfelter, O., W. J. Collins, and A. Yoon. 2006. Evaluating the Role of *Brown v. Board of Education* in School Equalization, Desegregation, and the Income of African Americans. *American Law and Economics Review* Advance Access. ⟨http://aler.oxfordjournals.org/papbyrecent.dtl⟩.

Barro, R. J., and X. Sala-i-Martin. 1992. Convergence. *Journal of Political Economy* 100: 223–251.

Berry, W. D., R. C. Fording, and R. L. Hanson. 2000. An Annual Cost of Living Index for the American States, 1960–1995. *Journal of Politics* 62: 550–567.

Borjas, G. J. 1987. Self-Selection and the Earnings of Immigrants. *American Economic Review* 77: 531–553.

Card, D., and A. Krueger. 1992. School Quality and Black/White Relative Earnings: A Direct Assessment. *Quarterly Journal of Economics* 107: 151–200.

Cascio, E. 2004. Schooling Attainment and the Introduction of Kindergartens into Public Schools. Working Paper. ⟨http://www.econ.ucdavis.edu/faculty/eucascio/cascio-kindergarten-apr04.pdf⟩.

Caselli, F., and W. J. Coleman II. 2001. The U.S. Structural Transformation and Regional Convergence: A Reinterpretation. *Journal of Political Economy* 109: 584–616.

Coelho, P.R.P., and J. F. Shepherd. 1979. The Impact of Regional Differences in Prices and Wages on Economic Growth: The United States in 1890. *Journal of Economic History* 39: 69–85.

Colberg, M. R. 1965. *Human Capital in Southern Development, 1939–1963*. Chapel Hill: University of North Carolina Press.

Connolly, M. P. 2004. Human Capital and Growth in the Post-Bellum South: A Separate but Unequal Story. *Journal of Economic History* 64: 363–399.

Donohue, J. J., and J. J. Heckman. 1991. Continuous versus Episodic Change: The Impact of Affirmative Action and Civil Rights Policy on the Economic Status of Blacks. *Journal of Economic Literature* 29: 1603–1644.

Donohue, J. J., J. J. Heckman, and P. Todd. 2002. The Schooling of Southern Blacks: The Roles of Legal Activism and Private Philanthropy, 1910–1960. *Quarterly Journal of Economics* 117: 225–268.

Fein, R. 1965. Educational Patterns in Southern Migration. *Southern Economic Journal* 32: 106–124.

Goldin, C. 1998. America's Graduation from High School: The Evolution and Spread of Secondary Schooling in the Twentieth Century. *Journal of Economic History* 58: 345–374.

Goldin, C., and L. F. Katz. 1997. Why the United States Led in Education: Lessons from Secondary School Expansion, 1910–1940. NBER (National Bureau of Economic Research) Working Paper 6144. ⟨http://www.nber.org/papers/W6144⟩.

Lleras-Muney, A. 2002. Were Compulsory Attendance and Child Labor Laws Effective? An Analysis from 1915 to 1939. *Journal of Law and Economics* 45: 401–435.

Margo, R. A. 1986. Race, Educational Attainment, and the 1940 Census. *Journal of Economic History* 46: 189–198.

———. 1990. *Race and Schooling in the South, 1880–1950: An Economic History*. Chicago: University of Chicago Press.

———. 2000. *Wages and Labor Markets in the United States, 1820–1860*. Chicago: University of Chicago Press.

———. 2004. The North-South Wage Gap, Before and After the Civil War. In *Slavery in the Development of the Americas*, ed. D. Eltis, F. Lewis, and K. Sokoloff, 324–351. New York: Cambridge University Press.

Margo, R. A., and W. J. Collins. 2006. Historical Perspectives on Race and Schooling: The United States. In *Handbook of the Economics of Education*, ed. E. Hanushek and F. Welch. New York: North-Holland.

Mitchener, K. J., and I. W. McLean. 1999. U.S. Regional Growth and Convergence, 1880–1980. *Journal of Economic History* 59: 1016–1042.

Neal, D. 2006. Black/White Differences in Human Capital: Causes and Consequences. In *Handbook of the Economics of Education*, ed. E. Hanushek and F. Welch. New York: North-Holland.

Nicholls, W. H. 1960. *Southern Tradition and Regional Progress*. Chapel Hill: University of North Carolina Press.

O'Rourke, K. H., and J. G. Williamson. 1997. Around the European Periphery, 1870–1913: Globalization, Schooling, and Growth. *European Review of Economic History* 1: 153–190.

Parker, W. N. 1980. The South in the National Economy, 1865–1970. *Southern Economic Journal* 46: 1019–1048.

Rosenbloom, J. L. 2002. *Looking for Work, Searching for Workers: American Labor Markets during Industrialization*. New York: Cambridge University Press.

Roy, A. D. 1951. Some Thoughts on the Distribution of Earnings. *Oxford Economic Papers* 3: 135–146.

Ruggles, S., M. Sobek, T. Alexander, C. A. Fitch, R. Goeken, P. K. Hall, M. King, and C. Ronnander. 2004. Integrated Public Use Microdata Series: Version 3.0. Machine-Readable Database. Minneapolis: Minnesota Population Center.

Sandberg, L. G. 1979. The Case of the Impoverished Sophisticate: Human Capital and Swedish Economic Growth before World War I. *Journal of Economic History* 39: 225–241.

Sundstrom, W. A., and J. L. Rosenbloom. 1993. Occupational Differences in the Dispersion of Wages and Working Hours: Labor Market Integration in the United States, 1890–1903. *Explorations in Economic History* 30: 379–408.

Suval, E. M., and C. H. Hamilton. 1965. Some New Evidence on Educational Selectivity in Migration to and from the South. *Social Forces* 43: 536–547.

Tindall, G. R. 1967. *The Emergence of the New South, 1913–1945*. Baton Rouge: Louisiana State University Press.

Tushnet, M. V. 1987. *The NAACP's Legal Strategy against Segregated Education, 1925–1950*. Chapel Hill: University of North Carolina Press.

Vigdor, J. L. 2002. The Pursuit of Opportunity: Explaining Selective Black Migration. *Journal of Urban Economics* 51: 391–417.

Williams, H. A. 2004. *Self-Taught: African American Education in Slavery and Freedom*. Chapel Hill: University of North Carolina Press.

Williamson, J. G. 1965. Regional Inequality and the Process of National Development: A Description of the Patterns. *Economic Development and Cultural Change* 13: 3–45.

———. 1980. Unbalanced Growth, Inequality, and Regional Development: Some Lessons from U.S. History. In *Alternatives to Confrontation: A National Policy Toward Regional Change*, ed. V. L. Arnold. Lexington, Mass.: Lexington Books.

———. 1996. Globalization, Convergence, and History. *Journal of Economic History* 56: 277–306.

Williamson, J. G., and P. H. Lindert. 1980. *American Inequality: A Macroeconomic History*. New York: Academic Press.

Woodward, C. V. 1951. *Origins of the New South, 1877–1913*. Baton Rouge: Louisiana State University Press.

Wright, G. 1986. *Old South, New South*. New York: Basic Books.

8 Democracy and Protectionism

Kevin H. O'Rourke and Alan M. Taylor

Does democracy encourage free trade, or do democratic reforms make it more difficult to achieve the market liberalizations that are necessary for economic growth? While democracy is obviously a non-negotiable moral imperative, this fundamental question is nonetheless one that has been posed periodically by policymakers and continues to be posed today. There are two positions on the issue, as might be expected. On the one hand, there are those who feel that political and economic openness, or democracy and markets, are inherently complementary. This sunny optimism has been expressed, among others, by former U.S. President William Jefferson Clinton, according to whom "Democracies don't attack each other. They make better trading partners, and partners in diplomacy" (Bliss and Russett 1998, 1126). On the other hand, there is a darker and more pessimistic tradition holding that democracy can undermine the political will to keep markets open, or alternatively, that it is only by stifling opposition that governments can impose free trade on an unwilling population.

There are certainly many individual case studies that can be appealed to by advocates of both positions. Most notable, perhaps, has been the embrace in the 1990s of both democracy and free trade by the countries of Eastern Europe, which had been denied both for so long. Other examples suggesting a complementary relationship between the two include mid-nineteenth-century Britain, which extended the franchise in 1832 and abolished the Corn Laws soon after; or the descent into dictatorship and autarky of much of Africa following independence in the 1950s and 1960s. But counterarguments are easy to come by as well. If those same African countries, as well as their counterparts in much of Asia, had been relatively open to trade prior to World War II (or World War I in the case of countries such as China and Japan), this was largely because they had been forced to open up by foreign military pressure, sometimes expressing itself as formal empire but always denying local people the right to self-determination in this policy domain. Famously, it was the autocratic Napoleon III who pushed the Cobden-Chevalier trade treaty through an unwilling French political system in 1860, while it took a bloody coup and a right-wing dictatorship to institute free market reforms in 1970s Chile. Most recently, a series of popular referendums in Europe seem to have undermined the drive toward ever-deeper integration in Europe, to the horror of Europe's political class, although whether this should be taken as a rejection of market liberalization or of bureaucratic *dirigisme* is a priori hard to say.

In the academic sphere there is no shortage of relevant literature, although systematic quantitative papers of the sort required to sift through the often-conflicting empirical evidence remain scarce. Polanyi (1957) is one obvious reference point; for him, "Socialism is, essentially, the tendency inherent in an industrial civilization to transcend the self-regulating market by consciously subordinating it to a democratic society" (234). And yet the growing social regulation to which democracy can give rise is not necessarily incompatible with open markets; indeed, the opposite seems to have been the case in nineteenth-century Europe, where newly enfranchised workers in countries such as Belgium *supported* free trade in exchange for a variety of labor market regulations and social insurance programs (Huberman 2006; Huberman and Lewchuk 2003). More generally, there is a theoretical tension between two opposing forces, as Garrett (2000) points out: "On the one hand, democracy makes leaders more accountable to their citizens, promoting trade liberalization to the extent that this is good for society as a whole. On the other hand, democracy also empowers distributional coalitions with intense interests, making higher levels of protectionism more likely" (973).[1]

Empirical work testing for an impact of democracy on the adoption of free trade policies has largely used the "gravity" framework to explore whether pairs of democratic countries trade more than would be expected if one or both were nondemocratic (Bliss and Russett 1998; Morrow, Siverson and Taberes 1998; Mansfield, Milner, and Rosendorff 2000). Such papers explore the determinants of the level of trade between country pairs; the real question, however, is whether democracies have more open trading policies than other countries, *ceteris paribus*. Furthermore, as the Garrett quotation suggests, the impact of democratization on trade policies may not be the same in all countries; a one-size-fits-all regression coefficient in an equation explaining trade policies as a function of democracy, as well as other control variables, is almost by definition going to give the wrong result. We need to do better than that.

There is another, well-developed literature on the political economy of trade policy, whose central purpose is to ask what determines countries' trade policies. The answer is that it all depends—on a country's relative endowments, which determine its comparative advantage vis-à-vis the rest of the world; and on the relative strength of the winning and losing sectors (Gourevitch 1986) or factors of production (Rogowski 1989). These studies typically do not focus on the question posed by this chapter, namely what effect does democratization have on trade policy. Indeed, such models, as well as more formal ones of the type associated with Mayer (1984), Findlay and Wellisz (1984), or Grossman and Helpman (2001), tend to take political institutions as given. The argument here is, however, that it is only by looking at our question through the lens of this political economy literature that a satisfactory answer can be formulated.

Our hypothesis is simple. Broadening the franchise involves transferring power from nonelected elites to the wider population, most of whom will be workers. Democratization will lead to more liberal trade policies in countries where workers stand to gain from free trade and to more protectionist policies in countries where workers will benefit from the imposition of tariffs and quotas. According to standard Heckscher-Ohlin theory, democratization will boost support for free trade in labor-abundant countries and lower it in labor-scarce economies. While debate still rages about the adequacy of such theory when it comes to explaining international distributional trends today, we know that the Heckscher-Ohlin theory does a good job in explaining distributional trends during the late nineteenth century, which was the epoch that motivated these two Swedish economists in the first place (O'Rourke and Williamson 1994; 1999; O'Rourke, Taylor, and Williamson 1996; Williamson 1996; 2002). If our hypothesis is valid, then the late nineteenth century should be a good place to test it; and in subsequent sections we do precisely this, using the cross-country data set pieced together by Williamson and his co-authors (Blattman, Clemens, and Williamson 2002; Clemens and Williamson 2004; Williamson 2003).

Three existing papers are particularly close in spirit to this one. The first one is Dutt and Mitra (2002), which looks at the impact of inequality on trade barriers in capital-abundant and capital-scarce economies. It assumes that societies are democratic, that voters are endowed with labor and capital, and that the median voter determines trade policy outcomes.

In more unequal societies, the median voter will own less capital, and thus policies will be more tilted toward labor, that is to say, they will be more pro–free trade in labor-abundant (capital-scarce) societies than in labor-scarce (capital-abundant) societies. Dutt and Mitra find empirical support for this proposition, using cross-national, late twentieth-century data.

This chapter can be seen as providing another test of median voter theory that is complementary to theirs and arguably more appropriate, at least in a nineteenth-century context. In time series for societies undergoing transformations toward or away from democracy, it is not the *endowments* of the median voter that are changing so much; rather, it is the *identity* of the median voter that is changing, as sections of the population are being enfranchised or disenfranchised. Like Dutt and Mitra, we assume that such shifts will have different impacts on different countries, depending on their factor endowments. Unlike them, however, we broaden the scope away from labor and capital because in order to understand the political economy of late nineteenth-century trade policy we have to consider the interests of land as well.[2]

We have to date been able to find two other papers whose arguments anticipate the one made here. The first is by Sachs and Warner (1995, 32), who titillate their readers by promising (in a later paper) a "detailed model of the timing of liberalization during the postwar period." In the preliminary regression included in the 1995 paper, they show that liberalization was earlier in countries with high labor-to-land ratios, which they had predicted on the basis that workers in these countries would gain from free trade; earlier, however (Sachs and Warner 1995, 20–21), they speculate that this mechanism would depend on the nature of political institutions in place in each country. We test that proposition explicitly here. The second paper is by Milner and Kubota (2005), of which we became aware since beginning our project. Their strategy is to run straightforward regressions of late twentieth-century trade policies on democracy, but to limit their sample of countries to developing countries, which are by assumption labor-abundant. The HO prediction is then that more democratic countries will be more open, and this prediction is confirmed by the data. Clearly, this finding is consistent with our argument; however, it does not exclude the possibility that more democratic countries are more open in the developed world as well, which would be completely at odds with the median voter mechanism proposed here.

In this chapter, we do not preassign countries to any particular category (e.g., labor-abundant or labor-scarce); rather, we let the data do this for us. This allows us to test our hypothesis for both rich and poor countries. It also lets us be more confident that what we are testing is indeed our preferred HO median voter theory linking democracy to policy, rather than some entirely different theory yielding a one-size-fits-all relationship applying to all countries. Moreover, we will explore the impact of both capital-labor and land-labor ratios on the democracy-policy link. According to Rogowski (1989), although both ratios could matter in principle, in practice it was the land-labor ratio that determined whether workers were in favor of free trade or protection. That is, in countries where land-labor ratios were high, workers should have been protectionist, and democracy should have been associated with higher tariffs, no matter what the capital-labor ratio, while the opposite should have been true in countries where land-labor ratios were low. It turns out that these predictions can be tested using the data at our disposal.

Democracy, the Median Voter, and Protection in a Three-Factor World

The literature we have reviewed conveys some mixed messages concerning the impact of increased democracy on the degree of protectionism. Can economic theory provide any clarification? In this section we review perhaps the most relevant benchmark model of the political economy of trade policy.

A Simple Median Voter Model

We start with the simple textbook 2×2 Heckscher-Ohlin framework, where the two factors are labor and land. To introduce political economy we employ the familiar median voter model. Individuals each own one unit of labor, but they differ in their endowments of land. This inequality in endowments leads not only to inequality in incomes but also to different preferences on trade policy among individuals (Mayer 1984; Dutt and Mitra 2002; Feenstra 2004, ch. 9).

We now adopt an assumption about the extension of the franchise that is broadly consistent with historical experience. The population is assumed to consist of a large set of individuals $i = 1, \ldots, L$, where the individuals are ordered according to decreasing levels of land endowment R^i, so that R^i is decreasing in i. Policy is decided by a majority of the popular vote among a subset of enfranchised individuals $i = 1, \ldots, 2M$. Here, $D = 2M/L < 1$ serves as an index of democracy (or the extent of the franchise) in the society, and we restrict attention to cases where the franchise is the exclusive preserve of the richest fraction D of the landowners.

In this setting, the median voter is individual M, and this voter owns R^M units of land.

Since voters differ on only one dimension—their land ownership—the median voter theorem can be applied, and the lessons of the venerable Stolper-Samuelson theorem can supply all the necessary intuition. So we must ask, when it comes to trade policy, what does individual M want? Individuals poorly endowed with land would vote in line with the preferences of a pure owner of labor—they will favor higher tariffs when labor is a scarce factor in the country relative to the rest of the world. Individuals richly endowed with land would tend to vote more in line with the preferences of a pure owner of land—they will favor higher tariffs when land is a scarce factor in the country relative to the rest of the world.

As the franchise is extended, M increases, and the median voter looks less like a landowner and more like a laborer. The implications are clear, when the median voter's preferences determine trade policy in this setting: *in a land-abundant country, democracy increases protectionism; in a land-scarce country, democracy reduces protectionism.*

Formally, the result is derived as follows (adapted from Feenstra 2004, ch. 9). Suppose each individual i has a quasi-linear utility function given by $c_0^i + U(c^i)$, where c_0^i is consumption of a *numéraire* export good, and c^i is the consumption of the import good. Consumers all have the same optimal consumption $c^i = d(p)$, with $d'(p) < 0$ and with any remaining income spent on the *numéraire* good, $c_0^i = I^i - pd(p)$. Then individual utility is

$$V(p, I^i) = I^i - pd(p) + U[d(p)] \qquad (1)$$

Both the export and import goods are produced using labor and land. The total endowments of labor and land are L and R, respectively. The fixed world price of the import is denoted by p^*, and this good has a specific tariff of t, so the domestic price is $p = p^* + t$. Let $y(p)$ denote the supply of the import-competing good, with $y'(p) > 0$. Imports are then $m(p) = d(p)L - y(p)$. Tariff revenue is equal to $T = tm(p)$, which we assume is redistributed via a poll subsidy. Let the wage be w and the rental price of land be q, so that individual income is $I^i = w + qR^i + (T/L)$, or

$$I^i = \frac{1}{L}(wL + qR^iL + T) = \frac{1}{L}(wL + \theta^i qR + T) \qquad (2)$$

where $\theta^i = R^i/(R/L)$ is the land-labor ratio for individual i relative to the overall land-labor ratio in the economy. Total GDP in the economy is $y_0(p) + py(p) = wL + qR$, where $y_0(p)$ represents the output of the *numéraire* good. Hence,

$$I^h = \frac{1}{L}[(\theta^i - 1)qR + y_0(p) + py(p) + T] \tag{3}$$

Differentiating individual utility in (1) with respect to the tariff, we obtain

$$\frac{dV^i}{dt} = -d(p) + \frac{dI^i}{dt}$$

$$= (\theta^i - 1)\frac{dq}{dp}\frac{R}{L} + \left[\frac{y_0'(p) + py'(p) + y(p)}{L} - d(p)\right] + \frac{1}{L}\frac{dT}{dt}$$

$$= (\theta^i - 1)\frac{dq}{dp}\frac{R}{L} + \left[\frac{y(p)}{L} - d(p)\right] + \frac{1}{L}\frac{dT}{dt}$$

$$= (\theta^i - 1)\frac{dq}{dp}\frac{R}{L} + \frac{t}{L}m'(p) \tag{4}$$

where the first line uses Roy's identity, the second line employs (3), the third line invokes the MRT-equals-price condition $y_0'(p) + py'(p) = 0$, and the fourth line exploits the fact that tariff revenue can be written $T = t[d(p)L - y(p)] = tm(p)$, implying $dT/dt = m(p) + tm'(p)$.

If the tariff is determined by majority vote, then the tariff prevailing will be that which maximizes the utility of the median voter. This voter's utility is $V^M = V(p, I^M)$, so the tariff will satisfy $dV^M/dt = 0$ (under standard conditions, $d^2V^M/dt^2 < 0$). Setting (4) equal to zero, the median voter's preferred tariff (or import subsidy, if negative) is

$$t^M = (1 - \theta^M)\frac{dq}{dp}\frac{R}{m'(p)} \tag{5}$$

We next examine the signs of the terms on the right-hand side of this expression.

• Clearly, $m'(p) < 0$, since imports fall as the price of the importable rises.

• Next, $\theta^M = R^M/(R/L)$ is the land-labor ratio for the median voter relative to the overall land-labor endowment of the economy. When democracy is limited, M is small, and θ^M will be well above 1, reflecting the privileged position of the voting class as large landowners. When the franchise is fully extended, M is large, and θ^M will be below 1, reflecting the fact that the median individual in society owns less than the average amount of land in an unequal society (Alesina and Rodrik 1994).

• Finally, when the import good is labor-intensive (the country is land-abundant), the Stolper-Samuelson theorem implies that $dq/dp < 0$; when the import good is land-intensive (the country is land-scarce), $dq/dp > 0$.

To sum up these results for empirical purposes, we expect, all else being equal,

• In land-scarce countries, tariffs will be high when democracy is limited but low when democracy is broad.

• In land-abundant countries, tariffs will be low when democracy is limited but high when democracy is broad.

Extending the Model to Three Factors

Of course, the real world is more complicated than such a simple 2×2 model, and thus the political economy of trade policy will be more complicated as well. In our empirical analysis, we explicitly take account of the fact that there are more than two factors of production. Indeed, we follow the classical economists of the period as well as a great many economic historians and consider a world in which there are three factors of production: land, labor, and capital. Of course, we could have replaced land with capital in the preceding analysis and obtained precisely the same predictions; in capital-scarce countries, extending the franchise should favor free trade, while the opposite should be the case in capital-abundant countries (Dutt and Mitra 2002).

It would also be a trivial extension of the model if land and capital were everywhere available in the same fixed proportions, for they could then be analyzed as a single composite factor of production with precisely the same results obtaining. More generally, one might presume that in economies where both capital-labor and land-labor ratios were high, extending the franchise would lead to greater protection; but that in economies where both capital and land were scarce relative to labor, democratization should lead to more liberal trade policies.

The problem is, however, that capital-land ratios vary greatly across countries. There are countries with high capital-labor ratios but low land-labor ratios; and countries with low capital-labor ratios and high land-labor ratios. What will be the effect of extending the franchise in such "mixed" cases? In a series of papers, Thompson (1985; 1986) has shown that in a three-factor two-good model, raising tariffs can either raise or lower the returns to any factor of production. Indeed, moving to free trade might even have "perverse" effects on factor prices, for example, lowering land rents in countries where they were initially below the world average. In such a setting, therefore, we are unlikely to obtain unambiguous theoretical predictions. Indeed, there is an even more fundamental theoretical problem because median voter models are difficult to set up in such a three-factor setting (Mayer 1984).

In his classic book, Rogowski (1989) simplifies by assuming that "the land-labor ratio informs us fully about any country's endowment of those two factors" (6). That is, in his basic schema he assumes that where land-labor ratios are high, labor is a relatively scarce factor and will thus favor protection regardless of capital-labor ratios; and that where land-labor ratios are low, labor is relatively abundant and will thus favor free trade regardless of capital-labor ratios. (He later relaxes this assumption and looks at the consequences of assuming that both land and labor are abundant/scarce relative to capital. In this case land and labor will hold similar positions on trade, the result being so-called "red-green" coalitions; the operative assumption throughout the book is, however, that such cases are relatively rare.) This seems to us to be a testable hypothesis, in that the prediction is that democratization will spur liberalization in all economies with high labor-land ratios regardless of capital-labor ratios; and that it will spur protection in all economies with low labor-land ratios regardless of capital-labor ratios. In the context of the late nineteenth century, Rogowski's basic assumption implies that democracy should have been associated with higher tariffs everywhere in the land-abundant New World, both in the more advanced societies of North America and Oceania and in the less industrialized countries of Latin America; and it should have been associated with lower tariffs everywhere in land-scarce Europe, as much in capital-abundant core countries such as the United Kingdom and Belgium as in capital-scarce countries on the southern and eastern peripheries.

Data and Econometric Results

Starting with the assumption that land-labor ratios provide a sufficient statistic for determining the preferences of the median voter, we set out to test our simple model using annual country-level panel data for the period 1870–1914. The sample of countries includes not just countries in Europe and North America but a total of 35 countries both developed and developing: Argentina, Australia, Austria-Hungary, Brazil, Burma,

Canada, Ceylon, Chile, China, Colombia, Cuba, Denmark, Egypt, France, Germany, Greece, India, Indonesia, Italy, Japan, Mexico, New Zealand, Norway, Peru, Philippines, Portugal, Russia, Serbia, Spain, Sweden, Thailand, Turkey, the United Kingdom, the United States, and Uruguay. As already mentioned, the data set was constructed by Williamson and his co-authors in a series of papers exploring the causes and consequences of protectionism in the late nineteenth and early twentieth centuries (Blattman, Clemens, and Williamson 2002; Clemens and Williamson 2004; Williamson 2003).

To test the basic median voter model with just two factors of production, land and labor, the econometric specification we adopt is as follows:

$$tariff_{it} = \beta_1 democ_{it} + \beta_2(democ_{it} \times \ln R_{it}/L_{it}) + u_i + \varepsilon_{it}. \qquad (6)$$

The variables are defined as follows. The dependent variable $tariff_{it}$ is the measure of protection, and as a proxy for this variable we use the ratio of duties to imports expressed in percent.

The measure of the breadth of the franchise is $democ_{it}$, which ranges over a 0–1 scale and is based on the index of democracy taken from the Polity database. However, we reason that the democratic forces captured in the median voter model can only generate changes in tariff policy if countries are free to set their own tariff policy. Many countries of the time were not allowed to pursue independent tariff policies even if they were not formal colonies. Some, like India or Indonesia, were run by European colonial powers, who imposed liberal trade policies on their possessions; others, like China or Turkey, while independent, were nevertheless obliged to run virtually free trade policies as a result of treaties with Western powers that were as often as not signed at the barrel of a gun. Hence we modify this variable as follows:

$$democ_{it} = \begin{cases} 0 & \text{if tariff autonomy} = 0 \\ (\text{Polity Score})/10 & \text{if tariff autonomy} = 1 \end{cases} \qquad (7)$$

Here, the Polity score is the measure of democracy on a 0–10 scale, and tariff autonomy is 1 except for countries that have no policy freedom to set their own tariffs. In our sample the no-autonomy observations are Burma, Ceylon, China, Egypt, India, Indonesia, Japan (before 1899), Thailand, and Turkey.[3]

The endowment measure is the log land-labor ratio $\ln R_{it}/L_{it}$, based on the estimated area of arable (food) crops in hectares divided by labor force. These data are taken from Clemens and Williamson (2004) and Blattman, Clemens, and Williamson (2002).

The scaling of the right-hand-side variables in equation (6) is of no great consequence. For convenience, we rescale $democ_{it}$ to take a value between 0 (low) and 1 (high), and we standardize the $\ln R_{it}/L_{it}$ variable to have a mean of 0 and a standard deviation of 1. Thus, $\ln R_{it}/L_{it}$ is negative for countries with below-average land-labor ratios, and it is important to bear this in mind when interpreting some of the results that follow. Summary statistics for the key variables of interest are shown in the chapter appendix.

The regression equation (6) also includes a fixed effect u_i and allows for a serially correlated error term ε_{it}, with autocorrelation coefficient ρ common to all countries. Inclusion of fixed effects controls for each country's "average" pattern of endowments and democracy over the length of the sample period as well as for any other country-specific factors leading to systematically higher or lower tariffs over time. The marginal effect of an increase in the extent of democracy is then captured by the slope coefficients. The identification of this effect is from a "within" regression, that is, the slope is estimated using the time dimension for each country in the panel. We are therefore seeking to answer the question, If a given country had changed its political institutions, then allowing for the country's factor endowments, what would have been the likely change in trade policy?

Table 8.1 shows the results of our estimation. In column 1 we estimate equation (6) without the interaction term to test a naive model inspired by those who argue that democracy is always associated with liberalization as well as those like Polanyi who argue that democracy provided a way for societies to mute the impact of markets. Neither of these positions finds much support in the data. Democracy was *not* associated with protection in this period, either positively or negatively.

Table 8.1
Democracy, Factor Endowments, and Protection: Land and Labor

Dependent Variable: *tariff*	(1) All Countries	(2) All Countries	(3) Noncolonies	(4) Tariff Autonomy
democ	0.261 (0.20)	0.691 (0.51)	1.337 (0.90)	0.094 (0.06)
democ × $\ln R/L$	—	1.551 (1.32)	2.292 (1.81)[a]	2.516 (1.87)[a]
No. of observations	1,262	1,262	1,172	1,087

Notes: Panel regression with fixed effects (not shown) and an AR(1) error term. Absolute value of *t*-statistics in parentheses.
a. Significant at 10 percent level.

In column 2 of table 8.1 we add the interaction term that allows for the impact of democracy on tariffs to vary depending on the country's factor endowment, as suggested by the two-factor median voter model. The positive coefficient on the interaction term implies that democratization raises tariffs in countries with sufficiently high land-labor ratios and lowers tariffs in countries with sufficiently low land-labor ratios. Still, the model finds only weak support here, with the coefficient on the interaction term statistically insignificant at conventional levels.

Some readers may say that our specification of the democracy variable, which takes into account not just the level of the franchise but also the freedom of the country in question to set its own tariffs, does not adequately deal with the fact that several countries in the sample did *not* enjoy tariff autonomy during this period. In order to address this, we include two additional sets of results in table 8.1. Column 3 excludes colonies from the sample, on the grounds that colonies might not have had true freedom to set their own tariff policies, and column 4 includes in the sample only those countries that enjoyed tariff autonomy over the relevant period. Of these two subsets, we prefer the latter because countries like Australia and Canada, while linked to Britain, did enjoy tariff autonomy and used it to raise tariffs, while other countries, such as Siam (Thailand) or China, which were nominally independent, had no such freedom. These results show that democracy is a statistically significant determinant of protectionism once factor endowments are included in the model, for this sample of countries. One possible reason for the difference between these results and those in column 2 is that in the countries without tariff autonomy, not only were tariff rates fixed at levels specified by the great powers for decades at a stretch, but as often as not there was no democracy, or any movement toward democracy, during the late nineteenth century. With both their tariff rates and democracy scores essentially fixed during the period, it may be no surprise that including such countries in the analysis reduces the variation in the data and weakens the statistical significance of the results.

Was democracy a quantitatively significant determinant of trade policy in countries enjoying tariff autonomy during the period? One simple way to gauge this is to look at the counterfactual changes in the implied tariff level predicted by the model as one changes the level of democracy while holding fixed factor endowments. Recall that the measure of the land-labor ratio was standardized, so a simple way to proceed is to use the model to forecast tariffs at all levels of democracy between 0 and 1, for

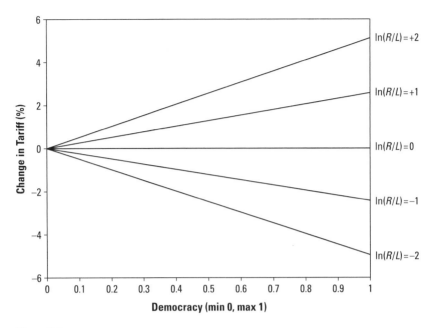

Figure 8.1
Democracy, factor endowments, and protection: Land and labor—five experiments. Data from table 8.1, column 4.

the average country, when the land-labor ratio is set to -2, -1, 0, 1, or 2 (corresponding to difference, in standard deviations, of the country's raw log land-labor ratio from the world average). These results are shown in figure 8.1, based on our preferred specification in table 8.1, column 4.

The model predicts that for a country with an average land-labor ratio, the change in tariffs would be minimal after a "full democratization" experiment, that is, an increase in democracy from the minimum of 0 to the maximum of 10. For a country with a land-labor ratio roughly one standard deviation below the mean (such as the United Kingdom, with a standardized log land-labor ratio of -0.93 in 1870), tariffs would be predicted to fall by about 2.5 percentage points. For a country with a land-labor ratio one standard deviation above the mean (such as the United States, with a standardized log land-labor ratio of $+0.83$ in 1870), tariffs would be predicted to rise by about 2.5 percentage points in the same experiment. For countries with even more extreme endowment vectors, the effects would be larger still. For example, in Argentina (with a standardized log land-labor ratio of $+2.15$ in 1870), the "full democratization" experiment would be predicted to raise tariffs by about 5 percentage points.

These results offer some insights into the evolution of national tariff policies in the nineteenth and early twentieth centuries. In land-abundant countries, the extension of the franchise raised popular pressure for protection, but in land-scarce countries the same democratic tendencies encouraged trade liberalization. The mechanism identified by the model is the different endowment bundles owned by median voters in the two groups of countries. While we should never take the median voter model too literally, given its simplistic assumptions and dubious implications about voting behavior, we think it nonetheless proves revealing as a way of illustrating the power of the middle-of-the-road electoral group to drive commercial policy.

Robustness Check: Three-Factor Model

In table 8.2, we extend our tests to a three-factor setting, in which the democracy variable interacts with capital-labor as well as with land-labor ratios. Building on equation (6), the estimating equation is now

$$tariff_{it} = \beta_1 democ_{it} + \beta_2(democ_{it} \times \ln R_{it}/L_{it})$$

$$+ \beta_3(democ_{it} \times \ln K_{it}/L_{it}) + u_i + \varepsilon_{it}. \qquad (8)$$

Obtaining historical capital-labor ratios for our sample is no simple task. The capital-labor ratio is physical capital per worker, based on the 1890–1914 *average* level for each country taken from Baier, Dwyer, and Tamura (2006). These capital stock estimates are based on standardized perpetual inventory methods (and guessed starting values). We consider only the average in the later part of the period 1890–1914 simply because perpetual inventory data are likely subject to wide initial estimation errors close to the start date of these series, which is no earlier than 1870 in most cases. It should be noted that these capital stock measures are only available for occasional benchmark dates. Since we average them, they contain no time series variation within each country. Furthermore, there are no capital stock data for the following countries: Ceylon, China, Colombia, Cuba, Egypt, Indonesia, Philippines, Russia, Serbia, Thailand, Turkey, Uruguay. For consistency in the presentation of the results, observations from these countries are excluded from all regressions reported in table 8.2.

For reference, column 1 replicates the specification used in table 8.1 for the new sample. The basic point of the simple land-labor median voter model is underscored again, and the coefficient on the interaction term even rises to the 5 percent significance level in this sample. The remaining

Table 8.2
Democracy, Factor Endowments, and Protection: Land, Labor, and Capital

Dependent Variable: *tariff*	(1) All Countries	(2) All Countries	(3) Noncolonies	(4) Tariff Autonomy
democ	2.680 (1.46)	2.487 (1.36)	4.753 (2.34)[a]	2.103 (1.13)
democ × ln R/L	3.595 (2.21)[a]	4.201 (2.56)[a]	6.467 (3.48)[b]	5.114 (2.92)[b]
democ × ln K/L	—	−4.762 (2.62)[b]	−4.089 (2.24)[a]	−4.034 (2.13)[a]
No. of observations	936	936	894	905

Notes: Sample is restricted to countries with data on capital-labor ratio. Panel regression with fixed effects (not shown) and an AR(1) error term. Absolute value of t-statistics in parentheses.
a. Significant at 5 percent level.
b. Significant at 1 percent level.

columns in table 8.2 can be viewed as a test of a more complex, three-factor model. As can be seen from the table, the capital-labor interaction terms are statistically significant, and negative. Moreover, this result is robust to the omission of colonies and countries without tariff autonomy during the period, as columns 3 and 4 show.[4]

Tables 8.3 and 8.4 provide additional sensitivity analysis, to gauge the robustness of the results. They concentrate throughout on the subsample of countries enjoying tariff autonomy, to make them consistent with our preferred specifications in column 4 of tables 8.1 and, especially, 8.2. Table 8.3 shows that the results are unaffected if random effects are used rather than fixed effects, and that they are also unaffected if time dummies are included alongside country dummies. This is particularly true for the three-factor specification reported in table 8.3, columns 4–6; the coefficients of interest are very similar in size to those reported in column 4 of table 8.2 and are all highly statistically significant. In the case of the two-factor model, the results also seem fairly robust, although the interaction term between democracy and the land-labor ratio becomes statistically insignificant at conventional levels when a random effects specification without time dummies is used. This does not concern us too much, however, since the three-factor model clearly fits the data better than the simpler two-factor model.

Table 8.4 addresses another possible concern, namely, that we have not controlled for other factors that might influence tariff levels. Since the regressions reported in tables 8.1 and 8.2 include country fixed effects,

Table 8.3
Robustness: Fixed versus Random Effects and Year Effects

Dependent Variable: *tariff*	(1) Tariff Autonomy	(2) Tariff Autonomy	(3) Tariff Autonomy
Year effects	Yes	No	Yes
Estimation	Fixed effects	Random effects	Random effects
democ	0.586	−0.414	−0.687
	(0.39)	(0.30)	(0.49)
democ × ln R/L	2.566	1.670	2.143
	(1.85)[a]	(1.44)	(1.81)[a]
democ × ln K/L	—	—	—
	—	—	—
No. of observations	1,087	1,112	1,112

Notes: Samples as in tables 8.1 and 8.2, column 4 (countries with tariff autonomy).
Panel regression with an AR(1) error term. Absolute value of *t*-statistics in parentheses.
a. Significant at 10 percent level.

we are picking up a lot of these factors already, but table 8.4 provides some extra reassurance by including two variables in the specification that have been found to be important in determining average tariff rates (Blattman, Clemens, and Williamson 2002; Williamson 2003; 2004). These are the lagged export/GDP share and lagged partner tariffs, and as table 8.4 shows, including them has virtually no effect on the coefficients of interest, whether we use fixed or random effects, or include time dummies or not.

Our results thus appear to be robust. What they imply is that, other things being equal, democratization had a stronger impact on lowering tariffs in rich, capital-abundant countries than in poor, capital-scarce countries. Such a finding seems at odds with the median voter model because, as mentioned earlier, we should in principle be able to replace land with capital in the model and derive precisely the same results. In order to understand this result, we need to step outside the rather limited confines of the model and enter the real world of late nineteenth-century politics.

Reality Check: Simulating the Rogowski Model
For purposes of illustration we now simulate the impact of "full democratization" on tariff policy as predicted by what we regard as our benchmark three-factor model for the sample of countries with tariff autonomy (table 8.2, column 4). What the coefficient sign patterns suggest is as follows. In land-scarce Europe, low land-labor ratios should have implied

Dependent Variable: *tariff*	(4) Tariff Autonomy	(5) Tariff Autonomy	(6) Tariff Autonomy
Year effects	Yes	No	Yes
Estimation	Fixed effects	Random effects	Random effects
democ	2.234 (1.16)	2.618 (1.65)[a]	2.415 (1.45)
democ × ln R/L	4.257 (2.30)[b]	4.571 (3.39)[c]	4.190 (3.01)[c]
democ × ln K/L	−4.114 (2.13)[b]	−4.044 (2.62)[c]	−4.040 (2.58)[c]
No. of observations	905	926	926

b. Significant at 5 percent level.
c. Significant at 1 percent level.

that democratization lowered tariffs, and in the capital-abundant north-western core, high capital-labor ratios should have reinforced this effect. Thus, in countries such as Britain or Belgium, democratization should have unambiguously lowered tariffs.

On the other hand, in poorer European countries such as Italy or Spain, low capital-labor ratios should have worked in the opposite direction, and democratization should have had a far less dramatic effect on liberalization. That is, democracy should have implied much lower tariffs in the European core, but the effect should have been weaker in the European periphery. Figure 8.2 illustrates the mechanism for two European countries, Britain and Italy. The preferred model of table 8.2, column 4, predicts that "full democratization" (moving from 0 to 1 on the horizontal axis) would, *ceteris paribus*, lower British tariffs by about 7 percentage points. In Italy the same democratic shift would have lowered tariffs by only 2 percentage points, a muted effect.

In the New World, the opposite logic applies. Everywhere in the New World, high land-labor ratios implied that democratization should have been associated with higher tariffs. However, in the richer parts of the New World, such as the United States, high capital-labor ratios should have muted this effect significantly. On the other hand, in poorer regions such as Latin America low capital-labor ratios should have reinforced the impact of high land-labor ratios, and thus democratization should have raised tariffs by a lot. Figure 8.2 shows the impact of increasing democracy in two New World economies, the United States and Argentina. The preferred model predicts that "full democratization" (moving from 0 to 1

Table 8.4
Robustness: Additional Regressors

Dependent Variable: *tariff*	(1) Tariff Autonomy	(2) Tariff Autonomy	(3) Tariff Autonomy	(4) Tariff Autonomy
Year effects	No	Yes	No	Yes
Estimation	Fixed effects	Fixed effects	Random effects	Random effects
democ	1.912	2.099	2.312	2.132
	(1.02)	(1.09)	(1.45)	(1.28)
democ × ln R/L	5.366	4.446	4.731	4.374
	(3.05)[b]	(2.41)[a]	(3.52)[b]	(3.16)[b]
democ × ln K/L	−4.357	−4.614	−4.385	−4.577
	(2.29)[a]	(2.40)[a]	(2.83)[b]	(2.93)[b]
No. of observations	904	904	925	925

Notes: Includes lagged export/GDP share and lagged partner tariffs (coefficients not reported).
Samples as in tables 8.1 and 8.2, column 4 (countries with tariff autonomy). Panel regression with an AR(1) error term. Absolute value of t-statistics in parentheses.
a. Significant at 5 percent level.
b. Significant at 1 percent level.

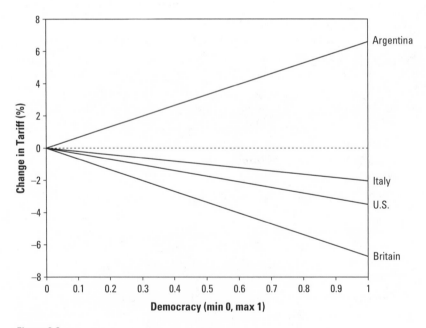

Figure 8.2
Democracy, factor endowments, and protection, land, labor, and capital—four country simulations. Data from table 8.2, column 4.

Table 8.5
Impact of Increasing Democracy on Tariffs in the Rogowski Model

	R/L Low	R/L High
K/L High	– A Rich europe	0 B Rich new world
K/L Low	0 C Poor europe	+ D Poor new world

Source: Based on Rogowski (1989, ch. 1).

on the horizontal axis) would, *ceteris paribus*, have raised Argentine tariffs by 7 percentage points. In the United States the same democratic shift would have actually lowered tariffs by a small 3 percentage points.

As mentioned, to understand the findings in figure 8.2, we have to move beyond the simple median voter model. What the coefficients in table 8.2 imply, in very broad terms, is that the sign of $d(tariff)/d(democ)$ corresponds to the qualitative predictions of the Rogowski model (in general, three-factor form) as summarized in table 8.5. We get an unambiguous result for the rich European core as well as for land-abundant but capital-scarce countries in Latin America and elsewhere. However, in poor land-scarce economies and in economies abundant in both capital and land, we do not expect much of an effect one way or another. This may not make sense in terms of the intuitions provided by the median voter model, but it does make sense in terms of nineteenth-century politics (Rogowski 1989).

What regions A and D in table 8.5 have in common is that in each case, capital and labor share the same interests as to trade policy. In region A, both capital and labor are pro–free trade, with only land being protectionist; and in region D, both capital and labor are protectionist, with only land being pro–free trade. Thus, in regions A and D, capital and labor formed coalitions against land, and political cleavages relating to trade took on an urban-rural nature. On the other hand, in regions B and C, capital and labor were on opposite sides of the trade debate. In region B, capital was pro–free trade, along with land, while labor was protectionist, whereas in region C, capital and land were both protectionist, with only labor supporting lower tariffs. In these cases, cleavages over trade policy took on a class nature, with labor being opposed to both capitalists and landowners.

What these results suggest is that democracy helped labor get its way on tariff policy, but only if it was supported by capital. In cases where labor was opposed by both capital and land, extending the franchise was not sufficient to allow labor to push trade policies in its preferred direction. Extending the logic of the two-factor model to a three-factor case, it would seem that the opposite should have been the case: in cases where labor was unambiguously scarce (abundant) relative to the two other factors of production, shifting the median voter in the direction of a "pure worker" should have unambiguously produced a more pro-labor tariff. The reason this was not the case is that in the real world politics is a more complicated affair than the median voter model would suggest. In particular, and especially (if not exclusively) in countries with proportional representation, coalition building is an essential requirement for constituencies trying to push particular policies.

The argument is well illustrated by the Belgian case (Huberman 2007). The country's socialist party, the *Parti Ouvrier Belge* (POB), was founded in 1885 and from the beginning supported free trade, as would be predicted by the Heckscher-Ohlin theory. However, it was not until the introduction of universal male suffrage in 1893 that the POB obtained enough votes to be represented in Parliament: its share of the vote was 13.2 percent in 1894, 21 percent in 1898, 22.5 percent in 1900, 26 percent in 1904, and 30.3 percent in 1914. The POB joined forces with the pro-business liberals in opposing tariffs, which were favored by the pro-landlord conservatives. Eventually, the POB and the liberals joined forces in government, with the POB using its support for free trade to extract welfare reforms from its laissez faire liberal allies. The net result is that there was no return to protection in Belgium during this period, unlike in France and Germany, where conservative agrarian interests gained the upper hand in the tariff debate. Crucially, neither the POB nor the liberals in Belgium had enough votes to govern on their own: throughout the period, both parties' share of the vote was much lower than that of the conservatives (which varied from a high of 51.1% in 1894 to a low of 41.4% in 1898). A POB-liberal coalition was necessary for free trade to hold, and this in turn required both the extension of the franchise and agreement between capital and labor on the trade issue. If the POB had been opposed by both land and capital on trade policy, it would not have had its way.

By contrast, in poorer regions of the European continent, labor was abundant but capital was scarce; thus capital and land joined forces on the trade issue. This was the case in countries like Spain, where Barcelona industrialists and large landowners agreed on a policy of rotation between conservative and liberal governments, both of which favored protection.

The franchise was gradually extended over the course of the late nineteenth century, but without a natural coalition partner, labor found its views on trade ignored, with a gradually mounting level of worker discontent, occasionally expressed through strikes and violent disturbances, being one consequence of this (Rogowski 1989, 41).

Conclusion

To the question, Does democracy promote free trade? we can only answer "it depends." Political economy considerations are crucial in answering such a question, and there is no reason to believe that the political economy of trade policy will be the same in every country. Indeed, standard trade theory suggests that it will vary greatly across countries. This chapter provides further evidence, if such were needed, of the power of the Heckscher-Ohlin factor endowment theory in understanding late nineteenth-century trade and politics. Democracy had directly opposite effects on tariff levels in rich Europe and the poor New World, and it had relatively small effects on tariffs in poor land-scarce regions and rich land-abundant ones.

Furthermore, it is important to reiterate the point that our results are based on variation across time, not across countries. Across time, the link between democracy and protection is complicated; across countries, it explains only a small proportion of the overall variance in the data. In all the regressions reported here, we found (but did not report) evidence of large country fixed effects, suggesting that other forces were at work in determining the variation of tariffs across countries—forces that were identified in a series of papers by Williamson and his co-authors (summarized in Williamson 2003; 2004). These were many and varied, and they included the need for governments to raise revenue, fears of deindustrialization in the periphery, increases in partner tariffs, and distributional concerns. For our preferred model in table 8.2, column 4, these fixed effects ranged from a high of 18 percent in Brazil, to a low of -10 percent in Austria-Hungary. To put it another way, our preferred specification in table 8.2, column 4, had an overall R^2 of 0.173, a between R^2 (due to the fixed effects) of 0.239, and a within R^2 of just 0.014. There was a strong relationship between democracy and factor endowments on the one hand and tariff levels on the other, but a whole range of country-specific factors mattered more for policy.

While our subject matter here is deliberately narrow, we suspect it has implications for broader debates. If the impact of democracy on trade liberalization is complicated, its impact on economic liberalization more generally and on economic growth is likely to be even more complicated. Democracy does not ensure pro-market policies, as some Western triumphalists would have it, nor does it fatally undermine such policies. Democracy does help produce policies that ordinary voters want, but what they want will vary dramatically across countries and over time.

Appendix: Summary Statistics

Table 8.A

Variable	No. of Observations	Mean	Standard Deviation	Minimum	Maximum
tariff	1,290	16.839	11.729	1.778	58.200
democ	1,290	0.344	0.350	0.000	1.000
ln R/L	1,290	0.000	1.000	−1.735	2.205
ln K/L	957	0.000	1.000	−1.850	1.708
democ × ln R/L	1,290	0.030	0.493	−1.125	1.797
democ × ln K/L	957	0.156	0.606	−1.218	1.708
colony	1,290	0.071	0.256	0.000	1.000
tariffautonomy	1,290	0.862	0.345	0.000	1.000

Notes

Taylor gratefully acknowledges the support of the John Simon Guggenheim Memorial Foundation. We are grateful to participants at the 2005 New Comparative Economic History conference and at the IIIS, INSEAD, Maynooth, Paris 1, and Sciences-Po seminars for their comments. Finally, we wish to thank Timothy Hatton, David Leblang, and anonymous referees for helpful suggestions, and Scott Baier and Jeff Williamson for generously sharing their data with us. We also thank Jeff for all his help and encouragement over the years.

1. Such considerations obviously relate strongly to two broader debates that are too vast to be adequately summarized here. The first concerns the relation between democracy and economic growth (see, e.g., Olson (1993) or Przeworski and Limongi (1993) for some of the theoretical arguments). Recent empirical papers include Rigobon and Rodrik (2005), who find a positive relationship between democracy and economic performance, and Rodrik and Wacziarg (2005), who argue that democratic transitions tend to have a positive effect on economic growth, even in the short run. On the other hand, Barro (1996) finds that once variables such as the rule of law, free markets, and government size have been controlled for, the effect of democracy on growth is weakly negative. There is also a large empirical literature on whether democracy promotes economic liberalization: for a flavor of this debate, see de Haan and Sturm (2003), and papers cited therein. This literature typically (but not always) finds that democracy promotes economic freedom; more interestingly, perhaps, a paper by Persson (2005) argues that the form of democracy matters for the adoption or otherwise of growth-promoting policies. In our view, however, different types of liberalization have different distributional effects and are thus likely to be affected differently by extending the franchise: it makes sense to look at individual policies separately.

2. As the previously cited publications make abundantly clear.

3. Based on a reading of Bairoch (1989), the standard English-language source on nineteenth-century trade policies.

4. In results not reported, we also found the result holds when missing data on democracy (e.g., for colonies excluded from Polity) are imputed by backfilling from the first available year. As an additional check, we also replaced our data on capital-labor ratios with data on output per capita, to see if the results were an artifact of our capital stock data. (The rationale for using output per capita is that one would expect rich countries to have high capital-labor ratios, other things being equal.) The results were robust to this change as well.

References

Alesina, A., and D. Rodrik. 1994. Distributive Politics and Economic Growth. *Quarterly Journal of Economics* 109 (2): 465–490.

Baier, S. L., G. P. Dwyer Jr., and R. Tamura. 2006. How Important Are Capital and Total Factor Productivity for Economic Growth? *Economic Inquiry* 44 (1): 23–49.

Bairoch, P. 1989. European Trade Policies, 1815–1914. In *The Cambridge Economic History of Europe*. Vol. 8, ed. P. Mathias and S. Pollard. Cambridge: Cambridge University Press.

Barro, R. J. 1996. Democracy and Growth. *Journal of Economic Growth* 1 (1): 1–27.

Blattman, C., M. A. Clemens, and J. G. Williamson. 2002. Who Protected and Why? Tariffs the World Around, 1870–1938. Paper presented at the Conference on the Political Economy of Globalization, Trinity College, Dublin, August 29–31.

Bliss, H., and B. Russett. 1998. Democratic Trading Partners: The Liberal Connection, 1962–1989. *Journal of Politics* 60 (4): 1126–1147.

Clemens, M. A., and J. G. Williamson. 2004. Why Did the Tariff-Growth Correlation Change after 1950? *Journal of Economic Growth* 9 (1): 5–46.

de Haan, J., and J.-E. Sturm. 2003. Does More Democracy Lead to Greater Economic Freedom? New Evidence for Developing Countries. *European Journal of Political Economy* 19 (3): 547–563.

Dutt, P., and D. Mitra. 2002. Endogenous Trade Policy through Majority Voting: An Empirical Investigation. *Journal of International Economics* 58 (1): 107–313.

Feenstra, R. C. 2004. *Advanced International Trade: Theory and Evidence*. Princeton, N.J.: Princeton University Press.

Findlay, R., and S. Wellisz. 1984. Endogenous Tariffs, the Political Economy of Trade Restrictions, and Welfare. In *Import Competition and Response*, ed. J. N. Bhagwati. Chicago: University of Chicago Press.

Garrett, G. 2000. The Causes of Globalization. *Comparative Political Studies* 33 (6–7): 941–991.

Gourevitch, P. 1986. *Politics in Hard Times: Comparative Responses to International Economic Crises*. Ithaca, N.Y.: Cornell University Press.

Grossman, G. M., and E. Helpman. 2001. *Special Interest Politics*. Cambridge, Mass.: MIT Press.

Huberman, M. 2007. A Ticket to Trade: Belgian Workers and Globalization before 1914. *Economic History Review*. Forthcoming.

Huberman, M., and W. Lewchuk. 2003. European Economic Integration and the Labor Compact, 1850–1913. *European Review of Economic History* 7 (1): 3–41.

Mansfield, E. D., H. V. Milner, and P. B. Rosendorff. 2000. Free to Trade: Democracies, Autocracies, and International Trade. *American Political Science Review* 94 (2): 305–321.

Mayer, W. 1984. Endogenous Tariff Formation. *American Economic Review* 74 (5): 970–985.

Milner, H. V., and K. Kubota. 2005. Why the Move to Free Trade? Democracy and Trade Policy in the Developing Countries. *International Organization* 59 (1): 107–143.

Morrow, J. D., R. M. Siverson, and T. E. Taberes. 1998. The Political Determinants of International Trade: The Major Powers, 1907–1990. *American Political Science Review* 92 (3): 649–661.

Olson, M. 1993. Dictatorship, Democracy, and Development. *American Political Science Review* 87 (3): 567–576.

O'Rourke, K. H., A. M. Taylor, and J. G. Williamson. 1996. Factor Price Convergence in the Late Nineteenth Century. *International Economic Review* 37 (3): 499–530.

O'Rourke, K. H., and J. G. Williamson. 1994. Late Nineteenth Century Anglo-American Factor Price Convergence: Were Heckscher and Ohlin Right? *Journal of Economic History* 54: 892–916.

———. 1999. *Globalization and History: The Evolution of the Nineteenth Century Atlantic Economy.* Cambridge, Mass.: MIT Press.

Persson, T. 2005. Forms of Democracy, Policy and Economic Development. NBER (National Bureau of Economic Research) Working Paper 11171. ⟨http://www.nber.org/papers/W11171⟩.

Polanyi, K. 1957. *The Great Transformation: The Political and Economic Origins of Our Time.* Boston: Beacon Press.

Przeworski, A., and F. Limongi. 1993. Political Regimes and Economic Growth. *Journal of Economic Perspectives* 7 (3): 51–69.

Rigobon, R., and D. Rodrik. 2005. Rule of Law, Democracy, Openness, and Income: Estimating the Interrelationships. *Economics of Transition* 13 (3): 533–564.

Rodrik, D., and R. Wacziarg. 2005. Do Democratic Transitions Produce Bad Economic Outcomes? *American Economic Review* 95 (2): 50–55.

Rogowski, R. 1989. *Commerce and Coalitions: How Trade Affects Domestic Political Alignments.* Princeton: Princeton University Press.

Sachs, J. D., and A. Warner. 1995. Economic Reform and the Process of Global Integration. *Brookings Papers on Economic Activity* 1: 1–118.

Thompson, H. 1985. Complementarity in a Simple General Equilibrium Production Model. *Canadian Journal of Economics* 18 (3): 616–621.

———. 1986. Free Trade and Factor-Price Polarization. *European Economic Review* 30 (2): 419–425.

Williamson, J. G. 1996. Globalization, Convergence, and History. *Journal of Economic History* 56 (2): 277–306.

———. 2002. Land, Labor, and Globalization in the Third World, 1870–1940. *Journal of Economic History* 62 (1): 55–85.

———. 2003. Stolper-Samuelson, Strategic Tariffs, and Revenue Needs: World Tariffs, 1789–1938. NBER (National Bureau of Economic Research) Working Paper 9656. ⟨http://www.nber.org/papers/W9656⟩.

———. 2004. The Tariff Response to World Market Integration in the Periphery before the Modern Era. Paper presented at the Market Integration Workshop, European University Institute, Fiesole, Italy. ⟨post.Economics.harvard.edu/faculty/jwilliam/papers/Fiesole04-text.pdf⟩.

9 A Dual Policy Paradox: Why Have Trade and Immigration Policies Always Differed in Labor-Scarce Economies?

Timothy J. Hatton and Jeffrey G. Williamson

We live in a world where trade policies are liberal and immigration policies are restrictive. Recent globalization discussions give the impression that this policy difference is a modern phenomenon (Wellisch and Walz 1998; Hillman and Weiss 1999), implying that trade policy was liberal and open a century ago. This conventional view is quite wrong. Instead, while most labor-scarce economies today have open trade and closed immigration policies, a century ago the labor-scarce economies had just the opposite, open immigration and closed trade policies. Thus, the inverse policy correlation has persisted over almost two centuries.

Why have policies toward the movement of labor and goods always been so different in labor-scarce economies? After all, importing labor-intensive products is pretty much like importing labor. So shouldn't trade and immigration policies reinforce each other? Consider for a moment the simple $2 \times 2 \times 2$ model in which trade is driven by factor endowments. Also, consider the country where labor is relatively scarce because that's the country for which immigration policies matter. Suppose such a country puts up a tariff to protect the scarce factor, labor. In the absence of immigration, wages will increase. But if labor is allowed to move across borders, the tariff-induced wage increase will be undone by immigration (Mundell 1957). By the same logic, an immigration policy designed to protect domestic labor will be undone by free trade: the desired effect will only be achieved by restricting both trade and immigration. Simple theory predicts that immigration and import restrictions should go together. In fact, they never have. Therein lies the policy paradox.

There are many reasons why reality might deviate from these simple Heckscher-Ohlin and Stolper-Samuelson predictions. Specific factors, increasing returns, and Ricardian differences in productivity are but three. Thus, trade and immigration may be less than perfect substitutes, or they might not be substitutes at all (Markusen 1983; Faini, deMelo,

and Zimmermann 1999). Nevertheless, the simple model is a useful starting point for exploring the persistent inverse correlation between trade
and immigration policies.

This chapter traces the histories of trade and immigration policies in
labor-scarce economies since the early nineteenth century. We find it
particularly useful to compare the two great globalization eras: the half
century from 1850 to World War I, and the half century from 1950 to
the present. Next, we explore some of the fundamentals that have influenced the evolution of trade and immigration policies. Key among them
are the decline in the costs of immigration and its impact on immigrant
selectivity; a secular switch in the net fiscal impact of trade relative to
immigration; and changes in the median voter and their impact on the
political economy of tariff and immigration policy. We also offer explanations for the variation between countries in voter attitudes toward trade
and immigration, and link this to the key forces underlying policy. We
conclude with some comments about current policies in historical
perspective.

The Evolution of a Dual Policy Paradox over Two Centuries

One could get the impression from today's labor-scarce economies that
there is something immutable about a world in which the movement of
labor is far more tightly constrained than the movement of goods. But
things were very different a century ago. The conventional wisdom views
the nineteenth century as the canonical liberal period in which globalization
was fostered by free trade and open immigration policies. Such conventional wisdom may fit the predictions of the simple $2 \times 2 \times 2$ model in which
trade and immigration policies go together, but it is a complete myth.

Consider first the evolution of tariff policy. Recent research has shown
that protection was at very high levels before 1914, much higher than is
often recognized and especially so in labor-scarce New World economies
(Coatsworth and Williamson 2004a; 2004b; Williamson 2006a; 2006b).
Figure 9.1 plots the average tariff rates, 1865–1938, for six regions, com-
prising 35 countries in total.[1] Tariffs were on the rise between 1870 and
1890, and from then until World War I they averaged around 16 percent,
a value exceeding every subsequent decade except the 1930s. The view
that the pre-1914 years were ones of relatively free trade stems from an
obsessive focus on the European industrial leaders, Britain, France, and
Germany, whose combined average tariff was no more than 6 or 7 percent. Even lower tariffs characterized Asia and the Middle East, most of

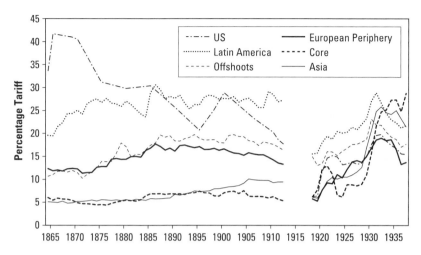

Figure 9.1
Average regional tariffs, 1865–1938.
Source: Williamson (2006a).

which was under the domination of the free-trading European imperial powers. The average for the European periphery was much higher, pretty close to the average for all 35 countries.

The big regional outliers from free trade policy were the labor-scarce European overseas offshoots. Latin America raised tariffs to almost 30 percent by the 1890s; the United States had average tariff rates above 30 percent as late as the 1880s, rates that were still equal to those of highly protective Latin America by 1900; and the remaining European offshoots reached tariff levels of about 20 percent, double or triple that of industrial Europe. Furthermore, tariffs in labor-scarce economies were far higher on imported manufactures than these averages would suggest. In short, labor-scarce countries with tariff autonomy imposed high and rising tariffs in the global century before World War I.

Interwar deglobalization saw tariffs soar (and nontariff barriers multiply).[2] This resurgence was led by the European core and its colonial empires (figure 9.1), and the rest of the world simply reconstructed the high protective walls they had erected before 1914. With the resumption of peace in 1945, average tariffs stood at about 15 percent, a figure similar to the average for 1870–1914. By the early 1960s, however, the trend in world tariff rates was steeply downward, so much so that by 1970 the average for these 35 countries was lower than at any previous period, barring the inflationary war years. The fact that much of the Third World remained highly protective does not change our characterization of the free trade trend because it is the labor-scarce OECD countries that matter to the policy paradox. Tariffs were lower in the half century following 1950 than they were in the half century following 1860, and they would look much lower if the comparison were restricted to the labor-scarce immigrant countries.

What about immigration policy? Here, there is no convenient summary statistic to describe immigration restriction, encouragement, or neutrality. Immigration policies typically involve rationing rather than taxing, so they don't generate tariff-equivalent measures. Furthermore, some countries used complex subsidies involving reduced steerage costs in transit, help with job search upon arrival, and cheap (or even free) land for settlement. The best we have is an index of policy stance constructed for five labor-scarce and immigrating New World countries from 1860 to 1930 (Timmer and Williamson 1998). The five are the United States, Canada, Argentina, Brazil, and Australia. Between 1860 and 1890 their average policy stance was mildly pro-immigration, but from the 1880s onwards there was a gradual tightening as some countries reduced or eliminated their immigrant subsidies and some started to experiment with outright barriers (Hatton and Williamson 2005, 158–159). This mild trend toward restriction was followed by a very sharp increase, led by the U.S. introduction of the literacy test in the Immigration Act of 1917 and a quota in 1921, the latter progressively tightened in 1924 and 1928. With the onset of the Great Depression and trouble in labor markets, there was a general clamp-down on immigration, not just in the five New World countries but all around the world. Nevertheless, up to 1914, immigration policy was still very open compared with the high tariff walls these labor-scarce economies had erected over a half century or more. Thus, the paradox: protective trade policy coexisted with open immigration policy in labor-scarce economies before 1914.

The immigration regime that emerged after World War II reflected the full panoply of controls that was the legacy of the interwar period—nationality laws, passport controls, entry visas, and above all, quotas. Some of these constraints were eased early on to accommodate refugee resettlement and guest worker programs in Europe and the United States, and migrant subsidies in Australia and New Zealand were also temporarily resumed. Labor-scarce countries also started to open their doors to immigrants from Latin America and the Third World, an important event that we discuss later. But by the early 1970s this partial liberalization had evaporated: guest worker programs in the West had ended, overseas migrant subsidies had been abandoned, skill-based points systems had been introduced, legislation penalizing employers of illegal immigrants had been passed, and so on. Immigration policies have become even tougher since the 1970s. The fact that immigration into the labor-scarce OECD has actually risen is not inconsistent with our characterization of the policy trend: world migration would have grown much more quickly had post–World War II policies been as liberal as pre–World War I policies, and a lower growth of immigration from poor countries would have yielded more open policies. That surge in world migration was triggered in large part by a release in Third World poverty constraints and by the help offered by rising numbers of previous immigrants resident in the OECD (Hatton and Williamson 2005, chs. 10 and 11).

Unfortunately, no immigration policy index exists for the recent era, and the best we can do is use the periodic surveys taken by the United Nations, which ask governments whether their policy aim is to reduce immigration, increase it, or keep it the same. The proportion of labor-scarce developed country governments seeking to reduce immigration increased from 18 percent in the mid-1970s to 60 percent in the mid-1990s (United Nations 2002, 18). While this measure reflects governments' intentions rather than their policy stances, it does suggest that immigration policies have become much more restrictive since the early 1970s. Thus, the paradox: liberal trade policy coexists with restrictive immigration policy today.

In summary, pro-immigration policies were established in labor-scarce economies early in the first global century, but trade policy was protectionist and it became even more so as the century progressed. Pro-trade policies eventually emerged in the labor-scarce OECD as the second global century unfolded, but immigration policies never underwent the same liberal reversal. There are, of course, national eccentricities that leave their mark on the timing and magnitude of individual country policy changes, but they share three common attributes: the fundamentals driving world migration and its selectivity; the net fiscal implications of trade and immigration; and the role of democracy in changing the median voter.

Immigrant Selectivity, Immigrant "Quality," and Immigration Policy
In the early nineteenth century European overseas emigration was a mere trickle compared with what came later. Those who did migrate came from the relatively developed European northwest and from the middle and upper parts of the income and wealth distribution. If the overseas native-born had a preference for western European immigrants, there was no

need for host governments to develop discriminatory policies to achieve that end because long distances, high transport costs, and poverty at home were barriers enough to prevent immigration from poorer countries in the south and east of Europe, or from Asia, or even by poorer individuals from the richer countries in the European northwest.

Anti-immigration voices got louder in labor-scarce host countries as the nineteenth century progressed, as the immigrant numbers rose, and most important, as their relative skills and education fell. The latter was induced by the gradual disappearance of poverty in Europe, carried by a spreading industrial revolution, and by the fall in the cost of the move, carried by a transportation revolution; both helped release the poverty constraint on the emigration of the poor (Hatton and Williamson 2005, ch. 4). The upper panel of table 9.1 documents this effect by reporting the ratio of the GDP per capita in source countries relative to the destination country, where the former are weighted by the changing shares of immigrants by source entering the destination country in question. U.S. contemporary observers made much of the declining "quality" of the new immigrants as their source shifted from the richer northwest Europe to the poorer south and east Europe. The U.S. index dropped from 92.3 in the 1870s to 49.5 in the 1900s, or by 46 percent. Over the same half-century, the Canadian and Argentine indices dropped by 42 and 50 percent, respectively.

Although anti-immigrant sentiment ebbed and flowed, there was no call for outright immigrant restriction in the United States during most of the nineteenth century, except for the demand for Chinese exclusion in the 1880s by West Coast interests.[3] When the United States did begin to close the door to immigrants, that policy move was driven largely by complaints from the median U.S. voter (the unskilled or semi-skilled worker in an urban occupation), who thought he was being crowded out by the relatively low-skilled "new immigrants" from southern and eastern Europe (Timmer and Williamson 1998). After more than two decades of debate, restrictive policy was introduced in 1917 with a literacy test (Goldin 1994), followed by country-of-origin quotas in 1921, 1924, and 1928. The U.S. quotas had two goals: reducing the total numbers, and reducing the share from poor source countries. In little more than a decade, every labor-scarce host country followed the U.S. lead by implementing measures that restricted immigration of the unskilled from poor source countries.

Things have evolved very differently during the second global century. First, discriminatory exclusion of those from poor source countries grad-

Table 9.1
GDP Per Capita Ratio: Average Source Country/Destination Country, 1860s–1990s

	1860s	1870s	1880s	1890s	1900s
United States	95.4	92.3	73.3	64.0	49.5
Canada	154.8	183.1	159.4	136.7	107.0
Argentina	114.2	110.2	89.8	68.4	54.6
	1950s	1960s	1970s	1980s	1990s
United States	49.1	40.8	29.8	24.0	22.4
Canada	64.5	60.0	40.8	33.7	30.8
Australia	73.4	75.4	64.5	55.5	49.0
Germany	95.6	70.1	61.1	51.1	44.7
United Kingdom	—	—	75.3	83.1	86.2

Sources: 1860s to 1900s: weights for gross immigration from Ferenczi and Willcox (1929), table 14, 274–287, by country with residuals by continent; GDP per capita from Maddison (1995), app. D, 194–206 (by country), and app. E, 212 (by broad region), with interpolations where necessary. Cross-border migration between the United States and Canada is excluded from the migration weights. 1950s to 1990s: weights for gross immigration, for the United States, from U.S. Immigration and Naturalization Service (2002), table 2, ⟨http://uscis.gov/ graphics/shared/aboutus/statistics/Immigs.htm⟩; for Canada, immigration data to 1979 kindly supplied by Don DeVoretz, and for 1980–2000 by Roger Bourque (Statistics Canada); for Australia, from DIMIA (2001), ⟨http://www.immi.gov.au/statistics/publications/ federation/body.pdf⟩; for Germany, data kindly supplied by Georgios Tassoukis; for the United Kingdom, from the data set used in Hatton (2005). Weights exclude cross-border migrants between the U.S. and Canada, and between the U.K. and Ireland; for Germany, they exclude flows of ethnic German *ausseidler*. GDP per capita for countries and regional residuals from Maddison (2001), app. C, 267–333.
Notes: Immigration weights by source country are constructed from data on annual gross immigration flows, summed by decade, where immigrants are classified by country of birth or last residence, and where those not classified are allocated to a residual group for each world region. These weights are applied to the mid-decade estimate of GDP per capita at constant purchasing power parity for individual countries or country groups.

ually disappeared, to be replaced by nondiscriminatory immigration policies, of which the 1965 Amendments to the U.S. Immigration Act and the abolition of the White Australia policy in the 1970s are but two examples. Removal of discriminatory exclusion might not have mattered much were it not for the fact that the poverty trap was at the same time also gradually unlocked in the poorer parts of the world and family reunification policies allowed the "friends and relatives effect" to do its multiplicative work. Compared with the native-born, the labor market quality of immigrants deteriorated in the major host countries, and it deteriorated at an even faster pace than it had in the previous century (Hatton 2000; Williamson 2004; Hatton and Williamson 2005, chs. 8 and 15).

What role did changing immigrant sources play? The lower panel of table 9.1 shows that the U.S. index of source versus destination country

GDP per capita fell by 54 percent over the half-century between the 1950s and 1990s. The Canadian and German indexes fell by almost exactly the same proportion. The Australian index fell by somewhat less, and the British index (at least from the 1970s) not at all.[4] It should be noted that these declines in source-to-destination GDP per capita occurred *despite* increasingly selective immigration policies that might have been expected to mitigate them. Having opened the door wider to the poorer parts of the world, restrictions on all potential immigrants had to be tightened with quotas and point systems in order to limit the size of the inflows and to raise the labor market quality of those admitted. Thus, immigration policy is much tougher now than a century ago simply because there are far more potential immigrants from poor countries to keep out.

The Fiscal Implications of Trade and Immigration

Trade and Revenue Tariffs Customs duties were a major source of central government revenue in the nineteenth century. In recently independent countries with little experience with tax collection, few bureaucratic resources to implement it efficiently, and limited access to foreign capital markets, customs revenues were an easy-to-collect fiscal source essential to support expenditures on defense and civil administration. This was certainly true of the United States and Latin America in the first half of the nineteenth century, although the United States had more success in gaining access to European capital markets. Furthermore, customs revenues were especially important for federal governments in labor-scarce and land-abundant countries because low population and taxpayer density made other forms of tax collection inefficient. The average share of customs duties in total revenues across eleven Latin American republics was 57.8 percent between 1820 and 1890, and the share was even higher for federal governments (65.6 percent) because local and state governments were typically reluctant to give up their limited tax weapons after joining a federation (Coatsworth and Williamson 2004a, 216). The share was no lower in the United States. Alexander Hamilton thought "the tariff was more important as a tool of fiscal policy than as an instrument for promoting manufactures" (Irwin 2002, 16) and subsequent nineteenth-century figures seem to prove him right.

The ratio of customs duties to total state revenue declined steeply in the labor-scarce world early in the twentieth century. The customs revenue share was 90 percent for both Australia and the United States in the 1850s. As late as the 1890s, the customs revenue share still averaged almost 58 percent for seven labor-scarce overseas countries, when it was less than 20 percent for the United Kingdom and France. By the time the second global century had emerged after World War II, the customs revenue share had fallen dramatically in the labor-scarce OECD and by the 1970s it was only about 4 percent. Of course, this reflects in part the fall in tariff rates, but most of it is driven by the rise in other tax revenue sources.

Immigrants and the Welfare State   In contrast, immigration had little or no fiscal impact in the first global century. Since welfare states were still very small, threats to the treasury from immigration were mostly irrelevant: migrants added little to tax revenues, and they received almost no federal transfers. Thus, tariffs brought plenty of fiscal benefits in the era before 1914, and immigrants brought no fiscal costs. With the sharp rise of the welfare state from the 1930s to the 1970s, social services expanded dramatically while federal and central governments diversified their sources of tax revenues. Between 1910 and 1970, social transfers (health, welfare, unemployment, pensions, housing subsidies) as a share in GDP rose in the United States from 0.6 to 10.4 percent, and from 0.7 to 14.8 percent for the median OECD country (Lindert 2004, table 1.2, 12–13). A clear OECD hierarchy had emerged in terms of commitment to the welfare state by 1980: the United States and Canada were at the bottom, and Germany, France, and Sweden were at the top. We show later how this hierarchy influenced public opinion about immigration.

The fact that New World immigrants in the late twentieth century suffered a far greater earnings disadvantage in labor markets than did those a century earlier has added further fuel to fiscal anti-immigration fires in the modern era. That is, while U.S. immigrant men earned 16.3 percent less than native-born men in 1990, they earned only 6.4 percent less in 1909 (Hatton and Williamson 2005, ch. 15). Relative to native-born, immigrants today are less productive than they were a century ago. Relative to native-born, immigrants today are therefore far more likely to need social transfers than they were a century ago (when, of course, such transfers were unavailable). Thus, U.S. poverty rates in 1959 were much lower for the foreign-born: 20.9 percent for households with native-born heads and 14.2 for households with foreign-born heads. Those relative rates had reversed dramatically by 1999: 11.8 percent for native-born and 17.4 percent for foreign-born (Hoynes, Page, and Stevens 2005).

Table 9.2 reports percentage point differences between European Union immigrants and nationals in their dependence on different welfare

Table 9.2
Welfare Dependence and Personal Characteristics, Immigrants and Nationals, 1994–1996

| | Percentage Point Difference between Immigrants and EU Nationals in Receipt of | | |
	Unemploy. Benefit	Family Benefit	Pension
Germany	1.6	—	—
Denmark	24.5	5.3	−17.9
Netherlands	7.0	7.9	−14.9
Belgium	6.7	1.1	−6.1
France	4.9	16.7	−12.8
United Kingdom	0.6	0.6	−23.4
Austria	8.9	8.1	−18.0
Finland	31.7	0.2	−12.7

Sources: Boeri, Hanson, and McCormick (2002, 74–75). Data for those aged 16 and above are from the European Community Household Panel.
Note: The first three columns refer to differences between non-EU citizens and EU citizens in the percentage receiving benefit. The next two columns are differences between the per-

benefits in the mid-1990s. For these eight European countries, immigrants have on average higher dependence on unemployment and family benefits. Their higher dependence on the welfare state reflects both demography (the immigrants have more children) and differences in labor market status (the immigrants have higher unemployment rates and lower levels of schooling). The lower impact of immigrants on pensions also reflects demography because they are younger on average. The table also documents important differences between countries. With the exception of Finland, those EU countries that have been able to positively select educated immigrants tend to have smaller differences in unemployment and welfare dependence. Those EU countries whose immigrants have fewer children have lower family benefit dependence. Immigrant characteristics and the generosity of the welfare state interact: the immigrant welfare burden is greatest where immigrants are poorly qualified for the market *and* the welfare state is relatively generous. (See also Boeri, Hanson, and McCormick 2002; Smith and Edmonston 1997; and Hatton and Williamson 2005, ch. 14.)

Voting Rights, Immigration Policy, and Trade Policy
It is one thing to identify changes in the immigrant mix and in budgetary imperatives as key elements in the clamor for restrictive policies. It is

	Difference in Characteristics between Immigrants and EU Nationals			
	Low Educated (%)	High Educated (%)	Age (years)	No. of Children/ household
Germany	21.2	−5.5	−8.6	0.54
Denmark	14.7	0.6	−7.8	0.47
Netherlands	22.7	5.3	−7.7	0.65
Belgium	10.6	−14.1	−2.5	0.12
France	22.5	−7.2	−3.6	1.10
United Kingdom	−15.4	21.2	−8.7	0.85
Austria	7.8	12.2	−10.6	0.35
Finland	−12.3	17.5	−7.4	0.04

centage with less than completed secondary school education and the percentage with college degrees. The age column is the difference in average age and the children column is the difference in number of children per household.

quite another to explain the process by which these translate into policy. There are two key questions: Who stood to gain, and who stood to lose? Who had the vote? The classic analysis of tariff protection starts from the Stolper-Samuelson theorem: owners of the scarce factor(s) should favor protection. Much of tariff history has been written in terms of a three-factor world: labor, capital, and land (Rogowski 1989). In land-abundant New World countries, the Stolper-Samuelson prediction is that labor should have searched for other scarce factors, like capital, to get enough votes to protect them from an invasion of imported labor-intensive manufactures. Owners of land and natural resources should have resisted, lobbying for free trade. But democracy matters, too. As O'Rourke and Taylor show in chapter 8 of this volume, extending the franchise increased the level of protection in countries that were labor-abundant and reduced it in countries that were labor-scarce. Such thinking seems to work relatively well for trade policy, but can it also be applied to immigration policy? We start with the question, Who had the vote?

Figure 9.2 shows the percent of adults voting in five New World countries between 1850 and 1940. By 1880 one-quarter of adults were voting in North America, although in South America the figure was less than 10 percent well into the twentieth century. Figure 9.3 shows a similar contrast between the industrial leaders and the continental followers until about 1910, which marked the beginning of a steep ascent to the interwar

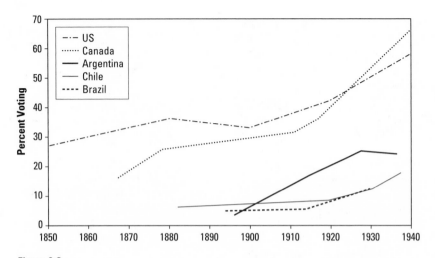

Figure 9.2
Percent of adults voting, New World, 1850–1940.
Source: Data from Engerman and Sokoloff (2005) kindly supplied by Ken Sokoloff.

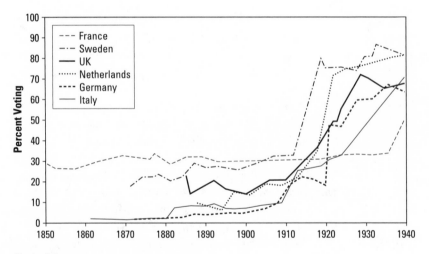

Figure 9.3
Percent of adults voting, Europe, 1850–1940.
Source: Data from Aidt et al. (2006) kindly supplied by Toke Aidt.

period. Although suffrage in the nineteenth century looks very limited, male voting rates were roughly twice those reported in figures 9.2 and 9.3, and they were higher still among white males in the United States. This means that in North America and in the European leader countries, voting percolated well down the hierarchy of class and income, giving a strong voice to urban unskilled labor. It may have extended down to the middle classes in South America and in the European follower countries, but not much beyond that.

The story of trade policy in western Europe is well known. The final abolition of the British Corn Laws in 1846 represents the triumph of labor and capital over landed interests, and it was underpinned by the combination of a shrinking share of agriculture and electoral reform that shifted the political balance toward urban interests. Stories that are similar in essence but different in detail and timing can be told for Belgium, Switzerland, and France (Rogowski 1989, 34–38). Farther to the east, the results were different, with Bismarck's marriage of iron and rye reflecting the political strength of a coalition of land and capital. Elsewhere in Europe, where land and capital were relatively scarce and where voting was restricted to a small minority, protectionist forces were in ascendance from mid-century. One might also have predicted that emigration would have been encouraged in western Europe and discouraged further south and east, but in fact there was little need for it. As noted, until late in the nineteenth century the main transatlantic flow came from the north and west of Europe. When south and east Europe joined the flow, governments found the cost of controlling emigration too great, and the benefits too limited, in the face of crumbling land-capital coalitions.

Labor-scarce United States, Canada, Australia, and New Zealand set their tariffs high: despite the importance of agriculture, scarce capital and scarce labor won the day in nineteenth-century tariff debates. But the story is complicated by the wide diffusion of both voting rights and land-holding. Here, tariff revenues were particularly important. They were used to buy the votes of the vast rural interiors in exchange for infrastructure development, particularly railways. In the antebellum United States, this played out as a coalition between the northeastern and the western states against the South (Irwin 2006), a coalition that was underpinned after 1862 by the expansion of settlement in the West under the Homestead Act and by Southern defeat in the Civil War. In Canada the National Policy of 1879 explicitly aimed to build on the Dominion Lands Act of 1877 to promote western settlement, principally by financing railways with tariff revenue (Pomfret 1981, 87). Australian post-federation policies explicitly aimed to promote a high-wage economy by protecting industry at the expense of agriculture.

Given that the capital-labor coalition had the upper hand in these countries, how do we explain the persistence of open immigration policies well into the twentieth century? Although anti-immigrant sentiment came and went with the Know Nothing movement in the United States, pressure began to build only at the end of the century, and for two reasons. One is that open immigration policy was explicitly linked to the expansion of tariff-financed infrastructure in the interior.[5] The second is that while the land-abundant frontier began to dry up in the late nineteenth century, mass migration of low-skilled workers from relatively poor countries gained momentum (table 9.1). Goldin (1994) has shown that the political balance eventually tipped in favor of restriction in 1917 after 20 years of debate and as wage competition shifted northern labor's attitudes against immigration, with southern support. Elsewhere, too, pressure for restriction mounted with the fact or the threat of low-skilled immigration.[6]

The continuation of open immigration policy in South America is easier to explain, as much of the political power lay in the hands of the free trading *Latifundia*. But things were not quite so straightforward because landowner power would also predict free trade, and contrary to popular belief, tariffs were higher in nineteenth-century South America than almost anywhere else. Given the literacy and wealth requirements for voting as well as the lack of secret ballots (Engerman and Sokoloff 2000, 226), urban capitalists formed the other half of the governing oligarchy. Both groups had strong interests in open immigration, but their interests in tariff protection typically diverged. While tariffs would have hurt the exporters of agricultural goods and minerals, the alternative of taxes on land and mineral rights would have been even more painful. As in North America, tariff revenues were important; indeed, recent empirical analysis suggests that revenues were the most important determinant of South American tariff levels (Coatsworth and Williamson 2004b). But the political imperatives for revenues were not just (or even mainly) infrastructure for the rural interior (much of which was financed from abroad). Above all, these revenues were used to fight the endemic wars that plagued the region.[7]

Thus three factors conditioned trade and immigration policies in the labor-scarce economies of the New World: revenue needs for development or war; sending country poverty constraints that kept immigration small and selective for most of the period; and the often-limited political franchise. But what about the second great globalization era after the 1950s? Agricultural interests had declined almost everywhere, and the extension of the franchise ensured that labor's voice gained increasing, if not overwhelming, weight. Democratic governments increasingly needed the support of grass roots public opinion for their policies. For the modern period we can examine individual attitudes directly.

Public Opinion and Public Policy

Policies should reflect public opinion where the franchise is universal. Thus, observers have focused on measuring and explaining individual attitudes toward immigrants and imports. We are interested here in two key questions. First, is public opinion more negative toward immigration than toward trade? If it is, we would then have an explanation as to why trade policies have been more liberal than immigration policies in the postwar era. If it is not, we need to offer an explanation for the apparent conflict between policy and public opinion. Second, what explains individual attitudes toward trade and immigration? What are the individual *and* the country characteristics that determine individual opinions?

Recent opinion surveys make it possible to measure the intensity of individual attitudes toward trade and immigration on the same basis across a large number of labor-scarce economies. The most widely used evidence is that taken from the national identity module of the International Social Survey Programme (ISSP), conducted in 24 countries in 1995. Here we assess data from 14 OECD countries of the ISSP survey so as to focus on opinion in relatively labor-scarce countries. Respondents were asked whether they would like to see immigration increased a lot, increased a little, kept the same, reduced a little, or reduced a lot. A similar question was asked about attitudes toward imports, and both sets of responses are placed on a scale of 1 to 5, with the value 5 representing the most intense opposition.

The average survey responses to these two questions are presented in table 9.3. Three features stand out. First, the average citizen would like to see both immigration and imports reduced. Second, there is very little difference between the average opposition to immigration and to imports. On the basis of this evidence, why has trade policy has been so much more liberal than immigration policy over the last three or four decades? We think there is a clear answer, which we take up later. Third, the correlation between attitudes toward immigration and imports across the

Table 9.3
Attitudes Toward Immigration and Trade, 1995

	Anti-Immigration Opinion[a]	Anti-Imports Opinion[a]	Correlation Coefficient	No. of Observations
Australia	3.768	3.999	0.271	2,318
Austria	3.808	3.907	0.267	923
Canada	3.311	3.292	0.284	1,310
Germany	4.270	3.283	0.370	1,630
Great Britain	4.060	3.772	0.325	955
Ireland	3.073	3.664	0.178	919
Italy	4.148	3.599	0.243	1,020
Japan	3.373	2.939	0.219	1,000
Netherlands	3.822	2.930	0.272	1,864
New Zealand	3.737	3.401	0.310	950
Norway	3.845	3.146	0.240	1,333
Spain	3.385	3.889	0.180	1,014
Sweden	3.970	3.254	0.253	1,132
United States	3.880	3.765	0.249	1,090
All countries	3.770	3.480	0.237	17,458

Source: Based on data from the 1995 International Social Survey Programme (ISSP), module on national identity, ⟨http://www.gesis.org/en/data_service/issp/data/1995_National _Identity.htm⟩.
Note:
a. Numbers represent average attitudes toward immigration and imports on a five-point scale, where 5 is strongly against and 1 is strongly in favor. The sample used here excludes cases where, for either immigration opinion or trade opinion, there was no response or a "don't know" response.

individuals in the survey is not particularly strong; the correlation coefficient is only about 0.24 for the full sample. Hence, opposition to imports and immigration could very well reflect the attitudes of rather different individuals.

Several studies have explored the association between attitudes toward immigration and socioeconomic characteristics of the respondents (O'Rourke 2006; Mayda 2004; O'Rourke and Sinnott 2006) as well as their attitudes toward imports (O'Rourke and Sinnott 2001; O'Rourke 2006; Mayda and Rodrik 2005). The regressions in table 9.4 follow their lead but with some differences.[8] Most important, we replace country dummies (country fixed effects) with a number of country-specific variables that allow us to assign explicit explanations to country differences in public attitudes. These country-specific variables are especially relevant

Table 9.4
The Determinants of Anti-Imports and Anti-Immigration Attitudes, 1995

Explanatory Variable	Anti-Immigration Opinion	Anti-Imports Opinion
Individual-Level Variables		
"Patriotism"	0.055 (1.81)	0.201 (7.39)
"Chauvinism"	0.374 (8.23)	0.397 (13.7)
Foreign-born	−0.035 (0.32)	−0.130 (1.99)
Second-generation immigrant	−0.283 (6.21)	0.085 (2.11)
Female	0.035 (1.13)	0.304 (11.3)
Age/100	0.009 (0.07)	−0.001 (1.08)
Married	0.038 (1.77)	0.029 (1.40)
Highly educated	−0.219 (7.13)	−0.280 (7.32)
Employed	−0.008 (0.51)	−0.032 (1.07)
Country-Level Variables		
Log GDP per capita	0.692 (2.58)	−0.294 (0.57)
Inequality	1.850 (2.26)	4.043 (2.23)
Log population	0.077 (1.51)	−0.072 (0.64)
Welfare expenditure/GDP	0.047 (7.26)	—
Share of population foreign	0.044 (3.13)	—
Imports/GDP	—	0.006 (0.28)
OECD trade/GDP	—	−0.009 (0.93)
R^2	0.207	0.219
No. of observations	14,820	14,820

Sources: 1995 ISSP data (see table 9.3 source). Sources for the country-specific variables are as follows: population and real GDP per capita at constant 1996 U.S. dollars, purchasing power parity adjusted, from A. Heston, R. Summers, and B. Aten, Penn World Table Version 6.1, Center for International Comparisons at the University of Pennsylvania (CICUP), October 2002, ⟨http://pwt.econ.upenn.edu/php_site/pwt61_form.php⟩. For inequality, Gini coefficients are taken from the World Bank's World Development Indicators, 2003, table 2.8, 64–66, ⟨http://www.worldbank.org/data/wdi2000/pdfs/tab2_8.pdf⟩. Welfare expenditure/GDP, imports/GDP, and OECD trade/GDP are from the World Bank's Global Development Network databases (government finance and macro time series), ⟨http://www.worldbank.org/research/growth/GDNdata.htm⟩. The share of foreign nationals in the population is taken from the Council of Europe's Demographic Yearbook, 2001, ⟨http://www.coe.int/t/e/social_cohesion/population/demographic_year_book/2001_Edition/default.asp⟩, and for non-European countries from Migration Information Source, ⟨http://www.migrationinformation.org/⟩. The numbers for countries for which only foreign-born data are available (as distinct from foreign nationals) were adjusted downward accordingly. All variables are for 1995 or the closest year available.
Notes: The countries included are those listed in table 9.3. The number of observations is reduced because data are missing for some of the individual-level explanatory variables. *t*-statistics in parentheses are from robust standard errors clustered by country.

to the preceding discussion about the evolution of policy since the mid-nineteenth century, but we are able to include only a few, given the limited number of countries in the ISSP sample. The results are displayed in table 9.4, with robust standard errors clustered by country.

Following O'Rourke and Sinnott (2006), we characterize prejudice against things foreign by the variables labeled "patriotism" and "chauvinism." Patriotism is measured by the average response to three questions that elicit the extent to which the individual believes that his or her country is superior to others. Chauvinism is measured by the average response to four questions that capture the individual's sense of loyalty to his or her country.[9] Both columns in table 9.4 illustrate that these variables contribute strongly and positively to individual anti-immigration and anti-imports sentiment. They provide compelling evidence that this kind of prejudice is an important component of individual attitudes.[10]

Relative to nonimmigrants, first-generation immigrants are opposed to immigration and imports, and second-generation immigrants strongly favor immigration but oppose expanding imports. Females have stronger anti-trade opinion than males, and age has very marginal effects in both equations. Consistent with other studies, the highly educated are less opposed to both immigration and imports. While they may have more enlightened views than the less educated, they may also suffer less from competition from low-skilled workers and may therefore fear immigration less. Being employed also lowers anti-immigration attitudes, but the effect is relatively small and not significant in either equation.[11]

The remaining variables in table 9.4 are the country-specific effects (taking one value for each country). The log of GDP per capita is strongly positive in the equation for immigration opinion but not in the equation for imports opinion. This is consistent with the view that immigration depends on absolute advantage, whereas trade depends on comparative advantage. Thus, individual attitudes are more anti-immigration in a richer country with a greater absolute income gap between it and potential source countries. The level of inequality has a positive effect on both types of opinion. This is consistent with Timmer and Williamson's (1998) finding that rising immigration restrictions after the 1880s were positively correlated with rising inequality and with falling source-relative-to-destination-country incomes (table 9.1). The population variable controls for country size, but it has opposite effects on opinion toward immigration and to imports, and it is not significant in either equation.[12]

Variables specific to the immigration opinion equation are the share of expenditure on welfare in GDP and the share of the population that is foreign nationals. Both of these have strong positive effects. Thus, the higher the percentage of foreign nationals in the population and the more generous the welfare net, the more public opinion opposes immigration. High levels of immigration have been associated with immigration from relatively poor source countries, and this, combined with generous destination country welfare systems, makes immigrants a bigger perceived fiscal threat to the median voter.[13]

In the imports opinion equation, we include the ratio of imports to GDP and the ratio of OECD trade (imports plus exports) to GDP. Import penetration has the expected positive sign—more imports are associated with more trade opposition—but with very low significance. We expect the coefficient on the OECD trade ratio to take on a negative sign (in the presence of the variable for overall imports penetration) because trade among rich countries is taken to be far less damaging to unskilled labor. The result is consistent with that prediction, but the coefficient is insignificant. In short, economywide variables seem to matter much less for imports than for immigration.

As we noted earlier, the fact that opposition to imports is nearly as intense as opposition to immigration seems inconsistent with observed policy outcomes. That puzzle can be resolved, at least in part, once we recognize that the share of immigrants strongly influences public opinion, whereas the trade share does not. If there is a political threshold beyond which negative opinion is translated into policy action, then immigration policy ought to be more restrictive than trade policy in order to gain similar levels of public acceptance. In the data underlying table 9.4, the mean ratio of foreign nationals to population is 6 percent, whereas the mean level of imports to GDP is a little more than 29 percent. Although these ratios are not really fully comparable, they are useful for illustration. If the foreign nationals share were raised by 23 percentage points (from 6 to 29 percent), then anti-immigration opinion would increase by $23 \times 0.044 = 1.01$. Thus, public opinion would become more negative by one full unit on a 1–5 scale. A smaller increase in foreign nationals share, say, 10 percentage points (well within the range of the data) would still increase anti-immigrant opinion by 0.44 units, which is greater than the standard deviation of the country means in table 9.3 (0.34). By contrast, policies that increase the import share by 10 percentage points would have only small effects given that the coefficient on the imports/GDP ratio is small and insignificant. Hence, the political costs of liberalization seem to be much greater for immigration than for trade.

Trade and Immigration Policies, Then and Now

We observe a policy paradox for labor-scarce economies in 1900—restricted trade but unrestricted immigration. We observe a policy paradox again today—restricted immigration but unrestricted trade. What accounts for the policy paradox, and why the switch?

We have argued that the progressive toughening of immigration policy and the progressive liberalization of tariff policy can be explained by a combination of factors. When the costs and risks of intercontinental migration were large, the "threat" of low-skilled immigration was muted because few could finance the move. Changes in the immigrant mix toward poorer source countries plus the increase in numbers of immigrants were the underlying anti-immigrant fundamentals at work, whereas macroeconomic shocks were the events that dictated the timing of the sharp changes toward more restrictive policies. As the gap between poor sending and rich receiving countries increased, the relative quality of the immigrants fell and their quantity rose, forcing tougher policy. Nineteenth-century immigrants might not have been a burden on the welfare state, but they certainly competed in labor markets with native-born workers because immigrant skills were so similar to the average native-born. The policy backlash was muted in some countries by a limited franchise and delayed in others by developmental coalitions and party politics. But eventually the backlash hit everywhere.

Today, country differences in anti-immigration opinion are driven by the scale of immigration, which represents the labor market threat; the size of the welfare state, which represents the potential welfare burden; and the universal franchise, which assures that those concerns are reflected in tough immigration policies. On the face of it, the puzzle might seem to be that public opinion isn't *more* negative toward immigration. Two explanations account for the puzzle. First, public opinion would be much more negative if immigration policies were more liberal. Second, the median voter today is far less threatened by labor market competition than the median worker was a century ago. As table 9.4 shows, the richer the country, the more anti-immigrant is public opinion, but more highly educated individuals are less anti-immigrant in attitude. The facts that the median voter is no longer unskilled and that the gap between the skills of native-born and immigrants has been widening offer important reasons that opinion isn't even more negative and immigration policies aren't even tougher than they are.

What about trade policies? Research has shown that they were much more restrictive in the past than has often been recognized, especially in labor-scarce economies. Why isn't the same true today? While the revenue motive was paramount in the nineteenth century, that imperative waned as revenue sources widened in the twentieth century. But that fact cannot fully explain the evolution from the high tariffs in the past to the low tariffs in the present. After all, there are other motives for protection besides revenue needs. Indeed, the results in table 9.4 suggest that anti-imports opinion is driven by much the same individual characteristics that determine anti-immigrant opinion. Thus, what applies to immigration also applies to imports: the median voter who is no longer unskilled faces less of a threat from the low-skilled labor embodied in imports from relatively poor countries. While "prejudice" does just as much damage to imports opinion as it does to immigration opinion, why should it change? The real difference between attitudes (and policies) toward imports and immigration cannot lie with "prejudice."

Some clues about the underlying fundamentals at work can be found in table 9.4. First, anti-immigration sentiment increases with the scale of immigration but anti-imports sentiment does not increase with the scale of imports, or at least not nearly as much. True, an increase in imports hurts some more than others: using the ISSP data, Mayda and Rodrik (2005) find that those who are employed in import-competing industries are substantially more anti-imports than those who are not. Indeed, those who have skills specific to export sectors might be expected to gain. One reason why tariffs were so high a century ago and are so low today is that the median voter is so different. Today there is a balance across voters between those who lose and those who gain from trade, because trade is more intraindustry than it was a century ago. Hence, an increase in imports has a more mixed effect on public opinion today than it did a century ago.

Second, higher GDP makes opinion more anti-immigration but not more anti-imports. The richer the country, the greater the immigration "threat" from low-income countries. For those well below the skills of the median voter, the threat is labor market competition. For the median voter, however, the threat is the fiscal implications of the welfare state. This part of the threat is far greater now than it was a century ago because of the rise of the welfare state and the fact that the poverty trap, which in the past held emigrants back in their poor sending countries, has been released, thus vastly widening the pool of potential poor and less skilled immigrants compared with the native-born.

Notes

We are grateful to Toke Aidt, Pieter Bevelander, Roger Bourque, Don DeVoretz, Peter Lindert, Jim Robinson, Ken Sokoloff, and Georgios Tassoukis for help with the data underlying this chapter. For useful comments on an earlier draft, we also acknowledge Jeff Frieden, Kevin O'Rourke, and Alan Taylor as well as participants at the 2005 New Comparative Economic History conference and the Harvard Political Economy lunch discussion group.

1. In addition to the United States, the countries included are three members of the European industrial core (France, Germany, United Kingdom); three English-speaking European offshoots (Australia, Canada, New Zealand); ten from the industrially lagging European periphery (Austria-Hungary, Denmark, Greece, Italy, Norway, Portugal, Russia, Serbia, Spain, Sweden); ten from the Asian and the Middle Eastern periphery (Burma, Ceylon, China, Egypt, India, Indonesia, Japan, the Philippines, Siam, Turkey); and eight from the Latin American periphery (Argentina, Brazil, Chile, Colombia, Cuba, Mexico, Peru, Uruguay).

2. Average tariff rates fell during the two World Wars. Most tariffs were imposed as specific duties a century ago, that is, cents per pound and yen per yard, not *ad valorem*, that is, percent of the total franc value. Thus, during inflation, the duties collected per value imported dropped as the value of the import rose, so the imputed *ad valorem* tariff rate fell. During postwar deflation, the opposite was true, when *ad valorem* tariff rates rose to resume their prewar levels.

3. The U.S. Congress did not debate immigration until the 1890s, when the numbers from the poorer parts of Europe began to surge. When incipient flows from poorer regions such as China and Japan began to offer an immigration "threat" to the West Coast of North America (the western U.S. states and British Columbia), exclusion was swift and decisive. Thus, the United States enacted the Chinese Exclusion Act as early as 1882.

4. The ratios in the bottom half of table 9.1 can be compared with those calculated by the OECD (2000, 191) for a larger set of countries for the single year 1997: Australia, 60.7; Belgium, 77.7; Canada, 44.4; Denmark, 70.4; Finland, 43.4; France, 28.3; Germany, 47.1; Italy, 40.8; Japan, 43.2; Netherlands, 73.4; Norway, 71.8, Sweden, 90.1; Switzerland, 76.3; United Kingdom, 71.5; United States, 22.0.

5. In the United States and elsewhere, those moving to the rural interior after mid-century were not necessarily immigrants, but immigration was nevertheless important. In an earlier study, we found that for every hundred immigrants to states in New England, the Mid-Atlantic, and East North Central, 40 nonimmigrants were displaced and moved west (Hatton and Williamson 1998, 167–169).

6. Several countries introduced a dictation test ahead of the United States. It was one of the first Acts of the newly federated Australian Commonwealth, and because the language was English (strictly speaking, it was at the discretion of the Immigration Officer), this formed the basis of what became known as the White Australia Policy.

7. Centeno (1997) lists 33 major international and civil wars between 1819 and 1880, although this excludes numerous small and medium-scale internal conflicts and a number of costly international wars.

8. Here we present ordinary least-squares regressions in order to facilitate comparison of the coefficients across the two different dependent variables; ordered probit regressions produced qualitatively similar results.

9. These variable clusters are those identified by O'Rourke and Sinnott (2006) using principal components analysis.

10. These variables do not capture racial attitudes directly; these are investigated for the United Kingdom by Dustmann and Preston (2004).

11. Following previous studies we also considered interacting the education dummy with the country's GDP per capita and with the country's inequality, but these interactions never proved to be significant when the country-level variables were also separately included, and hence they were eliminated.

12. The population variable was included in order to capture scale effects. For small countries the optimal, or acceptable, trade and immigration ratios may be higher, so the effect of scale is predicted to be positive (a given level of immigrant/imports penetration is less acceptable, the larger the country).

13. This interpretation is consistent with that of Facchini and Mayda (2006). Using the ISSP data, they find that high-income individuals are more opposed to immigration where the welfare state is large and where immigration is relatively unskilled.

References

Aidt, T. S., J. Dutta, and E. Loukoianova. 2006. Democracy Comes to Europe: Franchise Extension and Fiscal Outcomes, 1830–1938. *European Economic Review* 50: 249–283.

Boeri, T., G. Hanson, and B. McCormick, eds. 2002. *Immigration Policy and the Welfare System.* Oxford: Oxford University Press.

Centeno, M. A. 1997. Blood and Debt: War and Taxation in Nineteenth Century Latin America. *American Journal of Sociology* 102: 1565–1605.

Coatsworth, J. H., and J. G. Williamson. 2004a. Always Protectionist? Latin American Tariffs from Independence to Great Depression. *Journal of Latin American Studies* 36: 205–232.

———. 2004b. The Roots of Latin American Protectionism: Looking before the Great Depression. In *Integrating the Americas: FTAA and Beyond,* ed. A. Estevadeordal, D. Rodrik, A. M. Taylor, and A. Velasco. Cambridge, Mass.: Harvard University Press.

Dustmann, C., and I. Preston. 2004. Racial and Economic Factors in Attitudes to Immigration. IZA Discussion Paper 190. ⟨http://www.iza.org/⟩.

Engerman, S. L., and K. L. Sokoloff. 2000. History Lessons: Institutions, Factor Endowments, and Paths of Development in the New World. *Journal of Economic Perspectives* 14: 217–232.

———. 2005. The Evolution of Suffrage Institutions in the New World. *Journal of Economic History* 65: 891–921.

Facchini, G., and A. M. Mayda. 2006. Individual Attitudes towards Immigrants: Welfare-State Determinants across Countries. ⟨http://www.georgetown.edu/faculty/amm223/FacchiniMaydaWelfareImm05092006.pdf⟩.

Faini, R., J. de Melo, and K. F. Zimmermann, eds. 1999. *Migration: The Controversies and the Evidence.* Cambridge: Cambridge University Press.

Ferenczi, I., and W. F. Willcox. 1929. *International Migrations.* Vol. I. New York: National Bureau of Economic Research.

Goldin, C. 1994. The Political Economy of Immigration Restriction in the United States, 1890–1921. In *The Regulated Economy: A Historical Approach to Political Economy,* ed. C. Goldin and G. D. Libecap. Chicago: University of Chicago Press.

Hatton, T. J. 2000. How Much Did Immigrant Quality Decline in Late Nineteenth Century America? *Journal of Population Economics* 13: 509–525.

———. 2005. Explaining Trends in UK Immigration. *Journal of Population Economics* 18: 719–740.

Hatton, T. J., and J. G. Williamson. 1998. *The Age of Mass Migration: Causes and Economic Impact.* New York: Oxford University Press.

———. 2005. *Global Migration and the World Economy: Two Centuries of Policy and Performance.* Cambridge, Mass: MIT Press.

Hillman, A. L., and A. Weiss. 1999. Beyond International Factor Movements: Cultural Preferences, Endogenous Policies and the Migration of People. In *Migration: The Controversies and the Evidence,* ed. R. Faini, J. de Melo, and K. F. Zimmermann, 76–91. Cambridge: Cambridge University Press.

Hoynes, H., M. Page, and A. Stevens. 2005. Poverty in America: Trends and Explanations. NBER (National Bureau of Economic Research) Working Paper 11681. ⟨http://www.nber .org/papers/W11681⟩.

Irwin, D. A. 2002. The Early Trade Policy Experience of the United States, 1789–1820. Unpublished paper, Dartmouth College.

———. 2006. Antebellum Tariff Politics: Coalition Formation and Credible Commitments. NBER Working Paper 12161. ⟨http://www.nber.org/papers/W12161⟩.

Lindert, P. H. 2004. *Growing Public: Social Spending and Economics Growth since the Eighteenth Century.* Cambridge: Cambridge University Press.

Maddison, A. 1995. *Monitoring the World Economy, 1820–1992.* Paris: OECD.

———. 2001. *The World Economy: A Millennial Perspective.* Paris: OECD.

Markusen, J. R. 1983. Factor Movements and Commodity Trade as Complements. *Journal of International Economics* 13: 341–356.

Mayda, A. M. 2004. Who Is Against Immigration? A Cross-Country Investigation of Individual Attitudes toward Immigrants. IZA Discussion Paper 1115. ⟨http://www.iza.org/⟩.

Mayda, A. M., and D. Rodrik. 2005. Why Are Some People (and Countries) More Protectionist Than Others? *European Economic Review* 49: 1393–1430.

Mundell, R. A. 1957. International Trade and Factor Mobility. *American Economic Review* 47: 321–335.

OECD (Organisation for Economic Cooperation and Development). 2000. *Economic Outlook.* Paris.

O'Rourke, K. H. 2006. Heckscher-Ohlin Theory and Individual Attitudes Towards Globalization. In *Eli Heckscher, International Trade, and Economic History*, ed. R. Findlay, R. Henriksson, H. Lindgren, and M. Lundahl. Cambridge, Mass.: MIT Press.

O'Rourke, K. H., and R. Sinnott. 2001. What Determines Attitudes Towards Protection? In *Brookings Trade Forum 2001*, ed. S. M. Collins and D. Rodrik. Washington: Brookings Institution.

———. 2006. The Determinants of Individual Attitudes Towards Immigration. *European Journal of Political Economy* 22: 838–861.

Pomfret, R. 1981. *The Economic Development of Canada.* Toronto: Methuen.

Rogowski, R. 1989. *Commerce and Coalitions: How Trade Affects Domestic Political Alignments.* Princeton, N.J.: Princeton University Press.

Smith, J. P., and B. Edmonston, eds. 1997. *The New Americans: Economic, Demographic and Fiscal Effects of Immigration.* Washington: National Academy Press.

Timmer, A., and J. G. Williamson. 1998. Immigration Policy Prior to the 1930s: Markets, Policy Interactions, and Globalization Backlash. *Population and Development Review* 24: 739–771.

United Nations. 2002. *International Migration Report 2002.* New York.

Wellisch, D., and U. Walz. 1998. Why Do Rich Countries Prefer Free Trade over Free Migration? The Role of the Modern Welfare State. *European Economic Review* 42: 1592–1612.

Williamson, J. G. 2004. *The Political Economy of World Mass Migration: Comparing Two Global Centuries.* Washington: American Enterprise Institute.

———. 2006a. Explaining World Tariffs, 1870–1938: Stolper-Samuelson, Strategic Tariffs, and State Revenues. In *Eli Heckscher, International Trade, and Economic History*, ed. R. Findlay, R. Henriksson, H. Lindgren, and M. Lundahl. Cambridge, Mass.: MIT Press.

———. 2006b. *Globalization and the Poor Periphery before the Modern Era: The 2004 Ohlin Lectures.* Cambridge, Mass.: MIT Press.

10 Breaking the Fetters: Why Did Countries Exit the Interwar Gold Standard?

Holger C. Wolf and Tarik M. Yousef

Seventy years on, the scholarly debate on the causes of the Great Depression still fertilizes the contemporary policy debate. Over time, the foci and interpretations have markedly shifted. Most notably, the early U.S.-centric view has given way to a comparative inquiry in the tradition of Jeffrey Williamson, emphasizing systemic factors causing, propagating, and deepening the global recession. The monetary standard has naturally figured prominently among these systemic factors, charged with increasing susceptibility to international monetary shocks and depriving authorities of policy options to combat the deepening slump.

Indirect but compelling evidence on the restrictive nature of the standard is provided by the economic rebound enjoyed by most countries choosing to shed their "golden fetters" (Eichengreen and Sachs 1985; Campa 1990). Yet the evident benefits accruing to quitters proved unconvincing. Most governments retained gold and suffered deflation and recession. Many periphery countries were additionally hit by terms of trade declines and rising real indebtedness in the face of shrinking capital inflows. The choice of prolonged voluntary suffering is puzzling. Why, as Eichengreen (1992) asked, did countries stay "wedded to gold for so long...why were some more inclined than others to release their gold fetters?"

The answer is likely to be multifaceted, reflecting the multiple economic and political considerations shaping exchange rate regime choices. Intellectual conservatism certainly played a role. Resorting to the orthodox tools of deflation came naturally to most central bankers. The eventual exit of Britain, the intellectual standard bearer, was thus a shock, not just to the global economy but to the prevailing mentality (Eichengreen and Temin 2000). Yet a changing mentality—and for that matter any systemic feature—cannot be the whole story. Some countries quit well before Britain, eschewing the prevailing view. Others remained on gold long after Britain's departure had dealt orthodoxy a fatal blow. Conventional economic considerations are likely to provide another part of the answer (Hamilton 1987; Bernanke 1995). Certainly, industrialized countries blessed with ample reserves enjoyed greater discretion about their regime choice compared to reserve-poor developing countries facing adverse terms of trade shocks and dwindling capital inflows, and small open economies dependent on a dominant trading partner had little choice but to mimic the partner's choice.

While particulars differed, most countries enjoyed some nontrivial autonomy in choosing their exchange rate regime based on perceived trade-offs between the benefits of adherence and their costs in terms of prolonging deflation, recession, and political instability. A small empirical literature explores the factors influencing this choice, with a primary focus on the core countries (Zimmermann and Saalfeld 1988; Simmons 1994; Wandschneider 2005). The field, however, remains sparsely ploughed in comparison with the rich comparative literature on the economics of the period. In particular, little is known about the political economy of choices in the (non-European) periphery, a primary focus of our inquiry into the global dimensions of policymaking during this period.

We are fortunate in being able to draw on a rich conceptual framework developed over the last two decades by noted economic historians, including Michael Bordo, Carlos Díaz-Alejandro, Barry Eichengreen, Charles Kindleberger, Harold James, and Peter Temin, fruitfully complemented by a political science literature exploring the episode (Gourevitch 1984; Weir and Skocpol 1985; Drake 1989; Hall 1989; Simmons 1994; Berman 1998). The explanations advanced in these twin literatures are broadranging, encompassing the economic, social, and political spheres and emphasizing conditions at the country level as well as international factors, including financial shocks, social and government stability, international leadership, intellectual dogma, and the legacy of history.

In this chapter we take a Williamsonian comparative approach employing a rich data set covering close to 40 countries from the center and periphery to explore the relative importance of alternative determinants of regime choice. We begin with a condensed review of the debate, providing a background for developing four testable hypotheses. First, did countries with comparatively poor economic performance depart sooner? Second, did the combination of rising costs of signaling credibility and shrinking benefits from the "good housekeeping seal of approval" prompt borrowers to exit? Third, did national and systemic attachment to gold play a role? Finally, did the domestic political environment condition the exit decision?

The Rise and Fall of the Interwar Gold Standard

The classical gold standard ended with the suspension of convertibility and gold shipments following the outbreak of World War I. The suspension was expected to be temporary, to be reversed once hostilities ceased, consistent with the traditional contingency rule (Bordo and Schwartz 1994). Despite the unexpected length of the war, and its human and economic costs, an eventual return to gold remained a near-instinctive goal when the war finally drew to a close. Implementation proved difficult, however; by late 1919 only five countries had resumed convertibility. For most others, the return to gold proved difficult, whether it was because as newly independent countries they lacked reserves; or because of sustained fiscal problems, often reflecting social spending claims by the enlarged electorate; or because cumulative inflation prevented a return at the desired (prewar) parity or even led into outright hyperinflation (James 2001).

Restoring the International Financial System

Despite these difficulties, no credible alternative to the gold standard gained traction. The debates in Brussels and Genoa, while acknowledging and indeed occasioned by the difficulties facing many countries, illustrate the underlying consensus on the ultimate goal of reestablishing the gold link (Bordo, Edelstein, and Rockoff 1999), albeit with different motivations.

For Austria, Germany, and the other hyper- and high-inflation countries, the gold standard underpinned policy credibility and promised assurance against a relapse into fiscal profligacy, whereas in Britain the restoration of the gold standard at the prewar parity was closely intertwined with identity issues in the wake of U.S. ascendance.

For countries in the periphery, the trade-offs were multifaceted. As exporters of primary products prone to volatile terms of trade movements, these countries found strict adherence to gold prima facie less appealing (Blattman, Hwang, and Williamson 2004). Yet voluntarily donning the golden shackles while maintaining tight fiscal control—the model of the League of Nations stabilization loans, and the core program recommended by influential advisors such as Kemmerer[1]—promised compensating benefits by conferring the "good housekeeping seal of

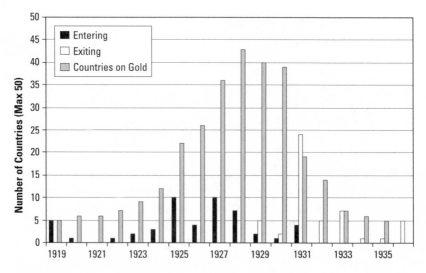

Figure 10.1
Entry and exit from the interwar gold standard, 1919–1936.

approval," facilitating access to the financial markets in London and New York and easing the task of attracting foreign direct investment (Yeager 1984; Bordo and Rockoff 1996).

Returning to gold thus simultaneously authenticated orthodox ideas of the era, satisfied the interests of international bankers, and legitimized proposals favored by ruling elites facing domestic opposition (Drake 1989).

As figure 10.1 shows, over time the golden lure coupled with an improving global economic outlook enabled a growing number of governments to vanquish domestic obstacles and join the emerging interwar gold standard. While only 7 countries joined between 1920 and 1924, 31 took the plunge in the next four years, bringing membership to a peak of 43 at the end of 1928.[2] Almost all classical gold standard members had now joined and so had the majority of newly independent states. The universal popularity of gold was, however, short-lived. Although three more countries joined the following year, 1929 also saw the first five exits.

At its peak the spatial and economic reach of the interwar standard matched its predecessor. Yet, as Keynes noted, the world had changed, and with it the economic and political framework encompassing the monetary system.[3] On a systemic level, the standard now rested on two central currencies while the leadership position once occupied by the Bank of England remained vacant (Kindleberger 1986). Specie shortages, aggravated by the failure of surplus countries to recycle gold, prompted increasing reliance on convertible foreign currency reserves, sidestepping the immediate problem of reserve shortage at the cost of enhanced fragility if the convertibility promise of the reserve currencies were to come into doubt, as happened in 1931 (Triffin 1947).

Economically, the increasing role played by organized labor, coupled with greater product differentiation and cartelization, reduced both wage and price flexibility, disabling a crucial adjustment channel (Eichengreen 1992). The rise of labor as a potent political force eroded support for the defense of the parity as the unquestioned monetary policy goal. Buttressed by the increased attention given by Cassel, Hawtrey, Keynes, and other prominent economists to the links between money and activity, employment stimulation emerged as a rival monetary policy objective, reducing support for international cooperation carrying perceived costs in terms of domestic employment and reducing the benefits of adherence to the standard (Simmons 1996).[4]

The Collapse of the Interwar Standard
Collectively, changed structures and objectives introduced a structural weakness into the interwar gold standard (Bordo and Eichengreen 1998). While temporarily camouflaged in the mid to late 1920s by robust growth and ample international capital flows, the inherent frailty soon became apparent in the wake of three re-enforcing shocks.

The slow demise began with the monetary tightening in the United States, forcing deficit countries to (belatedly) tackle their imbalances (Eichengreen and Portes 1986). Declining capital flows also eroded the perceived reward received by emerging countries in return for donning the golden fetters.[5] A first group of countries in the Americas—Argentina, Brazil, Canada, Paraguay, and Uruguay—responded to the changed incentives by abandoning gold in 1929. For a little while, they remained the exception as central banks in both mature and emerging economies resorted to the much impaired traditional tool of disinflation coupled with protectionism in an increasingly desperate ploy to defend the parity.[6]

The second act of the unfolding drama took place in Europe. Faced with an impending collapse of its banking system, the Austrian government guaranteed the deposits of the failing Creditanstalt, placing the convertibility promise in doubt. Whether at this point a speedy international loan might have stopped the crisis in time and sent a signal of systemic solidarity will remain an open question. In the event, no such support was forthcoming. Austria de facto exited the system, highlighting the absence of an effective multilateral support system and illustrating the resulting scarcity of policy options for countries perceived to be vulnerable.

Contagion was fast and furious. Within weeks, the Austrian crisis had spilled over to neighboring Germany.[7] With the gold standard in its death throes in both countries, attention shifted to Britain. A remarkably short two months after Germany's de facto exit, Britain succumbed. Unlike the prior departures, the British decision to exit—after having struggled so valiantly (if perhaps unwisely) to restore the prewar parity—irreparably harmed the gold standard mystique. With the Lord Keeper of the Seal itself ignominiously forced off gold, the credibility costs for periphery countries shedding their fetters evaporated; most countries in the British sphere of influence left with sterling,[8] a pattern repeated two years later when the United States exited.

In the periphery, the demise of the mentality had profound effects. As Díaz-Alejandro (1984) notes, "The disastrous news from the rest of the world...made policy-makers and informed opinion feel not only that local conditions were not so bad, after all, but also that no one knew, in Centre or Periphery, exactly what were the roots of the crisis nor how it could be overcome. After a terrible fright, this stimulated an almost exhilarated creativity. The old authorities and rules on economic policy were shattered. It was a time calling for reliance on one's discretion."

In the center, identification with the standard went deeper, and the shock of its collapse was more traumatic. The gold bloc mounted a spirited if ultimately futile defense, while the countries ingloriously forced off gold seemed paralyzed: in contrast to the "exhilarated creativity" of the newly unshackled emerging markets, uncertainty and risk aversion characterized the post-exit period of core countries as policymakers proved reluctant to plunder the newly available monetary policy armory to fight deflation (Simmons 1994).[9] The switch to "neo-orthodox" policies of devaluation, tariffs, and cartels in some countries and the rise of demand stimulation in others was slow and, absent a coordinated global expansionary policy, often took the form of beggar-thy-neighbor policies (Gourevitch 1984; Eichengreen 1992).

Despite the rather feeble use of the monetary arsenal, countries leaving the gold standard enjoyed economic recovery, while those remaining tethered to gold found themselves mired in unremitting economic depression (Eichengreen and Sachs 1985; Campa 1990; Eichengreen 1992; Eichengreen and Temin 2000). Combined with the adverse real exchange rate effects of devaluations elsewhere, the cost of retaining gold rose as more countries exited: the positive network effects supporting broad adoption (Meissner 2005) came into play on the downswing as well. With a delay, the experience of the escapees was not lost on those still on gold. "In the end, what led to that system's downfall was not just agitation on the left but the challenge to the hegemony of gold-standard ideology from the fact of economic and financial distress" (Eichengreen and Temin 2000, 201).

Toward a Political Economy of Policymaking

A large and productive literature examines the causes and consequences of the interwar gold standard and its eventual collapse.[10] We focus on one aspect of this debate: the timing and causes of the exit. By revealed preference, authorities in many countries who had initially thought it optimal to join the gold standard within a decade decided to exit. The decision was far from trivial: choosing to depart implied a sharp break with long-standing norms and policy practices. Yet in the end all governments exited the gold standard. What factors triggered the change? We explore the relative contribution of four factors: economic shocks, changed benefits from adherence, political developments, and shifting global fashions. Specifically, we propose and examine four testable hypotheses.

H1: Adverse domestic and external economic shocks, monetary and real, accelerated the exit from the gold standard.

Collapsing world trade, deflationary impulses, and for developing countries, adverse terms of trade shocks (Corbo 1992) contributed to the deepening global recession of the early 1930s and to frequent currency and banking crises. While endogenous to policy choices on the global level—notably the initially orthodox monetary policies adopted in the core—the decline in international trade and lending was largely exogenous for individual countries, particularly in the periphery. Thus, we explore whether countries suffering particularly acute adverse shocks exited earlier to avail themselves of more expansionary policies (including devaluation) and an increased potency of the lender-of-last-resort capacity. The proxies for adverse shocks include per capita output growth, the inflation rate, and the percentage change in the terms of trade.

H2: The "good housekeeping seal of approval" motive weakened in the face of dwindling capital flows and rising credibility problems.

While offering relief from the external shocks and domestic contraction, exits were not costless. As Bordo, Edelstein, and Rockoff (1999) have argued, for periphery countries and others suffering from credibility problems, adherence to the golden rule served as a good housekeeping seal of approval, facilitating access to international capital. Over time the weight of this motive may have weakened, initially in 1929 when the diminution of capital outflows from the United States reduced the payoff to perceived policy discipline, and terminally when Britain herself exited, reducing the credibility signal of adherence.[11] In some countries, reduced (external) perceptions of the benefits of commitment and its collateral damage to credibility were in turn reflected in (and aggravated by) widening yield spreads and exchange rate pressures, tilting the balance further in favor of exiting the system (Eichengreen 2002). We explore this hypothesis by looking at the role of the level of capital exports from creditor nations, the end-year spread of the country's long-term government bond vis-à-vis the U.K. consol, and the percentage change in the dollar exchange rate of a country's currency.

H3: The erosion of global attachment to gold (the mentality) hastened the exit, accelerated by network effects, while domestic attachment reflecting prior history delayed the exit.

Like any near-global monetary regime, the interwar gold standard exhibited strong network effects, both through the credibility effect and through the traditional trade links. As Meissner (2005) argues in the case of the nineteenth-century gold standard, these network effects can play an important role in the adoption of a gold peg. Network effects operate on the downside as well. The 1931 exit of Austria, Germany, and Britain undermined the "good housekeeping seal" argument for belonging to the club.[12]

Their exit also struck a blow at the prevailing mentality.[13] The degree to which shifting opinion patterns influenced national choices arguably depended on the strength of the national support for gold as the "right" monetary standard. We examine the mentality and network effects by a dummy variable of whether the country experienced high inflation before joining, by the number of countries on the standard in a given year, and by a dummy variable indicating whether a country's main trading partners (up to two) exited the system.

H4: Political instability and the extension of the franchise weakened the ability of countries to remain on gold in the face of the economic downturn.

Keynes's emphasis on the domestic politics of exchange rate regime choice remains prominent in the debate. Two linked themes are particularly prominent. First, the extension of the franchise and the rise of organized labor, coupled with greater attention to the potential of countercyclical policy, elevated full employment to a rival policy objective and challenged the unquestioned dominance of the gold peg in the prewar system (James 2001). Second, political instability in various forms—extraconstitutional changes in government, riots and unrest, frequent turnover of constitutional governments, highly fragmented political systems—impeded durable policy commitments, including defense of the peg and, at times, a consensus for exit (Eichengreen and Simmons 1995). We explore the role of political factors by including controls for political unrest, government instability, and democracy.

Exploring the Timing of Exit Decisions

In 1929 most of the world operated on gold. By 1933 the majority of countries had left. What caused this rapid change in the cost-benefit calculus? We have outlined four hypotheses to answer this question. To test their empirical content, we rely on duration or survival analysis[14] to explore the role of alternative variables in explaining the timing of exit from the interwar gold standard for a sample of 49 countries that had joined the system by or after 1919.

Our empirical strategy resembles that used by Meissner (2005) to examine the diffusion of the classical gold standard and by Wandschneider (2005) to analyze adherence to the interwar gold standard.[15] The dependent variable is the length of time on the interwar gold standard. A country enters the empirical analysis once it joins the system and drops from the analysis once it exits (see appendix A). While data availability for the explanatory variables and the need to use lags to minimize the problem of endogeneity reduces the sample size, the full-sample regressions include on average 37 countries and 230 country-years. Appendix B defines the explanatory variables chosen to capture the thrust of the four hypotheses while ensuring maximum data coverage across the center and, more important, the periphery countries.

Basic Empirical Results

Table 10.1 reveals that less severe deflation and milder recession prolonged the duration, consistent with the view that the double challenge of deflation and recession (themselves linked) undermined the willingness to remain wedded to gold. Negative terms of trade shocks significantly reduced the duration, consistent with the observation that external

Table 10.1
Duration of Adherence and Economic Factors, 1919–1936

Explanatory Variable	Expected Sign	Full Sample (1)	(2)	Center (3)	Periphery (4)
Output growth	+	3.795[a] (1.711)	4.870[a] (1.83)	12.575[a] (5.457)	3.973[b] (2.046)
Inflation	+	8.728[a] (1.833)	8.394[a] (2.559)	3.25 (8.76)	9.291[a] (1.662)
Terms of trade change	+	—	2.875[a] (1.186)	5.937 (4.456)	2.336[a] (1.233)
No. of observations		227	151	74	77
No. of countries		37	27	10	17
Log likelihood		−32.84	−22.11	−7	−14.05
Wald chi-square(1)		31.31	33.49	23.12	34.42

Notes: Robust standard errors in parentheses.
a. Significant at 5 percent level.
b. Significant at 10 percent level.

pressures on the current account affected the cost-benefit calculus of remaining under gold. The importance of the variables varies across the center and periphery countries. For the former, only output growth matters, whereas all three shocks appear relevant for the periphery countries.

Table 10.2 turns the spotlight to credibility. As expected, the trend in international capital exports conditioned the timing of exit. For debtor countries, the reversal in flows put pressure on reserves or undermined external confidence in the credibility of adherence to gold. The two country-specific variables that capture credibility problems—a higher yield spread relative to the consol and downward pressure on the exchange rate[16]—shorten duration as expected. The results are similar across the center and the periphery except in the case of yield spread, which solely operates through the periphery countries.

Table 10.3 turns the focus to the network and mentality effects. A history of high inflation prior to entry extended the life of the interwar standard, particularly in the center.[17] The number of countries on gold, measuring both network and mentality aspects, enters significantly for the center and periphery. The trading partner effect, proxied by whether one of the two main trading partners has exited, enters negatively for both groups. As the main partner tends to be either Britain or the United States, this variable also captures the damage to the gold standard mentality.

Table 10.2
Duration of Adherence and Credibility, 1919–1936

Explanatory Variable	Expected Sign	Full Sample (1)	(2)	Center (3)	Periphery (4)
Capital exports	+	0.901[a] (0.085)	1.258[a] (0.259)	1.317[a] (0.434)	1.271[a] (0.337)
Exchange rate pressure	+	—	2.079[a] (0.731)	4.012[a] (1.393)	1.063[a] (0.577)
Yield spread	–	—	−0.007[a] (0.002)	0.109 (0.244)	−0.003[b] (0.001)
No. of observations		307	134	61	73
No. of countries		49	24	9	15
Log likelihood		−19.34	−8.43	−2.63	−4.98
Wald chi-square(1)		111.49	57.05	19.18	55.12

Notes: Robust standard errors in parentheses.
a. Significant at 5 percent level.
b. Significant at 10 percent level.

Table 10.3
Duration of Adherence, Networks, and the Mentality, 1919–1936

Explanatory Variable	Expected Sign	Full Sample (1)	(2)	Center (3)	Periphery (4)
High inflation history	+	13.426[a] (1.04)	13.339[a] (1.049)	14.546[a] (1.118)	—
No. of countries on gold	+	0.056[a] (0.008)	0.054[a] (0.009)	0.058[a] (0.018)	0.058[a] (0.014)
Main trading partner exits	–	—	−1.307[a] (0.225)	−1.020[a] (0.662)	−1.222[a] (0.323)
No. of observations		238	238	101	137
No. of countries		38	38	12	26
Log likelihood		−33.91	−28.18	−8.27	−18.39
Wald chi-square(1)		182.83	232.67	183.57	47.77

Notes: Robust standard errors in parentheses.
a. Significant at 5 percent level.

Table 10.4
Duration of Adherence, Instability, and the Franchise, 1919–1936

Explanatory Variable	Expected Sign	Full Sample		Center	Periphery
		(1)	(2)	(3)	(4)
Riots, strikes, demonstrations	–	−0.081[a]	−0.115[a]	−0.154[a]	−0.043
		(0.03)	(0.032)	(0.022)	(0.164)
Government instability	–	−0.156[b]	−0.164[b]	−0.021	−0.251[a]
		(0.086)	(0.077)	(0.121)	(0.073)
Democracy	–	—	0.833[a]	−1.93	0.542
			(0.3)	(1.578)	(0.395)
No. of observations		278	278	101	177
No. of countries		45	45	12	33
Log likelihood		−48.28	−46.62	−11.36	−34.11
Wald chi-square(1)		8.56	21.63	69.08	13.39

Notes: Robust standard errors in parentheses.
a. Significant at 5 percent level.
b. Significant at 10 percent level.

Table 10.4 focuses on the role of politics. Political unrest, captured by the incidence of riots, strikes, and demonstrations, contributes to an earlier demise of the gold standard. Government instability also reduces the duration of the gold standard. The first is more important in the center countries, the second more pronounced in the periphery. More democratic countries remained longer on gold. The effect of democracy, however, differs across the two groups.[18] The effect on the center is negative, as predicted, but for periphery countries the effect is positive, although in both cases it is insignificant when the sample is divided.

Putting the Pieces Together

In tables 10.1–10.4 we separately explored the support for the four hypotheses. We now draw them together. Doing so comes at the unavoidable cost of losing some observations but allows an inference on proxy effects in the previous results. To minimize the loss of observations, we drop some variables like the yield spread and the high inflation history, which are only available for a small subset of countries. Similarly, we drop the country-specific inflation rate, which, despite being lagged, is arguably endogenous to the monetary regime. Table 10.5 reports the results, adding one group of variables at a time to a base specification with GDP growth and terms of trade shocks (column 1).

The results provide support for all four hypotheses. Domestic economic performance remains highly significant even after the inclusion of other

Table 10.5
Exit Decision across Hypotheses, 1919–1936

Explanatory Variable	(1)	(2)	(3)	(4)	(5)
Output growth	4.011[a]	3.175[b]	3.696[a]	3.774[a]	3.267[a]
	(1.643)	(1.829)	(1.829)	(1.582)	(1.43)
Terms of trade change	2.627[a]	2.781[a]	2.273[a]	2.481[a]	1.798[b]
	(0.687)	(0.948)	(0.874)	(0.935)	(1.22)
Capital exports	—	0.786[a]	0.007	0.883[a]	0.900[a]
		(0.182)	(0.22)	(0.173)	(0.164)
Exchange rate pressure	—	3.497[a]	2.214[a]	4.631[a]	4.521[a]
		(0.872)	(0.994)	(1.488)	(1.5)
No. of countries on gold	—	—	0.073[a]	—	—
			(0.015)		
Main trading partner exits	—	—	−0.645[a]	−1.080[a]	−1.088[a]
			(0.278)	(0.217)	(0.223)
Riots, strikes, demonstrations	—	—	—	0.096[b]	0.076[b]
				(0.05)	(0.038)
Government instability	—	—	—	0.238[b]	0.261[a]
				(0.127)	(0.129)
Democracy	—	—	—	—	0.596[b]
					(0.39)
No. of observations	220	169	169	145	145
No. of countries	35	32	32	31	31
Log likelihood	−36.13	−17.71	−13.19	−12.9	−12.4
Wald chi-square(1)	16.22	74.01	65.61	67.75	100.43

Notes: Robust standard errors in parentheses.
a. Significant at 5 percent level.
b. Significant at 10 percent level.

determinants. Weaker GDP growth and negative terms of trade shocks are robustly associated with shorter duration, *ceteris paribus*. The credibility indicators also remain significant when added to the economic factors (column 2), as do the two variables capturing the network and the mentality effects (column 3). As the number of countries on gold is highly correlated with the trend in international capital exports, we drop this variable before adding the political variables (column 4).

The two measures of political instability and democracy are significant, although riots, strikes and demonstrations and government instability switch sign in columns 4 and 5 as compared with table 10.4. In other words, political instability is associated with longer duration after taking into account other determinants. This is consistent with the political economy literature emphasizing the negative impact of instability on policy reform.[19]

The results in table 10.5 reaffirm our earlier findings: the exit decision from the interwar standard cannot be reduced to a single factor; it reflected traditional economic shocks, network effects, the strength of the domestic and international adherence to the standard as well as political factors.[20]

Conclusions

In 1919 there was little disagreement among countries that a return to gold was the right policy option. Within a decade, membership in the interwar standard rivaled its prewar antecedent. But while the latter system prospered for decades, the interwar system crumbled as soon as it had reached its peak membership. Two years later, fewer than ten countries remained on gold, and these exited soon thereafter.

The dramatic reversal accompanied by a wrenching global crisis has stimulated a rich literature exploring the linkages between the gold standard, monetary and fiscal policies, and the Great Depression. A prominent strand identifies prolonged adherence to the "barbarous relic" as a major culprit in the spread and depth of the Depression. Yet this conclusion raises further questions. What explains the costly failure to exit? Why were some countries willing to adhere until the bitter end while others showed little reluctance in withdrawing?

Drawing on the rich literature, this chapter has explored four broad complementary hypotheses to explain the timing of exit decisions from the standard. We find that all four hypotheses are supported by the data, suggesting that monocausal explanations cannot do justice to the episode. Standard economic shocks play an important role: countries suffering more severely from deflation and recession were likely to leave earlier. Network effects and the domestic and global adherence to the gold standard played a separate role: countries with greater national commitment to gold remained longer, while the exit of a trading partner and the erosion of global adherence accelerated exits. Third, the perceived costs and benefits of adhering to the gold standard as a "good housekeeping seal" influenced decisions. Finally, political instability exerted a separate influence.

The results open new avenues for inquiry. Two appear to be of particular interest. First, the importance of factors beyond the orthodox determinants of exchange rate regime choice in terms of the exit choice raises the question whether the entry timing was likewise influenced by non-traditional factors. Second, we have but scratched the issue of political determinants of exchange rate regime choice.

Appendix A: Entry and Exit from the Interwar Gold Standard

The dependent variable in our empirical analysis is the length of time a country adhered to the interwar gold standard, measured in years. We must thus specify the dates of entry into and exit from the system. While this might seem straightforward, it is not in this instance. As Obstfeld and Taylor (2003) note, the coding of these dates for the interwar gold standard involves a degree of "greater subjective judgment."

Problems arise on both sides. To set the entry date, we have to choose between the time of de facto stabilization under a fixed rate with full convertibility and a de jure adoption, which in some countries never came (Officer 2001). Similarly, on the exit side, a choice arises between de jure exits and the adoption of policies, such as controls on convertibility or a devaluation, that violated "the rules of the game."

Fortunately we are able to rely on the exhaustive work undertaken by Kemmerer (1954) for 54 countries. Although he does not discuss his criteria in any detail, his coding (with a few exceptions) is consistent with information published by the League of Nations on major decisions affecting the gold standard as well as Officer's (2001) more recent compilation of dates for an even larger sample relying on multiple sources, including Kemmerer.

We code a country as leaving the gold standard in a given year if it either officially suspended the gold standard or depreciated the value of the currency during that year. In most cases, countries did both sequentially, and often these actions occurred with, or were followed soon after by, the imposition of exchange controls. If the decisions occurred in subsequent years, we code the earlier year as the exit year.

For six countries in the periphery—Brazil, Chile, Honduras, New Zealand, South Africa, and Uruguay—Kemmerer's dating is not consistent with this rule. For these cases, or when Kemmerer does not provide exit dates, we followed the coding by Officer (2001), which is also consistent with information provided by the League of Nations. Other small discrepancies between Kemmerer and Officer appear to be due to the treatment of intrayear changes: Kemmerer considered a country as being on the gold standard in a given year if it remained on gold for up to six months, whereas we code countries as entering or leaving the standard if

Table 10.A
Adherence of 50 Countries to the Interwar Gold Standard, 1919–1936

	Starting Date (Kemmerer)	Ending Date[a] (Kemmerer)	(Officer)
Argentina	1927	**1929**	1929
Australia	1925	**1929**	1930
Austria	1923	**1931**	1931
Belgium	1925	**1935**	1935
Bolivia	1928	**1931**	1931
Brazil	1927	1930	**1929**
Bulgaria	1927	**1931**	1931
Canada	1926	**1931**	1929
Chile	1926	1932	**1931**
Colombia	1923	**1931**	1932
Costa Rica	1922	**1932**	1932
Cuba	1919	**1933**	—
Czechoslovakia	1926	**1931**	1931
Denmark	1927	**1931**	1931
Ecuador	1927	**1932**	1932
Egypt	1925	**1931**	1931
El Salvador	1920	**1931**	1931
Estonia	1928	**1931**	1931
Finland	1926	**1931**	1931
France	1928	**1936**	1936
Germany	1924	**1931**	1931
Greece	1928	**1931**	1932
Guatemala	1924	**1933**	1933
Honduras	1931	1934	**1933**
Hungary	1925	**1931**	1931
India	1927	**1931**	1931
Indonesia	1925	**1936**	1936
Italy	1927	**1934**	1934
Japan	1930	**1931**	1931
Mexico	1925	**1931**	1931
Netherlands	1925	**1936**	1936
New Zealand	1929	1931	**1930**
Nicaragua	1919	**1931**	1932
Norway	1928	**1931**	1931
Panama	1919	**1933**	—

	Month-Year of Measures Affecting Exit (League of Nations)		
	Suspension of Gold Standard	Imposition of Exchange Control	Depreciation Relative to Gold
Argentina	Dec-29	Oct-31	Nov-29
Australia	Dec-29	—	Mar-30
Austria	Apr-33	Oct-31	Sep-31
Belgium	Mar-35	Mar-35	Mar-35
Bolivia	Sep-31	Oct-31	Mar-30
Brazil	—	May-31	Dec-29
Bulgaria	—	—	—
Canada	Oct-31	—	Sep-31
Chile	Apr-32	Jul-31	Apr-32
Colombia	Sep-31	Sep-31	Jan-32
Costa Rica	—	Jan-32	Jan-32
Cuba	Nov-33	Jun-34	Apr-33
Czechoslovakia	—	Oct-31	Feb-34
Denmark	Sep-31	Nov-31	Sep-31
Ecuador	Feb-32	May-32	Jun-32
Egypt	Sep-31	—	Sep-31
El Salvador	Oct-31	Aug-33	Oct-31
Estonia	Jun-33	Nov-31	Jun-33
Finland	Oct-31	—	Oct-31
France	—	—	Sep-36
Germany	—	Jul-31	—
Greece	Apr-32	Sep-31	Apr-32
Guatemala	—	—	Apr-33
Honduras	—	Mar-34	Apr-33
Hungary	—	Jul-31	—
India	Sep-31	—	Sep-31
Indonesia	Sep-36	—	Sep-36
Italy	—	May-34	Mar-34
Japan	Dec-31	Jul-32	Dec-31
Mexico	Jul-31	—	Aug-31
Netherlands	Sep-36	—	Sep-36
New Zealand	Sep-31	—	Apr-30
Nicaragua	Nov-31	Nov-31	Jan-32
Norway	Sep-31	—	Sep-31
Panama	—	—	Apr-33

Table 10.A
(continued)

	Starting Date (Kemmerer)	Ending Date[a]	
		(Kemmerer)	(Officer)
Paraguay	1927	—	**1929**
Peru	1931	**1932**	1932
Philippines	1919	**1933**	1933
Poland	1927	**1936**	1936
Portugal	—	—	**1931**
Romania	1929	**1932**	1932
Siam	1928	**1932**	1932
South Africa	1925	1931	**1933**
Sweden	1924	**1931**	1931
Switzerland	1925	**1936**	1936
United Kingdom	1925	**1931**	1931
United States	1919	**1933**	1933
Uruguay	1928	1932	**1929**
Venezuela	1927	**1930**	1930
Yugoslavia	1931	**1931**	—

Sources: Kemmerer (1954), Officer (2001), League of Nations.
Note:
a. In cases where the exit date provided by Kemmerer (1954) differs from the coding rule we follow, or where Kemmerer (1954) does not provide an exit date, we code the exit according to Officer (2001). These years are shown in boldface.

they change any time during the year. As a robustness test, we also use an alternative coding that drops the years of entry and exit and counts only years completely spent on the gold standard.

Before describing the data in more detail, it is worth emphasizing areas we do *not* address. First, we do not distinguish between de jure and de facto adoption of the gold standard, nor between countries on a gold, gold coin, or gold exchange standard. We thus do not address the quality of adherence to the interwar standard compared to the classical gold standard. Second, we do not formally model the adoption decisions, although some of the control variables we use, such as whether the country had operated under the classical gold standard or whether it suffered a hyperinflation, may have influenced exchange rate regime choices.

Rather, our sole focus is on the decision to sever policy attachment to the system, particularly for the underresearched group of periphery coun-

	Month-Year of Measures Affecting Exit (League of Nations)		
	Suspension of Gold Standard	Imposition of Exchange Control	Depreciation Relative to Gold
Paraguay	—	Aug-32	Nov-29
Peru	May-32	—	May-32
Philippines	—	—	Apr-33
Poland	—	Apr-36	1936
Portugal	Dec-31	Oct-22	Oct-31
Romania	—	May-32	Jul-35
Siam	May-32	—	Jun-32
South Africa	Dec-32	Jan-33	—
Sweden	Sep-31	—	Sep-31
Switzerland	—	—	Sep-36
United Kingdom	Sep-31	—	Sep-31
United States	Apr-33	Mar-33	Apr-33
Uruguay	Dec-29	Sep-31	Apr-29
Venezuela	—	Dec-36	Sep-30
Yugoslavia	—	Oct-31	Jul-32

tries. With these considerations in mind, table 10.A presents the entry and exit dates for 50 countries on the interwar gold standard. Trivially, countries that never joined the system (such as Russia) are excluded. Since we are concerned with the duration of membership in the system, our analysis time begins in 1919 and ends in 1936, when the last countries exited. Definitions of the variables are provided in appendix B.

Appendix B: Variable Definitions

The database covers the period 1919–1936. The 12 core/center countries include Australia, Belgium, Canada, Denmark, France, Germany, Netherlands, New Zealand, Sweden, Switzerland, United Kingdom, and United States. The rest are coded as periphery countries.

Output Growth   Average annual change in real per capita GDP in the previous three years. Data are taken from Obstfeld and Taylor (2003), Blattman, Hwang, and Williamson (2004), and Maddison (2003).

Inflation   Average annual change in the consumer price index in the previous three years, transformed using $(\pi/1 + \pi)$. Data are taken from Obstfeld and Taylor (2003), Mitchell (2003a; 2003b; 2003c), and Astorga, Bergés, and Fitzgerald (2004).

Terms of Trade Change   Average annual change in the terms of trade in the previous three years. Data are taken from Obstfeld and Taylor (2003), Blattman, Hwang, and Williamson (2004), and Astorga, Bergés, and Fitzgerald (2004).

Capital Exports   Net global capital exports in millions of U.S. dollars from creditor nations in the world as calculated by Feinstein and Watson (1995) for the period 1924–1935.

Exchange Rate Pressure   Annual percentage change in the end-year exchange rate versus the U.S. dollar, transformed using $(\pi/1 + \pi)$. Data for 1922–1938 are from the League of Nations. This variable is measured so that an increase is an appreciation of the local currency versus the U.S. dollar.

Yield Spread   A measure of country risk calculated by the spread of a country's long-term bond yield versus London, measured in percentage points per annum. Data are taken from Obstfeld and Taylor (2003).

High Inflation History   A dummy variable indicating whether a country experienced high inflation before joining the interwar gold standard, defined as inflation in excess of 50 percent in any year between 1919 and the date of entry.

Number of Countries on Gold   Number of countries on the interwar gold standard for a given year, weighted by the size of their respective economies. The weight is the level of real per capita GDP from the same source as above.

Main Trading Partner Exits   A dummy variable indicating whether a country's major trading partner (up to two) had left the interwar gold standard. Data are taken from Mitchell (2003a; 2003b; 2003c).

Riots, Strikes, Demonstrations   A summary of the number of strikes, riots, and antigovernment demonstrations in a given year, calculated using principle components analysis. The underlying series correspond, respectively, to the variables s17f2, s18f1, and s17f6 in Banks (1971).

Government Instability   Number of times the premier position or 50 percent of the cabinet posts are occupied by new ministers in a given year. The variable corresponds to the field s22f2 in Banks (1971).

Democracy   Annual level of democracy as measured by the Polity (2005) database. The variable is a composite index of democracy and autocracy, ranging from -10 (most autocratic) to 10 (most democratic). The variable is transformed to range from 0 to 1.

Notes

The authors are grateful to Alan Taylor and Christopher Blattman for their generosity in sharing data; to Michael Bordo, Helge Berger, Stan Engerman, Richard Grossman, Timothy Hatton, Steve Heydemann, Kevin O'Rourke, Pierre Sicsic, Alan Taylor, and Peter Temin for helpful suggestions; and to Michael Robbins and David DeBartolo for able research assistance.

1. Brown (1942) provides a capsule summary of the prevalent model, encompassing steps "to balance national budgets and stop inflation; to direct the flow of long-term capital to countries financially and economically disorganized by the war and to safeguard that capital; to generalize and develop the institution of central banking and safeguard the independence of central banks; to adopt measures of gold economy; to reach a settlement of past debts." See Drake (1989) for a detailed account of how the model was promoted in the Andes.

2. There is some ambiguity in dating both entry and exit (as well as in allocating countries to the center and the periphery). The return to gold typically involved multiple steps, proceeding from fiscal to exchange rate stabilization to the de facto or de jure adoption of the gold standard (Officer 2001). Figure 10.1 is based on the entry and exit data presented in appendix A.

3. The differences are discussed in Eichengreen (1992; 1995), Bordo and Eichengreen (1998), Bordo, Edelstein, and Rockoff (1999), Bernanke and James (1991), and Officer (2001).

4. As Obstfeld and Taylor (2003) note, while under the classical standard, membership per se shaved off about half a percent of the borrowing spread, a richer set of determinants, including British Empire membership, public debt, and not least the exchange rate itself, influenced borrowing costs after the war.

5. A contemporary flavor of the unfolding events is provided in Fisher (1934) (Australia), Frankel (1933) (South Africa), Thomas (1935) (India), and Smith (1936) (Poland).

6. As Eichengreen and Temin (2000, 183) note, the influence of the dominant doctrine, already lamented by Keynes, remained crucial: "The most important barrier to actions that would have arrested or reversed the decline was the mentality of the gold standard."

7. The ultimate exit reflected the combination of the external shocks and their domestic repercussions with political (in)action, as detailed in Ferguson and Temin (2001), who diagnose a "failure of political will" as an important aspect of Germany's exit.

8. In the broader British sphere of influence, the only country remaining on gold in 1932 was the gold producer South Africa, which faced its share of troubles. As Frankel (1933, 98), writing two years later, notes, "It is ... clear that by the end of 1931, quite apart from the immediate crisis resulting from the currency change in Great Britain, South Africa was faced with the urgent need of undertaking the fundamental readjustments necessitated by the fall in export prices, the decline in national income, the increase in the burden of debt, the prevalent unemployment, and the rigidity of the domestic price structure."

9. Japan and Sweden provide partial exceptions.

10. The vast size of the literature prevents adequate referencing; key contributions include Friedman and Schwartz (1963), Hamilton (1987), Temin (1989), Eichengreen (1992), and Bernanke (1983).

11. See, for example, Díaz-Alejandro (1984, 22): "Peripheral shame and self-doubts gradually gave way to self-confidence, especially after Britain abandoned the gold standard in 1931 and Germany and the USA embarked on their own experiments."

12. The dilemma was particularly acute for countries in the British economic sphere, facing a choice between remaining on gold and accepting a steep real exchange rate appreciation.

13. See, for instance, Eichengreen and Temin (2000, 185): "Our argument is that the mentality of the gold standard was integral to the ideology of . . . those segments of society that controlled economic policies. . . . The world economy did not begin to recover when these people changed their minds; rather, recovery began when mass politics in its various guises removed them from office."

14. Specifically, we use an accelerated failure-time model that expresses the survival time (adherence to the gold standard, in our case) as a linear function of the covariates. This provides the convenience of interpreting all the results reported in tables 10.1–10.5 as the effects of covariates on the adherence to (survival of) the gold standard. All the results reported here are based on modeling the effects of covariates using an exponential distribution, although we obtain similar results with other parametric or semiparametric distributions. Although not reported, all regression results include a constant.

15. Duration methodology bears some similarity to standard probit regressions used to examine the determinants of exchange rate regimes, as in Edwards (1996) and Yeyati, Sturzenegger, and Reggio (2002), and the duration of pegs, as in Klein and Marion (1997). Our focus is, however, not so much whether a country was on gold or on a different standard in a specific year (for which a probit regression would be most appropriate) but rather the decision of how long to remain on gold after its widespread adoption in the mid 1920s.

16. As the variables are lagged one year, the exchange rate pressure (Bordo and Eichengreen 2002) measures the exchange rate movement relative to gold while the country operated under the standard; the rate thus captures whether the exchange rate moved closer to the gold point.

17. The high inflation dummy is dropped from the periphery regression in column 5 of table 10.3 because of collinearity. Few countries in our sample of the periphery experienced a high inflation history.

18. This may be due to the fact that democracies in the periphery were more fractionalized than in the center countries, although for both groups the correlation between the level of democracy and parliamentary fractionalization is positive and strong.

19. See, for example, Alesina and Tabellini (1990). This finding and the result that democracies tended to be politically more fractionalized during this period suggests that the exit decision was more likely in less polarized polities.

20. As a robustness check on these results and the duration methodology in general, we replicated the regressions in table 10.5 using a probit regression. Following Klein and Marion (1997), the dependent variable is coded 0 if a country operates on gold at the end of a year, and 1 if it exits during that year. We performed the analysis over the period 1925–1936. The evidence from the probit regressions is largely consistent with that obtained from duration analysis.

References

Alesina, A., and G. Tabellini. 1990. A Positive Theory of Budget Deficits and Government Debt. *Review of Economic Studies* 57: 403–414.

Astorga, P., A. R. Bergés, and V. Fitzgerald. 2004. *The Oxford Latin American Economic History Database (OxLAD)*. ⟨http://oxlad.qeh.ox.ac.uk/⟩.

Banks, A. 1971. *Cross-Polity Time Series*. Cambridge, Mass.: MIT Press.

Berman, S. 1998. *The Social Democratic Moment*. Cambridge, Mass.: Harvard University Press.

Bernanke, B. 1983. Nonmonetary Effects of the Financial Crisis in the Propagation of the Great Depression. *American Economic Review* 73: 259–276.

———. 1995. The Macroeconomics of the Great Depression: A Comparative Approach. *Journal of Money, Credit, and Banking* 27: 1–28.

Bernanke, B., and H. James. 1991. The Gold Standard, Deflation, and Financial Crisis in the Great Depression: An International Comparison. In *Financial Markets and Financial Crises*, ed. R. G. Hubbard, 33–68. Chicago: University of Chicago Press.

Blattman, C., J. Hwang, and J. G. Williamson. 2004. The Impact of the Terms of Trade on Economic Development in the Periphery, 1870–1939: Volatility and Secular Change. NBER (National Bureau of Economic Research) Working Paper 10600. ⟨http://www.nber.org/papers/W10600⟩.

Bordo, M., M. Edelstein, and H. Rockoff. 1999. Was Adherence to the Gold Standard a "Good Housekeeping Seal of Approval" during the Interwar Period? NBER (National Bureau of Economic Research) Working Paper 7186. ⟨http://www.nber.org/papers/W7186⟩.

Bordo, M., and B. Eichengreen. 1998. The Rise and Fall of a Barbarous Relic. NBER (National Bureau of Economic Research) Working Paper 6436. ⟨http://www.nber.org/papers/W6436⟩.

———. 2002. Crises Now and Then: What Lessons from the Last Era of Financial Globalization? NBER (National Bureau of Economic Research) Working Paper 8716. ⟨http://www.nber.org/papers/W8716⟩.

Bordo, M., and H. Rockoff. 1996. The Gold Standard as a "Good Housekeeping Seal of Approval." *Journal of Economic History* 56: 389–428.

Bordo, M., and A. Schwartz. 1994. The Specie Standard as a Contingent Rule. NBER (National Bureau of Economic Research) Working Paper 4860. ⟨http://www.nber.org/papers/W4860⟩.

Brown, W. A. 1942. The International Gold Standard Reinterpreted, 1914–1934. *Journal of Economic History* 2: 96–98.

Campa, J. M. 1990. Exchange Rates and Economic Recovery in the 1930s: An Extension to Latin America. *Journal of Economic History* 50: 677–682.

Corbo, V. 1992. Development Strategies and Policies in Latin America: A Historical Perspective. Paper 22. International Center for Economic Growth.

Cross-National Time-Series Data Archive. ⟨http://www.databanks.sitehosting.net/⟩.

Díaz-Alejandro, C. F. 1984. Latin America in the 1930s. In *Latin America in the 1930s: The Role of the Periphery in World Crisis*, ed. R. Thorp, 17–49. New York: Macmillan.

Drake, P. 1989. *The Money Doctor in the Andes: The Kemmerer Missions, 1923–1933*. Durham, N.C.: Duke University Press.

Edwards, S. 1996. The Determinants of the Choice Between Fixed and Flexible Exchange-Rate Regimes. NBER (National Bureau of Economic Research) Working Paper 5756. ⟨http://www.nber.org/papers/W5756⟩.

Eichengreen, B. 1992. *Golden Fetters: The Gold Standard and the Great Depression*. New York: Oxford University Press.

———. 1995. The Endogeneity of Exchange Rate Regimes. In *Understanding Independence: The Macroeconomics of the Open Economy*, ed. P. Kenen, 3–33. Princeton, N.J.: Princeton University Press.

———. 2002. Still Fettered after All These Years. NBER (National Bureau of Economic Research) Working Paper 9276. ⟨http://www.nber.org/papers/W9276⟩.

Eichengreen, B., and R. Portes. 1986. Debt and Default in the 1930s. *European Economic Review* 30: 599–640.

Eichengreen, B., and J. Sachs. 1985. Exchange Rates and Economic Recovery in the 1930s. *Journal of Economic History* 4: 925–946.

Eichengreen, B., and B. Simmons. 1995. International Economics and Domestic Politics: Notes from the 1920s. In *Banking, Currency and Finance in Europe Between the Wars*, ed. C. Feinstein, 131–149. Oxford: Clarendon Press.

Eichengreen, B., and P. Temin. 2000. The Gold Standard and the Great Depression. *Contemporary European History* 9: 183–207.

Feinstein, C., and K. Watson. 1995. Private International Capital Flows in Europe in the Inter-War Period. In *Banking, Currency and Finance in Europe Between the Wars*, ed. C. Feinstein, 94–130. Oxford: Clarendon Press.

Ferguson, T., and P. Temin. 2001. Made in Germany: The German Currency Crisis of July 1931. MIT Department of Economics Working Paper Series 01-07.

Fisher, A. 1934. Crisis and Readjustment in Australia. *Journal of Political Economy* 42: 753–782.

Frankel, S. H. 1933. The Situation in South Africa, 1929–1932. *Economic Journal* 43: 93–107.

Friedman, M., and A. Schwartz. 1963. *A Monetary History of the United States, 1867–1960*. Princeton, N.J.: Princeton University Press.

Gourevitch, P. A. 1984. Breaking with Orthodoxy: The Politics of Economic Policy Responses to the Depression of the 1930s. *International Organization* 38: 95–129.

Hall, P., ed. 1989. *The Political Power of Economic Ideas*. Princeton, N.J.: Princeton University Press.

Hamilton, J. 1987. Monetary Factors in the Great Depression. *Journal of Monetary Economics* 13: 145–169.

James, H. 2001. *The End of Globalization: Lessons from the Great Depression*. Cambridge, Mass.: Harvard University Press.

Kemmerer, D. 1954. Statement. In *Hearings on the Gold Reserve Act Amendments, U.S. Senate 83d Congress, Second Session*, 299–302. Washington: Government Printing Office.

Kindleberger, C. P. 1986. *The World in Depression, 1929–1939*. Berkeley: University of California Press.

Klein, M., and N. Marion. 1997. Explaining the Duration of Exchange Rate Pegs. *Journal of Development Economics* 54: 387–404.

Maddison, A. 2003. *The World Economy: Historical Statistics*. Paris: OECD.

Meissner, C. M. 2005. A New World Order: Explaining the International Diffusion of the Gold Standard, 1870–1913. *Journal of International Economics* 66: 385–406.

Mitchell, B. R. 2003a. *International Historical Statistics: Africa, Asia, and Oceania, 1750–2000*. 4th ed. New York: Palgrave Macmillan.

———. 2003b. *International Historical Statistics: Europe, 1750–2000*. 5th ed. New York: Palgrave Macmillan.

———. 2003c. *International Historical Statistics: The Americas, 1750–2000*. 5th ed. New York: Palgrave Macmillan.

Obstfeld, M., and A. M. Taylor. 2003. Soverign Risk, Credibility and the Gold Standard: 1870–1913 versus 1925–1931. *Economic Journal* 113: 241–275.

Officer, L. H. 2001. Gold Standard. In *EH.Net Encyclopedia*. ⟨http://eh.net/encyclopedia/article/officer.gold.standard⟩.

Polity. 2005. Polity IV Project: Political Regime Characteristics and Transitions, 1800–2003. ⟨http://www.cidcm.umd.edu/inscr/polity/⟩.

Simmons, B. 1994. *Who Adjusts? Domestic Sources of Foreign Economic Policy during the Interwar Years*. Princeton, N.J.: Princeton University Press.

———. 1996. Rulers of the Game: Central Bank Independence during the Interwar Years. *International Organization* 50: 407–443.

Smith, L. 1936. The Zloty, 1924–1936. *Journal of Political Economy* 44: 145–183.

Temin, P. 1989. *Lessons from the Great Depression.* Cambridge, Mass.: MIT Press.

Thomas, P. 1935. India in the World Depression. *Economic Journal* 45: 469–483.

Triffin, R. 1947. National Central Banking and the International Economy. *Review of Economic Studies* 14 (2): 53–75.

Wandschneider, K. 2005. The Stability of the Interwar Gold Exchange Standard: Did Politics Matter? Middlebury College Economics Discussion Paper 05-18. 〈http://ideas.repec.org/p/mdl/mdlpap/0518.html〉.

Weir, M., and T. Skocpol. 1985. State Structures and the Possibilities for Keynesian Responses to the Great Depression in Sweden, Britain, and the United States. In *Bringing the State Back In*, ed. P. Evans, D. Rueschemeyer, and T. Skocpol, 107–168. Chicago: University of Chicago Press.

Yeager, L. B. 1984. The Image of the Gold Standard. In *A Retrospective on the Classical Gold Standard, 1821–1931*, ed. M. Bordo and A. Schwartz. Chicago: University of Chicago Press.

Yeyati, E. L., F. Sturzenegger, and I. Reggio. 2002. On the Endogeneity of Exchange Rate Regimes. 〈http://ideas.repec.org/p/udt/wpbsdt/veintiuno.html〉.

Zimmermann, E., and T. Saalfeld. 1988. Economic and Political Reactions to the World Economic Crisis of the 1930s in Six European Countries. *International Studies Quarterly* 32: 305–334.

11 Were Jews Political Refugees or Economic Migrants? Assessing the Persecution Theory of Jewish Emigration, 1881–1914

Leah Platt Boustan

In 1881, 4.1 million Jews lived in the Russian empire. Over the next three decades, 1.5 million Russian Jews immigrated to the United States, and another 0.5 million left for other New World destinations, a mass migration surpassed in strength only by the Irish earlier in the century. Despite the intensity of Jewish migration, economic historians have paid little attention to this episode.[1] This is due, in part, to a lack of comparable data between Russia and the rest of continental Europe, but it also reflects the common belief that the exodus from Russia was a uniquely Jewish event and thus cannot be incorporated into a general model of migration as factor flows.

In this chapter, I argue that a confluence of demographic events, including population growth and internal migration from villages to larger cities, set the flow of Jewish migrants from Russia in motion. I further demonstrate that the timing of Jewish migration, once it had begun in earnest, was influenced both by periodic religious violence and by business cycles in the United States and Russia. Migration rates increased temporarily in the year after a documented persecution. In addition, by enlarging the stock of Jews living in the United States, many of whom joined emigrant aid societies or paid directly for their family's passage, temporary religious violence had modest long-run effects on the magnitude of the Jewish migration flow.

The Persecution Theory

Since the mid-eighteenth century, Jews in the Russian empire were forbidden to live outside the Pale of Settlement, an area that encompassed sections of Poland, Lithuania, Belorussia, and the Ukraine. The story of Jewish emigration usually begins with a full accounting of the pogroms, the anti-Jewish riots that swept through the Pale in the late nineteenth and early twentieth centuries. The first major riot took place in Odessa in 1871, during the relatively liberal reign of Alexander II.[2] Following Alexander's assassination ten years later, anti-Jewish violence again broke out in the south, this time in the city of Elizavetgrad, and spread northward for the next five months.[3] In the aftermath, the government of the new Tsar, Alexander III, publicly blamed the Jewish victims for instigating the riots and responded by passing the "May Laws," which, among other restrictions, forbade Jews from settling in rural areas (Dubnow 1918, 284–323; Rogger 1986, 58–70).

The next two decades were relatively quiet for the Jews of Russia.[4] One exception was the expulsion of Jews from Moscow in 1891. Because Jews were technically not allowed to live in the capital, this event was more symbolic than substantial, but the event stands out in the collective memory of the Russian Jewish experience.[5] A new round of pogroms erupted in 1903 in the Bessarabian capital of Kishinev. With the 1905 Revolution came widespread attacks, which affected some 650 Jewish communities in a single week, including the large urban centers of Odessa and Bialystok (Lambroza 1992, 226).

Proponents of the persecution theory define the year 1881 as a turning point in both the oppression of Russia's Jews and in their migration patterns. Ruppin (1934), an early Jewish sociologist, asserted that whereas before the pogroms of 1881, "the individual Jew would make up his mind to emigrate," perhaps because of "impossible economic conditions," after that year, "a mighty stream of emigrants broke forth; individual thinking gave way to a mass impulse, almost to a mass psychosis" (44).[6]

Attributing the takeoff of migration in 1881 to pogroms in that year begs the question: why did mass migration only begin in 1881, despite the frequent flare-ups of anti-Jewish violence before this date? The Odessa pogrom of 1871 notwithstanding, Kuznets (1975) estimates that only 31,000 Russian Jews migrated to the United States in the 1870s, compared with the nearly 150,000 who arrived in the 1880s. Migration was similarly unaffected by an earlier era of persecution under Nicholas I (1825–1855), whose government conscripted Jewish boys as young as eight into the Russian army and forced many of them to convert to Russian Orthodoxy (Stanislawski 1983).

One explanation for this pattern is that international migration may have become feasible only after certain economic and demographic factors were in place. While Jews were subject to a web of restrictions in their everyday lives—forbidden from living outside the Pale or in certain

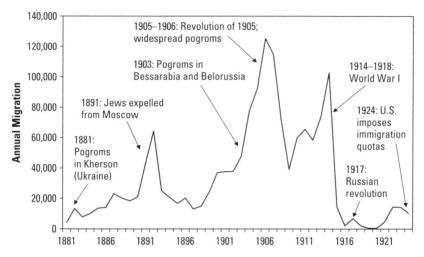

Figure 11.1
Annual Jewish migration from Russia to the United States, 1881–1924. Data from Joseph (1914), Ferenczi and Willcox (1929; 1932).

cities *within* the Pale, and from entering the professions—these constraints, on their own, may not have been enough to spark migration. An apt analogy is the migration of African-Americans from the South, which began in earnest only after 1915 despite decades of persecution under the Jim Crow laws.[7]

Furthermore, if the Jewish migration was solely a flight from violence rather than a search for higher wages or better living conditions, it should be subject to unique laws of motion, responding more to the dates of riots than to trends in economic variables. A first look at the pattern of Jewish migration seems to confirm a temporal relationship between migration and political hardship. Figure 11.1 annotates a graph of the annual migration flow of Russian Jews to the United States with important historical events. Immigration spiked in the 1891, the year that Jews were expelled from the Moscow, and again in 1904–1906, the turbulent years of the Kishinev massacre (1903), the Revolution of 1905, and the widespread riots of 1905–1906. This flow, which reached over 100,000 new migrants annually in the peak years of 1906 and 1914, came to a near standstill during the years of World War I and the Russian Revolution, rebounded slightly in the early 1920s, and was effectively halted with the immigration restrictions of 1924.

However, an emphasis on the uniqueness of the exodus from Russia obscures striking similarities between the timing of Jewish migration to

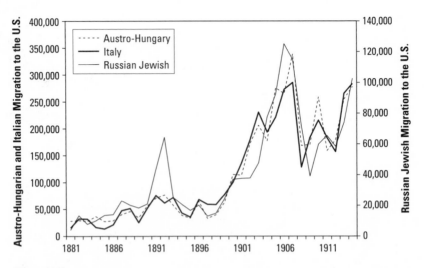

Figure 11.2
Annual Jewish migration from Russia to the United States, compared to other "new" migrant flows, 1881–1913. Data on Jewish entrants from Joseph (1914), Ferenczi and Willcox (1929; 1932); data on Italian and Austro-Hungarian migration flows from Ferenczi and Willcox (1929; 1932).

the United States and of other Eastern and Southern European migrant groups.[8] Figure 11.2 compares the annual migration flows to the United States of Russian Jews and of Austro-Hungarians and Italians in 1881–1914.[9] The correspondence between these time series is remarkable. This close relationship suggests that Jewish migration was sensitive to some of the same factors that drove migration from other southern and eastern European areas, with a likely candidate being economic conditions in the United States.

Economic and Demographic Determinants of Jewish Migration in the Long Run

In addition to political uncertainty and fear for physical safety, life in the Pale was marked by the demographic and economic pressures that are often associated with mass migrations. These include rapid population growth and a possible demographic transition, as well as urbanization, residential crowding, and ongoing industrialization. In this section, I suggest that it was the confluence of these forces rather than the violence in Elizavetgrad that ushered in an era of mass migration.

Demographic transitions are characterized by a burst of population growth as mortality rates, particularly those for infants and young chil-

Table 11.1
Population Growth among Jews and Non-Jews in the Russian Empire, 1825–1900

	Total (millions)				Growth Rates (annual percent)		
	1825	1850	1880	1900	1825–1850	1850–1880	1880–1900
Jewish							
Total	1.60	2.35	3.98	5.18	1.55	1.77	1.32
Lithuania, Belorussia	0.55	0.80	1.23	1.45	1.51	1.43	0.85
Congress Poland	0.40	0.58	1.01	1.33	1.46	1.88	1.40
Ukraine	0.63	0.93	1.60	2.20	1.58	1.84	1.61
Other	0.03	0.05	0.15	0.20	2.81	3.73	1.45
European Russia	49.8	61.6	85.6	111.2	0.85	1.10	1.32

Sources: Rows 1–5, Engelman (1949, 1185); row 6, Kuznets (1975, 63).

dren, decline in advance of reductions in fertility. Hatton and Williamson (1998) and Easterlin (1961) argue that demographic transitions may help explain the "long swings" of migration from Europe. Easterlin emphasizes that large cohorts crowd the home labor market, lowering wages and increasing the relative benefit of migration. Hatton and Williamson further suggest that, as the transition cohort reaches young adulthood, migration rates will increase simply because the young are more mobile.

Rapid population growth in the Jewish community over the nineteenth century is consistent with the presence of an early demographic transition. Throughout the nineteenth century, the total Jewish population of Russia grew at annual rates far above the rest of the empire (table 11.1). The growth rate for the overall population did not catch up to the rate in the Jewish community until after 1880, when the increase in the Jewish population was slowed by out-migration.[10]

A better measure is the rate of natural increase, which is not confounded by differential migration patterns (except indirectly through changes in the age structure). While the information necessary to calculate rates of natural increase over time does not exist for the Russian Jewish community, comparable data exist for other areas of Central and Eastern Europe. Table 11.2 presents birth and death rates for the Jewish communities of Prussia and Romania, as well as for the country as a whole. At the time, Prussia was more urbanized than Russia, and Romania was less so. In both places, the Jewish community grew faster than the overall population for some period—in Prussia at least through 1840 and in Romania until 1900—after which the positions reversed. The phase of

Table 11.2
Vital Rates (per Thousand) for Jews and for the Total Population of Prussia and Romania, 1820–1915

	Jews			Total		
	Birth Rate	Death Rate	Natural Increase	Birth Rate	Death Rate	Natural Increase
Prussia						
1822–1840	35.5	21.6	13.9	40.0	29.6	10.4
1876–1880	31.7	17.6	14.1	38.9	23.6	15.3
1886–1890	23.9	16.1	7.8	37.3	24.3	13.0
1896–1900	20.4	14.3	6.1	37.1	21.4	15.7
1906–1910	17.0	13.7	3.3	32.5	17.3	15.2
1911–1913	15.3	13.8	1.5	28.9	15.9	13.0
Romania						
1881–1886	46.8	26.0	20.8	41.3	26.3	15.0
1891–1895	43.2	23.5	19.7	41.0	31.0	10.0
1896–1900	40.1	21.4	18.7	40.1	27.4	12.7
1901–1905	32.6	21.2	11.4	39.5	25.7	13.8
1906–1910	29.6	17.4	12.2	40.4	26.5	13.9
1911–1915	26.6	16.1	10.5	42.7	24.8	17.9

Source: Kuznets (1975, 63–64).

rapid growth can be attributed to low Jewish mortality rates. Silber (1980) reports that by the late nineteenth century, Russian Jews exhibited the low fertility and mortality characteristic of Prussia at mid-century.[11]

At the same time, the Pale was undergoing a process of rapid transformation from a society of small villages (*shtetls*) to one of large urban centers. By 1897, 77.8 percent of Jews in the Pale lived in incorporated cities or other commercial centers (*miestechkos*), compared with just 15 percent of the Pale's non-Jewish population.[12] This urban concentration was the result of a century of rural-urban migration. The urban Jewish population grew faster than the Jewish population as a whole. Table 11.3 summarizes the available sources for major cities in the Pale.[13] The Jewish population expanded rapidly both in cities like Vilna, Minsk, and Warsaw, which were already home to established Jewish communities in the late eighteenth century (row 1), and in the new cities of Odessa, Ekaterinoslav, and Kiev (row 2).[14]

The direction of the theoretical relation between rural-urban migration within a country and migration across national borders is ambiguous. On the one hand, moving to a regional hub or capital city could substitute for

Table 11.3
Growth of the Jewish Population for Cities in the Pale, 1790–1910

Vilna			Minsk			Warsaw		
Year	Number	Annual Growth Rate (%)	Year	Number	Annual Growth Rate (%)	Year	Number	Annual Growth Rate (%)
1797	7,000	—	1802	2,700	—	1800	8,000	—
1832	20,000	3.04						
1847	23,050	0.94	1847	12,976	3.55			
1875	40,000	1.98				1876	100,000	3.37
1897	63,996	2.15	1897	47,562	2.63			
1910	72,323	0.95	1910	45,103	−0.50	1908	277,787	3.24

Odessa			Ekaterinoslav			Kiev		
Year	Number	Annual Growth Rate (%)	Year	Number	Annual Growth Rate (%)	Year	Number	Annual Growth Rate (%)
1795	246	—	1804	320	—	1797	207	—
1855	17,000	7.32	1857	3,365	4.54	1863	3,013	4.14
1897	138,915	5.13	1897	40,009	6.38	1897	31,801	7.17
1904	152,634	1.35	1910	69,012	4.38	1910	50,792	3.82

Source: Baron (1964, 64–67).

emigration abroad. However, internal migration could also facilitate the overseas journey, for instance, by introducing a new arrival to migration networks or by providing access to transportation. In the Russian Jewish case, one important effect of rural-urban migration was the weakening of the strong religious and communal bonds of *shtetl* life. After making their first break from traditional communal life, young people found it easier to take the larger leap to America, a step that was often shunned by village religious and community leaders.[15]

Given that demographic transition and rural-to-urban migration are both slow, long-run processes, might we need to appeal to pogroms to explain the sudden takeoff of Jewish migration in the 1880s? Not necessarily. Exponential growth is a common feature of many mass migrations, even from source areas without sudden catastrophic events, because of chain migration. Carrington, Detragiache, and Vishwanath (1996) have modeled this process as an endogenous decline in migration costs, whereby early migrants facilitate future waves by sending information and prepaid passage and by smoothing the transition to a new society. In such a framework, oppression can persist indefinitely without migration if the right economic conditions are not in place to encourage "pioneer" migrants, and conversely, migration can take off once it begins.

Explaining Annual Jewish Migration Rates: The Roles of Economic Opportunity and Religious Persecution

The previous section concerned the necessary conditions for a mass migration to begin. In this section, I turn to the timing of population flows once migration has started. I rely for my empirical framework on Hatton and Williamson's model of migration timing. The model posits that migration in a given year is driven by relative economic conditions in the sending and receiving countries and the size of the migrant stock in the destination area.[16] I find that this simple model, which includes only economic and demographic variables, is equally adept at explaining Jewish migration as at accounting for other European migrations. However, religious persecution is another important determinant of the timing of Jewish migration, with years after recorded violence posting above-trend migration.

Econometric Framework

Following Hatton and Williamson (1993, 1998) and Hatton (1995), I estimate a time series equation relating the emigration rate of Russian Jews to the United States to key economic variables. The equation is:

$$M/P_t = a_0 + a_1 \Delta \log(ER_f)_t + a_2 \Delta \log(ER_h)_t + a_3 \Delta \log(W_f/W_h)_t$$

$$+ a_4 \log(ER_f)_{t-1} + a_5 \log(ER_h)_{t-1} + a_6 \log(W_f/W_h)_{t-1}$$

$$+ a_7 \log(MST/P)_t + a_8(M/P)_{t-1} + \varepsilon_t \qquad (1)$$

where M/P is the Russian Jewish emigration rate, ER_f is the foreign (U.S.) employment rate, ER_h is the home (Russian) employment rate, W_f and W_h are the foreign and home real wages, MST is the stock of Jews living in the United States, and P is the Russian Jewish population.

Relative economic conditions are entered here as a ratio, constraining the coefficients on home and foreign variables to be equal and opposite, and thus emphasizing the comparative aspect of the migration decision. Alternatively, home and foreign conditions can be entered separately, either because migrants have more accurate information about home country wages or because economic conditions are measured with less error in the United States.

The specification includes two measures of chain migration—the migrant stock and the lagged dependent variable. The migrant stock measures the size of the whole émigré community, and the lagged dependent variable mirrors the fact that more recent migrants may have stronger ties to the home country.

To explore the importance of pogroms in the timing of Jewish migration, I focus on the following dates suggested by the historical literature: 1891, the year Jews were expelled from Moscow; 1903, the year of the Kishinev massacre; and 1905–1906, the period of pogroms following the 1905 Revolution. One simple test of the importance of religious persecution is to augment the model with dummy variables for the years in question, which will indicate whether the population outflow is significantly off-trend. Because the effect of a riot might not have been immediate, especially if prospective migrants needed to save money for their journey, I consider three specifications, respectively allowing an event in year t to have effect on migration in year t only, in year $t + 1$ only, or in both years $t + 1$ and year $t + 2$.

Measuring Jewish Migration

The model is estimated on annual data from 1886 to 1913. Because emigration was technically illegal, Russian officials never recorded the number of Jews leaving the empire (Rogger 1986, 176–187). I approximate emigration with gross annual *immigration* of Russian Jews to the United States, a reasonable proxy given that the United States absorbed 75 percent of the migrant flow and that return migration was very minor (Lestchinsky 1949; Gould 1980).[17]

Jewish immigration to United States is available from two sources: from 1881 to 1899 it must be inferred from the records of emigrant aid societies, and after 1899 the federal Immigration Service began counting Jewish migrants separately (under the category "Hebrew"). For the earlier period, I use figures compiled by Joseph (1914) for three ports—New York, Philadelphia, and Baltimore—which together account for the majority of Jewish arrivals.[18]

Arrivals were classified as "Hebrew" by the Immigration Service if they declared Yiddish as their mother tongue. According to the 1897 Census, 97 percent of Jews in the Russian empire met this criterion (Rubinow 1907, 488). Jews rarely left from Russian ports but rather sailed via Germany, France, and the United Kingdom.[19] Because the Immigration Service collected data by country of departure rather than country of last residence, these counts must be revised. I rely on Godley's adjustments (2001, 73–79).

Measuring the Determinants of Migration

Economic conditions in source and destination countries are measured here by wages and unemployment rates, which together can be conceptualized as a migrant's expected wage (Harris and Todaro 1970). I use real series of unskilled wages in the United States and factory wages in Russia (Williamson 1995; Gregory 1982). To adjust the Russian wages for purchasing power parity, I use food and rent prices for Moscow in 1913 and nationally representative expenditure budgets for Russia in 1927 (Zaleski 1955; *Workers' Family Budget* 1929).[20] The resulting calculations suggest that Russian factory wages around the turn of the twentieth century embodied 40 percent of the purchasing power of unskilled wages in the United Kingdom and only 30 percent of those in the United States.

I take estimates of the Jewish population from the *American Jewish Yearbook* to measure the stock of previous migrants in the United States. This value includes not only recent arrivals from Eastern Europe but also members of the earlier German immigrant wave. While the established German Jews often snubbed Eastern Europeans socially, they were also instrumental in funding emigrant aid societies (Rischin 1962).[21]

Estimation Results

I estimate the determinants of annual Jewish migration rates sequentially, starting only with economic variables, adding measures of chain migration, and finally supplementing the model with indicators of religious violence. In other words, I ask whether migration rates were above trend during episodes of persecution, given the prevailing economic conditions and the underlying logic of the migration chain.

The results of the time series estimation are presented in table 11.4. Column 1 includes only measures of the business cycle in the United States and Russia, and the wage ratio between the two countries. In a fuller specification (not shown), I include both contemporaneous and lagged variables. Migration rates respond to economic conditions in the current period in Russia and previous period in the United States, a pattern that is consistent with slow flows of information. I also include changes of all variables, of which only changes in U.S. employment rates

Table 11.4
Determinants of Emigration Rates of Russian Jews to the United States, 1886–1913

	Levels			Changes
	(1)	(2)	(3)	(4)
ln (U.S. employment rate), $t - 1$	148.764	119.521	90.669	198.532
	(37.129)	(38.245)	(30.639)	(46.348)
Δ ln (U.S. employment rate)	56.765	57.938	39.024	87.214
	(36.869)	(32.427)	(27.518)	(29.296)
Deviation from log trend,	−64.869	−30.024	−25.376	−32.742
Russian NNP, $t - 1$	(19.945)	(20.035)	(16.269)	(15.992)
ln (U.S./Russian wages), $t - 1$	34.584	4.795	—	—
	(7.369)	(11.907)		
ln (Jewish stock in U.S./		3.821	4.787	26.778
Russian Jewish population), $t - 1$		(2.263)	(1.136)	(34.682)
Migration rate, $t - 1$		0.466	0.244	
		(0.229)	(0.189)	
Migration rate, $t - 2$		−0.202	−0.114	
		(0.180)	(0.140)	
Event 1 (1891)			5.342	5.184
			(2.364)	(2.633)
Event 2 (1903)			4.932	8.483
			(2.441)	(2.639)
Event 3 (1905–1906)			6.182	−1.819
			(2.256)	(2.063)
Constant	−710.738	−537.203	−397.975	−1.772
	(168.051)	(170.224)	(138.588)	(2.402)
N	28	28	28	28
R^2	0.727	0.838	0.911	0.643
Breusch-Godfrey (p-value)[a]	0.078	0.828	0.732	0.053
Dickey-Fuller	−3.785[b]	−5.014[b]	−4.966[b]	—
Augmented D-F (4 lags)	−2.044[b]	−2.868[b]	−2.444[b]	—

Notes: Standard errors shown in parentheses. The dependent variable is the number of Russian Jewish immigrants to the United States divided by the total Russian Jewish population (Joseph 1914; Ferenczi and Willcox 1929; 1932; Kuznets 1975). The explanatory variables are U.S. employment rates (Vernon 1994; Lebergott 1957); Russian net national product, deviated from its fitted log trend (Gregory 1982); and the Jewish population in the United States (*American Jewish Yearbook*). The measures of religious persecution (events 1–3) are indicator variables for the years following recorded events.
a. The null hypothesis of the Breusch-Godfrey test of no auto-correlation is accepted in all cases, strongly in columns 2 and 3 and weakly in columns 1 and 4.
b. Significant at the 5 percent level. The critical value at that level for the Dickey-Fuller tests for cointegration is −1.95.

are a significant predictor of migration. In the reported results, I include the limited set of variables found to significantly affect migration. Higher employment and wages in the United States encouraged migration, as did improvements in employment, whereas better economic conditions in Russia discouraged it. When I break apart the wage ratio into U.S. and Russian wages, it appears that Jewish migration was responding only to wages in the United States (coeff. = 44.919, s.e. = 7.216).

The estimated pull of higher wages is not robust to adding a measure of the stock of Jews living in the United States (column 2). Both variables are increasing steadily throughout this period, and neither can be distinguished from a simple time trend. We can think of the stock measure as an economic interpretation of a time trend, that is, an explanation of why migration rates should be higher under equivalent economic conditions in the middle of a migration wave than at its inception. Column 2 also includes two lags of the migration rate, the first of which is large and positive.

The weakness of the wage ratio as a determinant of migration may be due to the fact that the wages series used are not representative of Jewish economic opportunities. Because the majority of Jewish immigrants worked in skilled handicrafts—tailoring was particularly common—the unskilled wage may not reflect relevant wage rates in the United States (Hersch 1931; Kahan 1978; Chiswick 1992). In addition, factory wages in Russia are available only for Moscow and St. Petersburg, which were unlikely to follow the same time trends as wages in the Pale.

We have scattered evidence that wage *levels* in cities like Vilna and Kiev were comparable to those in Moscow or St. Petersburg (Rubinow 1907). However, Russia's capital cities were receiving large migration flows from the surrounding countryside, likely suppressing wages there, while cities in the Pale were net exporters of labor.[22] Theory tells us that wages should rise in a source country as out-migration reduces the supply of labor. Migration should thus be a force for convergence. In contrast, the factory wage series for Moscow and St. Petersburg is stagnant over this period, while wages in the United States rise steadily.

Given these caveats, better measures of economic opportunities are employment rates, which receive the expected sign and are significant in all specifications. The economic determinants of Jewish migration are presented graphically in figure 11.3, which charts the migration rate against deviations from Russian NNP and from the U.S. employment trend. The time series correlations are apparent here. Migration rates spike in the early 1890s, when the Russian economy performs far below

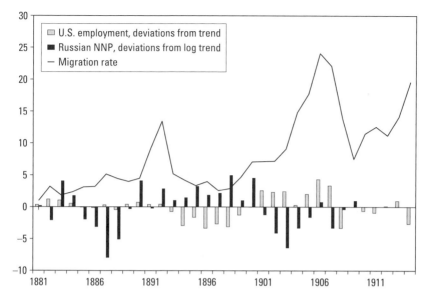

Figure 11.3
Annual Jewish immigration rates from Russia to the United States, compared to employment in the United States and Russian net national product, 1881–1913. U.S. employment
rates are deviated from a linear trend, and Russian NNP from a logarithmic trend. Data on
Jewish entrants from Joseph (1914), Ferenczi and Willcox (1929; 1932); Jacob Lestchinsky's
estimates of the Russian Jewish population are used to convert flows into rates (Kuznets
1975); U.S. employment rates from Vernon (1994) and Lebergott (1957); Russian net national product (NNP) from Gregory (1982).

trend, and again in 1904–1907, when the Russian economy is underper-
forming and U.S. employment is high.

It is interesting that both periods of extreme economic hardship in Russia coincide with recorded violence against the Jewish community. On the
one hand, this temporal link suggests that ignoring the economic fundamentals may lead to an unwarranted overemphasis on the role of pogroms. On the other hand, the correspondence of religious violence with
economic downturns may not be accidental. Riots may have started as
displaced workers attacked Jewish communities that they blamed for
their hardships.[23] Some argue that pogroms were implicitly or explicitly
supported by the Russian state as an outlet for dissatisfaction that may
have otherwise led to political unrest.[24] If pogroms are endogenous to
economic downturns, it becomes more difficult to definitively separate
the role of these two factors.

With this economic/demographic model of migration timing in place, I
include indicators of religious violence in the third column. In various

specifications (not shown), I allow the migration response to occur either in the event year or in the two years following an event. While migration rates are no higher in pogrom years themselves, they are significantly above trend in the year following such persecutions, and return to normal by the second post-pogrom year. The coefficients in column 3 indicate that migration rates increase by roughly five per thousand after each event, or nearly a full standard deviation (the mean migration rate in 1881–1913 is nine per thousand).

Interestingly, there is no evidence that migration rates responded to the severity of violence. There were no recorded deaths in the expulsion of Jews from Moscow, and only 45 deaths and 86 serious injuries reported in the 1903 pogroms; compare these figures to the 1,000 deaths and 7,000–8,000 wounded in 1905–1906 (Baron 1964, 57). Despite the fact that the number of casualties was an order of magnitude higher, the migration response in 1905–1906 was only 1.3 times larger than in 1891 or 1903. Jewish migrants may have been responding to rumors or a climate of fear rather than the true risk of personal harm.

To test the robustness of the pogrom response, I rerun the regression in first differences in the fourth column. The relation between migration rates and economic variables does not qualitatively change, but the Jewish stock variable is no longer significant. As before, the increase in migration rates in 1891–1892 and 1903–1904 are above trend. However, in changes, there is no demonstrable effect of the 1905–1906 pogroms, perhaps because it is hard to distinguish the 1905–1906 period from surrounding events, including the 1903 pogroms and the 1904–1905 Russo-Japanese war.

One way to disentangle the effect of pogroms from concurrent political events is to compare out-migration by region. Anti-Jewish violence was concentrated in the southern provinces, with 87 percent of the 1905–1906 riots occurring in the Ukraine or Bessarabia (Lambroza 1992, 230). While the immigration statistics do not distinguish newcomers by province, the 1920 U.S. Census asked the foreign-born to specify not only their country of origin but also their region of origin because of changes in European boundaries following World War I (Ruggles et al. 2004). Using the same criterion as contemporary immigration officials, I classify all immigrants who declare Yiddish as their mother tongue as Jews.

Figure 11.4 graphs the number of Jewish immigrants from either the violence-prone southern provinces (the Ukraine and Bessarabia) or the northern provinces (Poland and Lithuania) by year of entry into the United States.[25] From 1880 to 1900, immigration from these two regions

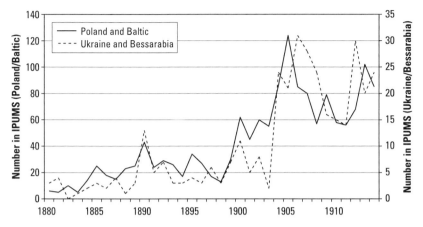

Figure 11.4
Estimated Jewish in-migration from the Russian Empire to the United States, by province, 1880–1914. Individual records from Ruggles et al. (2004). Immigrants are classified as Jewish if indicating mother tongue of Yiddish, Jewish, or Hebrew. Jewish immigrants are categorized by year of entry and place of birth.

moves in virtual lock step. From 1900 to 1903, relative southern immigration wanes. In the two postpogrom years (1903–1904 and 1905–1906), immigration from the south rebounds, in each case experiencing a change twice as large as in the rest of the Pale. However, these sharp increases only return the southern trend to that of the rest of the Pale. There is no evidence that immigration rates from the Ukraine and Bessarabia outstripped those from the rest of the Pale in the early 1900s, suggesting that the surge in migration was, in part, an empirewide phenomenon, reflecting the general turmoil surrounding the Revolution of 1905.

Magnitudes and Counterfactuals

Business cycles account for much of the volatility in migration rates. The lowest U.S. employment rate over a three-year stretch was 92 percent in the mid-1890s, and the highest was 97 percent ten years later. This five percentage point increase in employment rates is associated with an additional 4.5 migrants per thousand Russian Jews.

To evaluate the effect of chain migration, I follow Hatton and Williamson (1993) and assume that, in the long run, all economic variables and migration are in steady state (that is, I set changes equal to zero and equate M/P_t to M/P_{t-1}). Long-run coefficients are thus $a_x/(1 - a_8)$. Nearly one-half of the long-run rise in Jewish migration can be explained

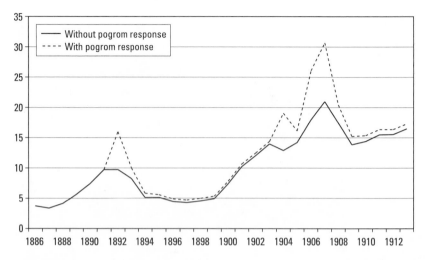

Figure 11.5
Simulated Jewish immigration rates from Russia to the United States, with and without pogrom response, 1881–1913. Annual migration rates are simulated using the coefficient estimates from table 11.4 (column 3) and actual data on economic conditions. Measures of
total Jewish stock and previous year's migration flow are updated in each year.

by an increase in the stock of Jews living in the United States. In the
1880s there were seven Jews in the United States for every 100 Russian
Jews. By the 1900s there were an average of 23 for every 100. The migration rate increased accordingly from 3 to 13 per thousand. If the Jewish
stock had remained at seven per 100 through the 1900s (70 percent lower
than it was), the average migration rate in that decade would have been
4.4 persons per thousand lower $(= (4.787/0.753) \cdot 0.7)$.

The effect of a pogrom shock on the migration flow appears to die out
after a single year. However, these short-term shocks can have long-run
effects by increasing the stock of Jews living in the United States. Figure
11.5 assesses the strength of this channel by simulating annual migration
rates using the coefficient estimates from table 11.4 (column 3). The first
scenario allows for the estimated migration response after years of persecution, and updates the measure of the total Jewish stock and the previous year's flow accordingly.[26] The second omits the pogrom response and
imagines that migration was determined only by prevailing economic
conditions. In comparing these two scenarios, it is clear that the dominant
effect of religious persecution is in the year immediately following an
event, in which the pogrom-response migration rate is around 50 percent
higher than the no-response rate.[27] After two years, the persecution rate

falls to within 9 percent of its no persecution counterpart, but because of the effect on the migrant stock, the two rates never fully converge. The comparison suggests that even after the initial migration response waned, an additional 18,900 Jews arrived in the United States who would not otherwise have made the journey in the ten years after the expulsion from Moscow (1894–1903).[28] The combined long-run effect of the Kishinev pogroms and the 1905–1906 turbulence was the sending of an additional 31,500 migrants from 1910 through 1913.

Assessing the Circumstantial Evidence for the Persecution Theory

Proponents of the persecution theory point to features of Jewish migrants—including their tendency to move in family units and their high rates of emigration relative to other ethnic groups in the Russian empire—as indirect evidence of the importance of religious persecution. Indeed, women made up 43 percent of Jewish entrants to the United States from 1899 to 1910, compared to only 31 percent of the total immigrant flow. Furthermore, while Jews comprised only 4 percent of the total population of the Russian empire, they represented nearly 50 percent of its intercontinental migration (Joseph 1914, 176–182). I argue here that neither of these facts are incompatible with the notion of Jews as economic migrants.

The underlying assumption of the first claim is that, because men are able to earn more than women, we should expect economically motivated migrants to be predominately male. The presence of women and children then becomes an indicator of a flight from violence or famine. If this is the case, we would expect there to be more women from those regions and during those periods in which Jews were subject to heavy persecution. Table 11.5 indicates that, within the Russian empire, Jews from the violence-prone southern provinces were more likely to send female migrants than Jews from Poland, but were *less* likely than Jews from the Baltic states to do so. Furthermore, Russian Jewish migrants as a whole were less likely than Jewish migrants from the relatively peaceful areas of Austro-Hungary, Romania, or Western Europe to be female.[29]

Was the female share of the migrant flow higher during known periods of persecution? Figure 11.6 plots three-year moving averages of the female share of Russian Jewish migrants by year of entry into the United States. The "pioneer" migrants arriving in the 1880s were predominately male.[30] The female share increased rapidly over this decade, peaking in 1893–1894 at 53.2 percent, perhaps as the first settlers sent for their

Table 11.5
Share of Jewish Migrant Stock in the United States That Is Female, by Region of Origin, 1920

	Share Female	Frequency
Russian Empire		
Baltic states	0.508	256
Russian Poland	0.463	579
Ukraine and Bessarabia	0.487	314
Russia, other	0.474	6,218
Outside of Empire		
Austro-Hungary	0.505	988
Romania	0.521	315
Western Europe and other	0.515	190

Source: Individual records from the 1920 integrated microsample of the U.S. Census (Ruggles et al. 2004).
Note: Immigrants are classified as Jewish if they indicate a mother tongue of Yiddish, Jewish, or Hebrew. Sample limited to arrivals between 1890 and 1914.

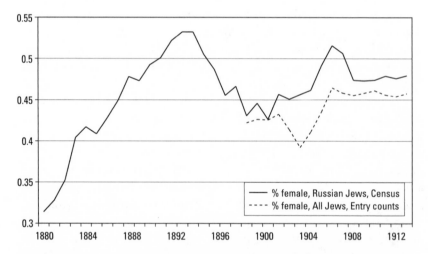

Figure 11.6
Female share of Russian Jewish immigrants to the United States, three-year moving averages, 1880–1914. For Russian Jews, the female share is calculated from the 1920 integrated micro-sample of the US Census Ruggles et al. (2004). Immigrants are classified as Jewish if indicating mother tongue of Yiddish, Jewish, or Hebrew. Russian empire includes Russian Poland, the Baltic States, Belorussia, the Ukraine, Bessarabia, and a large "other Russian" category. For comparison, also included is female share of all "Hebrew" immigrants, as collected by the Immigration Service from 1899 to 1914 (Ferenczi and Willcox 1929; 1932).

families. Following the panic of 1893 and the ensuing recession in the United States, the female share fell by 10 percentage points. By the mid-1900s, the female share had recovered. It is hard to disentangle the effect of the 1905–1906 pogroms from a temporary period of family reunification following the earlier recession. Whatever the case, it is clear that variation in the female share over time does not seem to be primarily driven by the time pattern of religious persecution.

A high female migration rate appears to be a feature of Jewish migration across areas and time periods. One explanation might be the cultural norm of endogamy, which persisted in the New World (Goldscheider and Zuckerman 1984). Another motivation might be the high labor force participation of women and children, who made up 30 percent of the Jewish labor force in the Pale in 1897 (Rubinow 1907, 524). Once arriving in the United States, Jews concentrated in the garment industry, whose decentralized structure allowed Jewish families to "use more of the labor resources of the household members [than] would have been possible within the framework of factory employment" (Kahan 1978, 240).

What should we make of the fact that Jews had higher emigration rates than any other group in the Russian empire? From 1899 to 1914, members of Russia's other ethnic minorities, including Poles, Lithuanians, Finns, and Germans, migrated to the United States at a rate of five per thousand, which is comparable to Jewish figures in the 1880s. Because it is common for migration to follow an inverted U-shaped pattern—accelerating with chain migration and eventually declining with wage convergence between source and destination—it is reasonable to imagine that this outflow would have continued were it not for the outbreak of World War I (Hatton and Williamson 1998). Thus, it may be more accurate to call Jews the first, rather than the only, ethnic group to leave the Empire.

Furthermore, while few ethnic Russians left the empire altogether, there were substantial population movements within the empire, both to the main cities of St. Petersburg and Moscow and to the eastern frontier. In the decade of the highest Jewish migration (1900s), the average rate of internal migration to Asiatic Russia was two per thousand from 1900 to 1904; it jumped to eight per thousand in the turbulent period after the 1905 Revolution (1905–1909).[31]

Conclusions

The timing of Jewish migration, like that of other migrations to the New World, responded to economic conditions. Jewish migration was particularly influenced by the health of the United States economy, perhaps because of its role as a financial constraint on migration networks. The single most important factor in the growth of out-migration rates from the Russian Jewish community was the size of the Jewish population in the United States. The path dependence of chain migration suggests that religious violence had both short- and long-term effects. Not only did migration notably increase in the years after anti-Jewish riots but the migration path was thereafter modestly higher due to the larger stock of Jews living in the United States. The power of the Hatton-Williamson model to explain annual Jewish migration rates casts doubt on previous attempts to set apart Jewish migration history from the context of European migrations to the New World.

Notes

This chapter grew out of Jeffrey Williamson's World Development course at Harvard University. I am indebted to his encouragement and intellectual guidance. I also acknowledge helpful comments from David Clingingsmith, Andrew Godley, Claudia Goldin, participants at Harvard's Graduate Economics History Tea, and the editors of this volume. Robert Allen kindly provided data on Russian wages.

1. Notable exceptions are Kuznets's (1975) thorough descriptive work and a section in Godley's (2001) book on Jewish entrepreneurial culture.

2. Odessa was also the site of smaller anti-Jewish riots in 1821, 1849, and 1859 (Klier 1992, 15–21).

3. Aronson (1990, 50–56), catalogs the anti-Jewish violence of 1881–1882 by date, province, and village.

4. Of this period, Dubnow (1918) writes: "Beginning with June, 1882, the pogroms assumed more and more a sporadic character.... In the course of the next twenty years, until the Kishinev massacre of 1903, no more than ten pogroms of any consequence may be enumerated, and these disorders were all isolated movements, with purely local coloring, and without the earmarks of a common organization or the force of an epidemic, such as characterized the pogrom campaigns of 1881, or those of 1903–1905." Löwe (2004) adds that over 95 percent of Russian pogroms occurred in either 1881–1882 or 1905–1906.

5. In 1881, only 53,574 Jews lived in the interior provinces, which establishes an upper bound on the number who may have lived in Moscow (Klier 1992, 5). Other estimates of the number exiled from Moscow range from 1,500 people to 14,000 heads of households (Baron 1964).

6. For a more complex reading of the events of 1881, see Frankel (1983). While he deems the year to be "of unique importance in modern Jewish history," he believes that the "shock of the pogroms ... accelerate[d] existing processes" rather than conjuring up the desire to migrate out of thin air (9,12). The existing processes he has in mind include Russian anti-Semitism, nascent Jewish emigration financed, in part, by Western funds, and an intellectual defense of Jewish self-determination.

7. Collins (1997) argues that African-American migration was delayed by the steady arrival of European migrants, taking off only as World War I bolstered the demand for industrial workers while simultaneously shutting off the immigrant labor supply. On the inadequacy of the persecution theory to explain black migration, see also Vickery (1977, 36–37).

8. This pattern was first noted by Hersch (1931), who noted that "Jewish immigration paralleled the total immigration to the United States" and concluded that "Jewish immigration arose partly from general causes ... and partly from circumstances peculiar to the life of the Jews" (475).

9. The data underlying this series are from Ferenczi and Willcox (1929, 384–393). Jews made up 9 percent of Austro-Hungarian migration from 1881 to 1910 (Joseph 1914, 110).

10. The fastest population growth in the Pale was in the Ukraine, and the slowest in the northern areas of Lithuania and Belorussia. This disparity could be due to internal migration to the Ukrainian cities of Odessa and Kiev or to higher outmigration rates from the North (Stampfer 1986).

11. While the growth paths of Jewish population in Prussia and Romania are consistent with an early demographic transition, some demographers argue that the Jewish community had *already* achieved a low fertility–low mortality equilibrium by the early nineteenth century because of its "absence of drunkenness, high standards of hygiene, devotion to children and close family ties" (Kuznets 1975, 67–68). For a synthesis of these two views, see Schmelz (1971).

12. Rubinow (1907, 493); Kuznets (1975, 70–71). The data come from the Russian census of 1897 and a private study conducted by the Jewish Colonization Society in 1898. The figure for the non-Jewish population of the Pale is imputed from the values for the Jewish and total populations.

13. Parenthetically, there is limited evidence for the importance of the 1882 May Laws, which prohibited Jews from settling in rural areas. The Jewish population of Vilna, which has the highest frequency data, grew at similar rates before and after the laws were promulgated (compare an annual growth rate of 1.98 from 1847 to 1875, and 2.15 from 1875 to 1897).

14. Jews were forbidden to live in the city of Kiev, though they were allowed to live in the surrounding province. This restriction, however, was not well enforced. On the legal prohibition, see Dubnow (1918, 151), and on its application, see Anderson (1980, 175).

15. Goldscheider and Zuckerman (1984, 100, 164). Some religious leaders condemned America as the *trayfa medina*, or impure land.

16. The microfoundations underlying this model can be found in Hatton (1995). Empirical applications are presented in Hatton and Williamson (1993, 1998).

17. Data on return flows from the United States are available only after 1908. The Jewish repatriation ratio in this period was 7.11 percent, the lowest of any European nationality or ethnic group (Gould 1980, 60). To convert the migrant flow into a rate, I divide by Lestchinsky's estimates of the Russian Jewish population, interpolated between decades (Kuznets 1975, 50). Annual migration series to two of Jews' other top destinations, Canada and Argentina, are available only from 1900 or 1904 onward (Hersch 1931).

18. The data underlying Joseph's (1914) figures were collected by the United Hebrew Charities in New York (1886–1899), the Association for the Protection of Jewish Immigrants in Philadelphia (1886–1899), and the Hebrew Benevolent Society of Baltimore (1891–1899). I use Godley's (2001) revisions to Joseph's data, which adjust for arrivals to other ports.

19. Wischnitzer (1948, 68) provides a detailed map of Jewish migration patterns out of Russia. Migrating in stages via other European ports was a common practice because of the nominal ban on emigration from the empire.

20. I thank Bob Allen for suggesting these data sources and discussing the PPP adjustment. These calculations rest on the strong assumption that prices in Moscow are representative of the country as a whole, and that postrevolutionary expenditure shares can be cast back to the 1880s.

21. Godley (2001) also applies the Hatton-Williamson model to Jewish migration from the Russian empire. His interest is primarily in comparing the Jewish migration flow to the United States and the United Kingdom, and thus he does not include indicators of anti-Jewish violence. A few other differences are worth noting. Godley uses per capita income in

European Russia as a proxy for standards of living, rather than factory wages. He also limits his definition of the migrant stock to Eastern European Jews in New York City, overlooking German Jews and Jews in the rest of the country. As a result, he finds that the migration rate was unaffected by the size of the migrant stock, which is at odds with the bulk of empirical work on European migration and with what we know of the Jewish migration experience from social histories.

22. To the best of my knowledge, there are no extant wages series for cities in the Pale at the turn of the century.

23. Aronson (1992) describes the economic context surrounding the 1881 Ukrainian pogroms as follows: "Landless peasants . . . were attracted to the relatively richer Ukraine from all over Russia. . . . New arrivals were unusually numerous in the spring of 1881, since an industrial depression . . . threw many factory hands . . . in Moscow and St. Petersburg out of work. . . . [In addition] local crop failures . . . led to near-famine conditions." See also Legge (1996) on an economic theory of anti-Semitism.

24. For a contrary view, see Rogger (1986, 28–33).

25. 78.6 percent of Jewish immigrants from the Russian empire in the 1920 Census do not indicate their province of birth. This comparison may be imperfect, then, given that it includes only the 21.4 percent who do.

26. In addition to adding the simulated migration flow to the stock, I allow the stock to grow by 3 percent in every year due to natural increase and the in-migration of Jews from the rest of the world.

27. The simulations in figure 11.5 do not include the twice-lagged migration rate, which is never statistically significant. When the negative effect of the twice-lagged rate is taken into account, the two migration rates converge soon after the date of a known pogrom (not shown). Thus, the figure represents an upper bound on the long-term effect of religious persecution.

28. From 1894 to 1903 the pogrom-response migration rate was, on average, 0.39 per thousand higher in each year than was the no-response rate. The Russian Jewish population was around 4.8 million in this decade, implying that in the long run the expulsion from Moscow led to the arrival of an additional 1,900 Jewish migrants in every year ($= 0.39 \times 4,800$).

29. 47.7 percent of Jewish migrants who entered the country between 1899 and 1910 and were enumerated in the 1920 Census were female, compared to 43 percent of new arrivals tallied by the Immigration Service over the same period. This disparity could be due to higher rates of male mortality.

30. Recovering the female share of the migrant flow from the 1920 Census will be increasingly biased because of differential mortality by gender the further one goes back in time. In 1920 the average Jewish immigrant who entered the United States in 1880 was 56.5 years old. If anything, this mortality will bias the female share in the 1880s upward, implying an even *larger* male majority among pioneer migrants.

31. Anderson (1980, 203) presents internal migration rates to Asiatic Russia in five-year intervals from 1885 to 1909 by province of origin. Migration to the agricultural frontier is an underestimate of total population mobility.

References

American Jewish Year Book. 1900–1920. Philadelphia: Jewish Publication Society of America. Various editions.

Anderson, B. 1980. *Internal Migration During Modernization in Late Nineteenth-Century Russia.* Princeton, N.J.: Princeton University Press.

Aronson, I. M. 1990. *Troubled Waters: The Origins of the 1881 Anti-Jewish Pogroms in Russia.* Pittsburgh: University of Pittsburgh Press.

————. 1992. The Anti-Jewish Pogroms in Russia in 1881. In *Pogroms: Anti-Jewish Violence in Modern Russian History*, ed. J. D. Klier and S. Lambroza. Cambridge: Cambridge University Press.

Baron, S. W. 1964. *The Russian Jew Under Tsars and Soviets.* New York: Macmillan.

Carrington, W. J., E. Detragiache, and T. Vishwanath (1996). Migration with Endogenous Moving Costs. *American Economic Review* 86: 909–930.

Chiswick, B. 1992. Jewish Immigrant Wages in America in 1909: An Analysis of the Dillingham Commission Data. *Explorations in Economic History* 29 (3): 274–289.

Collins, W. J. 1997. When the Tide Turned: Immigration and the Delay of the Great Black Migration. *Journal of Economic History* 57 (3): 607–632.

Dubnow, S. M. 1918. *History of the Jews in Russia and Poland.* Philadelphia: Jewish Publication Society of America.

Easterlin, R. 1961. Influences in European Overseas Emigration Before World War I. *Economic Development and Cultural Change* 9 (3): 331–351.

Engelman, U. Z. 1949. Sources of Jewish Statistics. In *The Jews: Their History, Culture, and Religion*, ed. L. Finkelstein. Philadelphia: Jewish Publication Society of America.

Ferenczi, I., and W. Willcox. 1929. *International Migrations.* Vol. 1. New York: National Bureau of Economic Research.

————. 1932. *International Migrations.* Vol. 2. New York: National Bureau of Economic Research.

Frankel, J. 1983. The Crisis of 1881–82 as a Turning Point in Modern Jewish History. In *The Legacy of Jewish Migration: 1881 and Its Impact*, ed. D. Berger. New York: Columbia University Press.

Godley, A. 2001. *Jewish Immigrant Entrepreneurship in New York and London, 1880–1914.* New York: Palgrave Macmillan.

Goldscheider, C., and A. S. Zuckerman. 1984. *The Transformation of the Jews.* Chicago: University of Chicago Press.

Gould, J. D. 1980. European Inter-Continental Emigration—The Road Home: Return Migration from the U.S.A. *Journal of European Economic History* 9 (1): 41–112.

Grant, O. 2003. Globalisation versus Decoupling: German Emigration and the Evolution of the Atlantic Labour Market, 1870–1913. *Explorations in Economic History* 40 (4): 387–418.

Gregory, P. R. 1982. *Russian National Income, 1885–1913.* Cambridge: Cambridge University Press.

Harris, J. R., and M. P. Todaro. 1970. Migration, Unemployment and Development: A Two-Sector Analysis. *American Economic Review* 60 (1): 126–142.

Hatton, T. J. 1995. A Model of UK Emigration, 1870–1913. *Review of Economics and Statistics* 77 (3): 407–415.

Hatton, T. J., and J. G. Williamson. 1993. After the Famine: Emigration from Ireland, 1850–1913. *Journal of Economic History* 53 (3): 575–600.

————. 1998. *The Age of Mass Migration.* New York: Oxford University Press.

Hersch, L. 1931. International Migration of the Jews. In *International Migrations*, ed. W. Willcox. New York: National Bureau of Economic Research.

Joseph, S. 1914. Jewish Immigration to the US, 1881–1910. *Studies in History, Economics, and Public Law* 59 (4): 7–209.

Kahan, A. 1978. Economic Opportunities and Some Pilgrims' Progress: Jewish Immigrants from Eastern Europe in the U.S., 1890–1914. *Journal of Economic History* 38 (1): 235–251.

————. 1986. *Essays in Jewish Social and Economic History.* Chicago: University of Chicago Press.

Klier, J. D. 1992. Russian Jewry on the Eve of the Pogroms. In *Pogroms: Anti-Jewish Violence in Modern Russian History*, ed. J. D. Klier and S. Lambroza. Cambridge: Cambridge University Press.

Kuznets, S. 1975. Immigration of Russian Jews to the United States: Background and Structure. *Perspectives in American History* 9: 35–124.

Lambroza, S. 1992. The Pogroms of 1903–1906. In *Pogroms: Anti-Jewish Violence in Modern Russian History*, ed. J. D. Klier and S. Lambroza. Cambridge: Cambridge University Press.

Lebergott, S. 1957. Annual Estimates of Unemployment in the United States, 1900–1954. In *The Measurement and Behavior of Unemployment: A Conference of the Universities–National Bureau Committee for Economic Research.* Princeton, N.J.: Princeton University Press.

Legge, J. 1996. An Economic Theory of Anti-Semitism: Exploring Attitudes in the New German State. *Political Research Quarterly* 49 (3): 617–630.

Lestchinsky, J. 1949. Jewish Migrations, 1840–1946. In *The Jews: Their History, Culture, and Religion*, ed. L. Finkelstein. Philadelphia: Jewish Publication Society of America.

Löwe, H.-D. 2004. Pogroms in Russia: Explanations, Comparisons, Suggestions. *Jewish Social Studies* 11 (1): 16–23.

Rischin, M. 1962. *The Promised City: New York's Jews, 1870–1914.* Cambridge, Mass.: Harvard University Press.

Rogger, H. 1986. *Jewish Policies and Right-Wing Politics in Imperial Russia.* Berkeley: University of California Press.

Rubinow, I. M. 1907. *Economic Condition of the Jews in Russia.* New York: Arno Press, 1975.

Ruggles, S., M. Sobek, T. Alexander, C. A. Fitch, R. Goeken, P. K. Hall, M. King, and C. Ronnander. 2004. Integrated Public Use Microdata Series: Version 3.0. Machine-Readable Database. Minneapolis: Minnesota Population Center.

Ruppin, A. 1934. *The Jews in the Modern World.* London: Macmillan.

Schmelz, U. O. 1971. *Infant and Early Childhood Mortality Among Jews of the Diaspora.* Jerusalem: Institute of Contemporary Jewry, Hebrew University of Jerusalem.

Silber, J. 1980. Some Demographic Characteristics of the Jewish Population in Russia at the End of the Nineteenth Century. *Jewish Social Studies* 42 (3–4): 269–280.

Stampfer, S. 1986. The Geographic Background of East European Jewish Migration to the United States before World War I. In *Migration Across Time and Nations: Population Mobility in Historical Contexts*, ed. I. A. Glazier and L. De Rosa. New York: Holmes and Meier.

Stanislawski, M. 1983. *Tsar Nicholas I and the Jews: The Transformation of Jewish Society in Russia, 1825–1855.* Philadelphia: Jewish Publication Society of America.

Vernon, J. R. 1994. Unemployment Rates in Postbellum America, 1869–1899. *Journal of Macroeconomics* 16 (4): 701–714.

Vickery, W. E. 1977. *The Economics of the Negro Migration, 1900–1960.* New York: Arno Press.

Williamson, J. G. 1995. The Evolution of Global Labor Markets since 1830: Background Evidence and Hypotheses. *Explorations in Economic History* 32 (2): 141–196.

Wischnitzer, M. 1948. *To Dwell in Safety: The Story of Jewish Migration since 1800.* Philadelphia: Jewish Publication Society of America.

Workers' Family Budget Enquiries in Soviet Russia. 1929. *International Labour Review* 20 (2): 568–576.

Zaleski, E. 1955. Les fluctuations des prix de détail en Union Soviétique. *Etudes et Conjonctures* 4: 329–384.

12 Inequality and Poverty in Latin America: A Long-Run Exploration

Leandro Prados de la Escosura

Latin America is today the world region in which inequality is highest, with an average Gini coefficient above 50 during the last four decades of the twentieth century (Deininger and Squire, 1996; 1998). A stable income distribution in the early postwar period worsened after 1980 (Altimir 1987; Morley 2000). Furthermore, no significant improvement in the relationship between income distribution and economic growth has taken place during the last decade (Londoño and Székely 2000), and inequality remains high despite episodes of sustained growth (ECLAC 2000).

Is today's high inequality a permanent feature of modern Latin American history? How has inequality affected poverty in the long run? These are pressing questions for social scientists. Unfortunately, no quantitative assessment of long-run inequality has been carried out for Latin America, except for Uruguay (Bértola 2005), but the perception of unrelenting inequality deeply rooted in the past is widespread (see, for example, Bourguignon and Morrisson's (2002) assumptions).

In this chapter I first examine long-run trends in inequality in modern Latin America and then, on the basis of trends in inequality and growth, make a preliminary attempt at calibrating their impact on poverty reduction.

When did inequality originate, and why has it persisted over time? Alternative interpretations have been put forward. Those that emphasize its colonial roots are worth stressing. According to Engerman and Sokoloff (1997), initial inequality of wealth, human capital, and political power conditioned institutional design, and hence performance, in Spanish America. Large-scale estates, built on pre-conquest social organization and an extensive supply of native labor, established the initial levels of inequality. In the post-independence world, elites designed institutions protecting their privileges. In such a path-dependent framework government policies and institutions restricted competition and offered opportunities to select groups (Sokoloff and Engerman 2000).

Acemoglu, Johnson, and Robinson (2002) provide a different explanation for the uneven fate of former colonies. Where abundant population showed relative affluence, "extractive institutions" were established, under which most of the population risks expropriation at the hands of the ruling elite or the government (forced labor and tributes, often existing already in the pre-colonial era, over the locals). With political power concentrated in the hands of an elite, this represented the most efficient choice for European colonizers despite its negative effects on long-term growth. This would be the case of the Iberian empires in the Americas, especially in its economic centers of Peru and New Spain.

The opening up to the international economy has been associated with a widening of income differences within and across countries. *Dependentists* have seen it as a cause of increasing inequality across and within countries, stressing the role of the terms of trade in Latin American retardation as countries either improved and shifted resources to primary production (Singer 1950) or deteriorated and provoked immiserizing growth (Prebisch 1950). Neoclassical trade theory predicts that trade liberalization after independence would allow Latin American countries to specialize along the lines of comparative advantage. The Heckscher-Ohlin model predicts that natural resources, as the abundant factor, will be intensively used and, as a result, their relative price in terms of labor will increase. This implies, in the Stolper-Samuelson extension of the Heckscher-Ohlin model, that insofar as land, the abundant factor, is more unequally distributed than labor, inequality will rise within national borders.

No evidence on inequality is available for the pre-1870 period with the exception of Argentina, for which Newland and Ortiz (2001) show that the expansion in the pastoral sector resulting from improved terms of trade increased the reward of capital and land, the most intensively used factors, while the farming sector contracted and the returns of its intensive factor, labor, declined, as confirmed by the drop in nominal wages. A redistribution of income in favor of owners of capital and land at the expense of workers took place in Argentina between 1820 and 1870. Williamson (1999) has explored the consequences for inequality of the early phase of globalization (1870–1914). On the basis of the wage-land rental ratio, he showed an increase of inequality within countries in Argentina and Uruguay that confirms empirically the Stolper-Samuelson theoretical predictions. As natural resources were the abundant productive factor in

Latin America, they were more intensively used in the production of exportable commodities. As a result, returns to land grew, relative to those of labor. Since the ownership of natural resources is more concentrated than that of labor, income distribution tended to be skewed toward landowners, and inequality rose over the decades prior to World War I. Presumably, inequality trends reversed in the interwar period, when globalization was interrupted, as suggested by the fact that the steep decline in the wage-rental ratio stopped in Argentina and Uruguay, and rose in the 1930s (Bértola and Williamson 2005). Globalization after 1980 has also been associated with rising inequality in Latin America.

Lewis's (1954) labor surplus model, in which the worker fails to share in GDP per capita growth because elastic labor supplies (migration of surplus labor from southern Europe, especially Spain and Italy) keep wages and living standards stable, also provides the basis of an interpretation of rising inequality in Argentina (Díaz-Alejandro 1970) and Brazil (Leff 1982) during the early phase of globalization.

But, can we quantify trends in income inequality in modern Latin America? Lack of historical household surveys prevents replication of modern inequality studies. Only after careful and painstaking research, country by country, can standard inequality measures be provided for Latin America's past.

An approach to assessing inequality has been proposed and applied to a wide international sample over 1870–1940 by Williamson (2002): the ratio of GDP per worker to unskilled wages. The rationale for this choice is that such a ratio confronts the returns to unskilled labor with the returns to all production factors, that is, GDP. Since unskilled labor is the more evenly distributed factor of production in developing countries, an increase in the ratio suggests that inequality is rising. So, in order to convey an idea of how inequality has evolved within Latin American societies, I have constructed Williamson's inequality index as the ratio of real GDP per worker to real wages, normalized with 1913 = 1 (see appendix).

Long-run trends in inequality derived with 11-year centered moving averages are presented for a group of main Latin American countries in figures 12.1a and 12.1b. A sustained rise in the inequality index from the late nineteenth century up to World War I is observed for the Southern Cone (no data available for Colombia) during the early phase of globalization (figure 12.1a). Conversely, a decline in inequality took place in the interwar years, as globalization was reversed. This view confirms the Stolper-Samuelson interpretation. The stabilization or decline of

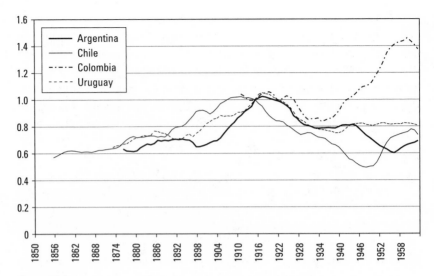

Figure 12.1a
Inequality indices in Argentina, Chile, Colombia, and Venezuela (1913 = 1).

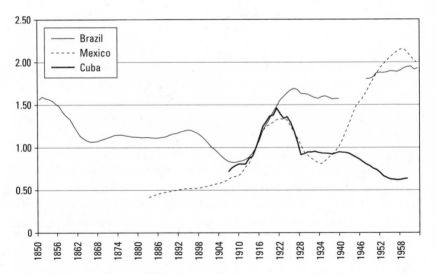

Figure 12.1b
Inequality indices in Brazil, Cuba, and Mexico (1913 = 1).

inequality during the mid-twentieth century could be related, as Bértola (2005) points out, to urbanization and the emerging role of government. Redistributive policies, as suggested by the rise of income tax share of government revenues in the thirties and forties (Astorga and Fitzgerald 1998, 346), are correlated with the decline in the inequality index in Argentina and Chile and its stagnation in Uruguay. The sustained rise in inequality exhibited between the late thirties and fifties in Colombia coincides with the "violencia" period (Palacios 1995).

In figure 12.1b trends in inequality are shown for Brazil, Cuba, and Mexico. Brazil presents a long-run decline up to 1913, with a flat phase between the late 1860s and 1890s, and Mexico shows a moderate increase in inequality between the 1880s and the revolution of 1910. Scattered evidence for Cuba suggests a similar pattern. A dramatic increase in inequality took place in the three countries after 1910 and well into the 1920s, followed by stabilization over the 1930s in Brazil and Cuba. A gradual rise in inequality in Brazil contrasts with the inequality reduction in Cuba between the early 1940s and the late 1950s. If the data on Cuba are taken at face value, the 1959 revolution would have occurred in a context of inequality stability after a sustained fall in a context of stagnated per capita income. The case of Mexico provides some perplexities, too. The aftermath of the 1910 revolution was a period of rising inequality followed by a dramatic inequality reduction. Then, between the mid-thirties and the mid-fifties—years of accelerating per capita GDP growth due to improving labor productivity and employment creation—a spectacular rise in the inequality would have taken place.

But how was the long-run evolution of inequality? A heuristic exercise in which available Gini coefficients (mainly from 1950 onward) are projected backward with the rate of variation of the "inequality indices," previously smoothed with 11-year moving averages, is provided in table 12.1, so conjectures about long-run inequality trends can be derived (see appendix). No doubt the pseudo-Gini indices derived prior to the mid-twentieth century are questionable. By using changes in the inequality index to project Gini coefficients backward, a new time series is created in which two different cardinal measures are used: the directly estimated Gini and the backward projection. These cardinal representations of ordinal inequality measures might result in large discrepancies. Nonetheless, it can be argued that because the inequality index can be interpreted as the ratio between a quantile of the income distribution (wage rates per day or hour) and the mean of the distribution (GDP per EAP), backward projections of Gini directly estimated coefficients could be consistent with

Table 12.1
Income Distribution in Latin America: Gini Estimates and Conjectures, 1850–1990

	1850	1860	1870	1880	1890	1900	1913
Argentina			39.1	39.7	43.6	42.0	61.8
Bolivia							
Brazil	46.2	37.2	32.9	33.0	34.4	29.8	29.5
Chile	36.6	40.7	41.3	47.2	51.9	58.5	65.5
Colombia							46.8
Costa Rica							
Dominican R.							
Ecuador							
El Salvador							
Guatemala							
Honduras							
Mexico							27.8
Nicaragua							
Panama							
Paraguay							
Peru							
Uruguay			29.6	33.1	32.2	38.4	45.9
Venezuela							
LatAm4			34.8	35.9	38.0	35.4	40.5
LatAm6							37.7
LatAm15							
LatAm16							

Note: Gini direct estimates are shown in bold; otherwise, pseudo-Gini (backward projection of Gini using variation of inequality indices).
LatAm4: population-weighted average of Argentina, Brazil, Chile, and Uruguay.
LatAm6: population-weighted average of Argentina, Brazil, Chile, Colombia, Mexico, and Uruguay.

"first-order inequality dominance." In other words, the amplitude of the swings in the pseudo-Gini indices could be wrong, but not the tendency.[1]

Several features in long-run inequality are worth highlighting. Inequality rose steadily until it reached a high plateau, which stabilized over the last four decades of the twentieth century. Moreover, persistent high inequality seems to be confirmed at least since the Great Depression. Another relevant feature is the wide variance across Latin American countries, with Gini indices ranging from 40 to almost 60. Nonetheless, countries' positions in the inequality ranking are not fixed. Southern Cone nations (Argentina and Chile) exhibited the highest inequality levels until the interwar years, when inequality rose in Mexico, Brazil, and Colombia, countries that by 1950 achieved an unenviable lead in inequality.

	1929	1938	1950	1960	1970	1980	1990
Argentina	49.3	50.0	**39.6**	**41.4**	**41.2**	**47.2**	**47.7**
Bolivia					**53.0**	**53.4**	**54.5**
Brazil	47.2	46.4	55.4	**57.0**	**57.1**	**57.1**	**57.3**
Chile	49.2	40.5	41.7	**48.2**	**47.4**	**53.1**	**54.7**
Colombia	40.2	**45.0**	**51.0**	**54.0**	**57.3**	**48.8**	**56.7**
Costa Rica			30.7	**50.0**	**44.5**	**48.5**	**46.0**
Dominican R.			32.4	34.6	**45.5**	**42.1**	**48.1**
Ecuador			57.1	61.0	60.1	54.2	**56.0**
El Salvador			44.0	**42.4**	**46.5**	**48.4**	**50.5**
Guatemala			**42.3**	28.6	**30.0**	**49.7**	**59.9**
Honduras			57.1	66.0	**61.8**	**54.9**	**57.0**
Mexico	24.3	30.4	**55.0**	**60.6**	**57.9**	**50.9**	**53.1**
Nicaragua				68.1	63.2	57.9	**56.7**
Panama			56.4	**50.0**	**58.4**	**47.5**	**56.3**
Paraguay						**45.1**	**57.0**
Peru			39.2	**61.0**	**48.5**	**43.0**	**46.4**
Uruguay	36.6	34.9	37.9	**37.0**	**42.8**	**43.6**	**40.6**
Venezuela			**61.3**	**46.2**	**48.0**	**44.7**	**44.0**
LatAm4	47.5	46.4	50.4	52.7	53.1	54.9	55.2
LatAm6	41.6	42.8	51.5	54.7	54.8	53.2	54.8
LatAm15			50.6	53.9	53.5	51.9	53.7
LatAm16				54.0	53.6	52.0	53.8

LatAm15: population-weighted average of all Latin American countries but Bolivia, Cuba, Haiti, Nicaragua, and Paraguay.
LatAm16: population-weighted average of all Latin American countries but Bolivia, Cuba, Haiti, and Paraguay.

It is also worth noticing the inequality decline in Venezuela during the 1950s and the worsening of Chilean income distribution of the 1970s and 1980s. Meanwhile, Uruguay appears to follow, at least until 1960, the European pattern of inequality.

An attempt to provide a regional view is shown in figure 12.2. Two phases of inequality expansion, one before 1929 and the other from World War II to 1960, are noticeable; and a fall in inequality is evident in the 1890s (associated with the Baring crisis) and in the Great Depression years. The sustained rise in inequality since 1900 reached a high plateau in the 1960s. This remained stable over the last four decades of the twentieth century and dwarfed the contraction in inequality of the 1970s and its rise during the 1980s.

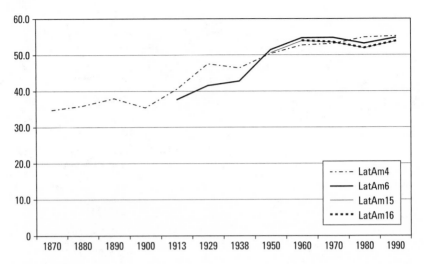

Figure 12.2
Gini estimates and conjectures for Latin America (population-weighted averages).

Inequality trends before World War I can be interpreted in Stolper-Samuelson terms. Thus, when Latin America opened up to international competition after independence, especially from the mid-nineteenth century to World War I, the relative position of land improved, and because land was unevenly distributed, inequality tended *ceteris paribus* to increase. Predictable are the reduction in inequality as the economy of Latin America closed up during the interwar period, and a new surge in inequality during the second wave of globalization (1950–1980). Naturally, the impact on income distribution of international trade and factor mobility is not the only force at play. Industrialization and redistributive forces from an increasing role of government also appear to have affected inequality reduction in Latin America during the twentieth century.

It is worth noting that inequality often appears to be positively correlated with economic growth, as suggested by the correspondence between rising inequality and per capita income before 1913 (especially in the Southern Cone) and after 1950, and their decline in the interwar period (see tables 12.1 and 12.2). Was there a trade-off between growth and inequality in Latin America? This question demands careful investigation.

Long-Run Trends in Poverty

Poverty reduction depends on the growth of average income and on how income is distributed, and is closely linked to the sensitivity of poverty to both (growth elasticity and inequality elasticity of poverty). Initial levels of development and inequality also condition the impact on poverty of growth and improvements in income distribution (Bourguignon 2003; Klasen 2004; López 2004; Ravallion 1997; 2004).

How did inequality and economic growth impinge on poverty in Latin America? In this section I focus on absolute growth of the poor's incomes (Ravallion and Chen 2003) rather than on whether a relatively disproportionate growth in the poor's incomes took place (Kakwani and Pernia 2000). In a heuristic exercise, I calibrate trends of absolute poverty from which hypotheses for further research can be derived.

A glance at Latin America's long-run economic growth is provided in table 12.2. In addition to country estimates, growth rates are presented for population-weighted averages of real GDP per head for different groups of Latin American countries (the lengthier the coverage, the lower the number of countries included). Some features can be noted. First, the origins of modern economic growth, as defined by a sustained increase in output per person, can be traced back to at least the mid-nineteenth century. Latin America experienced a sustained and steady growth over more than a century, only broken during the 1890s, the Great Depression, and especially the 1980s crisis. Fortunately, though, the picture of Latin America's performance seems quite robust. After a slow start in the mid-nineteenth century, Latin America appears to have grown significantly during the 1870s and 1880s and, after a slowdown in the 1890s, to have accelerated until World War I. Latin America's output per head slowed because of World War I and halted in the years of the Great Depression. After the Depression, its countries enjoyed their fastest phase of growth, which lasted more than four decades. Their somewhat better performance in the 1970s made up for slower growth in the so-called Golden Age (1950–1973). The 1980s represent a major break in the long-run performance of Latin America, only slightly offset by sluggish growth in the 1990s. Thus, while the growth of the early phase, 1860s–1929, was surpassed by the performance of the 1930s–1980, the post-1980 era is a phase of slowing down. To sum up, modern Latin America experienced sustained growth since the mid-nineteenth century, that was only brought to a halt during the 1980s.

Latin America consists of a heterogeneous group of countries that exhibit substantial discrepancies in their factor endowments and long-run performance. The high variance of growth rates of GDP per capita in Latin America proves it. In Argentina, Chile, and Mexico, income per head grew faster than Latin America's average between 1870 and 1913, whereas in Brazil, Colombia, Peru, and Venezuela this happened in

Table 12.2
Economic Growth in Main Latin American Countries, 1850–2000

	Argentina	Brazil	Chile	Colombia	Cuba	Mexico	Peru	Uruguay	Venezuela	LA6	LA10	LA15	LA20
1850–1870		0.2	1.7			0.0			−1.2				
1870–1890	3.3	0.2	2.0			2.0		0.4	2.6	1.7			
1890–1900	−0.8	−0.9	1.2			1.5		0.8	−1.5	0.4			
1900–1913	2.5	2.2	2.3	1.8	3.2	1.9	1.4	3.1	2.6	2.2	2.3		
1913–1929	0.9	1.4	0.9	3.9	−0.7	0.4	3.6	0.9	6.8	1.0	1.2	1.2	
1929–1938	−0.8	1.0	−0.8	1.4	0.2	0.4	0.1	0.1	0.5	0.1	0.2	0.1	
1938–1950	1.7	1.6	1.3	1.5	0.1	3.5	1.2	1.5	4.3	2.3	2.1	2.1	
1950–1960	1.1	3.7	1.5	1.6	0.3	2.3	2.9	0.6	3.4	2.4	2.3	2.3	2.3
1960–1970	3.9	3.1	1.9	2.2	−0.4	3.4	2.3	0.8	2.4	3.2	3.0	2.9	2.9
1970–1980	2.1	5.8	0.9	2.9	5.5	2.5	1.7	2.1	0.1	3.4	3.3	3.3	3.3
1980–1990	−2.4	−0.2	1.2	1.1	0.6	−0.1	−3.3	−0.2	−1.9	−0.5	−0.4	−0.5	−0.5
1990–2000	2.8	0.8	5.0	0.7	−7.1	1.7	2.3	2.1	−0.1	1.5	1.3	1.3	1.3
1870–1929	1.8	0.8	1.6	2.1	1.3	1.5	1.9	1.2	3.0	1.4			
1938–1980	2.1	3.4	1.4	0.9	−3.3	2.9	−0.5	1.4	2.6	2.7	2.6	2.6	2.9
1980–2000	0.2	0.3	3.1			0.8		0.9	−1.0	0.5	0.4	0.4	0.4
1870–1980	0.0	1.8	1.3			1.9		1.1	2.7	1.8			
1870–2000	0.0	1.6	1.6			1.8		1.1	2.1	1.6			

Notes: Logarithmic annual growth rates (percent).
LA6: population-weighted average of list exact countries. Argentina, Brazil, Chile, Mexico, Uruguay, and Venezuela.
LA10: population-weighted average of LA6 plus Colombia, Cuba, Ecuador, and Peru.
LA15: population-weighted average of LA10 plus Costa Rica, El Salvador, Guatemala, Honduras, and Paraguay.
LA20: population-weighted average of all Latin American countries.

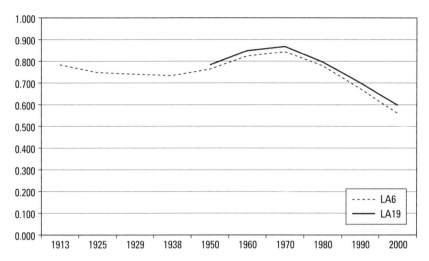

Figure 12.3
Dependence rate in Latin America (population-weighted averages).

1913–1938. On the whole, during the early phase of modern economic growth (1870–1929), Colombia, Peru, Venezuela, and to lesser extent Argentina grew faster than the region's average. In the second phase of sustained expansion (1938–1980), Mexico and especially Brazil exceeded the average, and Chile stands alone above the average in the last two decades of the twentieth century.

But did economic growth reach the lower deciles of income distribution and hence help reduce absolute poverty? High dependence rates in Latin America resulting from a delayed demographic transition help explain lower levels of GDP per person, and hence higher poverty, in Latin America (figure 12.3).[2] The persistence of high dependency rates in Latin America hint at the lack of incentives to reduce fertility provided by the institutional framework and at a weak demand for human capital, which had helped bring about the demographic transition in OECD countries (Galor 2004).

The poor are unevenly distributed and more concentrated in rural areas in Latin America. Improving labor productivity increases rural incomes and helps to reduce inequality as well as to promote growth; thus it may contribute to poverty reduction. Usually, rural-urban migration is accompanied by rising productivity in agriculture, and as a whole, rural-urban migration tends to have a positive impact on poverty reduction.

Table 12.3 provides evidence of a sustained decline in the share of agriculture in total employment, which fell below one-fifth of total employment

Table 12.3
Share of Economically Active Population in Agriculture, 1900–1990

	1900	1913	1929	1938	1950	1960	1970	1980	1990
Argentina	0.39	0.35	0.36	0.35	0.25	0.21	0.16	0.13	0.12
Bolivia					0.56	0.55	0.55	0.53	0.47
Brazil		0.71		0.69	0.62	0.55	0.47	0.37	0.23
Chile	0.37	0.37	0.37	0.36	0.33	0.30	0.24	0.21	0.19
Colombia				0.73	0.59	0.52	0.45	0.40	0.27
Costa Rica					0.57	0.51	0.43	0.35	0.26
Cuba					0.41	0.36	0.30	0.24	0.18
Dominican R.					0.73	0.64	0.48	0.32	0.25
Ecuador					0.65	0.59	0.52	0.40	0.33
El Salvador					0.65	0.62	0.57	0.44	0.36
Guatemala					0.69	0.66	0.61	0.54	0.52
Haiti					0.86	0.80	0.74	0.71	0.68
Honduras					0.75	0.72	0.67	0.57	0.41
Mexico	0.62	0.68	0.70	0.66	0.66	0.54	0.50	0.36	0.35
Nicaragua					0.70	0.63	0.51	0.40	0.29
Panama					0.56	0.51	0.42	0.29	0.26
Paraguay					0.54	0.54	0.50	0.45	0.39
Peru					0.58	0.52	0.48	0.40	0.36
Uruguay					0.24	0.21	0.19	0.17	0.14
Venezuela			0.59	0.54	0.43	0.33	0.26	0.15	0.12

Source: Astorga, Bergés, and Fitzgerald (2004).

in countries of the Southern Cone, Cuba, and Venezuela during the phase of sustained growth, 1938–1980. Alas, this trend cannot be generalized. Haiti, Guatemala, and Bolivia kept half or more of the labor force in the primary sector, and several others, including Mexico and Peru, still maintained more than one-third of workers in agriculture by 1990. The labor productivity gap between agriculture and the economy as a whole tended to close over the same period (table 12.4), but, again, the correspondence between those countries experiencing a long-run decline in agricultural employment and those in which the productivity gap exhibited a shrinking trend appears weak, and only includes Argentina, Uruguay, and Venezuela. Countries such as Brazil, Chile, and Cuba reduced the relative size of agricultural employment while keeping a substantial intersectoral productivity gap. Conversely, Colombia and Central America maintained high proportions of labor in agriculture while the average labor productivity gap was closing (actually, it closed completely in Nicaragua). Reliance on cash crops helps explain why this was the case.

Table 12.4
Relative Labor Productivity in Agriculture, 1900–1990

	1900	1913	1929	1938	1950	1960	1970	1980	1990
Argentina	0.74	0.70	0.64	0.62	0.68	0.77	0.82	0.85	1.20
Bolivia					0.46	0.44	0.31	0.28	0.32
Brazil		0.32		0.33	0.27	0.24	0.21	0.20	0.34
Chile	0.44	0.42	0.32	0.40	0.34	0.32	0.33	0.35	0.43
Colombia				0.64	0.64	0.63	0.63	0.62	0.91
Costa Rica					0.67	0.58	0.59	0.58	0.84
Cuba					0.51	0.52	0.64	0.52	0.51
Dominican R.					0.47	0.53	0.54	0.57	0.64
Ecuador					0.64	0.66	0.58	0.53	0.78
El Salvador					0.63	0.58	0.54	0.77	0.86
Guatemala					0.53	0.51	0.49	0.50	0.51
Haiti					0.61	0.62	0.68	0.56	0.58
Honduras					0.60	0.45	0.51	0.53	0.75
Mexico	0.45	0.37	0.28	0.30	0.28	0.30	0.23	0.24	0.22
Nicaragua					0.52	0.47	0.53	0.75	1.09
Panama					0.58	0.51	0.38	0.48	0.59
Paraguay					0.75	0.73	0.69	0.64	0.80
Peru					0.40	0.47	0.39	0.36	0.57
Uruguay					0.56	0.52	0.68	0.64	0.78
Venezuela				0.40	0.22	0.24	0.29	0.49	0.68

Source: Astorga, Bergés, and Fitzgerald (2004).

The shift from countryside to cities is confirmed by increasing urbanization (table 12.5), which reached beyond four-fifths of the population in
the Southern Cone, Brazil, and Venezuela in 2000 but still remained below half the population in Central America and Haiti.

Because low rural living standards relative to urban ones are said to be
an obstacle to the impact of growth on absolute poverty reduction (Klasen 2004), I have computed crude rural-urban gaps in terms of per capita
income. In order to do so, I assumed that incomes in the countryside
accrued mostly from agriculture. It is true that those living in rural areas
also produce services and light industrial goods, but the opposite could
also be said of some of those living in cities ("agro-cities," because they
continue supplying labor to agricultural tasks at peak season). If agricultural output is divided by population living in nonurban areas, a lower
bound for rural incomes can be obtained. Its ratio to average incomes
(per capita GDP) provides a crude indicator of the income gap between
countryside and the city (table 12.6).

Table 12.5
Urbanization Rates in Latin America, 1850–2000

	1850	1870	1890	1913	1929	1950	1960	1970	1980	1990	2000
Argentina	0.15	0.16	0.30	0.37	0.49	0.64	0.74	0.78	0.83	0.86	0.89
Bolivia					0.22	0.34	0.39	0.41	0.46	0.56	0.65
Brazil			0.15	0.21	0.28	0.36	0.45	0.56	0.66	0.75	0.81
Chile	0.08	0.15	0.21	0.33	0.43	0.57	0.68	0.75	0.81	0.83	0.85
Colombia			0.11	0.12	0.24	0.35	0.48	0.57	0.64	0.70	0.75
Costa Rica			0.24	0.15	0.20	0.34	0.37	0.40	0.43	0.46	0.52
Cuba	0.18	0.28	0.34	0.33	0.39	0.54	0.55	0.60	0.68	0.74	0.75
Dominican R.				0.11	0.14	0.24	0.30	0.40	0.50	0.58	0.65
Ecuador		0.10	0.20	0.25	0.23	0.29	0.34	0.39	0.47	0.55	0.62
El Salvador				0.26	0.45	0.37	0.38	0.39	0.42	0.44	0.47
Guatemala				0.30	0.25	0.25	0.32	0.36	0.37	0.38	0.40
Haiti						0.12	0.16	0.20	0.24	0.30	0.36
Honduras				0.18	0.24	0.31	0.23	0.29	0.35	0.42	0.47
Mexico			0.16	0.19	0.27	0.43	0.51	0.59	0.66	0.73	0.74
Nicaragua		0.20	0.18	0.23	0.24	0.35	0.40	0.47	0.50	0.53	0.65
Panama				0.14	0.25	0.36	0.41	0.48	0.50	0.54	0.58
Paraguay			0.20	0.37	0.24	0.35	0.36	0.37	0.42	0.49	0.56
Peru				0.12	0.25	0.42	0.46	0.57	0.65	0.69	0.73
Uruguay	0.16	0.29	0.44	0.44	0.49	0.63	0.80	0.82	0.85	0.89	0.91
Venezuela			0.11	0.13	0.27	0.43	0.61	0.72	0.79	0.84	0.87

Sources: Astorga, Bergés, and Fitzgerald (2004) backward projected with data in Flora (1973), except Chile; Cariola and Sunkel (1982, 144) for Chile, since 1870.

The evolution of the rural-urban income gap again yields ambiguous results. Although by the end of the twentieth century it closed dramatically in Colombia and Peru, and even reversed in Argentina, Uruguay, and Nicaragua, it remained large in Mexico, Central America, and the Caribbean. Thus the population residing in the countryside shrank throughout the twentieth century, and in many instances the rural-urban gap was reduced. Yet by 1990 a non-negligible share of the population, especially in the northern section of Latin America, remained in rural areas living on a substantially lower income than those in the city. Such high concentration of population in rural areas tends unequivocally to suggest poverty.

I then examine the evolution of absolute poverty as defined by a fixed international poverty line. Given the fact that Latin America, although exhibiting persistently high inequality, is not among the poorest regions of the world, I decided to use a poverty line (PL) equivalent to 1985

Table 12.6
Relative Rural Income per Head in Latin America, 1900–2000

	1900	1913	1929	1950	1960	1970	1980	1990	2000
Argentina	0.41	0.39	0.45	0.48	0.60	0.61	0.65	1.08	1.08
Bolivia				0.39	0.40	0.29	0.27	0.34	0.39
Brazil		0.29	0.32	0.26	0.24	0.23	0.21	0.31	0.47
Chile	0.21	0.23	0.21	0.26	0.30	0.32	0.39	0.48	0.40
Colombia	0.60	0.60	0.65	0.58	0.63	0.67	0.70	0.79	0.84
Costa Rica			0.25	0.58	0.47	0.42	0.36	0.40	0.25
Cuba				0.45	0.41	0.48	0.38	0.35	0.31
Dominican R.				0.45	0.48	0.43	0.37	0.38	0.39
Ecuador				0.59	0.60	0.49	0.40	0.58	0.66
El Salvador			0.79	0.65	0.58	0.51	0.57	0.56	0.42
Guatemala			0.48	0.49	0.49	0.47	0.43	0.44	0.41
Haiti				0.60	0.58	0.63	0.52	0.56	0.57
Honduras			0.74	0.65	0.42	0.49	0.47	0.53	0.52
Mexico	0.33	0.25	0.27	0.32	0.33	0.29	0.25	0.28	0.26
Nicaragua			0.87	0.56	0.49	0.51	0.60	0.67	1.05
Panama				0.51	0.44	0.30	0.28	0.33	0.29
Paraguay				0.62	0.61	0.54	0.49	0.61	0.70
Peru				0.39	0.45	0.44	0.41	0.66	0.85
Uruguay				0.36	0.55	0.71	0.71	0.99	1.15
Venezuela				0.16	0.20	0.26	0.35	0.51	0.59

Note: GDP per capita = 1.

Geary-Khamis $4 per day instead of just $1 or $2. Adjusted by the U.S. implicit GDP deflator, it represents in 1980 prices $3.1 per day (purchasing power adjusted), that is, $1,130 per person per year, or $4,521 per year for a four-member family unit.[3] On average, in Latin America, per capita income remained below the poverty line until World War I and did not double it until the 1960s.

In the ongoing debate on pro-poor growth, few views are shared. One of them is that a low level of development probably hampered the impact of growth on poverty reduction (Deiniger and Squire 1998). Moreover, the higher the initial level of inequality, the lower the reduction in poverty for a given rate of growth in GDP per head. Hence, the high levels of inequality shown in table 12.1 may have represented a deterrent for a deeper impact of growth on the poor. As Ravallion (2004) puts it, "Poverty responds slowly to growth in high inequality countries."

Measuring pro-poor growth is highly demanding in terms of empirical evidence, and data on income distribution, at least by quintile, are required. Alas, there are no microeconomic data available on household expenditures to compute historical trends and levels of poverty in Latin America. In these circumstances, Bourguignon and Morrisson's (2002) strategy of assuming that income distribution remained unaltered in Latin America from independence to the mid-twentieth century is very appealing. Given a fixed poverty line and the proportion of population below that line for the present, it would suffice to know the growth rate of GDP per head in order to compute levels of absolute poverty for the past. In fact, research findings state that a large proportion of long-run changes in poverty are accounted for by the growth in averages incomes (Kraay 2004), and hence they emphasize the protection of property rights, stable macroeconomic policies, and openness to international trade as means of growth and poverty suppression (Klasen 2004; OECD 2004). However, assuming a one-for-one reduction in poverty with per capita GDP growth seems a gross misrepresentation, and some economists have proposed to introduce a poverty elasticity of growth that would be lower, the higher the initial level of inequality (Ravallion 2004).

I carried out a calibration exercise of the impact on absolute poverty in Latin America resulting from the trends described for per capita GDP and inequality. To do so, I drew on López and Servén's (2006) empirical research that uses the largest and probably the best microdata set so far for a wide sample of developing and developed countries over the last four decades. They follow a parametric approach and find that the observed distribution of income is consistent with the hypothesis of log normality. Under log normality, the contribution of growth and inequality to changes in poverty levels only depends on the average incomes ratio to the defined poverty line and the degree of inequality as measured by the Gini coefficient:

$$P_0 = \Phi\left(\frac{\log(z/v)}{\sigma} + \frac{\sigma}{2}\right),$$

where $\sigma = \sqrt{2}\Phi^{-1}((1 + G)/2)$, and P_0 is the poverty head count, that is, the share of population below the poverty line; Φ is a cumulative normal distribution; v is average per capita income; z is the poverty line; σ is the standard deviation of the distribution; and G is the Gini coefficient.

Thus, all that is needed to carry out the poverty head count calibration is the poverty line/average income ratio and the Gini coefficient. Unfortunately, as noted, direct Gini estimates are available only for the late twentieth century. By splicing the inequality index with the Gini coefficients for the "statistical era," a long-run series of pseudo-Gini can be derived.

The highly tentative results from this heuristic exercise provide explicit conjectures on poverty trends and hopefully offer testable hypotheses for further research.

Table 12.7 summarizes the results of the conjectural exercise. A word of warning is necessary. The measurement error of the poverty levels is possibly high before the late twentieth century because I rely on Gini guesstimates. But trends in poverty are much better captured because the GDP per worker/unskilled wage ratio seems to capture inequality tendencies rather well. Moreover, the other element to be taken on board, the GDP per head/poverty line ratio, is much more accurately estimated and the López and Servén (2006) model employed in the calibration is one of the more robust measures of the complex relationship between growth, inequality, and poverty.

The main finding of the calibration exercise is that absolute poverty has experienced a long-run decline in Latin America since the late nineteenth century, only arrested in the 1890s and the 1930s and reversed in the 1980s (figure 12.4). In fact, the same two phases observed for Latin America's growth can be observed in the evolution of poverty reduction: 1870–1929, interrupted during the 1890s (Baring crisis years) and accelerated in the years from World War I to the Great Depression; and a steady acceleration in poverty decline between World War II and 1980. Once again, the 1980s stand out as an exceptional decade in which poverty increased across the board.

As regards the absolute number of poor, it grew over time as population expanded in response to high fertility rates; only in the 1970s did the number of poor actually fall, but it was to rise again in the 1980s. For an 18-country sample (all Latin America except Cuba and Haiti) the number of poor went from 93.8 million in 1980 to 127.4 million in 1990, when an absolute poverty line of 1985 Geary-Khamis $4 per day per person is used.

The high coincidence between phases of growth and poverty reduction makes sense; long-run inequality appears to rise to a high plateau, where it has approximately stabilized. It could be argued, along Kakwani and Pernia's (2000) lines, that as inequality remained relatively stable across Latin American countries throughout the second half of the twentieth century, economic growth resulted in proportional increases in the incomes of the poor, and hence pro-poor growth *stricto sensu* never occurred. Here, however, a less strict yardstick for the measurement of poverty is accepted, and a reduction in the share of population below the fixed poverty line is taken as a reduction in absolute poverty.

Table 12.7
Poverty Head Count in Latin America, 1850–1990

	1850	1860	1870	1880	1890	1900	1913
Argentina			64	60	53	56	58
Bolivia							
Brazil	93	96	96	96	95	98	93
Chile	94	89	84	74	71	70	65
Colombia							90
Costa Rica							
Dominican R.							
Ecuador							
El Salvador							
Guatemala							
Honduras							
Mexico							43
Nicaragua							
Panama							
Paraguay							
Peru							
Uruguay			45	48	42	43	32
Venezuela							
LatAm4			89	85	84	85	81
LatAm6							71
LatAm15							
LatAm16							

Notes: 1985 Geary-Kamis $4 per day per person—a calibration (percent).
LatAm4: population-weighted average of Argentina, Brazil, Chile, and Uruguay.
LatAm6: population-weighted average of Argentina, Brazil, Chile, Colombia, Mexico, and Uruguay.

Could it be said, then, that long-run poverty reduction in Latin America was led exclusively by the growth in average incomes? A glance at the numbers in tables 12.1, 12.2, and 12.6 indicates that when we descend to country level, this regularity is not confirmed. True, growth is the only force behind poverty reduction during 1870–1890 in Argentina and Chile, but this is not the case for the episode of substantial poverty contraction, 1913–1929, in which the fall in inequality played a significant role while per capita GDP growth decelerated, as confirmed by the national experiences of Argentina, Chile, and Uruguay. Growth, however, was the single force behind poverty decline in Brazil and almost exclusively in Colombia during the same period. A combination of inequality contraction and growth lies behind the fall in poverty levels in Argentina between the late

	1929	1938	1950	1960	1970	1980	1990
Argentina	41	45	24	22	10	11	17
Bolivia						65	71
Brazil	82	79	75	64	53	33	34
Chile	47	42	36	36	28	31	29
Colombia	70	65	61	57	52	32	37
Costa Rica			54	55	35	28	25
Dominican R.			83	71	64	43	53
Ecuador			87	84	79	66	43
El Salvador			74	66	58	58	64
Guatemala			63	52	37	44	59
Honduras			80	80	76	70	71
Mexico	31	36	43	41	27	13	15
Nicaragua				64	47	53	70
Panama			69	58	48	28	42
Paraguay						44	54
Peru			60	62	43	29	48
Uruguay	15	12	11	8	12	8	6
Venezuela			43	14	11	8	11
LatAm4	67	66	59	52	43	29	30
LatAm6	59	60	55	50	40	25	27
LatAm15			57	51	41	27	30
LatAm16			51	41	27	30

LatAm15: population-weighted average of all Latin American countries but Bolivia, Cuba, Haiti, Nicaragua, and Paraguay.
LatAm16: population-weighted average of all Latin American countries but Bolivia, Cuba, Haiti, and Paraguay.

1930s and the early 1950s, and in Venezuela and Peru during the 1950s and 1960s, respectively. Public redistributive policies (progressive taxes, transfers, and other government spending) seem to have mattered for poverty reduction (Astorga and Fitzgerald 1998).

In the second half of the twentieth century, however, growth emerges as the most prominent element underlying the reduction in absolute poverty. Examples are provided by Argentina and Brazil in the 1960s. This fact perhaps explains why absolute poverty levels remain high in 1990. Growth itself apparently did not suffice to cut down poverty sharply. High persistent inequality prevented a deeper impact on poverty reduction resulting from the intense growth of the 1950–1980 years, as the cases of Brazil and Colombia exemplify, with still one-third of their

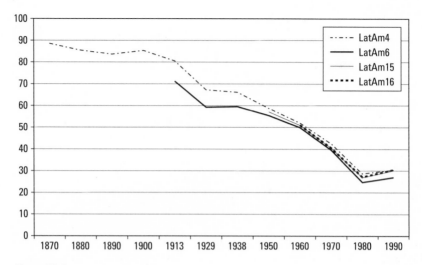

Figure 12.4
Poverty head count in Latin America (population-weighted averages).

populations below the poverty line. Despite sustained growth in the long run, absolute poverty remained high in Latin America at the end of the twentieth century (above one-fourth in 1980 and nearly one-third in 1990). Moreover, the variance across nations has widened (the unweighted coefficient of variation for a 15-country sample rose from 0.37 in 1950 to 1.08 in 1990). In 1980, for example, Brazil, Colombia, and Chile had a poverty head count of around one-third of their populations, and Venezuela and Uruguay were below two digits, and Mexico and Argentina slightly above. A look at small countries reveals that, for instance, in Central America, absolute poverty affected—if Costa Rica is excluded—half its population in 1980 and reached two-thirds in 1990. Andean countries (Bolivia, Ecuador, and Peru) also exhibited spectacular poverty levels in 1990. Actually, if Argentina, Uruguay, Venezuela, and Mexico are excluded, the poverty head count in Latin America reached one-half of the population at the end of the twentieth century.

Conclusions

This chapter has addressed some recurrent questions. Is inequality a long-run curse? How did trends in inequality and growth affect poverty? Unfortunately, only tentative conclusions that provide hypotheses for further research can be offered.

Persistent high inequality is confirmed by historical evidence, with Gini indices ranging from 40 to almost 60. However, inequality has not remained stable, as is usually assumed in the literature; it experienced a long-run rise until it reached a stable plateau in the late twentieth century. Openness conditioned to some extent how much inequality contributed to poverty reduction. Trade usually raised inequality, and in globalization phases poverty reduction tended to come from growth. Conversely, in isolationist phases Stolper-Samuelson forces led to inequality decline and hence to poverty reduction.

Absolute poverty experienced a long-run decline in Latin America from the late nineteenth century on, its evolution shadowing that of per capita income growth. Long-run poverty reduction in Latin America was led, but not exclusively conditioned, by the growth in average incomes, especially in the second half of the twentieth century. A lower degree of initial inequality, it can be conjectured, would have implied that Latin American growth had a larger payoff in terms of poverty reduction.

Appendix: Data Sources

GDP per Capita and per Worker Volume Indices

In order to facilitate comparisons over space and time, I linked volume estimates computed at national relative prices to benchmark estimates for the year 1980 expressed in 1980 Geary-Khamis dollars available for most Latin American countries from the UN's International Comparisons Project (ICP IV).

Data for twentieth-century Latin American GDP volumes and total population and economically active population comes, unless stated, from Astorga and Fitzgerald (1998), Astorga, Bergés, and Fitzgerald (2004), and Mitchell (1993).

Argentina della Paolera, Taylor, and Bózzoli (2003), GDP, 1884–1990, spliced with Cortés-Conde (1997) for 1875–1884. I assumed the level for 1870 was identical to that of 1875.

Brazil GDP, Goldsmith (1986), 1850–1980.

Chile Díaz, Lüders, and Wagner (1998) and Braun et al. (1998).

Colombia GRECO (2002), since 1906. I assumed the level for 1900 was identical to that of 1906.

Mexico INEGI (1995), 1850–1990. GDP figures from 1845 to 1896, interpolated from the original benchmark estimates.

Uruguay   Bértola (1998), since 1870.

Venezuela   Baptista (1997).

Central America (Costa Rica, El Salvador, Guatemala, Honduras, and Nicaragua)   I obtained the level for 1913 by assuming a growth for 1913–1920 identical to that of 1920–1925, the latter taken from Astorga, Bergés, and Fitzgerald (2004).

Real Wages

I used Williamson's (1995) real wages, updated in 1996 and 2002, for Argentina, Brazil, Colombia, Cuba, Mexico, and Uruguay, and completed the series up to 1960 for Colombia (GRECO 2002), Cuba (Zanetti and García 1976), and Mexico (INEGI 1995). For Chile, I used data in Braun et al. (1998).

Gini Coefficients

1990   Székely (2001), except Guatemala from Londoño and Székely (2000).

1970–1980   Londoño and Székely (2000) for Brazil, Chile, Colombia, and Costa Rica; Altimir estimates reproduced in Hofman (2001) for Argentina and Bolivia, 1980; WIDER (2004) for the Dominican Republic, 1980; Deininger and Squire (1996) for Bolivia, Ecuador, El Salvador, Guatemala, 1970; Honduras, 1980; Paraguay, 1980; and Uruguay.

1938–1960   Altimir (1998) estimates reproduced in Astorga and Fitzgerald (1998) and Hofman (2001), except for Costa Rica, El Salvador, Guatemala, and Peru from Deininger and Squire (1996, updated).

Gini Backward Projections

Gini coefficients projected backward with inequality indices constructed as the ratio between unskilled wage indices and GDP per worker, with 1913 = 1.

Notes

Comments, on an earlier draft of this chapter, by Pablo Astorga, Luis Bértola, Stefan Houpt, Humberto López, Giovanni Vecchi, and Jeff Williamson are most appreciated. Roberto Vélez Grajales provided excellent research assistance, and Humberto López and Patricia Macchi helped me with the calibration of poverty head count. Humberto López and Luis Servén kindly allowed me access to their unpublished research. I received valuable feedback from seminar participants at Harvard, Oxford, Universidad de la República (Montevideo), Lund, Carlos III, and Granada. I am solely responsible for any errors.

1. EAP stands for "economically active population." A regression of direct estimates of Gini coefficients on backward projections of Gini for 1980 with inequality indices yields a partial correlation of 0.86.

2. Population-weighted averages computed from Astorga, Bergés, and Fitzgerald (2004).

3. This is twice as much in 2004 prices, according to EH.net (S. H. Williamson 2004).

References

Acemoglu, D., S. Johnson, and J. A. Robinson. 2002. Reversal of Fortune: Geography and Institutions in the Making of the Modern World Income Distribution. *Quarterly Journal of Economics* 117 (4): 1231–1294.

Altimir, O. 1987. Income Distribution Statistics in Latin America and Their Reliability. *Review of Income and Wealth* 33 (2): 111–155.

———. 1998. Income Distribution. In *Progress, Poverty and Exclusion: An Economic History of Latin America in the Twentieth Century*, ed. R. Thorp. Washington: Inter-American Development Bank.

Astorga, P., A. R. Bergés, and V. Fitzgerald. 2004. *The Oxford Latin American Economic History Database (OxLAD)*. ⟨http://oxlad.qeh.ox.ac.uk/⟩.

Astorga, P., and V. Fitzgerald. 1998. Statistical Appendix. In *Progress, Poverty and Exclusion: An Economic History of Latin America in the Twentieth Century*, ed. R. Thorp, 307–365. Washington: Inter-American Development Bank.

Baptista, A. 1997. *Bases Cuantitativas de la Economía Venezolana, 1830–1995*. Caracas: Fundación Polar.

Bértola, L. 1998. *El PBI de Uruguay, 1870–1936 y Otras Estimaciones*. Montevideo: Universidad de la República.

———. 2005. A 50 años de la curva de Kuznets, una reivindicación sustantiva: distribución del ingreso y crecimiento económico en Uruguay y otros países de nuevo asentamiento desde 1870. Working Paper, Series 05-04, Universidad Carlos III de Madrid.

Bértola, L., and J. G. Williamson. 2003. Globalization in Latin America before 1940. NBER (National Bureau of Economic Research) Working Paper 9687. ⟨http://www.nber .org/papers/W9687⟩.

Bourguignon, F. 2003. The Growth Elasticity of Poverty Reduction: Explaining Heterogeneity across Countries and Time Periods. In *Inequality and Growth: Theory and Policy Implications*, ed. T. Eichner and S. Turnovsky. Cambridge, Mass.: MIT Press.

Bourguignon, F., and C. Morrisson. 2002. Inequality among World Citizens. *American Economic Review* 92 (4): 727–744.

Braun, J., M. Braun, I. Briones, and J. Díaz. 1998. Economía Chilena, 1810–1995. Working Paper 187, Pontificia Universidad Católica de Chile.

Cariola, C., and O. Sunkel. 1982. *La Historia Económica de Chile, 1830–1930: Dos ensayos y una bibliografía*. Madrid: Instituto de Cooperación Iberoamericana.

Cortés-Conde, R. 1997. *La Economía Argentina en el Largo Plazo, Siglos XIX y XX*. Buenos Aires: Editorial Sudamericana–Universidad de San Andrés.

Deininger, K., and L. Squire. 1996. A New Data Set Measuring Income Inequality. *World Bank Economic Review* 10 (3): 565–591.

———. 1998. New Ways of Looking at Old Issues: Inequality and Growth. *Journal of Development Economics* 57 (2): 257–285.

della Paolera, G., A. M. Taylor, and G. Bózzoli. 2003. Historical Statistics. In *A New Economic History of Argentina*, ed. G. Della-Paolera and A. M. Taylor, 376–385. New York: Cambridge University Press.

Díaz, J., R. Lüders, and G. Wagner. 1998. Economía Chilena, 1810–1995: Evolución Cuantitativa del Producto Total y Sectorial. Working Paper 186, Pontificia Universidad Católica de Chile.

Díaz-Alejandro, C. F. 1970. *Essays on the Economic History of the Argentine Republic.* New Haven, Conn.: Yale University Press.

ECLAC (Economic Commission for Latin America and the Caribbean). 2000. *The Equity Gap: A Second Assessment.* ⟨http://www.eclac.org/publicaciones/SecretariaEjecutiva/6/lcg2096/equitygapII.pdf⟩.

Engerman, S. L., and K. L. Sokoloff. 1997. Factor Endowments, Institutions, and Differential Paths of Growth among New World Economies. In *How Latin America Fell Behind: Essays on the Economic Histories of Brazil and Mexico, 1800–1914,* ed. S. Haber, 260–304. Stanford, Calif.: Stanford University Press.

Flora, P. 1973. Historical Processes of Social Mobilization: Urbanization and Literacy, 1850–1965. In *Building States and Nations: Models and Data Resources,* ed. S. N. Eisenstadt and S. Rokkan, 213–258. London: Sage.

Galor, O. 2004. The Demographic Transition and the Emergence of Sustained Economic Growth. Discussion Paper 4714, Centre for Economic Policy Research (CEPR), London.

Goldsmith, R. W. 1986. *Brasil 1850–1984: Desenvolvimento financeiro sob um século de inflaçao.* São Paulo: Harper and Row.

GRECO (Grupo de Estudios de Crecimiento Económico). 2002. *El Crecimiento Económico Colombiano en el Siglo XX.* Bogotá: Banco de la República–Fondo de Cultura Económica.

Hofman, A. A. 2001. Long-Run Economic Development in Latin America in a Comparative Perspective: Proximate and Ultimate Causes. Macroeconomía del Desarrollo Series 8. Economic Commission for Latin America and the Caribbean (ECLAC).

INEGI (Instituto Nacional de Estroística Geografia e Informática). 1995. *Estadísticas Históricas de México.*

Kakwani, N., and E. Pernia. 2000. What Is Pro-Poor Growth? *Asian Development Review* 18 (1): 1–16.

Klasen, S. 2004. In Search of the Holy Grail: How to Achieve Pro-Poor Growth? In *Toward Pro-Poor Policies: Aid, Institutions, Globalization,* ed. B. Tungodden, N. Stern, and I. Kolstad, 63–93. New York: Oxford University Press.

Kraay, A. 2004. When Is Growth Pro-Poor? Cross-Country Evidence. Working Paper 04/47, International Monetary Fund.

Krongkaew, M., and N. Kakwani. 2003. The Growth-Equity Trade-off in Modern Economic Development: The Case of Thailand. *Journal of Asian Economics* 14: 735–757.

Leff, N. 1982. *Underdevelopment and Development in Brazil.* London: Allen and Unwin.

Lewis, W. A. 1954. Economic Development with Unlimited Supplies of Labour. *Manchester School of Economic and Social Studies* 22: 139–191.

Londoño, J. L., and M. Székely. 2000. Persistent Poverty and Excess Inequality: Latin America, 1970–1995. *Journal of Applied Economics* 3 (1): 93–134.

López, J. H. 2004. Pro-Poor Pro-Growth: Is There a Trade-off? Policy Research Working Paper 3378, World Bank.

López, J. H., and L. Servén. 2006. A Normal Relationship? Poverty, Growth, and Inequality. Policy Research Working Paper 3814, World Bank.

Maddison, A. 1995. *Monitoring the World Economy, 1820–1992.* Paris: OECD.

———. 2003. *The World Economy: Historical Statistics.* Paris: OECD.

Mitchell, B. R. 2003. *International Historical Statistics: The Americas, 1750–2000.* 5th ed. New York: Palgrave Macmillan.

Morley, S. 2000. *La Distribución del Ingreso en América Latina y el Caribe.* Santiago de Chile: Fondo de Cultura Económica and Comisión Económica para América Latina y el Caribe (CEPAL).

Newland, C., and J. Ortiz. 2001. The Economic Consequences of Argentine Independence. *Cuadernos de Economía* 115: 275–290.

OECD (Organisation for Economic Cooperation and Development). 2004. *Accelerating Pro-Poor Growth through Support for the Private Sector Development. An Analytical Framework*. Paris: OECD.

Palacios, M. 1995. *Entre la Legitimidad y la Violencia: Colombia 1875–1994*. Bogotá: Norma.

Prados de la Escosura, L. 2007. When Did Latin America Fall Behind? In *The Decline of Latin American Economies*, ed. S. Edwards, G. Esquivel, and G. Márquez, 22–94. Chicago: University of Chicago Press.

Prebisch, R. 1950. *The Economic Development of Latin America and Its Principal Problems*. New York: United Nations.

Ramos, J. R. 1996. Poverty and Inequality in Latin America: A Neostructural Perspective. *Journal of Interamerican Studies and World Affairs* 38: 141–158.

Ravallion, M. 1997. Can High Inequality Development Countries Escape Absolute Poverty? *Economics Letters* 56: 51–57.

———. 2004. Pro-Poor Growth: A Primer. Policy Research Working Paper 3242, World Bank.

Ravallion, M., and S. Chen. 2003. Measuring Pro-Poor Growth. *Economics Letters* 78 (1): 93–99.

Singer, H. W. 1950. The Distribution of Gains Between Investing and Borrowing Countries. *American Economic Review* 40: 473–485.

Sokoloff, K., and S. L. Engerman. 2000. Institutions, Factor Endowments, and Paths of Development in the New World. *Journal of Economic Perspectives* 14 (3): 217–232.

Stein, S. J., and B. H. Stein. 1970. *The Colonial Heritage of Latin America: Essays on Economic Dependence in Perspective*. New York: Oxford University Press.

Székely, M. 2001. The 1990s in Latin America: Another Decade of Persistent Inequality, but with Somewhat Lower Poverty. Working Paper 454, Inter-American Development Bank.

WIDER (World Institute for Development Economics Research). 2004. World Income Database. Helsinki: UNO/WIDER/UNDP.

Williamson, J. G. 1995. The Evolution of Global Markets since 1830: Background Evidence and Hypotheses. *Explorations in Economic History* 32: 141–196.

———. 1999. Real Wage Inequality and Globalization in Latin America before 1940. *Revista de Historia Económica* 17: 101–142.

———. 2002. Land, Labor, and Globalization in the Third World, 1870–1940. *Journal of Economic History* 62 (1): 55–85.

Williamson, S. H. 2004. What Is the Relative Value? Economic History Services. ⟨http://eh.net/hmit/compare/⟩.

Zanetti, O., and A. Garcia, eds. 1976. *United Fruit Company: Un Caso del Dominio Imperialista en Cuba*. Havana: Ciencias Sociales.

13 The Convergence of Living Standards in the Atlantic Economy, 1870–1930

George R. Boyer

The four decades leading up to the First World War witnessed rapid globalization, income convergence in the Atlantic economy, and mass migration from Europe to the New World. Recent work by Jeffrey Williamson and his co-authors has greatly increased our understanding of the process of globalization during these years by documenting the convergence in real wages and the trends in mass migration and explaining what brought them about.[1] This chapter complements Williamson's work by examining the convergence of nonincome measures of well-being, including life expectancy, educational opportunities, and discretionary time, for 15 countries in the Atlantic economy from 1870 to the beginning of the Great Depression.[2]

Why is it important to examine nonincome aspects of the standard of living? The data presented here show that GDP per capita and real wages are not good proxies for nonincome measures of well-being. Life expectancy, educational attainment, and discretionary time measure aspects of the standard of living that are not captured by income measures. To determine the effects of the rapid globalization of the late nineteenth century on living standards, broadly defined, it is therefore necessary to examine the extent of convergence in nonincome aspects of well-being as well as in real wages. Moreover, some share of potential emigrants took life expectancy, educational opportunities, discretionary time, and the size of social safety nets, as well as real wages, into account when making migration decisions. Thus, the growth of nonincome aspects of the standard of living might help to explain the patterns of western European emigration from 1870 to 1910.

The chapter begins by presenting data on GDP per capita, real wages, and five nonincome measures of living standards for 15 countries for the benchmark years 1870, 1910, and 1930. It then examines the extent of convergence over time in each of the measures and shows that life expectancy, educational opportunities, and discretionary time converged even more rapidly than did real wage rates or GDP per capita. I then turn to a discussion of the relation between nonincome measures of living standards and European mass migration. I contend that the slowdown in emigration from northwestern Europe in the two decades leading up to the First World War was caused by increases in nonincome measures of living standards and the adoption of social safety nets in origin countries as well as by increasing real wages and the ending of the demographic transition.

The Measurement of Living Standards

The most widely used measure to compare living standards across countries is GNP (or GDP) per capita, which measures a nation's aggregate command over resources. Economists accept that GNP and GDP are measures of production and that "the goal of economic activity ... is consumption" (Nordhaus and Tobin 1973, 512). If national differences in life expectancy, infant mortality, and school enrollment largely are explained by differences in GDP per capita—the wealthier a country is, the more it can spend on health care and educating its children—then per capita income is a reasonable proxy for living standards. However, recent research shows that "there is no automatic and direct connection" between GNP per capita and nonincome measures of well-being (Morris 1979; Szreter 1997; Easterlin 2004). This conclusion has led economists studying the standard of living to examine, in addition to income, various nonincome measures of well-being, such as life expectancy, education, and voluntary leisure time.[3]

Life expectancy at birth is the most often used biological measure of well being; increased longevity is assumed to be a good thing in and of itself, and longevity also is a proxy for the state of health of those living (United Nations 1990, 11). Other measures of biological well being used by economists include infant mortality rates and height by age, a proxy for net nutrition in childhood and adolescence (Steckel and Floud 1997).

Workers gain satisfaction from leisure as well as income, and there is plenty of evidence from the twentieth century that workers desire reductions in hours of work as well as increases in wages. Kuznets (1952, 68–69) maintained that "it is impossible to understand why [the American] national product grew as it did ... unless we pay attention to the choices that people made between hours of work and hours of leisure." The decline in annual hours of work that occurred in virtually all industrialized nations after 1870 "did not come about as an accident" and resulted in a significant increase in workers' voluntary leisure time, which should be included in a measure of living standards (Fogel 2000, 184–186).[4]

Insecurity of income was a reality of working-class life in the nineteenth century. Despite rapid increases in real wages from 1850 to 1913, the majority of workers still lived life "close to the margin," so that prolonged spells of unemployment or sickness led to financial distress (Floud 1997, 22–23; Boyer 2006). In the 1870s, the social safety net was quite small throughout the Atlantic economy, consisting almost entirely of the Poor Law. However, several European countries adopted social insurance programs during the three decades from 1883 to 1913, and social spending increased sharply from 1880 to 1930 (Lindert 1994; 2004; Huberman and Lewchuk 2003). This widening of the social safety net reduced workers' financial insecurity and improved their standard of living in a way that is missed by data on GNP per capita or real wages.[5]

The following section presents data on GDP per capita, real wages, and five nonincome measures of living standards for countries in the Atlantic economy over the period 1870 to 1910, and examines whether income and nonincome measures tended to move together, and whether nonincome measures converged at a more or less rapid rate than did GDP per capita or real wages.

Living Standards before the First World War, 1870–1910

Keynes (1919, 10–11) called the four decades preceding the First World War "an extraordinary episode in the economic progress of man." It was a period of "rapid globalization: capital and labor flowed across national frontiers in unprecedented quantities, and commodity trade boomed as transport costs dropped sharply" (Williamson 1998, 51). Real wages and GDP per capita rapidly converged within the Atlantic economy, driven by the migration of upwards of 50 million Europeans to New World destinations (Hatton and Williamson 1998).

Table 13.1 shows data for seven measures of the standard of living for 15 countries in 1870 and 1910: GDP per capita, real wages for manual laborers, life expectancy at birth, literacy, school enrollment, discretionary (leisure) time, and social spending. GDP per capita is measured in 1990 international dollars. The real wage series is an index, with wages in the United Kingdom in 1905 set equal to 100 (Williamson 1995). The

Table 13.1
Income and Nonincome Measures of Living Standards, 1870 and 1910

	GDP per capita 1870	Wages 1870	Life Expectancy 1870	Literacy 1870	School Enrollment 1870	Discretionary Hours 1870	Social Spending 1880
Argentina	1311.0	58.3	33.0	22.5	146	na	0.00
Australia	3667.0	127.0	48.0	73.1	605	1368	0.00
Belgium	2633.0	59.0	40.0	64.3	384	677	0.17
Canada	1641.0	100.5	42.6	77.0	836	1315	0.00
Denmark	1922.0	35.5	45.5	86.3	472	726	0.96
France	1869.5	59.0	42.0	69.0	436	992	0.46
Germany	1902.0	69.0	36.2	84.8	743	876	0.50
Ireland	1773.0	48.7	41.3	74.2	298	1052	0.86
Italy	1470.0	26.0	28.0	31.5	263	1160	0.00
Netherlands	2647.5	54.7	38.9	77.8	495	886	0.29
Norway	1308.5	31.7	49.3	72.5	647	725	1.07
Spain	1376.0	31.0	33.7	31.3	409	1192	0.00
Sweden	1674.0	34.3	45.8	83.8	603	724	0.72
United Kingdom	3342.0	66.0	41.3	74.3	561	1405	0.86
United States	2482.5	113.0	45.3	80.0	787	1064	0.29
COV[a]	0.354	0.505	0.146	0.311	0.386	0.249	0.957

Sources: GDP per capita, Maddison (1995); real wages, Williamson (1995); revised series for Belgium, the Netherlands, Norway, Spain, and the U.K. constructed for O'Rourke and Williamson (1997), obtained from the authors; life expectancy, Dublin, Lotka, and Spieqel-man (1949) and Crafts (1997b); United States, Haines (1994) and U.S. Census Bureau (2003); literacy, Flora (1973) except Ireland, 1870, assumed same as U.K., and Ireland, 1910, Crafts (1997b); school enrollment, Lindert (2004, vol. 2) and revised numbers from

school enrollment rate is defined as primary and secondary school students per 1,000 children aged 5–14. Annual discretionary (leisure) time is defined as 4,160 hours minus the average annual number of hours worked.[6] Social spending is defined as the percentage of national product devoted to social transfer spending.

There was a general improvement in both income and nonincome measures of well-being during the golden age of globalization, which was shared by workers throughout the Atlantic economy. Real wages increased by 75 percent on average from 1870 to 1910, and GDP per capita increased by 71 percent. Average life expectancy at birth rose from 40.6 years in 1870 to 52.2 years in 1910. The average literacy rate rose from 67 percent to 86 percent, and school enrollment rates increased by 31 percent. The annual number of hours worked declined on average by

	GDP per capita 1910	Wages 1910	Life Expec- tancy 1910	Literacy 1910	School Enroll- ment 1910	Discre- tionary Hours 1913	Social Spending 1910
Argentina	3755.7	92.3	46.3	62.5	417	na	0.00
Australia	5461.0	131.7	59.1	95.5	895	1946	1.12
Belgium	3975.0	85.3	49.6	86.6	355	1319	0.43
Canada	3830.0	204.0	52.5	92.5	917	1292	0.00
Denmark	3592.7	101.3	57.7	97.0	730	1429	1.75
France	3097.7	70.3	50.4	88.1	862	1227	0.81
Germany	3526.0	87.0	49.0	97.0	791	1437	1.75
Ireland	2733.0	91.3	53.8	91.0	607	1470	1.38
Italy	2359.3	50.3	47.2	60.7	433	1207	0.00
Netherlands	3704.0	76.3	56.1	92.5	449	1218	0.39
Norway	2049.3	82.3	57.2	97.0	731	1422	1.18
Spain	2164.7	35.7	41.8	47.8	485	1559	0.02
Sweden	2930.3	99.7	57.0	98.5	720	1415	1.03
United Kingdom	4714.0	95.3	53.4	92.5	720	1504	1.38
United States	5015.0	169.3	51.9	92.3	944	1260	0.56
COV[a]	0.287	0.435	0.094	0.183	0.298	0.136	0.809

⟨http://www.econ.ucdavis.edu/faculty/fzlinder/⟩; discretionary time, calculated by author from data on annual hours worked obtained from Huberman (2004), Norway calculated as average of Denmark and Sweden; social spending, Lindert (2004, vol. 1).
a. Coefficient of variation.

nearly 400 from 1870 to 1910, giving workers an extra 7.5 hours of discretionary time per week.

A glance at the seven series for either year shows that a country's ranking in the league table depends on which measure of the standard of living is being considered. In 1910 the United States ranked first in school enrollment rates, second in GDP per capita and in real wages, but ninth in life expectancy and in social spending, and eleventh in discretionary time. Norway ranked fifteenth in GDP per capita and eleventh in real wages, but second in literacy, third in life expectancy, and fifth in social spending. For some countries, however, the data tell a consistent story. Italy ranked thirteenth or below in every measure, and Australia ranked first in three measures and third or above in six. Table 13.1 also makes clear that the ranking of countries in terms of material living standards differs depending on whether GDP per capita or real wages is used to measure income.

The bottom row in each column of table 13.1 gives the coefficient of variation (COV), which measures the extent of dispersion across countries for each measure of living standards. In both 1870 and 1910, dispersion was greatest in social spending and wage rates, and lowest in life expectancy and discretionary hours. The dispersion in nonincome measures of well-being was significantly less than that in wage rates because the exceptionally high wages of the English-speaking European offshoots were not mirrored by similar advantages in the three l's (longevity, learning, and leisure). Indeed, workers in the three Scandinavian countries had higher literacy rates than workers in Australia, Canada, or the United States throughout the period, higher life expectancies than workers in Canada or the United States, and after 1890, more discretionary time than U.S. or Canadian workers.

The period from 1870 to 1910 witnessed a convergence in every measure of well-being, although nonincome measures converged more rapidly than did GDP per capita or real wages. The coefficient of variation of real wages declined from 0.505 in 1870 to 0.435 in 1910; the COV for life expectancy declined from 0.145 to 0.094, and that for school enrollment fell from 0.386 to 0.298. The differing trends in convergence of income and nonincome measures is most prominent in the decade from 1900 to 1910. Dispersion in GDP per capita remained roughly constant during the decade, and real wage rates, which converged sharply from 1870 to 1900, diverged after 1900—the COV increased from 0.402 in 1900 to 0.435 in 1910. The convergence in wage rates was caused by Europe (especially Scandinavia and Ireland) catching up to the English-speaking (and high-wage) European offshoots, and the divergence from 1900 to 1910 was driven by the sharp increase in Canadian wages during the decade.[7] In contrast, the nonincome measures of well-being—life expectancy, education, and discretionary income—continued to converge from 1900 to 1910.

Diverging Wages but Converging Living Standards, 1910–1930

The First World War and its aftermath was a major shock to the Atlantic economy, which led to the speeding up of a "globalization backlash" that was already underway in several New World countries (Timmer and Williamson 1998). As part of this backlash, each of the main immigrant destinations—Argentina, Australia, Canada, and the United States—imposed increasingly severe restrictions on immigration.

Table 13.2 presents data for the seven measures of the standard of living for 1929–1930. It also shows real wage data for 1914.[8] The divergence

Table 13.2
Income and Nonincome Measures of Living Standards, 1930

	Real Wages		GDP per capita	Life Expec- tancy	Liter- acy	School Enroll- ment	Discre- tionary Hours	Social Spend- ing
	1914	1929	1929	1930	1930	1930	1930	1930
Argentina	71.0	102.0	4246.0	54.5	74.5	632	na	0.00
Australia	111.0	137.0	5035.7	65.5	97.0	916	2023	2.11
Belgium	41.0	47.3	4950.0	57.9	94.1	731	1682	0.56
Canada	120.0	122.7	4752.3	60.3	95.7	1000	1519	0.31
Denmark	92.0	151.7	4875.0	62.4	98.5	752	1722	3.11
France	69.0	69.7	4515.0	57.5	94.7	673	1557	1.05
Germany	86.0	94.7	4230.7	61.3	98.5	793	1753	4.82
Ireland	88.0	106.0	2883.0	58.3	94.5	802	1779	3.74
Italy	50.0	50.7	2943.3	54.5	76.9	580	1566	0.10
Netherlands	78.0	130.0	5533.0	64.4	97.0	797	1608	1.03
Norway	101.0	114.0	3145.0	64.2	97.0	770	1730	2.39
Spain	39.0	54.7	2852.3	49.0	67.5	732	1857	0.07
Sweden	79.0	112.0	3821.0	63.2	99.0	819	1739	2.59
United Kingdom	85.0	100.7	5188.3	60.3	97.0	701	1846	2.24
United States	124.0	172.7	6568.0	59.5	95.7	1000	1553	0.56
COV	0.316	0.353	0.248	0.075	0.109	0.154	0.083	0.906

Sources: See table 13.1. Discretionary hours estimated using data from Maddison (1995) and Huberman (2004).

in real wages in the Atlantic economy that began in the first decade of the twentieth century continued in the interwar period, partly as a result of the globalization backlash. From 1914 to 1929, the coefficient of variation of wages for the 15 countries increased from 0.316 to 0.353. The increase in dispersion was driven by a 39 percent increase in real wages in the already high-wage United States, and the slow wage growth in France and Italy. By 1929 real wages in the United States were three times greater than wages in Italy, Spain, and Belgium, and nearly two-and-a-half times greater than wages in France. Unlike wages, GDP per capita continued to converge after 1910, largely as a result of the poor macroeconomic performance of two of the leaders, Australia and the United Kingdom. From 1910 to 1929, GDP per capita declined by 8 percent in Australia and increased by only 10 percent in the United Kingdom.[9] In terms of material well being, whether measured by GDP or real wages, the United States was the dominant nation in the decade after the First World War.

The disruption to the Atlantic economy caused by war and the New World's antiglobalization backlash did not stop the convergence in nonincome measures of well-being; life expectancy, education, and discretionary time all converged from 1910 to 1930. Convergence was especially pronounced in school enrollment; its COV declined from 0.298 in 1910 to 0.154 in 1930 as a result of rapid increases in enrollment rates in Belgium, the Netherlands, Spain, Argentina, and Italy. Of course, the speed of convergence after 1910 would have been even greater in a counterfactual world in which neither the war nor the migration restrictions occurred. Social spending diverged in the 1920s, as a result of sharp increases in spending by Germany, Ireland, Denmark, and Sweden. As of 1930 social spending exceeded 3 percent of national income in Germany, Ireland, and Denmark but remained below 1 percent of national income in six countries, including the United States and Canada.

As in previous years, the ranking of countries in 1929 depends on how well-being is defined. The United States ranked first in GDP per capita, real wages, and school enrollment but ninth in life expectancy, thirteenth in discretionary time, and tenth in social spending. By contrast, Sweden ranked eleventh in GDP per capita and seventh in real wages but first in literacy and fourth in life expectancy, school enrollment, and social spending.

It is possible to examine the extent of convergence over the longer period from 1870 to 1929 for all measures of well-being except real wages.[10] All measures converged over the six decades, but the three *l*'s—longevity, learning, and leisure—converged much more rapidly than did GDP per capita. By focusing on income measures, economists have underestimated the extent of convergence in living standards that occurred in the Atlantic economy after 1870.

Broad Measures of Living Standards: The Human Development Index

The finding that income and nonincome measures of the standard of living do not necessarily move together has led to the development of new indices that combine economic, biological, and social variables to form more comprehensive measures of the quality of life. The most influential of these is the Human Development Index (HDI), produced by the United Nations Development Programme (UNDP) and originally presented in the 1990 *Human Development Report*. The HDI is calculated as an unweighted sum of three indices, measuring GDP per capita, life expectancy at birth, and education (literacy and mean years of schooling). The HDI has been widely used by development economists and economic historians, but it is open to criticism.[11] Per capita GDP includes income from sources other than labor and is "much too coarse" an instrument for measuring material living standards (Williamson 1995, 143). There is little justification given for the decision to weigh income, life expectancy, and education equally in the index. There are potentially serious problems of double-counting because income "can be used to acquire and/or produce either of the other two indicators (improved health or education)" (Kelley 1991, 319). The fact that income is an input to other measures of well-being suggests that it should be given a weight greater than one-third in the HDI. Finally, the HDI has been accused of comparing apples and oranges—GDP per capita is measured in monetary units, life expectancy in units of time, and education as a combination of a unit of time (school enrollment) and a percentage (literacy). In sum, the HDI offers a useful and simple way to combine income and nonincome measures into a single measure of the standard of living, but one should be cautious in interpreting the results obtained from the index.

Table 13.3 presents the Human Development Index for 1870, 1890, 1910, and 1930, constructed using the data in tables 13.1 and 13.2. For each of the three components, an index is created by assuming maximum and minimum values for the variable and defining the measure so that each country's value falls between 0 and 1. For example, I_{ij} is the indicator for country j with respect to variable i, and is defined as: $I_{ij} = (X_{ij} - \min X_i)/(\max X_i - \min X_i)$.

For GDP per capita, the maximum is set at \$6,568 (1990 international dollars), the value achieved by the United States in 1930, and the minimum at \$200.[12] Following Crafts (1997b), I set the maximum life expectancy at 85 and the minimum at 25. For literacy and school enrollment, the maximum is 100 percent and the minimum is 0 percent. The index for education is constructed giving literacy a weight twice that of school enrollment.

Columns 1–4 of table 13.3 present the conventionally defined HDI for 1870, 1890, 1910, and 1930, constructed as the unweighted average of the indices for GDP per capita, life expectancy, and education. In columns 5–7 the HDI (Wages) is calculated for 1870–1910 with Williamson's (1995) real wage data substituted for GDP per capita as the index's

Table 13.3
Human Development Index, 1870–1930

	HDI				HDI(Wages)			
	1870	1890	1910	1930	1870	1890	1910	1930
Argentina	0.169	0.296	0.490	0.611	0.170	0.281	0.425	0.546
Australia	0.539	0.676	0.777	0.795	0.541	0.627	0.693	0.755
Belgium	0.396	0.483	0.566	0.722	0.330	0.421	0.477	0.516
Canada	0.437	0.515	0.650	0.758	0.498	0.642	0.783	0.706
Denmark	0.448	0.535	0.656	0.755	0.377	0.475	0.616	0.751
France	0.384	0.466	0.584	0.692	0.358	0.422	0.514	0.551
Germany	0.422	0.507	0.611	0.720	0.412	0.474	0.549	0.642
Ireland	0.371	0.472	0.562	0.625	0.331	0.459	0.549	0.638
Italy	0.182	0.291	0.419	0.543	0.118	0.238	0.352	0.448
Netherlands	0.433	0.510	0.612	0.802	0.359	0.450	0.521	0.723
Norway	0.426	0.500	0.572	0.673	0.380	0.478	0.579	0.688
Spain	0.225	0.274	0.356	0.503	0.174	0.190	0.273	0.421
Sweden	0.446	0.537	0.620	0.713	0.385	0.498	0.611	0.689
United Kingdom	0.482	0.574	0.680	0.751	0.392	0.488	0.570	0.634
United States	0.497	0.579	0.711	0.849	0.536	0.622	0.719	0.797
COV	0.286	0.235	0.182	0.137	0.350	0.294	0.244	0.180

income component. Column 8 presents the HDI(Wages) for 1930, using the real wage data from Williamson's 1914–1945 wage series.[13]

Australia had the highest HDI scores in 1870 and 1910, followed by the United States and the United Kingdom. The United States had the highest HDI score in 1930, followed by the Netherlands and Australia. The results are slightly altered when real wages are substituted for GDP per capita—in 1910 Canada has the highest HDI score, followed by the United States and Australia. The rankings of countries by HDI scores are at times significantly different than the rankings by income in tables 13.1 and 13.2. For example, in 1870 Sweden ranked tenth in GDP per capita and twelfth in real wages but fifth in HDI and sixth in HDI(Wages), as a result of its high life expectancy and literacy rates. Conversely, Argentina in 1910 ranked sixth in GDP per capita and seventh in real wages but thirteenth in HDI and HDI(Wages).

Both the HDI and HDI(Wages) converged sharply from 1870 to 1910. The HDI continued to converge from 1910 to 1930, by which time its co-efficient of variation was half its 1870 level. The COV for the HDI(Wages) also declined in the 1920s, from 0.223 in 1914 to 0.180 in 1929, despite the increased dispersion in real wages.[14] Thus, the standard of living, broadly defined to include both income and nonincome components, converged throughout the period from 1870 to the Great Depression.

Causes of Convergence in Living Standards

Tables 13.1–13.3 show that there was a strong convergence in living standards, no matter how defined, in the Atlantic economy in the second half of the nineteenth century. What caused this convergence? O'Rourke and Williamson (1997) have shown that the convergence in wage rates and GDP per capita were driven by factor market and commodity market integration. One particular aspect of globalization, the mass migration from Europe to the New World, explained 40–65 percent of Scandinavian real wage convergence on the United States from 1870 to 1910, and all of Irish and Italian convergence (O'Rourke and Williamson 1997, 185). Following Taylor and Williamson (1997), Hatton and Williamson (1998, 224) report that in the absence of immigration during these decades, real wages in 1910 would have been 15 percent higher than their actual level in the United States, 28 percent higher in Australia, and 31 percent higher in Canada. By contrast, in the absence of emigration, real wages in 1910 would have been 33 percent lower than their actual level in Italy, 36 percent lower in Ireland, and 11–15 percent lower in Scandinavia. The coefficient of variation for their 1910 counterfactual wage rates for the 15-country sample is 0.611. A comparison of this result with the COV for actual wages in table 13.1 shows that if there had been zero net migration from 1870 to 1910, real wages in the Atlantic economy would have diverged, rather than converged, in the four decades leading up to the First World War.

What is less clear is the effect of mass migration on nonincome measures of living standards. The United States and Canada, two countries with high rates of net immigration, had below-average absolute increases in life expectancy, literacy, and discretionary hours from 1870 to 1910. Conversely, several European countries with high emigration rates had above-average increases in longevity, learning, and leisure. In 1870 life expectancy in Denmark and Sweden was 3–6 months higher than in the United States; by 1910 the gap had widened to 5–6 years. Life expectancy in Germany was 9 years less than in the United States in 1870 but only 3 years less in 1910. The available height data tell a similar story. The average height of adult U.S. males declined by 1.1 cm from 1850 to 1900; over the same period, average height increased by 6.4 cm in Germany, 4.2 cm in Sweden, 3.8 cm in Denmark, and 2.6 cm in the Netherlands.[15] Some of North America's relative decline in health after 1870 might have been caused by its high immigration rates, although part must be attributed to improved nutrition and increased spending on public health in parts of western Europe, in particular Scandinavia and Germany.[16]

High immigration rates might also have lowered the ability of North American workers to reduce the length of their work week. From 1870 to 1910, the average Canadian worker gained no additional discretionary time, and the average U.S. worker gained about 200 hours per year. In contrast, the average Scandinavian worker gained about 700 hours of discretionary time per year, and the average German worker gained 560.

If one assumes that the large inflow of migrants had no impact on non-income measures of well-being in either sending or receiving countries— that is, life expectancy and education would have remained at their actual 1910 levels if there had been zero net migration from 1870 to 1910—then it is possible to calculate the extent of convergence in living standards in a world without mass migration by recalculating the HDI(Wages) in 1910 using the counterfactual wage rates reported in Hatton and Williamson (1998, 224). The coefficient of variation for HDI(Wages) would have been 0.281 in 1910 in the counterfactual case, as opposed to the actual value of 0.244. Living standards still would have converged after 1870, but the decline in the COV would have been 0.052 (0.333 − 0.281) rather than 0.089—more than 40 percent of the actual convergence would not have occurred.

This calculation provides a lower-bound estimate of the impact of zero migration on the dispersion of living standards. If mass migration led to a deterioration in the quality of life in receiving countries and an increase in quality of life in sending countries, then in a counterfactual world of zero net migration after 1870, life expectancy and education would have been higher in the New World and lower in Europe. As a result, the already large gap in HDI(Wages) scores between the English-speaking New World countries and Europe in 1910 would have been even larger, raising the dispersion in living standards. However, back-of-the-envelope calculations suggest that for any realistic estimates of the changes in life expectancy and education associated with the zero migration counterfactual, living standards broadly defined still would have converged in the Atlantic economy from 1870 to 1910.

Differing Patterns of Growth in Living Standards

Tables 13.1–13.3 show that there is no set relation between income levels and nonincome measures of well-being. One way to get a better idea of

Table 13.4
Comparison of Living Standards at GDP per Capita Near $3,000

	Year	GDP per capita	Real Wages	Life Expec- tancy	Liter- acy	School Enroll- ment	Leisure Hours	Social Spend- ing
United Kingdom	1870	3342	66.0	41.3	74.3	561	1405	na
United States	1880	3110	113.3	40.5	83.0	809	1116	0.29
Netherlands	1880	3000	73.3	41.7	80.1	479	966	0.96
Belgium	1880	2962	67.3	45.4	69.1	385	816	0.17
Germany	1900	3066	84.0	44.4	96.3	796	1104	0.59
Denmark	1900	2909	86.0	53.1	96.3	731	1418	1.41
Argentina	1900	2818	106.3	41.9	52.5	329	na	0.00
France	1910	3098	70.3	50.4	88.1	862	1227	0.81
Sweden	1910	2930	99.7	57.0	98.5	720	1415	1.03
Norway	1930	3145	na	64.2	97.0	770	1730	2.39
Italy	1930	2943	na	54.5	76.9	580	1566	0.10

Sources: See tables 13.1 and 13.2.

the differing patterns of development is to compare several countries at roughly the same level of GDP per capita. Table 13.4 presents data on various measures of living standards for 11 countries with per capita income of about $3,000. The date at which this income level was achieved ranged from before 1870 for the United Kingdom to 1930 for Norway and Italy. A per capita GDP of $3,000 is associated with life expectancy ranging from 41 to 64 years, literacy rates from 52.5 percent to 98.5 percent, and school enrollment rates from 329 per thousand to 809 per thousand.

The Scandinavian countries stand out for their relatively high quality of life at any given level of GDP per capita. This is best seen by comparing Denmark, Sweden, and Norway with countries that achieved a per capita income of $3,000 at the same time. Life expectancy in Denmark in 1900 was nearly nine years longer than in Germany, and eleven years longer than in Argentina. Danish education levels were similar to those in Germany but far above those in Argentina. Denmark had a higher level of social spending than either country, and its workers enjoyed significantly more discretionary time than did German workers. The differences between Sweden and France in 1910, and between Norway and Italy in 1930, are equally striking. Swedes lived nearly seven years longer than Frenchmen, had a 13 percent higher literacy rate, and enjoyed more leisure time. Norwegians in 1930 lived 9.7 years longer than Italians, were better educated, and had more discretionary time and a much larger social safety net.

Another way to address the same issue is to compare the level of GDP per capita or the real wage at which countries achieved an average life expectancy of 50. Once again Scandinavia leads the way. Norway reached a life expectancy of 50 in the early 1880s, at a per capita income level of about $1,500. Sweden came next, at about $1,900, followed by Denmark at $2,500. By comparison, France reached this milestone at a per capita income of $3,000, the Netherlands and Germany at about $3,500, Belgium at $4,000, and the United States and the United Kingdom at about $4,500. In terms of wages, Norway achieved a life expectancy of 50 at a real wage of about 45, Denmark at a real wage of 60, Sweden and the Netherlands at a real wage of 80, Belgium and Germany at about 88, the United Kingdom at about 100, and the United States and Canada at 120. The data pose a challenge to McKeown and Record's (1962) assertion that the major cause of the late nineteenth-century decline in mortality was improvements in nutrition resulting from increasing real wages.[17]

A third piece of evidence concerning different patterns of development is the effect of industrialization on heights. British and U.S. men appear to have "paid a biological price" for economic growth. In Britain adult male height declined by as much as 5.4 cm from the birth cohort of 1820 to the birth cohort of 1850; in the United States male height declined by 4.0 cm from 1830 to 1890. German males experienced a "small and short-lived" decline in stature during industrialization (Steckel and Floud 1997, 429–430). In contrast, the average height of male Swedes increased by about 3 cm during their industrialization phase from 1870 to the First World War (Sandberg and Steckel 1997, 129).[18] In Denmark male stature increased by about 2 cm from the 1880s to 1913, and in Norway stature increased by 2 cm from 1890 to 1920 (Floud 1994, 16–18).

Why didn't Scandinavians pay a biological penalty for their late nineteenth-century economic growth? Or, to put the question another way, how was Scandinavia able to achieve a higher average life expectancy than that in the United States or the United Kingdom despite having lower material living standards? The answer largely has to do with the timing of public health investments. Swedish cities responded quickly to an 1857 statute and constructed sewer and water systems, which reduced the health problems associated with urbanization (Sandberg and Steckel 1997, 143–145). In contrast, British cities responded very slowly to the Public Health Act of 1848, and as a result infant mortality rates did not appreciably decline until the first decade of the twentieth century.[19] U.S. cities also were late in adopting sewers and water filtration systems—in

1900 only 6.2 percent of the urban population received filtered water, rising to 26 percent in 1910 (Haines 2000, 139, 176).

In sum, there is not a simple linear relation between a country's GNP per capita or average real wage rate and its citizens' well-being. The different patterns of development are most clearly revealed by comparing North America with Scandinavia. Tables 13.1–13.3 show that workers in both regions had high living standards, compared with workers elsewhere in the Atlantic economy, but they achieved these living standards in different ways. North Americans had exceptionally high real wages but life expectancies only slightly above average. Scandinavians had lower wage rates but greater life expectancies, higher literacy rates, more discretionary hours, and a larger social safety net. In short, North Americans had a greater command over resources, but Scandinavians had a higher quality of life.

The United States and Scandinavia continued to follow different paths of economic development throughout the twentieth century. According to the United Nations (2004) *Human Development Report*, in 2002 the United States ranked fourth in the world in per capita GNP, sixteenth in school enrollment, and twenty-seventh in life expectancy. Sweden ranked twenty-first in GNP per capita, second in life expectancy, and first in school enrollment.

Nonincome Measures of Living Standards and European Mass Migration

During the half century leading up to the First World War, nearly 50 million Europeans migrated to New World destinations. Hatton and Williamson (1998; 2005) have shown that this mass migration was driven by real wage gaps between origin and destination countries, wage rates and demographic trends in origin countries, and the size of the emigrant stock abroad. They also found that emigration from most European countries followed an inverted-U-shaped pattern—emigration rates rose steeply at first, then leveled off, and subsequently declined (Hatton and Williamson 1998, 46–51). The life cycle pattern was most marked for Germany and the Scandinavian countries. Hatton and Williamson contend that the downswings in emigration experienced by these countries in the decades before World War I were caused by the ending of the demographic transition and by shrinking real wage gaps.

People who "are satisfied with their lot ... have no motives to migrate" (Burgdörfer 1931, 341). Satisfaction comes not only from wage rates but also from health, educational opportunities, discretionary time, and financial security. Perhaps the late nineteenth-century growth in life expectancy, discretionary hours, and social spending in Scandinavia and Germany caused some potential migrants to decide to remain at home.

Table 13.5 presents home country–to–United States ratios for four measures of living standards—real wages, life expectancy at birth, school enrollments, and discretionary time—and for the adjusted Human Development Index in 1870, 1890, and 1910, for eight European countries that sent a large share of their emigrants to the United States.[20] For each measure of well-being, the eight countries, on average, improved relative to the United States from 1870 to 1910, as can be seen in the table's final column. However, the extent of improvement and the value of the ratios differed significantly across measures of well-being. The average gap in life expectancy and discretionary time between the United States and western Europe was eliminated by 1890, and by 1913 both longevity and leisure were greater in western Europe than in the United States. On the other hand, real wage gaps remained large throughout the period; the average ratio of European to U.S. wages increased from 0.40 in 1870 to 0.50 in 1910. The gap in school enrollment rates also remained large; the average ratio increased by only 0.04 from 1870 to 1910, and the ratio declined for Germany, Norway, and the Netherlands. The ratio of European to U.S. HDI(Wages) scores increased from 0.64 in 1870 to 0.76 in 1910—convergence was especially pronounced for the three Scandinavian countries, Italy, and Ireland.

Table 13.5 also reports the value of the social insurance index (SII) for each country, as calculated by Huberman and Lewchuk (2003). The four social insurance entitlements included in the index are accident compensation, unemployment insurance, sickness insurance, and old age insurance; an index value of 1.0 signifies that the country had in place compulsory programs for all four entitlements. In 1870 no European country had adopted a social insurance safety net. By 1913 all eight countries had adopted at least a partial safety net—the value of the SII ranged from 0.5 for Italy to 1.0 for the United Kingdom and Ireland. The United States had no safety net until 1911–1913, when about half the states enacted workers' compensation legislation; the value of the SII for the United States was 0.0 for 1900 and perhaps 0.125 for 1913.

Finally, table 13.5 reports decadal emigration rates for each European country. The data clearly show the life cycle pattern of emigration discussed by Hatton and Williamson (1998). Emigration rates from Scandinavia and Germany reached their peak in the 1880s (Irish emigration

Table 13.5
European/United States Ratios, 1870–1910

	Den-mark	Ger-many	Ireland	Italy	Nether-lands	Nor-way	Sweden	U.K.	Mean Ratio
Real wages ratio									
1870	0.31	0.61	0.43	0.23	0.48	0.28	0.30	0.58	0.40
1890	0.39	0.52	0.54	0.25	0.56	0.37	0.41	0.63	0.46
1910	0.60	0.51	0.54	0.30	0.45	0.49	0.59	0.56	0.50
Life expectancy ratio									
1870	1.01	0.80	0.91	0.62	0.86	1.09	1.01	0.91	0.90
1890	1.03	0.87	0.98	0.84	0.98	1.09	1.09	0.98	0.98
1910	1.11	0.94	1.04	0.91	1.08	1.10	1.10	1.03	1.04
School enrollment ratio									
1870	0.60	0.94	0.38	0.33	0.63	0.82	0.77	0.71	0.65
1890	0.82	0.90	0.61	0.41	0.53	0.78	0.80	0.63	0.69
1910	0.77	0.84	0.64	0.46	0.48	0.77	0.76	0.76	0.69
Discretionary time ratio									
1870	0.68	0.82	0.99	1.09	0.83	0.68	0.68	1.32	0.89
1890	1.04	0.89	1.10	0.98	0.90	1.04	1.04	1.27	1.03
1913	1.13	1.14	1.17	0.96	0.97	1.13	1.12	1.19	1.10
HDI(Wages) ratio									
1870	0.70	0.77	0.62	0.22	0.67	0.71	0.72	0.73	0.64
1890	0.76	0.76	0.74	0.38	0.72	0.77	0.80	0.78	0.71
1910	0.86	0.76	0.76	0.49	0.72	0.81	0.85	0.79	0.76
Social insurance index									
1870	0.00	0.00	0.00	0.00	0.00	0.00	0.00	0.00	
1900	0.625	0.75	0.25	0.50	0.125	0.25	0.125	0.25	
1913	0.75	0.75	1.00	0.50	0.75	0.75	0.625	1.00	
Emigration rate									
1870–1879	1.97	1.35	11.28	4.29	2.66	4.33	2.96	3.87	
1880–1889	3.74	2.91	16.04	6.09	4.06	10.16	8.25	5.71	
1890–1899	2.60	1.18	9.70	8.65	4.62	4.56	5.32	3.92	
1900–1913	2.80	0.43	7.93	17.97	5.36	7.15	4.49	7.08	

Sources: For real wages, life expectancy, school enrollment, and discretionary time, see table 13.1; social insurance index, Huberman and Lewchuk (2003); emigration rate, Hatton and Williamson (1998, 33).
Notes: Ratios for real wages, life expectancy, school enrollment, discretionary time, and HDI(Wages) calculated as $X_{ij}/X_{US,j}$, where X is the measure of well-being, i is the European country, and j is the year. Emigration rate is calculated as gross emigrants per thousand population per annum decade averages.

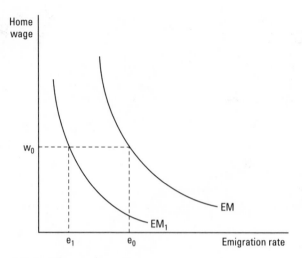

Figure 13.1
Stylized emigration responses
Source: Adapted from Hatton and Williamson (1998, 36).

rates peaked before 1870) and then declined, while Dutch and especially Italian emigration rates increased throughout the period.

A European contemplating emigration to the United States, if he or she had perfect access to information, would be able to compare home and destination living standards across several measures of well-being. For example, a Danish potential emigrant in 1910 observed a real wage gap of 40 percent between Denmark and the United States, a school enrollment rate 82 percent as high as in the United States, an average life expectancy 3 percent greater than the U.S. one, and a value for HDI(Wages) 76 percent as high as the U.S. one.

The data in table 13.5 suggest that the slowdown in emigration from Germany, Scandinavia, and Ireland in the two decades leading up to World War I might have been driven by factors in addition to declining wage gaps and the ending of the demographic transition. The story is best envisioned by considering figure 13.1. Changes in a country's emigration rate occur because of movements along the downward-sloping home country emigration function (EM) and because of shifts in the function. Hatton and Williamson (1998, 36–37) contend that during a country's industrialization, its emigration function shifts outward (to the right), which generates an increase in its emigration rate. At some level of development, the EM function stabilizes, so that further increases in home wages slow down emigration.

However, it is possible that for some countries the EM function does not remain stable at high levels of development but rather shifts back to the left. Consider the following scenario. Some share of potential migrants take nonincome measures of well-being and the size of social safety nets, as well as real wages, into consideration when making migration decisions. Moreover, some countries, upon reaching a high level of development, devote additional resources to public health, education, and safety nets. The resulting increases in life expectancy, educational opportunities, and social insurance causes the EM function to shift leftward (to EM_1), which reduces the emigration rate for any given real wage.

Such a scenario could help to explain the sharp reductions in emigration from Germany, Scandinavia, and Ireland to the United States after 1890. From 1890 to 1910, Germany experienced an 18 percent increase in real wages. Over the same two decades, life expectancy increased by 8.5 years (a 21 percent increase), and annual discretionary time increased by 37 percent (385 hours). The increase in longevity and leisure, combined with the reduction in financial insecurity resulting from the adoption of Bismarck's social insurance system, might have caused a leftward shift in the EM function and a subsequent decline in emigration. In a paper on German emigration, Khoudour-Casteras (2004) envisions such a scenario. He contends that the social insurance legislation adopted by Bismarck in the 1880s raised "indirect wages" and reduced the incentives of risk-averse Germans to emigrate. He estimates that in the absence of social insurance, German emigration rates from 1886 to 1913 would have been more than double their actual level.

Ireland experienced a 19 percent increase in real wages from 1890 to 1910, an 18 percent increase in life expectancy (8.1 years), a 14 percent increase in discretionary hours, and a 15 percent increase in its school enrollment rate. All three Scandinavian countries experienced very rapid wage increases after 1890, but they also had sharp increases in life expectancy and leisure time, and adopted social safety nets. The increase in Scandinavians' living standards was a result not just of rising wages but also of improvements in longevity, leisure, and security. In sum, the slowdown in emigration from northwestern Europe in the two decades leading up to the First World War probably was caused by increases in nonincome measures of living standards and the adoption of social safety nets as well as by increasing real wages and the ending of the demographic transition.

The United States still had a lot to offer to potential migrants in the first decade of the twentieth century. Real wages and educational opportunities were significantly higher than in western Europe. Potential emigrants from northwestern Europe had to weigh the high U.S. wages against the inherent risks associated with international migration and the high life expectancies, more discretionary time, and better developed social safety nets of home. Some who made this calculation put a high weight on income and educational opportunities, whereas others put a high weight on health, leisure, and social insurance. Those who chose to emigrate to the United States were people for whom the prospective income gains— for their children as well as themselves—mattered most and the non-income aspects of well-being mattered least. As a result of this process of self-selection, the United States attracted the most enterprising and the least risk-averse among the pool of potential migrants.[21]

From 1901 to 1910, over 460,000 persons migrated from Scandinavia to the United States.[22] In a sense, this move was like the move from "Sweet Auburn" to Sheffield in the 1830s discussed by Williamson (1981; 1982) in his papers on urban disamenties and living standards in industrializing Britain—migrants traded quality of life for greater purchasing power. Those who left Scandinavia for the United States placed a high value on purchasing power and education, whereas many of those who chose to remain at home must have placed a relatively high value on quality of life.

Could this self-selection of migrants help to explain certain aspects of U.S. social policy? Throughout the first half of the twentieth century the United States was a leader in education but a laggard in other aspects of social welfare spending (Lindert 2004). Perhaps the U.S. "peculiar distaste" for welfare is related to its immigration experience. Survey data show that U.S. and western European populations have sharply differing views about poverty and the poor—those in the United States are far more likely to believe that the poor are lazy and that people can work their way out of poverty (Alesina, Glaeser, and Sacerdote 2001). While some historians have traced such views back to the Puritans, these attitudes were reinforced by the influx of self-selected immigrants from Europe, who pulled themselves up by their own bootstraps and believed that all in their new country could do the same. A similar story might help to explain the U.S. leadership in education. Many immigrants to the United States saw human capital accumulation as the key to economic success for their children. Immigrants were willing to pay taxes to fund a first-rate educational system because education enabled their families to improve their economic status. However, they were unwilling to pay for social welfare policies, partly because they believed that their families would have little need for a social safety net and partly because they believed that many of those who would benefit from welfare policies were undeserving of public assistance. Immigrants' views toward education and social welfare differed from the views of their stay-at-home European cousins, who placed higher weight on health and social welfare and therefore chose not to emigrate to the United States. To sum up, U.S. "exceptionalism" existed before the late nineteenth-century influx of immigrants, but those who immigrated typically shared U.S. attitudes toward work, education, and welfare, and therefore helped to maintain U.S. social policies.

Hatton and Williamson (2005, 199–200) contend that even in the absence of war, immigration quotas, and the Great Depression, emigration from Europe to the United States would have declined after 1914 because countries in southern and eastern Europe would have undergone the same life cycle pattern that occurred in northwestern Europe before 1914. An examination of nonincome measures of living standards suggests that they are correct but that immigration rates might have remained high for at least two or three decades after 1914. School enrollment rates and social spending remained low in most southern and eastern European countries in 1930 (Lindert 1994; 2004). Life expectancy in the United States in 1930 was 5 years greater than in Italy, 10 years greater than in Spain, and 9.5 years greater than in Poland or Hungary (Dublin, Lotka, and Spiegelman 1949). Indeed, life expectancy in southern and eastern Europe in 1930 was below that of Scandinavia in 1900. Unlike Scandinavia or Germany in the 1890s, southern and eastern Europe in 1930 remained far below the United States in all aspects of the standard of living. As a result, emigration rates probably would have remained high throughout the 1920s and 1930s in the absence of quotas or the Depression.

Conclusions

The half century from the end of the American Civil War to the beginning of the First World War was a time of rapid convergence of living standards and mass migration in the Atlantic economy. Jeffrey Williamson and his co-authors have documented the convergence in real wage rates and explained what brought it about. This chapter has shown that nonincome measures of well-being—life expectancy, educational opportunities, and discretionary time—converged even more rapidly than income from 1870 to 1910, and they continued to converge from 1910 to 1929, a time of diverging real wage rates. By focusing on income measures, economists have underestimated the extent of convergence in living standards that occurred in the Atlantic economy after 1870.

The data on nonincome measures of living standards yield insights into the process of mass migration that occurred from 1870 to 1913, and in particular into the life cycle trend in emigration found by Hatton and Williamson (1998). Potential migrants cared about health, leisure, educational opportunities, and government safety nets as well as real wages. The investment by Germany and the Scandinavian countries in public health, education, and social safety nets in the late nineteenth century led to increases in nonincome aspects of the standard of living, which along with increasing real wages and the ending of the demographic transition, explain the slowdown in emigration from northwestern Europe in the two decades leading up to the First World War.

Notes

I thank Stan Engerman, Tim Hatton, Peter Lindert, Jeffrey Williamson, and the participants at the New Comparative Economic History conference for their helpful comments on an earlier draft of this chapter.

1. See, in particular, Williamson (1995; 1996; 1997; 1998), O'Rourke and Williamson (1997; 1999), Taylor and Williamson (1997), Hatton and Williamson (1998; 2005), and Lindert and Williamson (2003).

2. My data set includes 11 European countries and 4 European offshoots: Argentina, Australia, Belgium, Canada, Denmark, France, Germany, Ireland, Italy, the Netherlands, Norway, Spain, Sweden, the United Kingdom, and the United States. All 15 countries are included in Williamson's (1995) real wage database. The countries in Williamson's database not included here, because of lack of data for certain key variables, are Portugal and Brazil.

3. See, for example, Morris (1979), Sen (1987), Dasgupta and Weale (1992), Anand and Ravallion (1993), and Crafts (1997a; 1997b). Engerman (1997) provides a useful discussion of the relation between national income and welfare.

4. Kuznets (1952, 63–69) calculated the changing value of leisure in the United States from 1869 to 1948, and added it to the "flow of consumer goods" to obtain an estimate of the "final product of the economy reaching ultimate consumers." Similarly, Nordhaus and Tobin (1973) included an imputed value for leisure time in their "measure of economic welfare."

5. Most developed countries had systems of poor relief throughout the nineteenth century. However, the assistance given by the Poor Law typically was minimal, and during the period 1840–1880 relief expenditures rarely exceeded 1 percent of GDP (Lindert 1998, 113–114).

6. While this definition is open to criticism, it should not affect the ranking of countries in terms of leisure. I chose 4,160 hours as the maximum length of the work year. It is equal to 52 times 80 hours per week. This assumes that the remaining 88 hours in the week are necessary for sleep, meals, chores, and travel to and from work. One could instead assume that these activities take 12 hours per day, making the maximum possible number of hours worked per year 12 times 365, or 4,380. This definition would simply increase workers' discretionary leisure time in all countries without affecting the ranking. Fogel (2000, 184) estimates that sleep, meals, chores, and commuting take 13 hours per day.

7. From 1870 to 1900 real wages increased by more than 140 percent in Denmark, Norway, and Sweden, and by 88 percent in Ireland, all countries with below-average wages in 1870.

In contrast, the three highest-wage countries in 1870—Australia, the United States, and Canada—experienced wage increases of 8 percent, 38 percent, and 62 percent, respectively. The convergence is even more striking if Spain, whose real wages declined from 1870 to 1910, is left out of the calculation.

8. Williamson (1995) constructs separate wage data sets for the period up to 1913 and for 1914–1945. Each of the wage series is linked to a distinct PPP real wage benchmark. The 1910 data in table 13.1 use the first wage series, and the data for 1914 in table 13.2 use the second wage series.

9. The average increase in per capita income for the 15 countries was 24 percent. If Australia and the United Kingdom are removed from the data set, the other 13 countries experienced a divergence in GDP per capita from 1910 to 1929. GDP per capita is measured for the three years centered on 1910 and 1929; thus, the measure for 1929 includes the first full year of the Great Depression, 1930. Australia's decline in per capita income is not simply a result of including 1930 in the calculation. GDP per capita peaked in Australia in 1925 and declined by 11 percent from 1925 to 1929; it declined by 6 percent from 1929 to 1930. For the United Kingdom, GDP per capita declined by only 1 percent from 1929 to 1930. By contrast, in the United States, GDP per capita fell by 10 percent in the first year of the Depression.

10. Similar comparisons cannot be made for the measures that include real wages because the 1870–1910 data set and the 1914–1929 data set use different wage series. See note 8.

11. On the use of the human development index by economic historians, see in particular Crafts (1997a; 1997b) and various chapters in Steckel and Flood (1997). For an economist's critique of the human development index, see Kelley (1991). There is a discussion of various criticisms of the HDI in United Nations (1993, 104–114).

12. The United Nations Development Programme (UNDP) discounts income above a certain level, on the assumption that additional income above the threshold only marginally increases human development. While discounting income may make sense in the context of the UNDP's focus on poverty, it seems more reasonable, when comparing living standards across developed countries, to assume that an additional dollar is equally valuable at any level of income, and that is what I do here. Crafts (1997b) calculated the HDI using both definitions of income for a set of countries in 1870, 1913, and 1950.

13. The 1930 estimates for HDI(Wages) are not strictly comparable to the 1870 and 1910 estimates because they are based on Williamson's 1914–1945 wage series, whereas the earlier estimates are based on his wage series that ends in 1913. They therefore should not be used to examine the trend in HDI scores from 1910 to 1930. However, they can be used to compare HDI rankings across countries in 1930.

14. The convergence occurs even if we reweight the index by raising the weight of the income component (GDP per capita or real wages) to 0.5 and reducing the weights for life expectancy and education to 0.25 each.

15. The height data are from Flood (1994) and Steckel and Flood (1997).

16. This was not the case for Australia, another country with high immigration rates, where life expectancy, literacy, school enrollment, discretionary hours, and social spending all increased at average or above-average rates from 1870 to 1910. Given the high living standards, more European emigrants should have chosen Australia as a destination over the United States, Canada, or Argentina during the age of mass migration. It would appear that Australian workers were protected to some degree by "the tyranny of distance."

17. To be fair, McKeown and Record (1962) were trying to explain the decline in English mortality rates over time, not differences in life expectancy across countries. Still, the wide range of real wages associated with a life expectancy of 50 seems to support Easterlin's (2004, 102) conclusion that "life expectancy cannot be taken to be simply a byproduct of economic growth. . . . Public policy initiatives have been essential to the improvement of life expectancy, and these can be, and, in fact, have been, undertaken in the absence of economic growth." On the relation between public policy and falling death rates in Victorian Britain,

see Szreter (1988; 1997). Kunitz and Engerman (1992) provide a detailed discussion of the relation between trends in real wages and mortality.

18. During this same period, average male height in the United States increased by about 1 cm (Costa and Steckel 1997, 72).

19. The sluggish response of British cities was largely a result of what Williamson (1990) calls "public sector failure"—the determination of shopkeepers, landlords, and other small tradesmen to keep their regressive property taxes as low as possible. Lindert (2004) provides an excellent discussion of the negative effects on social spending resulting from extending the franchise to the lower middle class, as occurred in Britain in 1832.

20. According to Hatton and Williamson (1998, 54), in the 1890s French emigrants predominantly went to Canada, and Spanish migrants to Argentina. Belgium sent only 7.2 percent of its emigrants to the United States.

21. On self-selection and immigration, see Borjas (1991).

22. The breakdown of migrants to the United States by country was as follows: about 65,000 from Denmark, 180,000 from Norway, and 220,000 from Sweden. During this decade nearly 90 percent of Danish emigrants to non-European countries, 94 percent of Norwegian emigrants, and 98 percent of Swedish emigrants went to the United States. Emigration data are from Jensen (1931, 289, 297).

References

Alesina, A., E. Glaeser, and B. Sacerdote. 2001. Why Doesn't the United States Have a European-Style Welfare State? *Brookings Papers on Economic Activity* 2: 187–254.

Anand, S., and M. Ravallion. 1993. Human Development in Poor Countries: On the Role of Private Incomes and Public Services. *Journal of Economic Perspectives* 7 (1): 133–150.

Borjas, G. J. 1991. Immigration and Self-Selection. In *Immigration, Trade, and the Labor Market*, ed. J. M. Abowd and R. B. Freeman. Chicago: University of Chicago Press.

Boyer, G. R. 2006. Insecurity, Safety Nets, and Self-Help in Victorian Britain. Unpublished Manuscript, Cornell University.

Burgdörfer, F. 1931. Migration across the Frontiers of Germany. In *International Migrations*. Vol. 2, *Interpretations*, ed. W. F. Willcox. New York: National Bureau of Economic Research.

Costa, D. L., and R. H. Steckel. 1997. Long-Term Trends in Health, Welfare, and Economic Growth in the United States. In *Health and Welfare during Industrialization*, ed. R. H. Steckel and R. Floud. Chicago: University of Chicago Press.

Crafts, N. F. R. 1997a. Some Dimensions of the "Quality of Life" during the British Industrial Revolution. *Economic History Review* 50 (4): 617–639.

———. 1997b. The Human Development Index and Changes in Standards of Living: Some Historical Comparisons. *European Review of Economic History* 1 (3): 299–322.

Dasgupta, P., and M. Weale. 1992. On Measuring the Quality of Life. *World Development* 20: 119–131.

Dublin, L. I., A. J. Lotka, and M. Spiegelman. 1949. *Length of Life: A Study of the Life Table*. New York: Ronald Press.

Easterlin, R. A. 2004. *The Reluctant Economist: Perspectives on Economics, Economic History, and Demography*. Cambridge: Cambridge University Press.

Engerman, S. 1997. The Standard of Living Debate in International Perspective: Measures and Indicators. In *Health and Welfare during Industrialization*, ed. R. H. Steckel and R. Floud. Chicago: University of Chicago Press.

Flora, P. 1973. Historical Processes of Social Mobilization: Urbanization and Literacy, 1850–1965. In *Building States and Nations: Models and Data Resources*, ed. S. N. Eisenstadt and S. Rokkan. Vol. 1. London: Sage.

Floud, R. 1994. The Heights of Europeans since 1750: A New Source for European Economic History. In *Stature, Living Standards, and Economic Development: Essays in Anthropometric History*, ed. J. Komlos. Chicago: University of Chicago Press.

———. 1997. *The People and the British Economy, 1830–1914*. Oxford: Oxford University Press.

Floud, R., K. Wachter, and A. Gregory. 1990. *Height, Health and History: Nutritional Status in the United Kingdom, 1750–1980*. Cambridge: Cambridge University Press.

Fogel, R. W. 2000. *The Fourth Great Awakening and the Future of Egalitarianism*. Chicago: University of Chicago Press.

Haines, M. R. 1994. Estimated Life Tables for the United States, 1850–1900. NBER (National Bureau of Economic Research) Historical Working Paper 59. ⟨http://www.nber.org/papers/H0059⟩.

———. 2000. The Population of the United States, 1790–1920. In *Cambridge Economic History of the United States*. Vol. 2, *The Long Nineteenth Century*, ed. S. L. Engerman and R. E. Gallman. Cambridge: Cambridge University Press.

Hatton, T. J. and J. G. Williamson. 1998. *The Age of Mass Migration: Causes and Economic Impact*. Oxford: Oxford University Press.

———. 2005. *Global Migration and the World Economy: Two Centuries of Policy and Performance*. Cambridge, Mass.: MIT Press.

Huberman, M. 2004. Working Hours of the World Unite? New International Evidence of Worktime, 1870–1913. *Journal of Economic History* 64 (4): 964–1001.

Huberman, M., and W. Lewchuk. 2003. European Economic Integration and the Labour Compact, 1850–1913. *European Review of Economic History* 7 (1): 3–41.

Jensen, A. 1931. Migration Statistics of Denmark, Norway, and Sweden. In *International Migrations*. Vol. 2, *Interpretations*, ed. W. F. Willcox. New York: National Bureau of Economic Research.

Kelley, A. 1991. The Human Development Index: "Handle with Care." *Population and Development Review* 17 (2): 315–324.

Keynes, J. M. 1919. *The Economic Consequences of the Peace*. London: Macmillan.

Khoudour-Casteras, D. 2004. The Impact of Bismarck's Social Legislation on German Emigration before World War I. Unpublished Manuscript, University of California.

Kunitz, S. J. and S. L. Engerman. 1992. The Ranks of Death: Secular Trends in Income and Mortality. *Health Transition Review* 2 (Suppl.): 29–46.

Kuznets, S. 1952. Long-Term Changes in the National Income of the United States of America since 1870. In *Income and Wealth of the United States: Trends and Structure*, ed. S. Kuznets. Cambridge: Bowes and Bowes.

Lindert, P. H. 1994. The Rise of Social Spending, 1880–1930. *Explorations in Economic History* 31 (1): 1–37.

———. 1998. Poor Relief before the Welfare State: Britain versus the Continent, 1780–1880. *European Review of Economic History* 2 (2): 101–140.

———. 2004. *Growing Public: Social Spending and Economic Growth since the Eighteenth Century*. Cambridge: Cambridge University Press.

Lindert, P. H., and J. G. Williamson. 2003. Does Globalization Make the World More Unequal? In *Globalization in Historical Perspective*, ed. M. D. Bordo, A. M. Taylor, and J. G. Williamson. Chicago: University of Chicago Press.

Maddison, A. 1995. *Monitoring the World Economy, 1820–1992*. Paris: OECD.

McKeown, T., and R. G. Record. 1962. Reasons for the Decline of Mortality in England and Wales during the Nineteenth Century. *Population Studies* 16 (2): 94–122.

Morris, M. D. 1979. *Measuring the Condition of the World's Poor: The Physical Quality of Life Index*. New York: Pergamon Press.

Nordhaus, W. D., and J. Tobin. 1973. Is Growth Obsolete? In *The Measurement of Economic and Social Performance*, ed. M. Moss. New York: National Bureau of Economic Research.

O'Rourke, K. H., and J. G. Williamson. 1997. Around the European Periphery, 1870–1913: Globalization, Schooling and Growth. *European Review of Economic History* 1 (2): 153–190.

————. 1999. *Globalization and History: The Evolution of a Nineteenth-Century Atlantic Economy*. Cambridge, Mass.: MIT Press.

Sandberg, L. G., and R. H. Steckel. 1997. Was Industrialization Hazardous to Your Health? Not in Sweden! In *Health and Welfare during Industrialization*, ed. by R. H. Steckel and R. Floud. Chicago: University of Chicago Press.

Sen, A. 1987. *The Standard of Living*. Cambridge: Cambridge University Press.

Steckel, R. H., and R. Floud, eds. 1997. *Health and Welfare during Industrialization*. Chicago: University of Chicago Press.

Szreter, S. 1988. The Importance of Social Intervention in Britain's Mortality Decline c. 1850–1914: A Re-interpretation of the Role of Public Health. *Social History of Medicine* 1 (1): 1–37.

————. 1997. Economic Growth, Disruption, Deprivation, Disease, and Death: On the Importance of the Politics of Public Health for Development. *Population and Development Review* 23 (4): 693–728.

Taylor, A. M., and J. G. Williamson. 1997. Convergence in the Age of Mass Migration. *European Review of Economic History* 1 (1): 27–63.

Timmer, A. S., and J. G. Williamson. 1998. Immigration Policy Prior to the 1930s: Labor Markets, Policy Interactions, and Globalization Backlash. *Population and Development Review* 24 (4): 739–771.

United Nations. 1990. *Human Development Report 1990*. Oxford: Oxford University Press.

————. 1993. *Human Development Report 1993*. Oxford: Oxford University Press.

————. 2004. *Human Development Report 2004*. Oxford: Oxford University Press.

U.S. Census Bureau. 2003. *Statistical Abstract of the United States: 2003*. Washington: Government Printing Office.

Williamson, J. G. 1981. Urban Disamenities, Dark Satanic Mills, and the British Standard of Living Debate. *Journal of Economic History* 41 (1): 75–83.

————. 1982. Was the Industrial Revolution Worth It? Disamenities and Death in Nineteenth-Century British Towns. *Explorations in Economic History* 19 (3): 221–245.

————. 1990. *Coping with City Growth during the British Industrial Revolution*. Cambridge: Cambridge University Press.

————. 1995. The Evolution of Global Labor Markets since 1830: Background Evidence and Hypotheses. *Explorations in Economic History* 32 (2): 141–196.

————. 1996. Globalization, Convergence, and History. *Journal of Economic History* 56 (2): 277–306.

————. 1997. Globalization and Inequality, Past and Present. *World Bank Research Observer* 12 (2): 117–135.

————. 1998. Globalization, Labor Markets, and Policy Backlash in the Past. *Journal of Economic Perspectives* 12 (4): 51–72.

You Take the High Road and I'll Take the Low Road:
Economic Success and Well-Being in the Longer Run

Cormac Ó Gráda

The focus of this chapter is not on explaining growth but on the consumption and welfare implications of the different routes taken by two pairs of economies in the past. The case studies considered are (1) the Dutch and British economies between the sixteenth and nineteenth centuries, and (2) the Irish and Italian economies during the second half of the twentieth century. In each case, both economies begin and end with roughly equal levels of output and consumption per head, but the different routes taken involve initial divergence, or forging ahead by one country followed by the other's catching up. In the Anglo-Dutch case, it was the Netherlands that opened up a lead during the Dutch Golden Age (c. 1580–1670) only to be tagged by industrializing Britain more than a century later. In the case of Ireland and Italy, both economies set out at roughly the same point in terms of productivity and consumption in mid-century. Between the 1950s and the 1980s, Italy forged ahead, only to be caught up by a late surge from Ireland in the 1990s. Both Italy and the Netherlands enjoyed higher consumption and living standards between start and end points. Other things being equal, growing fast and then slowly would seem preferable to growing slowly first, and then fast. The chapter is about the measurement and some welfare implications of the different paths traveled.

The Dutch Republic and Great Britain

For much of the seventeenth century the Dutch Republic was Britain's main economic rival in Europe. Although Britain's beggar-my-neighbor commercial policies prevailed over the Dutch in the long run, for decades travelers to Holland and leaders of British public opinion marveled at Dutch ingenuity and success. Gregory King's national accounts imply that by the end of the Golden Age the Dutch Republic was the richest economy in Europe (de Vries 1974, 242–243). The population of Amsterdam surged from 30,000 in 1550 to 175,000 by 1650, making it the fourth city in Europe by 1650 (after London, Paris, and Naples) (de Vries 1984, 271). Historians have celebrated Dutch "precocity" and "primacy in world trade" during the Golden Age. The ability of a small nation—the Netherlands contained only 1.5 million people in 1600, compared to Britain's six million and France's 18.5 million—to thrive on a thin natural resource base was the envy of its rivals (Schama 1987; Israel 1989).

Three decades ago, de Vries (1976, 251, 252) described the economy of the Golden Age era as "high-level traditionalist," which by the eighteenth century had sunk "into a complacent stagnation." Soltow and van Zanden (2001, 31) support this assessment; they dubbed the growth of the Golden Age era "premodern" because it failed to generate significant gains in living standards and could not sustain itself in the long run. Others, however, have stressed Dutch breakthroughs in agriculture, financial institutions, shipping, and public finance. De Vries and van der Woude (1997) have described the early modern Dutch economy as the first to experience "modern economic growth."

Either way, for all its earlier successes, the Dutch economy was widely deemed a failure by the early nineteenth century. Some historians link "the non-event of [Dutch] economic stagnation" (Mokyr 1976, 84) relative to industrializing Britain—or, indeed, to Belgium—to its own earlier success. They blame the institutional sclerosis of a high-wage economy encumbered by a generous social welfare regime, unable to cope with competition from the latecomers Belgium and Great Britain (de Vries 1974; Mokyr 1976; de Vries and van der Woude 1997; van Zanden 2002a, 2002b; van Zanden and van Riel 2004). The historiography of the post–Golden Age economy is somber in tone. And according to Maddison's estimates, Dutch GDP rose only by 7 percent between 1700 and 1820, whereas Belgium's doubled and the United Kingdom's more than trebled. Over the same period, Dutch GDP per head fell.

In the late seventeenth century Gregory King reckoned that Dutch national income exceeded that of England by 10 to 15 percent. This gap is much less than that allowed by Maddison, who implies that for over three centuries the Dutch enjoyed higher output per head than anyone else and that in 1700 Dutch GDP per head was 1.7 times the U.K. level (de Vries 1974, 242–243; Maddison 2001, table B21). Maddison implies that the Dutch and British economies had roughly the same GDP per head c. 1500. The Netherlands then forged ahead, only to lose ground from the late seventeenth century on, and be overtaken c. 1800. This, and the sense that the Netherlands paid a price for being an "early starter," suggests the case for taking a longer perspective in assessing the performance of the early modern Dutch economy and for focusing on the period 1500–1800 as a whole.

Here I rely on an amended version of Maddison's estimates, which imply that GDP per head in the Netherlands and the United Kingdom were roughly equal c. 1500 and again c. 1835. In between, the Dutch built up a lead that reached its peak in proportional terms in the 1690s; from then on, the lead was slowly whittled away. However, since the historiography is really about Anglo-Dutch rivalry, Maddison's GDP per head data must be adjusted to exclude Ireland. The adjustment matters because Irish GDP per head was much less than the British in this period, and Irish population was a significant proportion of the U.K. total, rising from about one-fifth c. 1500 to one-third c. 1820 (Ó Gráda 1997b). I assume, arbitrarily, that Irish GDP per head was half the British throughout. Figure 14.1 plots the trends in Dutch, U.K., and British GDP per head between 1500 and 1900, as inferred from Maddison's data.

Van Zanden's reconstructions of Dutch GDP imply a very different trajectory before c. 1820. Whereas Maddison implies only a small Dutch advantage over the United Kingdom c. 1500, van Zanden implies an advantage of nearly three-fifths. And while Maddison reckons that real GDP per head in the Netherlands rose by 140 percent between 1500 and

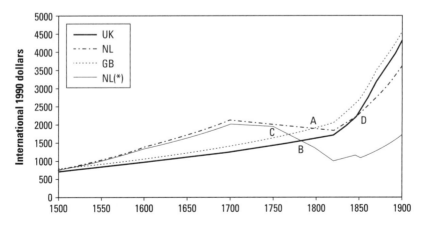

Figure 14.1
GDP per head in the United Kingdom, the Netherlands, and Great Britain, 1500–1900. *nl* traces Dutch GDP per head; *nl(*)* Dutch GDP per head after adjusting for lower Dutch population growth; *uk* GDP per head for United Kingdom; *gb* omits Ireland. The exclusion of Ireland allows *gb* to overtake *nl* half a century earlier (A versus D). Slower Dutch population growth entails closing the gap even earlier (C versus A).

Table 14.1
Estimates of Dutch GDP per Head, 1500–1820

Year	(1) Maddison	(2) van Zanden	(2)/(1)
c. 1500	761	1,252	1.65
c. 1650	1,700	2,411	1.42
c. 1700	2,100	2,386	1.14
c. 1750	1,985	2,337	1.28
1820	1,838	1,838	1.00

Sources: Maddison (2001), 1500, 1700, and 1820; van Zanden (2001, table 4.3); Maddison (2005, 25); my interpolations for Maddison, c. 1650 and c. 1750.

1820, van Zanden's best guess is that the rise was about one-third of that (Maddison 2001, table B21; van Zanden 2001; compare Federico 2002). The contrasting Maddison and van Zanden trajectories are summarized in table 14.1. Meanwhile de Vries and van der Woude (1997, 709–710) refuse to "venture an estimate" of the growth rate of the Dutch economy before the 1660s, but nonetheless they are confident that income per capita rose, pointing to significant productivity increases in agriculture, services, and shipping, and the big rise in energy consumption in the previous two centuries or so. It is enough to point out here that if van Zanden's estimate for 1500 is correct, then the Anglo-Dutch gap would have opened up earlier and all the following calculations will underestimate the gap.

By Maddison's reckoning Dutch GDP per head overtook British GDP per head in the mid-1510s and maintained its edge until mid-1790s. How much was the extra Dutch output worth? Between 1514–1515 and 1794–1795, the average gap was one-fifth of Dutch GDP per head. Alternatively, adding together the annual gaps yields a sum equivalent to 52 times 1795 GDP per head! Assuming that the ratio of consumption to GDP did not differ greatly between the two economies in this period, the average gap is a measure of the premium in living standards enjoyed by the Dutch. It would be nice to know the relevant ratios of household consumption and GNI to GDP; in the absence of such data, it bears noting that the ratios of external wealth to GDP in both economies at the end of the period were still very small, and both investment and government expenditure were relatively small percentages of GDP in both economies c. 1800.[1] Henceforth, I use GDP as a proxy for consumption.[2]

It would take a long time before faster British growth "recouped" the accumulated Dutch advantage. By 1850 only about 12 percent of the accumulated gap in annual GDPs per head had been "recouped." Six

Table 14.2
Population and GDP per Head, the Netherlands and Great Britain, 1500–1820

Year	Population (thousands)		GDP per Head (1990 international $)	
	Netherlands	Great Britain	Netherlands	Great Britain
1500	950	3,142	754	795
1600	1,500	5,700	1,368	1,060
1700	1,900	6,640	2,110	1,408
1820	2,355	14,139	1,821	2,048

Source: Netherlands data from Maddison (2001, tables B10 and B21).

decades or so later, only three-fifths of the gap had been made up. These calculations take no account of any major differences in the rates of population growth. In assessing economic performance, however, account should also be taken of extensive growth. In what follows, when comparing economic welfare and performance, I simply add the rate of population growth to that in GDP per head. An economy in which GDP per head doubles over a given period while population remains the same is deemed to perform as well as an economy where GDP per head fails to grow but population doubles. In other words, this means comparing growth rates in real GDP. Since Britain's population grew faster than the Dutch over the period (table 14.2), allowing for differences in population growth attenuates the Dutch advantage somewhat, to 39 times 1795 GDP per head. In figure 14.1, the $nl(*)$ schedule tracks Dutch GDP per head, weighted by an index that sets Dutch population relative to British in 1500 at unity. Here the British subsequently "recoup" more quickly, by 1858.

Whether the consumption streams should be discounted is rather a moot point. Discounting is equivalent to treating all those who lived in the country for part or whole of the period in question as if they were represented by a lone individual with no thought for the next generation and with "no family or friends interested in his (her) survival" (Williamson 1984, 158). Whatever the validity of such an analogy for periods of a few decades, the Anglo-Dutch case refers to a period necessarily involving successive cohorts of individuals. There is no reason why the average individual living in 1620–1650 should be valued more than the average individual living in 1720–1750. A second reason for not discounting is time inconsistency: those same young people who tend to heavily discount the future regret in retrospect what seems like careless overspending (van den Berg 2002).[3]

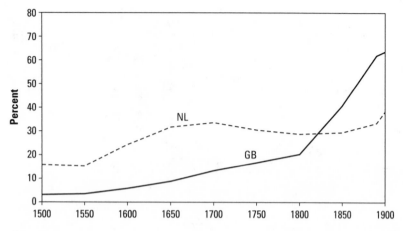

Figure 14.2
Urbanization rates in Great Britain and the Netherlands, 1500–1900. From de Vries (1984, 39, 45–46). Urbanization is measured as the percentage of the population living in towns and cities with a population of ten thousand or more.

Allowing for Urbanization

Dutch economic precocity was founded on a highly productive agricultural sector, a strong commercial sector, and precocious urbanization. As Wrigley et al. (1997, 204) warn, however, "the severity of the urban penalty should not be underestimated." Figure 14.2 describes urbanization rates (where "urban" includes towns and cities of ten thousand or more) in the Netherlands and Great Britain, 1500–1900. Dutch urbanization rates, unparalleled in early modern Europe, imposed a toll in terms of morbidity and life expectancy. Williamson's (1981) research on British cities during the Industrial Revolution is eloquent on this score. Although it remains unclear whether the nutritional status of urban populations generally was inferior to that of rural populations, they certainly suffered from congestion, poor sanitation, adulterated food, and endemic diseases (Riley 2001, 161–163). Urbanites everywhere were also smaller in stature. Many rich citizens, aware of the increased mortality risk, left the cities for their rural retreats during the summer. The poor did not have that choice.

In 1673 England's former ambassador at the Hague described the Dutch "as generally not so long-liv'd as in better Airs; and begin to decay early, both men and women, especially in *Amsterdam*," singling out "Diseases of the Climate [which] all hot and dry Summers bring... that are infectious among them, especially into Amsterdam and Leyden" (Temple

1673, 161). Alas, the data to test these claims are lacking. Pre-1800 Dutch demographic data are poor, and how Amsterdam achieved its remarkable population growth in the century or so after 1580 remains somewhat of a mystery. The high proportions of widowed household heads in Dutch towns and cities, and the Dutch obsession with cleanliness in the Golden Age era, are consistent with the presumption that mortality was high in a congested, damp environment (van Strien 1993, 212–213, 231 n. 95; van der Woude 1972, 311–313; Schama 1987, 375–384).[4] However, hard evidence on immigration, mortality, and the main causes of death is lacking, prompting some "controlled conjectures" (de Vries 1985, 664; van der Woude 1983, 197–209; de Vries and van der Woude 1997; van Leeuwen and Oeppen 1993).

An important contribution by Alter (1983, 33) reports life expectancy, $e_0 = 25.3$ years for the lives of nominees in the Amsterdam life annuities of 1586–1590, and $e_0 = 30.0$ years for those of 1672–1674.[5] Plainly, the social rank of the annuitants and their residence in Amsterdam are factors: these were prosperous people living in a port city. Although some claim that because infectious disease did not discriminate between rich and poor, mortality differed less by class in early modern Europe than later,[6] evidence suggests that Alter's estimates should be taken very much as an upper bound of life expectancy in the Netherlands at the time. The low life expectancies yielded by the trickle of evidence from local studies are corroborative. Life expectancy in the Maasland (south Netherlands) in 1730–1759 was strikingly low (26.5 years), and in a cluster of five Catholic communities living in the northern clay lands around Groningen in 1731–1770, it was just over 30 years (Noordam 1986; Paping 1988).

The paucity of Dutch data means that the evidence from urban communities in neighboring countries is also worth considering. English data (tables 14.3 and 14.4) imply a very substantial urban penalty in terms of life expectancy before 1800 (Woods 2000; Szreter and Mooney 1998).[7] The impact of class may be gauged from comparing the life expectancy of Londoners in general with that of London Quakers, a largely middle-class group. Quaker life expectancy was 28.8 years in 1650–1699, 24 years in 1700–1749, 29.8 years in 1750–1799, and 35.5 years in 1800–1849 (Landers 1993, 158). This implies a gap of six to seven years between London Quakers and other Londoners in the eighteenth century, although London Quakers still died younger than rural Englishmen and Englishwomen. In seventeenth-century Geneva the class gradient was just as steep as in London. In 1650–1684 the life expectancy of Genevan workers, male and female together, was 20.5 years, that of the middle

Table 14.3
Life Expectancy in England and Wales (years), 1750s–1900s

	London	Large Towns	Small Towns	Rural
1751–1760	20.1	—	27.5	41.3
1801–1810	35.0	32.0	34.2	42.2
1821–1830	36.9	32.7	36.2	43.3
1841–1850	36.7	32.0	36.0	43.5
1861–1870	37.7	33.0	38.0	46.5
1881–1890	42.6	39.0	44.0	51.0
1901–1910	49.4	46.3	50.5	56.5

Source: Woods (2000, 369).

Table 14.4
Life Expectancy in London and in England and Wales, 1700s–1860s

	(1) England and Wales	(2) London	(1) – (2)
1700s	38.5	18.5	20.0
1730s	31.8	18.2	13.6
1740s	33.5	17.6	15.9
1750s	37.0	20.1	16.9
1760s	34.6	20.5	13.9
1770s	36.9	21.6	15.3
1780s	35.3	25.5	9.8
1790s	37.1	27.5	9.6
1800s	37.2	28.0	9.2
1810s	37.8	32.4	5.4
1820s	39.6	34.4	5.2
1830s	40.5	36.9	3.6
1840s	40.0	36.7	3.3
1850s	40.0	38.0	2.0
1860s	40.8	37.7	3.1

Sources: Landers (2000, 171), London 1730s–1820s; Woods (2000, 365), London 1700s, 1830s–1860s; Wrigley and Schofield (1981, 230), England and Wales.

class 26.0 years, and that of the elite 36.8 years (de Vries 1984, 184; Perrenoud 1975).[8] In the light of such data, Alter's estimates for Amsterdam annuitants' middle-class nominees reveal very short lives indeed for Amsterdamers. A six-year gap between the middle class and the population as a whole would indicate life expectancies in the cities of less than 20 years in the 1580s and 23–25 years in the 1670s.

Given the high rate of Dutch urbanization at a time when the urban mortality disadvantage was so high, it is surely not far-fetched to assume

Table 14.5
The Gap in "True" Living Standards (multiples of 1795 British GDP per head)

	GDP per Head	"True" Measure $\beta = 1$	"True" Measure $\beta = 0.45$
Gap relative to 1795 GDP per head	52	34	10
Allowing for extensive growth	39	21	-3

that urbanization reduced the average life span in the Netherlands by an average of three years below British levels during the *longue durée* analyzed here.

Building on Usher (1973), Williamson (1984) explained how to factor in increasing life expectancy in assessments of the economic performance of industrializing Britain. Usher's widely used measure reduces to the expression

$$G_{\hat{C}} = G_C + \frac{1}{\beta} G_L$$

where $G_{\hat{C}}$ represents growth rate of $\hat{C}$, the "true" standard of living after taking the change in life expectancy into account, G_C the growth rate of GDP per head, β the elasticity of utility with respect to GDP per head, and G_L the change in life expectancy. In this simple model the role of β is pivotal; in his study of Britain c. 1780–1930, Williamson worked with values of $\beta = 0.25$ to 0.45. An even simpler but serviceable way of dealing with the issue is that proposed by Lichtenberg (2003).[9] He defines expected individual lifetime well-being (EILW) as $Y_A \cdot e_A$, where Y_A is average income and e_A is expectation of life at birth in economy A. Relative EILW at a point in time then is measured as $[Y_A \cdot e_A]/[Y_B \cdot e_B]$. This amounts to assuming that the marginal utility from additions to Y and e is constant. In effect, Lichtenberg's measure of "true" change implies $\beta = 1$.

In table 14.5 I report the implications of factoring in the cost of lower Dutch life expectancy for values of $\beta = 0.45$ and $\beta = 1$. Even $\beta = 1$ reduces the cumulative gains built up between 1515 and 1795 considerably; assuming $\beta = 0.45$ erodes all the Dutch advantage, once differential population growth is also allowed for.

Ireland and Italy

In the year of *il sorpasso*, 1987, Italian GDP briefly overtook that of Great Britain (Maddison 2001, tables C1b and C1c).[10] For Ireland, 1999, when GDP per head overtook that of the United Kingdom, marked a similar defining moment. In 1998 Irish GDP per head also overtook that of Italy. By the mid-2000s Ireland was well ahead of the United Kingdom in terms of GDP per head.

During the 1990s much was made of the dynamism of the Irish economy. It seemed as if the Irish had just unlocked the secret to fast, sustained economic growth. The celebratory commentary on that era from far and near (e.g., Gray 1997), and the eagerness elsewhere to learn from Ireland, might seem to imply that the Celtic Tiger's growth compensated for the earlier delay: the main thing is that Ireland got there eventually. The Anglo-Dutch example suggests otherwise: it suggests that Ireland's route of underachievement followed by convergence and even overshooting may have exacted a heavy price in economic welfare.

If a shift in economic policy was a precondition for the economic boom that began in the late 1980s and made Ireland "Europe's star-performing economy," by the same token earlier underperformance can be blamed largely on policy failure. Inward-looking economic policies, including tariff protection and restrictions on capital imports, were mainly responsible for the stagnation of the 1950s. The opening up of the economy in the late 1950s yielded results in the following decade, but the gains were negated by the disastrous policy response to the second oil crisis of the late 1970s. That response sought to match the impact of the price shock through fiscal expansion, with the result that public expenditure rose to levels that by the early 1980s threatened national bankruptcy. There followed a period of fiscal rectitude and high unemployment. The public debt/GDP ratio peaked at 129 percent in 1986; in that same year the unemployment rate was 18 percent, and it would remain above 10 percent for another decade.

Between 1987 and 2000 the economy grew at an annual rate of 7 percent, faster than any other OECD economy. Even today Irish economic growth continues to exceed OECD and EU averages. This suggests that there is more to the achievement of the Irish economy than catch-up or belated convergence. However, compensation for underperformance since mid-century is a crucial part of the story. Two features of economic growth in this period support this view. First, when adjusted for the effects of transfer pricing, productivity growth in the 1990s was by no means spectacular (Honohan and Walsh 2002, 45–46). Second, when the spare capacity accumulated since the early 1980s had been mopped up, the rate of economic growth slowed down, although it still remained considerably above the EU average.

The course of the Irish economy since 1950—initial underperformance, mitigated by rapid advance from the late 1980s on—prompts an analysis of the last half century or so of Irish economic history as a unit.[11] Although dwarfing Ireland in terms of both population and output,[12] Italy offers a useful comparative perspective because both economies were backward by west European standards in mid-century, with GDPs per head barely half those of the United Kingdom, Sweden, or Denmark.[13] Of course, the two economies differed in obvious ways that conditioned their very different trajectories. In geographic terms, Italy is located in the heart of Europe, whereas Ireland is on the periphery. At the outset Italy benefited from generous doses of Marshall Plan aid and from the stimulus of European economic integration. Ireland's gains from European integration and foreign largesse would come toward the end of the century, at a time when the tyranny of distance mattered much less than in mid-century.

In the 1950s and 1960s real Irish consumption per head fell way behind the Italian; the gap narrowed thereafter, but it took the hectic growth of the Celtic Tiger era to bridge it once more. The contrasting paths taken by the two economies are described in figures 14.3 and 14.4. Figure 14.3 describes the gaps in consumption and GDP per head, and figure 14.4 outlines the contrasting demographic trajectories. In Italy, GDP and

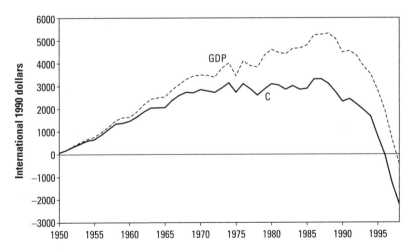

Figure 14.3
Gaps between GDP and C (consumption) per capita, 1950–1998. GDP data GDP(IT) and GDP(IRL) from Maddison (2001); conversion of GDP to C based on Mitchell (1975, 793) and United Nations (2006).

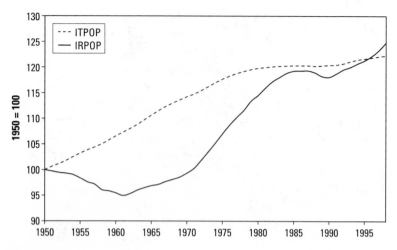

Figure 14.4
Population in Ireland and Italy, 1950–1998. From Maddison (2001).

consumption per head grew steadily until near the end of the period, while the rate of population growth fell from 0.6 percent in the 1950s and 1960s to close to zero today. In Ireland, the rate of consumption and GDP growth per head accelerated over the half century, even during the years of gloom and doom in the 1980s. Short-run movements in the two economies were poorly correlated: whereas the 1950s are deemed Ireland's "lost decade," in Italy they were years of the "economic miracle," and while Italy was enjoying its "splendid eighties," Ireland was finding its way out of a deep economic crisis.[14] Short-term population movements differed, too. While Italian population growth decelerated over the half century, Irish population growth was subject to wide fluctuations. The half century included two stretches of decline when emigration was substantial and a time in the late 1960s and 1970s when population grew by over 1 percent annually.

Imagine for a moment that statistical artifact, the average citizen, faced with the choice of either the Italian or Irish route to affluence in 1950. Since our interest is in economic well-being, our primary focus would be on consumption (private plus public) rather than on GDP.[15] The cumulative difference in consumption to 1998 is 33 times the Irish 1950 consumption per head, or six times 1998 consumption per head. Alternatively, had Ireland followed the Italian road, Irish consumption per head would have been over one-third higher on average in the interim. Discounting forward at 2 percent gives ratios of 20 times Irish 1950 con-

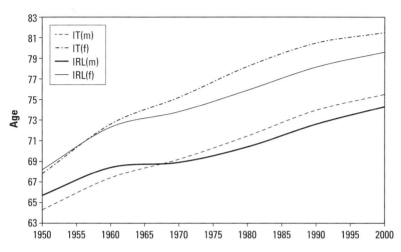

Figure 14.5
Life expectancy for males and females in Italy and Ireland, 1950–2000.

sumption per head and 3.8 times 1998 consumption per head, and discounting forward at 3 percent gives ratios of 16 and 3.0. Discounting or
no discounting, the cost of slower growth in the early phases was clearly
large.

Demographic Considerations

As figure 14.4 shows, although the population growth rates in Ireland and
Italy over the period as a whole were similar, short-term trends were very
different. In the 1950s and 1960s, in particular, the gaps in rates of population growth were considerable, with negative implications for Ireland's
relative economic performance. The wedge between population growth–
augmented consumption per head was nearly eight times 1998 Irish consumption per head (as opposed to six times when population is not taken
into account).

In assessing the two growth paths, the influence of improvements in life
expectancy should also be factored in. In 1950 Irish males stood to live
1.4 years longer than their Italian peers, and Irish females 0.4 years
longer. Half a century later the gap was reversed, with Italian males
expected to outlive Irish males by 1.2 years, and Italian females to outlive
Irish females by 1.9 years (figure 14.5). Thus, allowing for differences in
the changes in the expectation of life at age zero, or $e(0)$, between 1950
and 2000 would marginally increase Italy's advantage. The timing of the

catch-up obviously matters. Italian women overtook Irish women in the mid-1950s, and Italian men overtook Irish men a decade or so later. Here we work with the average.

For Ireland-Italy, I compare $U = \Sigma Y_i \cdot \bar{e}_i$, where Y_i is consumption per head in year i, and $\bar{e}_i$ is life expectancy in year i relative to life expectancy in 1950. Combining the data summarized in figures 14.3 and 14.5 and adding up over the entire period implies a gap 17.9 percent greater than before.[16] Here I follow Williamson (1984, 162–165) and others in assuming that the improvements in life expectancy in this period were mainly due to exogenous factors such as improvements in medical technology and public health. Taking into account demographic factors just reinforces the point that the extra consumption that Italy gained by being the early starter was considerable.

Did Inequality Matter?

In Ireland affluence has not brought a reduction in income inequality. To what extent might differences in income inequality trends in Ireland and Italy affect the preceding comparisons? International comparisons of income distribution are a minefield, and broadly comparable Irish and Italian data are available only from the early 1970s on (Atkinson and Brandolini 2001; Nolan and Smeeding 2005; Brandolini 2004).[17] Table 14.6 suggests that income inequality in Italy was considerably greater than in Ireland in the 1970s but that the gap closed quickly thereafter, and that by turn of the century inequality in Ireland was marginally greater.[18]

Trends in the regional variation of incomes are also worth considering. In Italy the gap between richer and poorer regions was greater throughout than in Ireland. The long-standing backwardness of the Mezzogiorno

Table 14.6
Gini Index for Ireland and Italy, 1973–2000

Year	Italy	Ireland
1973	42.0	36.7
1980	37.0	36.0
1987	34.4	35.2
1994–1995	36.3	36.2
2000	36.0	37.5

Note: The data refer to gross value added (GVA) per head in Irish planning regions.

is an important factor here.[19] In both economies there is evidence of considerable convergence between provinces or regions during the 1960s and 1970s, and of marking time in the 1980s and 1990s. In Italy the coefficient of variation of regional GDP per head across Italy's 20 provinces fell from 0.35 in the early 1960s to 0.27 in the late 1970s, but it was still 0.25 at the turn of the century.[20] Data are available on gross value added per head in Irish regions since 1973 and on personal income or disposable income per head since 1960.[21] Throughout, not surprisingly, the regional variation in disposable income was less than that in value added. Allowing for regional inequality makes Ireland look comparatively better throughout the period, but this outcome is the product of the different histories and geographies of the two economies. More to the point, regional inequality decreased slightly more in Italy than in Ireland.

Conclusions

Economic historians tend to have less time than their colleagues in political and military history for past heroics. They are used to entrepreneurs being replaceable, to social savings being "small," and to economic growth during the Industrial Revolution being "modest." Their answers to "How big is big?" are conditioned by a belief in Harberger triangles and a confidence that inputs, both animate and inanimate, are highly substitutable. Against such a historiographic tradition, the "savings" or "costs" of the alternative routes described in this chapter are very significant. When the Irish route to the present is evaluated against the Italian, the cost of policy "failures" in the 1950s and 1970s was indeed large, just as the benefits of Dutch economic precociousness in the sixteenth and seventeenth centuries, even when set against later retardation, were considerable.

Appendix: Dutch and English Wages

In the debate about incomes in the early modern Netherlands and Britain, wage data only muddy the waters further. Estimates by Allen (2001) suggest that building laborers (BL) and building craftsmen (BC) in London (L, representing England) were better paid than their counterparts in Amsterdam (A, representing the Netherlands) in the first half of the sixteenth century, but that they lost their lead thereafter and did not regain it for a century or more. Allen's data also suggest that real wages in Amsterdam were about one-fifth higher in 1750–1799 than they had been

Table 14.7
Wages in Southern England and Belgium, c. 1500–1540

Item (quantity per daily wage)	(1) England, 1501–1505	(2) Antwerp, 1501–1505	(1)/(2)
Wine (litres)	3.47	2.92	1.19
Herrings (no.)	43.32	48.45	0.89
Peas (litres)	40.27	19.70	. 2.05
Wheat (litres)	22.25	19.84	1.12
Sugar (kilos)	0.94	1.02	0.92

Item (quantity per daily wage)	(3) England, 1536–1540	(4) Antwerp, 1536–1540	(3)/(4)
Wine (litres)	2.64	3.49	0.76
Herrings (no.)	38.17	45.48	0.84
Peas (litres)	30.50	21.38	1.43
Wheat (litres)	21.90	17.15	1.28
Sugar (kilos)	0.39	0.74	0.52

Source: Munro (2001, table 16).

in 1550–1549, whereas in London they were about the same in both periods. Meticulous research by Munro (2001), from which table 14.7 is taken, corroborates Allen's findings for the early sixteenth century. It reveals that wage earners in England c. 1500 had the edge over wage earners in the Antwerp region—generally conceded to be as economically advanced as Holland at this time—but that they lost it during the following few decades. Such data are not so readily squared with van Zanden's claim that Dutch GDP per head was 1.58 times the British c. 1500, nor with the assertion that "real wages declined a lot between 1500 and 1800" (van Zanden 2001; 2002a, 154); but they are not so easily reconciled either with the almost threefold rise in GDP per head indicated by Maddison over the same period. Van Zanden (2001, 78–79) concedes that English GDP per head in 1650 was unlikely to be "only about half the Dutch level."

Notes

This chapter is a considerably revised version of the paper presented at the Harvard conference. Thanks to Bob Allen, Kevin Denny, Tim Guinnane, David Madden, Angus Maddison, Gunnar Persson, Brendan Walsh, the editors, and conference participants for comments on the earlier draft, and to Andrea Brandolini, Gianfranco di Viao, and Brian Nolan for income distribution and regional income data.

1. In an analysis of the British national debt toward the end of our period, Clark (2001, 426, 434–436) dubs the amount in foreign hands "pitiably small"; compare Neal (1990, 68–72).

2. In comparing Italy and Ireland, I use consumption rather than GDP.

3. Discounting might seem appropriate in a scenario in which countries are running current account deficits in order to allow expenditure to exceed income.

4. De Vries (1985, 669) notes that, in the 1730s, Amsterdam parish registers recorded an annual average of 3,300 girls born; 25 years later, an annual average of 1,410 Amsterdam-born women were wed. The ratio seems to imply high mortality, but this makes no allowance for the relative importance of inward and outward migration, celibacy, and the likely under-registration of births.

5. The disappearance of plague was the main cause of the improvement between the two dates. These are Alter's (1983) "non-select" estimates, which exclude the first years of each annuity in order to minimize selection bias. In Amsterdam in 1636 the plague killed over 17,000 people, or one-seventh of the population; in Leiden and in Haarlem, too, it killed significant proportions of the inhabitants.

6. The estimates of life expectancy yielded by van Leeuwen and Oeppen's (1993) Generalized Inverse Projection modeling are generally *higher* than those derived from annuities between the 1670s and 1720s; I do not invoke them here for that reason.

7. Death-by-age data for London as a whole become available only in the early eighteenth century.

8. Life expectancy in Geneva grew roughly in tandem with London: from 23.9 years in 1625–1649 to 34.3 years a century later, and 39.9 years in 1800–1820 (Perrenoud 1978, 223).

9. For more recent applied work on this topic, compare Nordhaus (2002) and Becker Philipson, and Soares (2005).

10. The *sorpasso* emerged when the Italian statistical service revised its estimate of the black economy upward.

11. For an account of the Irish economy before the boom, see Ó Gráda (1997a). For an earlier attempt at an Ireland-Italy comparison, see Ó Gráda and O'Rourke (2000).

12. In mid-century the Italian economy was 16 times the size of Ireland's.

13. Italy had been worse affected by World War II than neutral Ireland, and its recovery between 1945 and 1950, spurred by the Marshall Plan, was accordingly faster. However, by mid-century the rates of growth in both economies had declined to levels sustained in the following decade.

14. For an excellent overview of the Italian economy between 1945 and the mid-1990s, see Rossi and Toniolo (1996).

15. This also finesses the point that pairwise GDP comparisons are usually misleading when Ireland is involved, since they ignore the significant gap between Irish GDP and GNP, due to transfer pricing and the repatriation of royalties and profits by foreign multinationals. In mid-century this gap was insignificant, but by the mid-1980s Irish GDP was only 90 percent of GNP, and today it is only 85 percent. Thus while Irish GDP per head overtook the Italian in 1997–1998, the gap between Irish GNP per head and Italian GDP per head was not closed until 2001.

16. In partial mitigation, over the half century the number of hours worked per employee in Ireland dropped more than in Italy: by 25.8 percent versus 18.9 percent; compare Gordon (2004).

17. An earlier estimate for urban Ireland can be inferred from data on gross weekly household incomes in Irish cities and towns in 1965–1966 (as reported in Geary 1977, 172–175). It implies a G of 0.345 but is not readily comparable to my later estimates.

18. I owe the 2000 Irish estimate to Brian Nolan, who estimated it from the Household Budget Survey.

19. The problems of the Italian South, or Mezzogiorno, have been the focus of a huge literature from a variety of disciplines. For nuanced studies of the Mezzogiorno in the 1990s, with some background on earlier trends, see Barca (2001) and di Vaio (2004).

20. Calculations based on weighted standard deviations yield broadly similar results.
21. Both Irish measures involve splicing data and shifts in definition. The income data splices two series: (1) the 1960–1977 estimates refer to estimates of personal income (which includes transfers). These are mainly the work of Micheál Ross and were originally published by NESC (1980); (2) the 1980–1994 data are taken from Boyle, McCarthy, and Walsh (1999), and the 2000 figure derives from Irish Central Statistics Office (CSO) estimates of disposable income by county, ⟨http://www.cso.ie/releasespublications/documents/economy/2001/regincome_2001.pdf⟩. The gross value added series combines that of O'Leary (2003) for 1960–1996 with CSO data for 2000, adjusted downward from 0.213 to 0.177 to allow for the effect of transfer pricing. This reflects the gap between O'Leary's estimate for 1996 (0.156) and the uncorrected CSO data (0.188). I assume that the coefficients of variation changed at a constant rate in years between observations.

References

Allen, R. C. 2001. The Great Divergence in European Wages and Prices from the Middle Ages to the First World War. *Explorations in Economic History* 38: 411–447.

Alter, G. 1983. Plague and the Amsterdam Annuitant: A New Look at Life Annuities as a Source for Historical Demography. *Population Studies* 37 (1): 23–41.

Atkinson, A. B., and A. Brandolini. 2001. Promises and Pitfalls in the Use of "Secondary" Data Sets: Income Inequality in OECD Countries as a Case Study. *Journal of Economic Literature* 39 (3): 771–799.

Barca. F. 2001. New Trends and the Policy Shift in the Italian Mezzogiorno. *Daedalus* 130 (2): 93–113.

Becker, G. S., T. J. Philipson, and R. R. Soares. 2005. The Quality and Quantity of Life and the Evolution of World Inequality. *American Economic Review* 95: 277–291.

Boyle, J. G., T. McCarthy, and J. Walsh. 1999. Regional Income Differentials and the Issue of Regional Equalisation in Ireland. *Journal of the Statistical and Social Inquiry Society of Ireland* 28 (1): 157–196.

Brandolini, A. 1999. The Distribution of Personal Income in Post-War Italy: Source Description, Data Quality, and the Time Pattern of Income Inequality. Discussion Paper 350, Bank of Italy, Rome. ⟨http://www.bancaditalia.it/ricerca/consultazioni/temidi/td99/tema_350_99.pdf⟩.

———. 2004. Income Inequality and Poverty in Italy: A Statistical Compendium. Rome: Bank of Italy. Mimeo.

Clark, G. 2001. Debt, Deficits, and Crowding Out: England, 1727–1840. *European Review of Economic History* 5: 403–436.

de Vries, J. 1974. *The Dutch Rural Economy in the Golden Age.* New Haven, Conn.: Yale University Press.

———. 1976. *The Economy of Europe in an Age of Crisis, 1600–1750.* Cambridge: Cambridge University Press.

———. 1984. *European Urbanization, 1500–1850.* London: Methuen.

———. 1985. The Population and Economy of the Preindustrial Netherlands. *Journal of Interdisciplinary History* 15 (4): 661–682.

de Vries, J., and A. van der Woude. 1997. *The First Modern Economy: Success, Failure, and Perseverance of the Dutch Economy.* Cambridge: Cambridge University Press.

Di Vaio, G. 2004. Economic Changes and Public Policies in the Mezzogiorno during the 1990s: An Assessment. *Economia Società e Istituzioni* 16 (1): 77–115.

Federico, G. 2002. The World Economy, A.D. 0–200: A Review Article. *European Review of Economic History* 6: 111–121.

Fogel, R. W. 2004. *The Escape from Hunger and Premature Death, 1700–2100.* Cambridge: Cambridge University Press.

Geary, P. T. 1977. Wages, Prices, Income, and Wealth. In *Economic Activity in Ireland: A Study of Two Open Economies,* ed. N. Gibson and J. Spencer, 149–189. Dublin: Gill and Macmillan.

Gordon, R. J. 2004. Two Centuries of Economic Growth: Europe Chasing the American Frontier. NBER (National Bureau of Economic Research) Working Paper 10662. ⟨http://www.nber.org/papers/W10662⟩.

Gray, A., ed. 1997. *International Perspectives on the Irish Economy.* Dublin: Indecon Economic Consultants.

Harris, W. 1699. *A Description of the King's Royal Gardens at Loo. Together with a Short Account of Holland.* London: Roberts.

Honohan, P., and B. M. Walsh. 2002. Catching up with the Leaders: The Irish Hare. *Brookings Papers on Economic Activity* 1: 1–57.

Hughes, C., ed. 1903. *Shakespeare's Europe: Unpublished Chapters of Fynes Moryson's Itinerary.* London: Sherratt and Hughes.

Israel, J. 1989. *Dutch Primacy in World Trade, 1585–1740.* Oxford: Clarendon Press.

Landers, J. 1993. *Death and the Metropolis: Studies in the Demographic History of London, 1670–1830.* Cambridge: Cambridge University Press.

Lichtenberg, F. L. 2003. Pharmaceutical Innovation, Mortality Reduction, and Economic Growth. In *Measuring the Gains from Medical Research: An Economic Approach,* ed. K. M. Murphy and R. H. Topel, 74–109. Chicago: University of Chicago Press.

Maddison, A. 2001. *The World Economy: A Millennial Perspective.* Paris: OECD.

———. 2005. Measuring and Interpreting World Economic Performance, 1500–2001. *Review of Income and Wealth* 51: 1–35.

Mitchell, B. R. 1975. *European Historical Statistics.* London: Macmillan.

Mokyr, J. 1976. *The Industrialization of the Low Countries, 1795–1850.* New Haven, Conn.: Yale University Press.

Munro, J. H. 2001. Money, Wages, and Real Incomes in the Age of Erasmus: The Purchasing Power of Coins and of Building Craftsmen's Wages in England and the Low Countries, 1500–1540. ⟨http://www.economics.utoronto.ca/ecipa/archive/UT-ECIPA-MUNRO-01-01.html⟩.

Neal, L. 1990. *The Rise of Financial Capitalism.* Cambridge: Cambridge University Press.

NESC (National Economic and Social Council). 1980. Personal Incomes by Region. Paper 8683. Dublin: Stationary Office.

Nolan, B., and B. Mâitre. 2000. A Comparative Perspective on Trends in Income Inequality in Ireland. *Economic and Social Review* 31 (4): 329–350.

Nolan, B., and T. M. Smeeding. 2005. Ireland's Income Distribution in Comparative Perspective. *Review of Income and Wealth* 51: 537.

Noordam, D. J. 1986. *Leven in Maasland: Een Hoogontwikkelde Plattelandssamenleving in de Achttiende en het Begin van de Negentiende Eeuw.* Hilversum, Netherlands: Verloren.

Nordhaus, W. D. 2002. The Health of Nations: The Contribution of Improved Health to Living Standards. NBER (National Bureau of Economic Research) Working Paper 8818. ⟨http://www.nber.org/papers/W8818⟩.

O'Brien, P., and D. Keene, eds. 2001. *Urban Achievement in Early Modern Europe: Golden Ages in Antwerp, Amsterdam, and London.* New York: Cambridge University Press.

Ó Gráda, C. 1997a. *A Rocky Road: The Irish Economy since the 1920s.* Manchester: Manchester University Press.

———. 1997b. Les fluctuations de la population irlandaise avant 1700. In *Histoire des populations de l'Europe. I. Origines aux prémices de la revolution démographique,* ed. J.-P. Bardet and J. Dupâquier, 382–387. Paris: Fayard.

Ó Gráda, C., and K. H. O'Rourke. 2000. Living Standards and Growth. In *The Economy of Ireland: Policy and Performance of a European Region*, ed. J. O'Hagan, 178–204. Dublin: Gill and Macmillan.

O'Leary, E. 2003. Aggregate and Sectoral Convergence among Irish Regions: The Role of Structural Change, 1960–1996. *International Regional Science Review* 26 (4): 483–501.

Paping, R.J.F. 1988. Papisten in de Ommelanden, 1730–1810. Ph.D. diss., University of Groningen.

Perrenoud, A. 1975. L'inégalité sociale devant la mort à Genève au XVIIe siècle. *Population* 30: 236.

———. 1978. La mortalité à Genève de 1625 à 1825. *Annales de demographie historique*, 209–233.

Riley, J. C. 2001. *Rising Life Expectancy: A Global History*. Cambridge: Cambridge University Press.

Rossi, N., and G. Toniolo. 1996. Italy. In *Economic Growth in Europe since 1945*, ed. N. Crafts and G. Toniolo, 427–454. Cambridge: Cambridge University Press.

Schama, S. 1987. *The Embarrassment of Riches: An Interpretation of Dutch Culture in the Golden Age*. New York: Knopf.

Soltow, L., and J. L. van Zanden, eds. 2001. *Income and Wealth Inequality in the Netherlands, 16th–20th Century*. Amsterdam: Het Spinhuis.

Szreter, S., and G. Mooney. 1998. Urbanization, Mortality, and the Standard of Living Debate: New Estimates of the Expectation of Life at Birth in Nineteenth-Century British Cities. *Economic History Review* 51 (1): 84–112.

Temple, Sir W. 1673. *Observations upon the United Provinces of the Netherlands*. Farnborough, U.K.: Gregg, 1971. Photographic reprint of the original.

United Nations. 2006. Statistics Division National Accounts Database. ⟨http://unstats.un.org/unsd/nationalaccount/nadefault.htm⟩.

Usher, D. 1973. An Imputation to the Measurement of Economic Growth for Changes in Life Expectancy. In *The Measurement of Economic and Social Performance*, ed. M. Moss. New York: Columbia University Press.

van den Berg, H. 2002. Does Annual Real Gross Domestic Product Per Capita Overstate or Understate the Growth of Individual Welfare over the Past Two Centuries? *Independent Review* 7 (2): 181–196. ⟨http://www.independent.org/pdf/tir/tir_07_2_vandenberg.pdf⟩.

van der Woude, A. M. 1972. Variations in the Size and Composition of the Household in the United Provinces of the Netherlands. In *Household and Family in Past Time*, ed. P. Laslett, 299–318. Cambridge: Cambridge University Press.

———. 1983. *Het Noorderqkwartier*. Utrecht: H&S.

van Leeuwen, M.H.D., and J. E. Oeppen. 1993. Reconstructing the Demographic Regime of Amsterdam, 1681–1920. In *Economic and Social History in the Netherlands*. Vol. 5, 61–102. Amsterdam: Nederlandsch Economisch-Historisch Archief (NEHA).

van Strien, C. D. 1993. *British Travellers in Holland during the Stuart Period*. Leiden: Brill.

van Zanden, J. L. 1995. Tracing the Beginning of the Kuznets Curve: Western Europe during the Early Modern Period. *Economic History Review* 48 (4): 643–664.

———. 2001. A Survey of the European Economy, 1500–2000. In *Early Modern Capitalism: Economic and Social Change in Europe, 1400–1800*, ed. M. R. Prak London: Routledge.

———. 2002a. Taking the Measure of the Early Modern Economy: Historical National Accounts for Holland in 1510–1514. *European Review of Economic History* 6 (1): 131–163.

———. 2002b. The Revolt of the Early Modernists and the First Modern Economy: An Assessment. *Economic History Review* 55 (4): 619–641.

van Zanden, J. L., and A. van Riel. 2004. *The Strictures of Inheritance: The Dutch Economy in the Nineteenth Century*. Princeton, N.J.: Princeton University Press.

Williamson, J. G. 1981. Urban Disamenities, Dark Satanic Mills, and the British Standard of Living Debate. *Journal of Economic History* 41 (1): 75–83.

———. 1984. British Mortality and the Value of Life. *Population Studies* 38: 157–172.

Woods, R. 2000. *The Demography of Victorian England and Wales*. Cambridge: Cambridge University Press.

Wrigley, E. A., R. Davies, J. Oeppen, and R. S. Schofield. 1997. *English Population History from Family Reconstitution, 1580–1837*. Cambridge: Cambridge University Press.

Wrigley, E. A., and R. S. Schofield. 1981. *The Population History of England: A Reconstruction*. London: Arnold.

15 Euro-Productivity and Euro-Jobs since the 1960s: Which Institutions Really Mattered?

Gayle J. Allard and Peter H. Lindert

The flagging performance of productivity and employment in Europe since the mid-1970s has puzzled researchers for years. In the search for explanations, economists have focused on unemployment rates and a narrow range of variables, countries, and time periods. Their results have often been less than robust, causing some researchers to doubt whether clear and credible explanations for these problems could be extracted from the complex macroreality.

We believe that in the spirit of the New Comparative Economic History, a broader approach should be taken to these pressing issues, which involve the workings of entire macroeconomies. In this chapter, we search eclectically for data and avoid discarding information while matching our tests more closely to real social issues. Our results contradict theories on the negative effects of the welfare state and contain important messages about Europe's productivity lag and the insider-outsider divide in rigid labor markets. Specifically, we find that

• Employment protection legislation (EPL) redistributes human capital formation from youths and women to senior males. This shows up as a delayed loss in labor productivity rather than as a net effect on jobs.

• Product-market regulations may have also reduced productivity, although this result is not robust.

• Coordinated wage bargaining boosts productivity, presumably by affecting wage moderation and macropolicy.

• Tax wedges and transfer payments, often blamed for slow European job growth, have no clear cost in jobs or productivity. Past studies showed negative effects because they failed to separate transitory from durable effects, and because some researchers accepted theory as an empirical test.

Here we broaden the empirical debate in several ways. First, we examine effects on jobs and productivity together, shedding extra light on both. This crucial step is missed by both the labor market and GDP growth literatures.[1] We also combine institutions that have been considered separately in the labor market or growth literature. Finally, we offer new historical estimates of two labor market institutions and new econometric tests, which point to a new reading of the verdicts on different institutional suspects. Past studies missed some of these verdicts by discarding fixed effects as mere control variables when the effects in fact offer telling clues on the roles of different institutions. Our conclusions counter some of the recent pessimism about the usefulness of international macropanel evidence.

Better Measures of Labor Market Institutions

Blanchard and Wolfers (2000) write, "Explanations (of high unemployment) based solely on institutions . . . run . . . into a major empirical problem: many of these institutions were already present when unemployment was low. . . . Thus, while labour market institutions can potentially explain cross-country differences today, they do not appear able to explain the general evolution of unemployment over time" (2).[2] This concern has led to the view that since institutional suspects antedate the onset of high unemployment and slow productivity growth in the 1970s, they cannot explain it. However, this view is based on imperfect impressions of the history of labor market institutions. Better measures show that the main suspects—strict EPL, generous unemployment compensation, and high tax rates—arrived on the scene before European jobs and productivity growth began to suffer. Even if the problems that began in the 1970s owed much to the oil shocks, the causal mechanisms cannot be uncovered without a correct charting of institutional history. We provide this history with improved measures from 1950 of two key labor market institutions in OECD economies: the generosity of unemployment compensation and the strictness of employee protection legislation (Allard 2003; 2005a; 2005b).

Unemployment Compensation: The Net Reservation Wage

Unemployment compensation is clearly a work disincentive in the short run. How large a disincentive it is depends on three components of unemployment compensation:

• *Replacement rate*, (benefits per recipient) divided by (market wage), after taxes

• *Eligibility of jobless for benefits*, including legal job search requirements and sanctions for noncompliance

• *Duration* of coverage

Many studies measuring unemployment compensation focus on the replacement rate, omitting the other components. Others consider duration but do not put the whole picture together for a long time span. There are "no comprehensive time series data on the coverage of the [unemployment compensation] system or on the strictness with which it is administered" (Nickell, Nunziata, and Ochell 2005, 4).

We introduce estimates that incorporate all three components of unemployment compensation into a single measure of the net reservation wage: the expected value of unemployment compensation as a percent of the median market wage after taxes.[3]

The new picture of unemployment compensation shown in figure 15.1 reveals important differences in the timing of more generous benefits. Benefits rose from 1967 in most of the core countries of the European Community, well before the post-1973 macroshocks. Other countries escalated benefits after the first oil shock. Generous unemployment benefits never reached Greece and Portugal or Pacific Rim countries besides New Zealand. Clearly, unemployment compensation differed in its timing as well as in long-run national averages.

Employment Protection Legislation

Lack of data has restricted past studies to a few limited snapshots of EPL. This study draws on an extended index of EPL strictness that dates back to 1950,[4] which reveals that job protection was neither fixed over time nor the same across countries. The view that strict EPL was already in place in the low-unemployment era before 1973 is incorrect except for Spain and Portugal, where it dates to the Franco and Salazar dictatorships (but where democracy brought greater job protection). Figure 15.2 illustrates the differences in timing across countries since 1960. As with the dole, EPL rose at varying times and to different extents across countries, and strict EPL often antedated other institutional changes and poorer macroperformance by a few years. Italy was a leader, tightening worker protection in formal sectors in the 1960s, three decades before it instituted generous unemployment benefits. France, Germany, and the

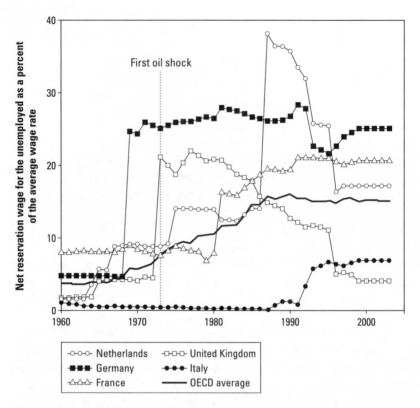

Figure 15.1
Unemployment compensation, 1960–2003: core European Union countries (*left*) and other
countries (*right*). From Allard (2003).

Netherlands also tightened EPL in the years of union strength and full
employment between 1967 and 1973. Other countries such as Sweden,
the United Kingdom, and Ireland raised EPL after the first oil shock hit.
Since the mid-1980s, EPL, like unemployment benefits, has hardly re-
treated in the OECD as a whole, and cross-country differences persist.

Other Institutions
The only labor market institution that was present in the low-
unemployment 1960s was coordinated wage bargaining, which brings
employer groups and organized labor together to negotiate wages and
working conditions for most of the economy. Such bargains are outside
the ordinary functioning of decentralized markets and thus qualify as interventionist, even when the government does not participate. To plot the

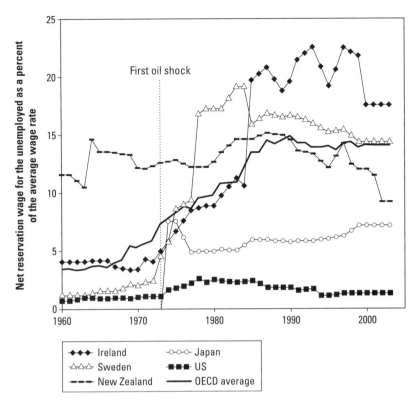

Figure 15.1
(continued)

history of coordinated wage bargaining, we use recent estimates by Ochel (2000). Over the last four decades of the twentieth century, the nature of coordinated wage bargaining was stable for about half the OECD countries; some clung to coordination and others consistently rejected it. In some cases coordinated bargaining broke down, as in Spain and Portugal after the dictatorships, Britain under Thatcher, and New Zealand in 1990. In Scandinavia it weakened yet did not collapse. In contrast, it strengthened in Ireland in the 1990s. For the OECD as a whole, the degree of coordination shows very little trend.

Other government institutions rose gradually in importance, especially after the oil shocks. Tax rates and tax wedges on labor earnings followed the upward path noted with unemployment compensation. Active labor market policies, such as subsidies for retraining and job search, rose later, from the mid-1980s. The only interventionist policy to decline was

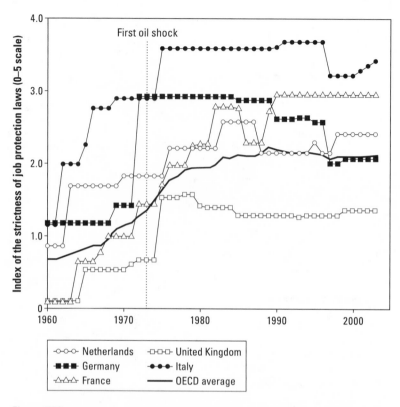

Figure 15.2
Employment protection legislation, 1960–2003: core European Union countries (*left*) and other countries (*right*). From Allard (2003).

product-market regulation; a seven-sector index developed by the OECD shows gradual declines since 1980.

Better Tests

With improved institutional measures in hand, we next expand the range of tests. We concentrate on macropanel tests despite the pessimism about whether international macropanels can effectively judge national institutions. We agree that microstudies of individual countries can yield important evidence if they draw on true policy experiments. Yet better evidence can be squeezed from the international contrasts than recent authors have acknowledged.

Our specifications of the determinants of international job and productivity performance differ from past studies. However, our most durable

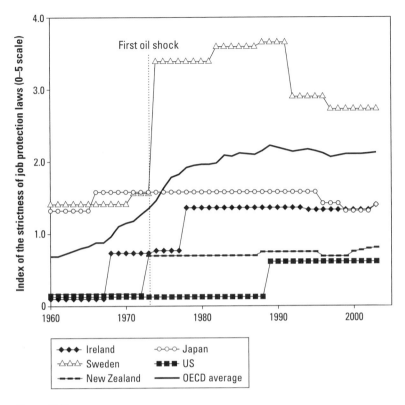

Figure 15.2
(continued)

results do not depend on the details of variable inclusion or functional form. The main points emerge simply because we combine job and productivity determinants into a single system, retest with different periods and countries, and reinterpret fixed effects that showed up in other studies.

The Basic Equation Set

We explore the effects of a common set of control variables and institutions on jobs, productivity, and growth using the following basic equation defined over $j = (1, \ldots, J)$ countries and $t = (1, \ldots, T)$ time periods:

$$Y_{jt} = \beta_k \, X_{kjt} + u_{jt} \tag{1}$$

where Y represents the job and productivity variables to be explained; X_k, the k identified influences on Y; and u_{jt}, the error term. The choice of behavioral X should envelope competing theories. The X variables can be instrumented or not and can have time lags or not. The choices of X variables depend on data availability, as do the countries and time periods. To reduce serial correlation, we use three-year averages as the time dimension of each observation. Having more complete data permits us to span the 1963–1965 to 1999–2001 period in a single set of equations. However, for the following discussion we split that period into two overlapping samples, 1963–1965 to 1978–1980 and 1978–1980 to 1999–2001, because of structural shifts.

The independent influences (X_k) on jobs, productivity, and growth are summarized in table 15.1. The dependent variables are the five job outcomes, four productivity and GDP outcomes, and one growth rate listed in the first row of the table. Next come some control variables often used in the literature. For most equations the lagged dependent variable must be included because the behavior of jobs and productivity depends strongly on influences that also influenced the previous period's jobs and productivity. One can deal with this feedback in various familiar ways, including first differencing. One differencing approach is the simple growth equation in the middle column. We do not explore complete first differencing here because we argue that the fixed country effects that differencing is designed to finesse often contain vital information for judging institutions.

The other control variables are familiar. The lagged term for GDP per capita relative to the United States, a proxy for catching-up potential, has the effects one expects from the growth convergence literature: a poorer recent past lowers current productivity but raises the growth rate. Educational attainment is a familiar source of productivity, although its influence is sometimes obscured here by the inclusion of the lagged dependent variable. The age shares of the young and old also have familiar effects on employment and productivity.

Global or national aggregate demand and aggregate supply shocks strongly affect jobs and productivity in all studies. Macroeconomists use various proxies for them. We take a cautious approach, capturing key influences while minimizing risk of simultaneity bias. As a proxy for aggregate demand shocks we use OECD-wide inflation minus unemployment, and for aggregate supply shocks we use the "misery index," the sum of inflation and unemployment at the same global level.[5]

Table 15.1 lists the institutional and budgetary variables at the heart of the debates over European jobs and growth. Product-market institutions are represented by the OECD index of product-market regulation and the

Table 15.1
Sets of Second-Stage Equations to Explain Employment, Unemployment, Productivity, and Growth in the OECD, 1963–2001

	Main Equations	Growth Equations	Results Displayed
Job Outcomes			
Employment ratio, 15–64, pop.	Dep		table 15.2
Employment ratio, 15–64, women	Dep		—
Unemployment rate, overall	Dep		—
Unemployment rate, women/men	Dep		table 15.3
Unemployment rate, youth/men	Dep		table 15.3
Productivity and GDP Outcomes			
ln (GDP/person employed)	Dep		table 15.2
ln (GDP per labor hr)	Dep		table 15.2
ln (GDP per person, 15–64)	Dep		table 15.2
ln (GDP per capita)	Dep		
3-yr log growth rate, GDP per capita		Dep	table 15.2
Basic Control Variables			
Dependent variable, 3 yr lag[a]	X	—	
ln (GDP per capita/U.S. GDP per capita), 10 yr lag	X	X	
Educational attainments of adults	X	X	
Young (0–15 share)	X	X	
Old (share 65 and up)	X	X	
Global demand shocks (OECD infl. − unempl.)	X	X	
Global supply shocks (OECD infl. + unempl.)	X	X	
Institutional Forces			
Product-market regs. in 7 sectors	X	X	post-1978 sample only
Int. open policies (Freedom House)	X	X	
Employment protection laws (EPL)	—	—	
12 yrs ago	X	X	
Change from 12 yrs to 6 yrs ago	X	X	
Change from 6 yrs ago to now	X, IV	X, IV	IVs in table 15.2
12 yrs ago, interacted with levels of coord.	X	X	
Coord. wage setting intermediate	X	X	
Coord. wage setting strong	X	X	

Table 15.1
(continued)

	Main Equations	Growth Equations	Results Displayed
Budgetary Policies			
Unempl. comp. (and squared, cubed)	X, IV	X, IV	IVs in table 15.2
Total taxes/GDP (and squared, cubed)	X, IV	X, IV	IVs in table 15.2
Income and property tax share of tot. taxes	X, IV	X, IV	IVs in table 15.2
Consumption tax share of tot. taxes	X, IV	X, IV	IVs in table 15.2
Social transfer share of tot. taxes	X, IV	X, IV	IVs in table 15.2
Fixed country binaries[b]	s	s	
Fixed time binaries	s	s	

Notes:
a. For the female and youth rates of employment and unemployment, the lagged dependent variable is the lagged overall rate, not the rate specific to women or youth.
b. For Germany, there are two different binary-variable fixed countries: West Germany through 1989, then all Germany from 1990 on.
Dep = dependent variable explained in one of this set of equations; X = exogenous variable used in all variations of this equation; IV = predicted value based on instruments in a first-stage OLS equation; s = exogenous variable used in some variants of this equation, not others.

The sample is a balanced panel of 21 OECD countries times three-year time periods. The 21 countries are Australia, Austria, Belgium, Canada, Denmark, Finland, France, Germany (West to 1989, all Germany 1990 on), Greece, Ireland, Italy, Japan, Netherlands, New Zealand, Norway, Portugal, Spain, Sweden, Switzerland, United Kingdom, United States. However, Spain and Portugal were omitted from the pre-1980 sample for want of OECD measures of social transfer spending.

The three-year time periods are 1978–1980 to 1999–2001 (so that $n = 21 \times 8$ periods = 168), 1963–1965 to 1978–1980 (so that $n = 19 \times 6$ periods = 114), and in some nondisplayed variants, the whole period 1963–1965 to 1999–2001 ($n = 19 \times 13 = 247$).

The employment ratio is employment divided by the 15–64 population.

EPL is an index (0–5) of the strictness of employment protection laws, updated from Allard (2003). Coordinated wage setting is an index (1–3), from Ochel (2000), with 1999 values extended through 2001. An intermediate level of wage coordination was any Ochel rating 2.0–2.5, inclusive. A strong level of wage coordination was any case with rating 3.0. (There were no cases between 2.5 and 3.0.)

For a sketch of the first-stage equations generating the predicted values from instruments, see Allard and Lindert (2006), appendix A. These refer only to the Instrumental Variable (IV) variants, of course. For data sources, see Allard (2003) and the Allard-Lindert OECD data sets 1950–2001 at ⟨http://www.econ.ucdavis.edu/faculty/fzlinder/⟩.

Freedom House index of business leaders' opinions on how open countries' markets are. The OECD regulation index covers seven sectors (airlines, telecommunications, electricity, gas, post, rail, and road freight) but omits sectors that have stood out in recent technological advances, such as retailing. Arguably these omitted sectors grew faster in the United States than in Europe because of European regulations on land use and work hours. The Freedom House measure of openness seems appropriate because it tries to capture policy, not geography. However, since this variable has been almost constant in the OECD countries since the 1970s, it explains little.

We use the long reach of the new EPL estimates to capture the possible dynamics of employment protection laws. As conjectured, EPL may save jobs and encourage productivity in the first few years, when it protects working-age men and increases their human capital. However, it could cost jobs and productivity later, as the share of unprotected youths and women in the labor force rises. To explore the dynamics and test for the durable net effects, we use one level of lagged EPL and a couple of changes in EPL. The level is the oldest, with a 12-year lag.

Next comes the Ochel (2000) index of coordination in functional forms designed to test some ideas in the literature. One idea dating back at least to Calmfors and Driffil (1988) is that wage-setting coordination has a U-shaped effect on jobs. It promotes employment at the two extremes, when bargaining is either fully decentralized or centralized, whereas semicoordinated bargaining costs jobs.[6] We test this, and also test whether EPL and coordinated bargaining, which both pursue stable jobs and costs, are substitutes or complements.

The consensus view on budgetary policies is that higher taxes or transfers cut jobs, and some reduce productivity as well. The main suspects are taxes on productive labor and subsidies to the unemployed. Surprisingly few studies test for a familiar corollary: the output loss from a tax wedge or a nonwork subsidy should increase nonlinearly. Perhaps this frequent oversight is another casualty of emphasizing job effects at the expense of output effects. The corollary can be tested with cubic functions to explore the differences in the effects of consecutive tax or transfer increases of the same size.

In addition to the total tax burden and unemployment compensation, we explore the effects of the tax and spending mix. On the tax side, we follow the shares of income, property, and consumption taxes, and omit social security contributions. On the expenditure side, we follow the share of social transfers and omit nonsocial expenditures plus net budget surplus minus nontax revenue.

Durable and Transitory Influences

As some theories hint, we should anticipate the possibility that a kth independent variable X_k has different slopes for its durable influence (call it X_{kd}) and its transitory residual (x_{kjt}). That kind of split is important whenever behavior reacts differently to durable and transitory influences, as in Milton Friedman's permanent income hypothesis of the consumption function. Therefore we prefer this generalization of the basic equation:

$$Y_{jt} = B_k x_{kjt} + A_k X_{kd} + u_{jt} \qquad (2)$$

Fortunate researchers find the same coefficients for the two component parts of X_{kjt}, so that each $B_k = A_k = \beta_k$, yielding the usual panel equation in equation (1), $Y_{jt} = \beta_k X_{kjt} + u_{jt}$. Yet that is not the case in recent OECD experience, so we need to distinguish durable from transitory effects.

Durable influences pose one important problem. The estimation task gets complicated if the durable influences, $(A_k X_{kd})$, behave like linear combinations of conventional fixed place binaries and fixed time binaries, as with the budgetary variables here. When this happens, equation (2) behaves like

$$Y_{jt} = B_k x_{kjt} + C_{kj} X_{kj} + D_{kt} X_{kt} + U_j + V_t + e_{jt} \qquad (3)$$

where B, C, and D represent coefficients; X_{kj}, fixed country profiles of the durable influences; X_{kt}, fixed time profiles of the durable influences; U_j and V_t, vectors of coefficients on conventional place and time binaries; and e_{jt}, the new error term. A serious identification problem looms in this case because the durable behavioral influences, X_{kj} and X_{kt}, will be linear combinations of the conventional fixed effect binaries. We cannot separately estimate X_{kj} and U_j, or X_{kt} and V_t. We return to this complication later, after examining the results from omitting conventional fixed effects in the spirit of equation (2).

An analogy to the econometrics of the familiar consumption function underlines the difference between durable ($A_k X_{kd}$) and transitory effects ($B_k x_{kjt}$) and their problematic relation to conventional fixed effects. Suppose that we had data on consumption, income, and other attributes of 500 people in a ten-year panel, and we were estimating how a permanent income gain would affect consumption. The permanent income hypothesis suggests that the marginal propensity to consume is much higher when income is permanently raised than when it is raised only one year. Yet the standard approach to pooled estimation includes fixed effects for individuals, places, or time and then discards them, reporting only the slope with respect to transitory changes. In the consumption function case, that would amount to hiding a long-run marginal propensity to consume of perhaps 0.9 and then presenting the transitory slope of perhaps 0.2 as the predicted effect of raising income permanently. The usual way of hiding the durable effect is to shorten the regression table by simply indicating whether fixed effects were added to the equation. Yet fixed effects are often the closest approximation to the effects of durable influences for which long-run moving averages stand in as proxies. This difference matters greatly to the debate over European institutions. We return to it when confronting the role of fixed effects in the international macroestimates of job and productivity determinants.

Institutional Influences on Euro-Jobs and Euro-Productivity, 1978–2001

The Basic Verdicts

Our international macropanel tests, approached on these terms, offer new insights on which institutions matter and which do not. Although we encounter some of the ambiguities that have troubled past authors, eclecticism offers a net gain, once we have presented better tests, separated durable from transitory influences, extended the time span, and visited other countries. We begin with the same data period as most studies (1980–2001).[7] We display results only for the instrumented version of each equation because the choice between IV and single-equation estimates did not affect the signs or magnitudes of the institutional effects.

Of the dependent variables introduced in table 15.1, we focus on six key measures of job and output performance.[8] They do not include the unemployment rate, which has dominated labor market literature. It has the drawback of giving equal weight to two labor transitions that are unequal in importance: the key transition between being employed and being inactive, and the transition between two inactive states, being in or out of the registered labor force. To focus on the first transition and link to the results on labor productivity, we follow the gross employment ratio for the 15–64 population. Later we examine unemployment rates for demographic subgroups.

Control Variables   Before turning to the featured institutional effects, we note that the control variables in table 15.1 performed as expected. The strongest influence was the lagged dependent variable, whose coefficient was always between 0.5 and 1. It should never be dropped or replaced with first differencing. A related dynamic variable is the catch-up variable, this country's income gap behind the United States ten years earlier. As expected, backwardness raised growth but had no clear effect on employment or productivity levels.

The nonperforming control variable is educational attainment. It proved insignificant in productivity and growth equations, probably because its gradual effect is eclipsed by the lagged dependent variable and the catch-up variable.

Having large shares of old or young population dragged down employment, productivity, and GDP growth, presumably because middle-aged groups are more productive.

Another strong set of control variables, OECD-wide shocks to aggregate demand and aggregate supply, performed as expected. Strong demand raised jobs, productivity, output, and the growth rate; and bad supply shocks (here meaning the oil shocks) cut jobs, productivity, output, and growth.

The results for institutions and budgetary policies are illustrated with test statistics on some very large institutional increments in table 15.2.[9]

Product-Market Regulations   While European governments have retained most of their job protection, unemployment compensation, and high taxes, they have been steadily dismantling product-market regulations since 1980. The first row in table 15.2 suggests that this boosted output per employed person or per labor hour everywhere, possibly by large amounts. The average OECD country cut product-market regulations by a little over two points (on a 0–6 scale) since 1980, which should have raised GDP per worker or hour by more than 1 percent in each of the initial three years, or by up to 10 percent over the whole sample period, once feedback through the lagged dependent variable is included. Plausible as this may seem, we think the true unit effects of product-market deregulation may be both larger and smaller than our coefficients show. Larger, because OECD measures of product-market regulations cover only seven sectors, missing the effects of deregulation in others. Smaller, because in other plausible specifications of the same equations the product-regulation variable shown in table 15.2 is less significant. Deregulation probably did help OECD-wide growth, but the evidence is not robust. A related product-market institution, trade policy (not shown in table 15.2), did not have significant effects because it hardly differed over time or across these 21 countries since 1980.

Employment Protection Laws (EPL)   The debate over European jobs has devoted attention to the charge that EPL costs jobs and raises unemployment. Our estimates suggest a possible negative net effect on jobs that could easily be zero. This matches the conclusion by Nickell, Nunziata, and Ochel (2005): "Evidence that they [EPLs] have a decisive impact on overall rates of unemployment is mixed, at best" (10).[10]

As we hinted earlier, EPL has clearer effects on productivity, especially with a 12-year lag. Interestingly, that effect depends on whether the country uses coordinated wage bargaining as an alternative job protection device. Table 15.2 presents two sets of results on EPL, one for countries with little or no wage coordination, and one for countries with closely coordinated wage setting. In the no-coordination context, increased job protection did not reduce productivity. This may be because the extra job protection was implemented where protection was initially low, so that it protected a large number of relatively productive insiders while delaying the careers of few outsiders, yielding positive net effects on productivity. Examples would be protection against collective dismissal under Reagan and Bush in 1988–1989 and similar modest initial increases in EPL in Canada, 1984–1985, or Australia, 1992–1993. By contrast, where wage coordination is strong, extra EPL lowers productivity significantly. In these settings, EPL was older and its negative effects on productivity had time to appear. One example was Ireland in the decades after EPL was tightened in 1977–1978. Another was Spain after the end of the Franco era, in the dozen years when new power and security for insiders coincided with lingering coordination that in fact did little to moderate wages.

Coordination in Wage Bargaining   Even though OECD studies played down the effects of coordinated wage setting, many econometric studies show that it had a positive effect on jobs. We get a similar positive result, with two significant changes: coordination seems to raise productivity rather than jobs, and it appears to be strongest in economies where EPL is low. Thus coordination in wage bargaining affects productivity and output growth results as strongly as it affected employment results in past studies.[11] Its positive role fits the fuller, more secure employment achieved without strict EPL in the late 1990s in Ireland, and to a lesser extent in Austria, Denmark, and the Netherlands (Auer 2000).

Table 15.2
The Three-Year Effects of Selected Institutional Changes on Jobs and GDP, 1978–2001

Institutional Changes (Independent Variables)	Percentage Estimated Effects on				
	Jobs	GDP/ Worker	GDP/ Hour	GDP/ Person 15–64	3-Year Growth Rate of GDP per Capita
Market Regulations					
Raising the index of product-market regulations by 1	−0.06 (0.34)	−1.23[a] (0.45)	−1.13[a] (0.36)	−2.16[a] (0.74)	0.30 (0.40)
Tightening employment protection laws (EPL), by 1 index point for 12 years or more					
(a) with little or no wage-setting coordination	−0.66 (0.75)	1.70[b] (0.90)	1.66[a] (0.67)	−1.26 (1.42)	0.51 (0.91)
(b) with high wage-setting coordination	−0.52 (1.30)	−6.06[a] (1.50)	−3.50[a] (1.13)	−5.16[c] (2.49)	−3.66 (1.45)
Shifting the index of coordinated wage setting from no coordination to high					
(a) with weak EPL	2.92 (2.49)	22.62[a] (3.09)	15.31[a] (2.79)	20.64[a] (4.92)	14.70 (2.83)
(b) with strict EPL	3.39 (2.61)	−4.14 (2.76)	−1.87 (1.75)	6.47 (4.78)	0.59 (2.78)
The "double jump": from low (0.4) to high (3.5) EPL, and from no to high wage coordination	1.33 (2.14)	5.59[c] (2.54)	6.18[a] (1.76)	5.14 (4.09)	4.70 (2.60)
Fiscal Wedges in the Labor Market					
Raising the unemployment compensation support ratio					
(a) from 0% (e.g., Italy 1979) to 1%	−0.20 (0.21)	−0.39[b] (0.22)	−0.05 (0.19)	−0.82[c] (0.34)	−0.18 (0.22)
(b) from 15% (e.g., France 1982) to 16%	0.04 (0.07)	−0.06 (0.08)	0.12[d] (0.06)	−0.10 (0.12)	0.03 (0.07)
(c) from 30% (e.g., Belgium 1982) to 31%	−0.25[c] (0.12)	−0.10 (0.16)	0.19 (0.12)	−0.28 (0.22)	−0.15 (0.14)
Broader Fiscal Shifts					
Raising all taxes and transfers in proportion					
(a) taxes up from 27% of GDP (U.S.) to 28%	0.13 (0.19)	0.35[d] (0.20)	−0.16 (0.16)	0.36 (0.33)	0.62 (0.21)
(b) taxes up from 35% of GDP (Italy 1985) to 36%	−0.01 (0.10)	0.33[a] (0.10)	0.37[a] (0.08)	0.29[d] (0.16)	0.09 (0.11)
(c) taxes up from 45% of GDP (Belgium 1985) to 46%	0.20 (0.14)	−0.10 (0.15)	−0.44[a] (0.10)	0.61[c] (0.27)	0.06 (0.15)

Table 15.2
(continued)

Institutional Changes (Independent Variables)	Percentage Estimated Effects on				
	Jobs	GDP/ Worker	GDP/ Hour	GDP/ Person 15–64	3-Year Growth Rate of GDP per Capita
Raising taxes and spending them only on extra transfers					
(a) taxes up from 27% of GDP (U.S.)	0.17	0.37	−0.20	0.56	0.57
to 28%	(0.23)	(0.25)	(0.20)	(0.41)	(0.26)
(b) taxes up from 35% of GDP (Italy	0.03	0.34^c	0.33^c	0.44^d	0.05
1985) to 36%	(0.14)	(0.17)	(0.13)	(0.25)	(0.18)
(c) taxes up from 45% of GDP	0.22	−0.09	−0.46^a	0.71^c	0.04
(Belgium 1985) to 46%	(0.16)	(0.17)	(0.12)	(0.30)	(0.17)
Coefficient on the lagged dependent	0.98^a	0.86^a	0.89^a	0.76^a	
variable^e	(0.03)	(0.02)	(0.02)	(0.04)	

Notes:
a. Significant at the 1 percent level (two-tail).
b. Significant at the 7 percent level.
c. Significant at the 5 percent level.
d. Significant at the 10 percent level.
e. To compute eventual steady-state impacts, multiply the (logged) 3-year coefficients by $1/(1 -$ this coefficient).

Standard errors in parentheses. For the structures of the equations, see table 15.1. All equations displayed here have highly significant F-statistics.

Jobs = ratio of employed persons to adult population of working age (15–64); min, mean, max of its natural log = −0.78, −0.43, −0.16.

Productivity per worker = real GDP per employed person; min, mean, max of its natural log = 9.9, 10.57, 11.1.

Productivity per hour = GDP per labor hour; min, mean, max of its natural log = 9.9, 10.55, 11.0.

Product-market regulation = index of degree of regulatory intervention in product markets; min, mean, max = 1.00, 4.1455, 5.98.

Index of strictness of EPL ranges from 0 to 5 (Allard 2003); min, mean, max = 0.10, 2.09, 3.83; "weak" EPL has index of 0.4 (U.S.), "strict" EPL has index of 3.5 (Italy).

Index of collective wage setting ranges from 1 to 3 (Ochel 2000); min, mean, max = 1.0, 1.98, 3.0; "little or no coordination" has index of 1, "high" coordination has index of 3.

Overall generosity and use of compensation to the unemployed is the Allard "net reservation wage." More specifically, it is measured as the product of (1) the marginal "replacement rate," or (benefits per recipient) divided by (market wage), net of taxes; (2) probability of collecting benefits, scored based on reading of national legislation; and (3) duration of coverage over the first year.

Welfare state social transfers as a share of GDP include public pensions, public health, unemployment compensation, family assistance, and public housing; min, mean, max = 7.64 percent, 20.50 percent, 32.80 percent.

The variants here exclude nonhuman capital formation from the set of regressors, implicitly endogenizing capital formation and the capital stock.

The equation for GDP per person 15–64 is estimated directly, not derived from the employment and productivity estimates shown in earlier columns.

How can that be? Scholars have identified some channels through which coordination could raise productivity over time. Coordination spawns wage moderation, which may tame sectoral rent seeking with job security. The consensus it builds can also cut the personnel costs of supervising workers (Gordon 1994; Teulings and Hartog 1998). It may facilitate stable macropolicy by promoting trust (Auer 2000; Blanchard 2004b).

The favorable effects of coordination (presumably with wage moderation) are so strong that in combination with strict EPL they significantly raise productivity. This would explain the "double jump" test statistics in the middle rows of table 15.2. Again, the GDP gain seems to come mainly through productivity, suggesting the need for deeper research into how such institutional packages affect human capital formation over the longer run.

Unemployment Compensation   To explore budget-related institutions, we must use the distinction between durable and transitory effects. Employment and productivity seem to react very differently to the durable and transitory components of unemployment compensation rules, taxes, and transfers. The regressions confirmed this difference, which probably has two explanations. One is that optimizing employers and members of the work force perceive the difference between durable and temporary changes in taxes and transfers. The other source is econometric: no amount of instrumenting seems to remove all short-run cyclical effects from tax and transfer shares of GDP. We therefore explore the durable influences of fiscal variables (X_{kd}), and omit transitory elements (X_{kjt}) from the underlying equations. The durable effects can be represented by countries' sample averages of the relevant fiscal parameters because these parameters tended to stay on a plateau in the 1978–1980 to 1999–2001 sample.

For the post-1980 period, the effects of more generous unemployment compensation are negative, as expected. The slopes shown in table 15.2 reveal that raising benefits reduces employment and overall GDP somewhat at the bottom and top of the range of generosity experienced in the OECD. Starting with essentially zero benefits, as in Italy in 1979, unemployment compensation when introduced cuts GDP slightly. Then, across the more typical middle ranges, with unemployment compensation at about 15 percent of median wage, more support to the unemployed has no clear effect. At the high end, such as the 31 percent support ratio offered in Belgium in 1982, more compensation reduces jobs and (probably) GDP. While the effects tend to be negative, they are not dramatically large. Probably the main reason for this is a simple point high-lighted by the new estimates of the generosity of unemployment benefits: the benefits did not cause large drops in employment because those benefits never exceeded one-third of median wage for production workers.

Broader Fiscal Shifts The effects of higher tax and transfer rates for the economy as a whole, in contrast, departed sharply from conventional wisdom. The "broader fiscal shifts" rows of table 15.2 show that higher tax and expenditure rates actually *raised* employment and output, whether the extra taxes were spent entirely on social transfers or on all kinds of expenditures in fixed proportions. The only exception is the negative effect on productivity per hour from raising taxes above 45 percent of GDP, as in Belgium in 1985.

As previous scholars have noted, this seldom-announced positive result should not seem strange, once one factors in both sides of government budgets.[12] Higher taxes and spending may not drag down growth in high-budget welfare states, which have some of the world's least corrupt governments. Since much of the extra public expenditure is spent on efficiency-building public health, education, and infrastructure, it outweighs the GDP costs of transfers like early retirement or unemployment compensation. It also seems likely that some of the productivity gain comes from the stronger demand-smoothing effect of automatic stabilizers in the higher-budget countries.

Different Effects for Different Worker Groups Many labor market institutions, particularly those that raise the costs of turnover, could affect the employment of different groups in diverse ways. The laws separating protected from unprotected workers could boost the pay and productivity of protected insiders at the expense of outsiders. In particular, many institutions raise the jobs and pay of males over 25 at the expense of females and youths (here 15–24) in the labor force. The differential employment effects can be tested for[13] by examining the outsider-insider ratios of unemployment rates, with women and youths as the outsiders. We choose unemployment rates rather than employment ratios because the latter are complicated by school enrollment (especially for the young) and other influences on female labor force participation.

The clearest result, shown in table 15.3, is that EPL strongly redistributes unemployment toward women and youths, to the advantage of males over 25. As conjectured earlier, this insider-outside difference is one reason why EPL might have positive effects when it is first instituted, and

Table 15.3
Three-Year Effects of Selected Institutional Changes on the Relative Unemployment of Women and Young Adults, 1978–2001

Institutional Changes (Independent Variables)	Estimated Effects on Female / Male Unemployment among Persons Aged 15–64		Youth (Ages 15–24) Unemployment / Unemployment among Males Aged 15–64	
Market Regulations				
Raising the index of product-market regulations by 1	0.065	(0.024)[a]	−0.226	(0.05)[a]
Tightening employment protection laws (EPL) by 1 index point for 12 years or more				
(a) with little or no wage-setting coordination	0.197	(0.052)[a]	0.482	(0.10)[a]
(b) with high wage-setting coordination	0.288	(0.101)[a]	0.420	(0.13)[a]
Shifting the index of coordinated wage setting from no coordination to high				
(a) with weak EPL	−0.516	(0.232)[b]	0.085	(0.28)
(b) with strict EPL	−0.233	(0.124)[c]	−0.107	(0.22)[d]
The "double jump": from low (0.4) to high (3.5) EPL, and from no to high wage coordination (from 1.0 to 3.0)	0.282	(0.148)[c]	1.328	(0.30)[a]
Fiscal Wedges in the Labor Market				
Raising the unemployment compensation support ratio				
(a) from 0% (e.g., Italy 1979) to 1%	−0.052	(0.016)[a]	−0.179	(0.03)[a]
(b) from 15% (e.g., France 1982) to 16%	−0.013	(0.006)[b]	−0.066	(0.01)[a]
(c) from 30% (e.g., Belgium 1982) to 31%	0.015	(0.012)	−0.150	(0.04)[a]

negative later on. When first implemented, EPL protects a large share of the labor force and may do no net damage to on-the-job skill formation. With the passage of time, however, a rising share of workers spends a longer time queuing for protected jobs, causing a net drop in human capital. Table 15.3 supports this story: where EPL is stricter, outsiders have higher unemployment rates.

Other institutions have mixed effects on female and youth unemployment. Strict product-market regulations seem to discourage female employment and help youth employment, for unknown reasons. Closer wage coordination has the opposite tendency. The combination of strong

Institutional Changes (Independent Variables)	Estimated Effects on Female / Male Unemployment among Persons Aged 15–64		Youth (Ages 15–24) Unemployment / Unemployment among Males Aged 15–64	
Broader Fiscal Shifts				
Raising all taxes and transfers in proportion				
(a) taxes up from 27% of GDP (U.S.) to 28%	0.016	(0.014)	0.095	(0.03)[a]
(b) taxes up from 35% of GDP (Italy 1985) to 36%	−0.014	(0.008)[d]	0.043	(0.01)[a]
(c) taxes up from 45% of GDP (Belgium 1985) to 46%	−0.019	(0.010)[b]	0.023	(0.02)
Raising taxes and spending them only on extra transfers				
(a) from 27% of GDP (U.S.) to 28%	0.033	(0.018)[c]	0.077	(0.03)[b]
(b) from 35% of GDP (Italy 1985) to 36%	−0.001	(0.011)	0.030	(0.02)
(c) from 45% of GDP (Belgium 1985) to 46%	−0.011	(0.011)	0.014	(0.02)
Coefficient on the lagged ln(employment ratio), 15–64	−1.802	(0.238)[a]	−1.956	(0.37)[a]

Notes:
a. Significant at the 1 percent level (two-tail).
b. Significant at the 5 percent level.
c. Significant at the 7 percent level.
d. Significant at the 10 percent level.

Standard errors in parentheses. For the structures of the equations, see table 15.1; table 15.2 notes apply here also. Female/male ratio of unemployment rates in the 15–64 age range has a 21-country min, average, max = 0.57, 1.35, 2.88. Youth/adult male ratio has sample min, average, max = 1.1, 2.31, 5.4; its sample consists of 14 countries: Australia, Canada, Finland, France, Germany, Ireland, Italy, Japan, Netherlands, Norway, Portugal, Spain, Sweden, United States.

EPL and wage coordination still shifts unemployment to outsiders, so that EPL's discriminatory effect outweighs the more equal treatment implied by wage coordination. Table 15.3 seems to show that more generous unemployment compensation favors employment of outsiders, but the result should be read through its male denominator: unemployment compensation allows more males over 25 to be officially unemployed. Finally, raising taxes in general shifts unemployment toward youth, perhaps because social security taxes raise the cost of an initial hire.

If the insider-outsider effect of EPL is so strong, it should show up in the raw data, not just in multivariate regressions. It does, both in the broad movements over time and in the differences across countries. It was in the 1970s that unemployment became dramatically higher for youths and women, relative to men. This timing correlates with the rise in EPL, and the shift toward unemployed women and youths was stronger in the high-EPL Mediterranean and Belgium than elsewhere. Today's international pattern shows the likely link to EPL even more clearly. Unemployment rate ratios tilt strongly toward women and youths in the high-EPL Mediterranean countries, in a way that was much less apparent before the rise in Mediterranean EPL. The strongest conclusion so far is that employment protection laws clearly redistribute jobs toward males over 25 at the expense of others.

Some Institutions Not Featured Here

Not all institutions can be analyzed here. The closest near-miss is the mix of tax types within the overall tax bill. We did test for differences in jobs and productivity caused by shifts among three tax categories: consumption taxes, social security payroll deductions, and income plus property taxes. We did not find robust results, however, so that any hunches about the merits of consumption taxation must remain hunches.[14]

Despite a determined effort to include the effects of active labor market policies, we have been unable to pin down their effects from this panel. The basic reason is that we could not reliably separate such policies from the cyclically sensitive outlays associated with them. We note the optimism about such activist policies in recent literature but cannot confirm or reject it here.[15]

Some other leading suspects escape trial for want of sufficient data. So it was with minimum wage laws, early retirement subsidies, the productivity revolution in retailing, and research and development policies.

Those Vexing Fixed Effects (UFOs)

Institutional results for all studies of European employment are strongly affected by the inclusion or exclusion of conventional time or country fixed effects. The usual practice is to hide these effects behind rows that simply indicate whether fixed effects are included. We feel this is a mistake where the real influences are durable rather than transitory, as in the recent history of jobs and growth in the OECD. Recall from equation (3) that durable behaviors can be linear combinations of the coefficients of those binaries by time and place, posing a tough problem of interpretation. A researcher must decide: Should linear combinations of binary fixed effects be selected so as to capture durable forces at work in the economy (X_{kd}), or should the standard approach be used, adding $J - 1$ fixed place effects and $T - 1$ fixed time effects to the regression?

In the name of reserving judgment, economists have chosen the latter path and have thrown away information. The usual fixed effects interpretation reveals a belief in mysterious UFOs (unidentified fixed objects), which are presented as though they were forces known to be separate from X. But what are they? Can we find what lies behind them? It turns out that the UFOs correlate strongly with the country average components of some variables but not others. For the 1978–2001 sample, country fixed effects correlate strongly and positively with big government (total tax share) in all job, productivity, and growth equations. One can even run regressions with the country UFOs as a dependent variable explained by the tax share and a few other X_{kd}, and get suggestive results. Doing so is a big first step toward endogenizing the UFOs. Experimenting with such regressions gives back the main conclusions featured in connection with table 15.2.[16]

Figure 15.3 dramatizes the same point by comparing the fixed country effects for the log of GDP per person with the share of all taxes in GDP. How should people interpret such striking patterns? Attributing them to separate "unobservable" forces seems inadequate. We recommend viewing such patterns as revealing information that researchers should have featured all along. The durable effects of institutional packages are often captured in the fixed effects and may be larger than the transitory coefficients that economists report. Focusing on durable effects corresponds with the kind of question that motivated our research: What would happen if an institution were durably changed, and not reversed the next year?

A Deeper History: How the 1960s–1970s Were Different

Institutional influences on employment and growth appear to evolve over time, and we have suggested some reasons for this. To track this evolution, we compare the preceding results with those from a similar panel for 19 countries over six three-year periods, 1963–1965 to 1978–1980.[17]

For this earlier period, control variables also explained most of the temporal changes in employment and productivity. The shocks to aggregate demand and supply, especially the oil shocks, account for much of the change from 1973 on. Lagged dependent variables and age variables also played the same strong roles as in the later era.

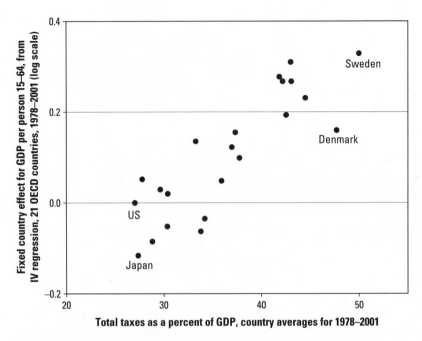

Figure 15.3
A pattern explaining fixed country effects (UFOs) for GDP per person in the OECD, 1978–2001.

The institutional effects, however, seem to have been evolving. The contrasts between the test statistics for the 1960s and 1970s are quite different from those shown for the later era in table 15.2.[18]

Before 1980, employment protection laws did not seem to have the negative effects they have delivered since 1980. Whether strict EPL had a positive effect depended on whether the tightening occurred in a context of coordinated wage bargaining. Without coordinated settlements, tighter EPL may have had no clear effects within this time period. With coordination, tightening EPL seems to have boosted jobs and GDP over the 1960s and 1970s, even though it eventually dragged down productivity, as shown in table 15.2. Combining strict EPL with coordinated wage setting worked well in Scandinavia in these early years.

We tentatively interpret EPL's effects over time in terms of the insider-outsider model and the career cycle. In the 1960s and 1970s, EPL was new in most of western Europe, except on the Iberian peninsula. It protected a large share of workers and initially denied work to relatively few outsiders, so the job effect was positive during cyclical shocks, and productivity was not yet compromised. As the century wore on, however, the outsider share of the labor force rose steadily and its favorable job and human capital effects were overwhelmed by the negative effects on outsiders' careers, yielding the numbers in tables 15.2 and 15.3.[19]

On the fiscal front, the results for the 1960s and 1970s differ from the fiscal effects in the post-1980 era. Raising unemployment compensation from zero to low levels promoted jobs and productivity in the way predicted by the Sinn (1995) model. General fiscal expansion, on the other hand, had negative effects in the bottom and top budget ranges and indeterminate effects on the heavily represented middle range. We offer no explanation why raising taxes and spending had a negative effect on results for the 1960s and 1970s yet lacked clear negative effects in other plausible specifications for these same decades or for the period after 1980.[20]

Two Kinds of Verdicts

This chapter demonstrates how eclecticism in pursuing evidence pays off by delivering clearer verdicts than a narrower empirical exercise might have yielded. Our wider range of tests brings us to two different kinds of verdicts, familiar from U.S. trial law: reasonable doubt verdicts and preponderance-of-evidence verdicts.

The reasonable doubt rule, as practiced in U.S. criminal cases, is demanding if a case is to be made against a defendant (here, institutions). If some evidence doesn't fit, the defendant must be acquitted. Robustness is one econometric translation of the reasonable doubt yardstick. Only one of our conclusions delivers this demanding a verdict against any of Europe's labor market or fiscal institutions. This verdict is that employment protection laws have created labor market insiders and outsiders, as portrayed by Lindbeck and Snower (2001), reducing employment and earning power for women and youths relative to males over 25.

However, our eclectic body of evidence has yielded several preponderance-of-evidence verdicts.[21] The preponderance-of-evidence suggests that the effects of EPL on employment and GDP have become less positive and more negative over time. When first instituted, EPL can boost employment without compromising productivity, as in the 1960s and 1970s. Over time, however, the employment gain evaporates as outsiders become a rising share of the labor force. At the same time, negative productivity effects creep in, as a declining share of the work force's career history is spent as protected insiders. Product-market regulations also appear guilty of lowering productivity, although the evidence against them leaves reasonable doubt. By the 1980s and 1990s unemployment compensation had also drifted toward the negative effect predicted by theory.

Other institutions are acquitted, even on the preponderance-of-evidence criterion. Coordinated wage setting seems to have very positive job and productivity effects. And the overall bundle of welfare state transfers shows no negative effects on either jobs or output, at least not since 1980.

Notes

The authors are indebted to Matthew Pearson for able research assistance, and to seminar audiences at Berkeley, British Columbia, Copenhagen, Cornell, Harvard, Oxford, and the World Bank for helpful comments on earlier drafts of this chapter. Any remaining errors are ours.

1. The employment literature has revolved around the Organisation for Economic Cooperation and Development (OECD) consensus that Europeans have lost their jobs to product and labor market rigidities, high tax rates on labor, and overgenerous unemployment compensation and early retirement subsidies. Baker et al. (2005) and Freeman (2005) criticize the OECD panel econometric literature, suggesting that economists adjusted institutional data to match their conclusions, and that there is "a yawning gap between the confidence with which the case for labor market deregulation has been asserted and the evidence that the regulating institutions are the culprits." Freeman calls for forsaking the macropanel approach in favor of microeconomic studies of individual country labor markets. Blanchard and Wolfers (2000) say a key reason for the failure of macropanels to yield clear answers is that the institutional variables are essentially fixed country effects. In contrast, the literature on comparative economic growth concludes that western Europe lags behind North America because of differences in technology policy, telecommunications taxes and restrictions, education, taxes, the welfare state, restrictions on product-market competition, and policies toward big-box retail stores. Employment protection laws, coordinated wage bargaining and minimum wages receive little attention, and productivity friendly institutions like public health systems with controlled prices and universal insurance coverage receive none. The only overlapping variables are some taxes and spending, which are found to reduce GDP. The most persuasive study in this genre is Kneller, Bleaney, and Gemmell (1999), which classifies taxes by whether they discourage investments, and divides expenditures into productive and unproductive uses, finding that distortionary taxes hurt growth if they finance unproductive expenditures, while nondistortionary taxes do not; and productive government expenditures enhance growth, while unproductive ones do not. A strong case can be made for merging these separate literatures because they have missed the chance to test the employment and productivity effects of each institution together. Common sense also predicts that the effects should unfold with different time lags, allowing another opportunity for testing by exploring the two kinds of effects simultaneously.

The debate over employment protection legislation (EPL), which raises the costs of worker dismissal, illustrates the need to test for job and productivity effects together. Although theory argues that EPL creates insiders and outsiders, protecting the jobs of the former and reducing incentives to hire the latter, few writings have quantified total and separate effects, even though the marginal data cost is minimal. And while advocates of job protection have long asserted that EPL raises productivity by stabilizing jobs, in this case for protected "insiders," strict EPL also denies new jobs to outsiders. This delays their human capital formation and reduces later productivity. To evaluate these contradictory effects on productivity over time, we propose a new test: can the negative productivity effects of exogenously tightening EPL rise for two or three decades? Our results suggest that they do, making the productivity effects of older, longer-standing EPL more negative than newly instituted protections. Other institutions also affect both jobs and productivity in ways that allow extra testing of each leading hypothesis from labor or growth economics.

2. Similarly, Blanchard (2004b, 3): "European labor market institutions did not come into being in the early 1970s. For the most part, both the architecture and the level of social protection were put in place earlier, and were then consistent with low unemployment."

3. These measures, from Allard (2005b), are based on rules and statutes. Observed expenditure behavior may show different movements from what the rules imply at face value.

4. Before these new estimates, based on Allard (2003; 2005a; 2005b), the historically deepest set of estimates was that of Lazear (1990).

5. To capture these two shocks, we used four variables. The first two are the (inflation minus unemployment) and (inflation plus unemployment) shocks for the whole OECD, multiplied by the individual country's trade openness (exports plus imports divided by GDP). The other two are the same multiplied by a dummy for the United States. This reflects the fact that the United States carries a considerably greater weight than any other country in the OECD-wide averages for inflation and unemployment.

6. A similar idea is presented by Freeman (1998).

7. 2001 is the last year for OECD social spending data.

8. To focus on the most meaningful conclusions about institutional impacts, tables 15.2, 15.3, and 15.6 present results based primarily on test statistics for linear combinations of coefficients, rather than on single coefficients.

9. Tables 15.2 and 15.3 display very large increments in institutions and budgetary policies for rhetorical purposes. Such jumps never actually occurred from one three-year period to the next, even though all the institutional combinations actually occurred in the sample. The counterfactuals shown in these tables violate the "speed limit" described in Lindert (2004, II, 29–30).

10. For a similar conclusion, see Addison and Teixeira (2003).

11. Baker et al. (2005) and studies cited there.

12. See, for example, Helms (1985), Atkinson (1999), and Lindert (2004, ch. 10, ch. 18). The results of Kneller, Bleaney, and Gemmell (1999) agree about higher taxes spent on government purchases but not about higher taxes for transfer spending.

13. See, in particular, Bertola, Blau, and Kahn (2001; 2002). Some of their tests trace the effects of unionization rather than the institutions emphasized here, but unionization rates and these institutions are sufficiently correlated to make the results comparable.

14. Clearer results were announced by Kneller, Bleaney, and Gemmell (1999). Yet we prefer our regression specification and could not confirm their results with our chosen equations.

15. Nickell, Nunziata, and Ochel (2005, 6) are relatively upbeat about the policies' ability to cut unemployment, citing macrostudies by Scarpetta (1996), Nickell (1997), and Elmeskov, Martin, and Scarpetta (1998) and the microeconometric studies summarized in Martin (2000).

16. We have done so in unreported regressions on 22 fixed country effects (21 countries minus the base country, with different effects for Germany before and after 1990). The same UFO regressions should have more power when there are more fixed place effects, as in interstate regression analyses of the 50 United States.

17. The 19 countries are those listed in the notes to table 15.1, minus Portugal and Spain, for whom we lack data on social transfers. The earlier sample also lacks the OECD index of product-market regulations.

18. The differences in structure make it unwise to combine the 1963–2001 era into a single sample, unless one can cleverly specify equations that capture the structural evolution.

19. Studies for countries outside the OECD support the idea that EPL has negative effects on jobs. For Latin America and the Caribbean, institutions that make labor markets less flexible seem to have reduced formal-sector employment and output, as in western

Europe since about 1980. Latin American and Caribbean experience also shows that EPL has lowered formal sector employment, mainly for women and youths. In Chile, where dismissal costs were raised in 1966, slashed in 1974, and raised in 1985 and 1991, surveys in Santiago showed that tighter EPL raised employment for prime working-aged males and reduced employment for women and youths. In Brazil, responses to two increases in dismissal costs confirm that job tenure for youths and women declined relative to males 25 and older; see Gonzaga (2003). A differences-in-differences analysis shows that men over 25 gained in job tenure relative to women and youths, even though the net effect on total jobs is unclear. For India and Southern Africa, the effects are more broadly negative; see Besley and Burgess (2004). Labor market restrictions similarly seem to account for much of Zimbabwe's unemployment since independence.

20. For alternative specifications over both historical samples, see Lindert (2004, II, app. E).

21. The econometric analogy to a preponderance-of-evidence verdict is Sala-i-Martin's (1997) acceptance-of-confidence-interval verdicts from repeated trials instead of stricter interpretations of "robustness."

References

Addison, J. T., and P. Teixeira. 2003. The Economics of Employment Protection. *Journal of Labor Research* 24 (1): 85–129.

Agell, J. 1999. On the Benefits from Rigid Labour Markets: Norms, Market Failures, and Social Insurance. *Economic Journal* 108: 143–164.

Allard, G. J. 2003. Jobs and Labor Market Institutions in the OECD. Ph.D. diss., University of California, Davis.

———. 2005a. Measuring Job Security over Time: In Search of a Historical Indicator for EPL (Employment Protection Legislation). Working Paper WP05-17, Instituto de Empresa, Madrid.

———. 2005b. Measuring the Changing Generosity of Unemployment Benefits: Beyond Existing Indicators. Working Paper WP05-18, Instituto de Empresa, Madrid.

Allard, G. J., and P. H. Lindert. 2006. Euro-Productivity and Euro-Jobs since the 1960s: Which Institutions Really Mattered? NBER Working Paper 12460. Cambridge, Mass.: NBER.

Atkinson, A. B. 1999. *The Economic Consequences of Rolling Back the Welfare State*. Cambridge, Mass.: MIT Press.

Auer, P. 2000. *Employment Revival in Europe: Labour Market Success in Austria, Denmark, Ireland, and the Netherlands.* Geneva: International Labour Organization.

Baker, D., A. Glyn, D. Howell, and J. Schmitt. 2005. Labor Market Institutions and Unemployment: A Critical Assessment of the Cross-Country Evidence. In *Fighting Unemployment*, ed. D. Howell, 72–118. Oxford: Oxford University Press.

Bassanini, A., S. Scarpetta, and P. Hemmings. 2001. Economic Growth: The Role of Policies and Institutions: Panel Evidence from OECD Countries. OECD Economics Department Working Paper 283.

Bean, C. 1994. European Unemployment: A Survey. *Journal of Economic Literature* 32 (2): 573–619.

Bertola, G., F. D. Blau, and L. M. Kahn. 2001. Comparative Analysis of Labor Market Outcomes: Lessons for the U.S. from International Long-Run Evidence. In *The Roaring Nineties: Can Full Employment Be Sustained?* ed. A. B. Krueger and R. Solow. New York: Russell Sage Foundation.

———. 2002. Labor Market Institutions and Demographic Employment Patterns. NBER (National Bureau of Economic Research) Working Paper 9043. ⟨http://www.nber.org/papers/W9043⟩.

Besley, T., and R. Burgess. 2004. Can Labor Regulation Hinder Economic Performance? Evidence from India. *Quarterly Journal of Economics* 119 (1): 91–134.

Blanchard, O. 2004a. The Economic Future of Europe. *Journal of Economic Perspectives* 18 (4): 3–26.

———. 2004b. Explaining European Unemployment. *NBER Reporter Online.* ⟨http://www.nber.org/reporter/summer04/⟩.

Blanchard, O., and J. Wolfers. 2000. The Role of Shocks and Institutions in the Rise of European Unemployment: The Aggregate Evidence. *Economic Journal* 110: 1–33.

Bruno, M., and J. Sachs. 1985. *The Economics of Worldwide Stagflation.* Cambridge, Mass.: Harvard University Press.

Calmfors, L., and J. Driffil. 1988. Bargaining Structure, Corporatism, and Macroeconomic Performance. *Economic Policy* 3: 13–61.

Elmeskov, J., J. Martin, and S. Scarpetta. 1998. Key Lessons for Labor Market Reforms: Evidence from OECD Countries Experience. *Swedish Economic Policy Review* 5 (2): 205–252.

Fallon, P. R., and R. E. B. Lucas. 1991. The Impact of Changes in Job Security Regulations in India and Zimbabwe. *World Bank Economic Review* 5 (3): 395–413.

Flanagan, R. J. 1988. Unemployment as a Hiring Problem. *OECD Economic Studies* 11 (Autumn): 123–154.

———. 1999. Macroeconomic Performance and Collective Bargaining: An International Perspective. *Journal of Economic Literature* 37 (3): 1150–1175.

Freeman, R. B. 1998. Single-Peaked vs. Diversified Capitalism: The Relation between Economic Institutions and Outcomes. NBER (National Bureau of Economic Research) Working Paper 7556. ⟨http://www.nber.org/papers/W7556⟩.

———. 2005. Labour Market Institutions without Blinders: The Debate over Flexibility and Labour Market Performance. NBER (National Bureau of Economic Research) Working Paper 11286. ⟨http://www.nber.org/papers/W11286⟩.

Freeman, R. B., and J. L. Medoff. 1984. *What Do Unions Do?* New York: Basic Books.

Freeman, R. B., and R. Schettkat. 2005. Marketization of Production and the U.S.-Europe Employment Gap. *Economic Policy* 20 (41): 6–50.

Gonzaga, G. 2003. Labor Turnover and Labor Legislation in Brazil. *Economia* 4 (1): 165–207.

Gordon, D. 1994. Bosses of Different Stripes: A Cross-National Perspective on Monitoring and Supervision. *American Economic Review* 84 (2): 375–379.

Gordon, R. J. 2004. Why Was Europe Left at the Station When America's Productivity Locomotive Departed? NBER (National Bureau of Economic Research) Working Paper 10661. ⟨http://www.nber.org/papers/W10661⟩.

Gordon, R. J., and I. Dew-Becker. 2005. Why Did Europe's Productivity Catch-up Sputter Out? A Tale of Tigers and Tortoises. In *Proceedings of the Conference on Productivity Growth, Federal Reserve Bank of San Francisco.*

Heckman, J., and C. Pagés, eds. 2004. *Law and Employment: Lessons from Latin America and the Caribbean.* Chicago: University of Chicago Press,

Helms, L. J. 1985. The Effects of State and Local Taxes on Economic Growth: A Time Series Cross-Section Approach. *Review of Economics and Statistics* 67 (4): 574–582.

Kneller, R., M. Bleaney, and N. Gemmell. 1999. Fiscal Policy and Growth: Evidence from OECD Countries. *Journal of Public Economics* 74 (2): 171–190.

Lazear, E. P. 1990. Job Security Provisions and Employment. *Quarterly Journal of Economics* 105: 699–726.

Lindbeck, A., and D. J. Snower. 2001. Insiders versus Outsiders. *Journal of Economic Perspectives* 15 (1): 165–188.

Lindert, P. H. 2004. *Growing Public: Social Spending and Economic Growth since the Eighteenth Century.* 2 vols. Cambridge: Cambridge University Press.

Martin, J. P. 2000. What Works among Active Labour Market Policies: Evidence from OECD Countries' Experiences. *OECD Economic Studies* 30: 79–113.

Montenegro, C. E., and C. Pagés. 2004. Who Benefits from Labor Market Regulations? Chile, 1960–1998. In *Law and Employment: Lessons from Latin America and the Caribbean,* ed. J. Heckman and C. Pagés, 401–434. Chicago: University of Chicago Press.

Nickell, S. J. 1997. Unemployment and Labor Market Rigidities: Europe versus North America. *Journal of Economic Perspectives* 11 (3): 55–74.

———. 2004. Employment and Taxes. Discussion Paper 634. Centre for Economic Performance, London School of Economics and Political Science.

Nickell, S. J., and R. Layard. 1999. Labor Market Institutions and Economic Performance. In *Handbook of Labor Economics.* Vol. 3, ed. O. Ashenfelter and D. Card. Amsterdam: North Holland.

Nickell, S. J., L. Nunziata, and W. Ochel. 2005. Unemployment in the OECD since the 1960s: What Do We Know? *Economic Journal* 115 (500): 1–27.

Ochel, W. 2000. Collective Bargaining. Ifo Institute for Economic Research, Munich.

OECD (Organisation for Economic Cooperation and Development). 1985. *Social Expenditure, 1960–1990.* Paris.

———. 1994. *The OECD Jobs Study: Evidence and Explanations.* 2 vols. Paris.

Polachek, S. W., and W. S. Siebert. 1993. *The Economics of Earnings.* New York: Cambridge University Press.

Sala-i-Martin, X. 1997. I Just Ran Two Million Regressions. *American Economic Review* 87 (2): 178–183.

Scarpetta, S. 1996. Assessing the Role of Labour Market Policies and Institutional Settings on Unemployment: A Cross-Country Study. *OECD Economic Studies* 26 (1): 43–98.

Schneider, F., and R. Klinglmair. 2004. Shadow Economies around the World: What Do We Know? CESifo Working Paper 1167. Ifo Institute for Economic Research, Munich.

Siebert, H. 1997. Labor Market Rigidities: At the Root of Unemployment in Europe. *Journal of Economic Perspectives* 11 (3): 37–54.

Sinn, H.-W. 1995. A Theory of the Welfare State. *Scandinavian Journal of Economics* 97 (4): 495–526.

———. 1996. Social Insurance, Incentives, and Risk Taking. *International Tax and Public Finance* 3 (3): 259–280.

Teulings, C., and J. Hartog. 1998. *Corporatism or Competition? Labour Contracts, Institutions, and Wage Structures in International Comparison.* Cambridge: Cambridge University Press.

Afterword

Lawrence H. Summers

Following an introduction by John H. Coatsworth, Professor of History and Monroe Gutman Professor of Latin American Affairs at Harvard University, the following remarks were delivered in honor of Jeffrey G. Williamson, Laird Bell Professor of Economics, by Lawrence H. Summers, President of Harvard University, at the Jeffrey Williamson Festschrift, on November 4, 2005.

Thank you very much, John, for that very kind introduction. It brings back to mind what Lyndon Johnson used to say when he was very generously introduced: "I wish my parents had been here for that. My father would have appreciated it, and my mother would have believed it."

Actually, in a certain sense, it reminds me of an experience I had when I was in Washington, and I was asked to introduce President Clinton to a financial group he was going to speak to. I explained the President's great financial virtues, commitment to deficit reduction, and so forth, with great emphasis, and even great exaggeration, if truth be told. The President stood up and he said, "Larry, that was terrific. You have just illustrated one of my first laws of political life: Whenever possible, be introduced by someone who works within an organization you lead, or whose budget you help determine."

I am here for two reasons. The secondary reason, which I will address first, is to say a few words about the field of economic history. The primary reason I am here is to say a few words about Jeff Williamson.

I have been sensible enough to think that economic history was of profound importance for understanding economics, and for understanding our society more broadly, for as long as I have been thinking about being an economist. But I confess that, as I have aged, I have come to a much greater sense of the importance of economic history, and the importance of our understanding of economic history for the contemporary world, for almost every question that economists think about.

In a sense, I was reminded of this very powerfully three or four years ago when I had an interaction with my children. I have, as some of you know, twin daughters, Pam and Ruth.

I saw Ruth, and I asked her, "What are you learning in social studies?"

And Ruthie said, "We're studying the Industrial Revolution."

So I said, "Oh, what have you learned about the Industrial Revolution, Ruthie?"

And Ruthie said, "Well, Daddy, I get that it was good, because we have television and stuff now. But it was really bad for all those people, because they had to go work with the machines in the city, and they had to go work with the looms and get their fingers cut off. So it was really terrible for the people then, but I guess it's good for the people now."

So I said, "Is that really what they taught you about the Industrial Revolution, Ruthie?"

Ruthie said, "Yes."

I said, "You're sure, Ruthie?"

"Yes."

And so fifteen minutes passed, Ruthie went into the kitchen to get something to eat, and Pam came into the room. One of the great things about having identical twins as a social scientist is that it permits parallel experimentation.

So I said, "Pammy, what are you learning in school about the Industrial Revolution?"

She said, "How did you know we were studying the Industrial Revolution?"

"Well, I talked to Ruthie. So what are you learning, Pammy?"

"Well," she said, "it was really bad, Daddy. With all those people working in all those mills and all the terrible things that happened to them, I guess it maybe it had to be okay. But, gosh, it was really bad for the people."

I said, "Really. Well, what about the fact that they could have stayed in the fields, and they chose to come to the city?"

"Well, they must have been made to do that because no one would have wanted to work in those mills."

"Is that really what they taught you?"

"Yes."

I said, "Do you and Ruthie have the same teacher?"

"No."

"Do you have the book that you're studying?"

And so they brought me the textbook, and it said basically what they were saying to me. It said that there was some good stuff, but basically the Industrial Revolution was an act of repression. I was really quite struck by this because it did not fit with my understanding of the Industrial Revolution. So I talked to Jeff and he basically confirmed my economic prejudices.

He said that, yes, of course there were some increases in inequality, and yes, there were some increased accidents, but basically people were moving from the rural areas to the cities because of the opportunities there. Life was terrible by today's standards, but it was better than it had been before, and we moved into a period where the standards of living changed significantly.

I then asked some other historians who were not affiliated with the field of economic history about the question, and their answers were a little more like what Pam and Ruth had heard in class.

On one level, it is a sort of a funny story, and the people who are economists like me probably are tending to maintain a sense of superiority and enthusiasm about the Industrial Revolution. But on another level, this story is actually, I think, about something that is very important, because, if one believes that the process of globalization and industrialization is one that has the enormous potential to transform the lives of millions of people who are destitute today—if we cannot convince people that the Industrial Revolution was a good thing, we are going to have a very difficult time convincing people globally that modernization is a good thing as well. It really is very much that understanding of economic history that is actually very shaping and revealing as to the source of attitudes towards a very fundamental kind of question.

Keynes famously wrote about the distilled frenzy of academic scribblers. I am not sure that everyone who has written on the Industrial Revolution quite qualifies as having risen to a frenzy, but it is one of many examples of our understanding of the past and how that understanding of the past changes into the general understanding. Where leaders of economic history have a profound impact on today's world, whether it is thinking about what the 1929 crash meant, whether it is the different ways in which the experience of slavery is seen, whether it is the understanding of myth or the understanding of reality regarding the settlement of the American Frontier, whether it is the role of colonizing power, the images and the understanding of economic history, I believe, are very much part of the shaping of economic views that have a profound impact on the way in which the world moves.

Questions like the ones that are on the agenda for this conference are of such very great importance. That is why I think the work that Jeff Williamson has done and the leadership that Jeff has provided to the profession and to this university over a very long time are so important. I am told that, at one meeting, Jeff's colleagues gave him an Energizer Bunny, and that Energizer Bunny still sits in his office as a symbol of his attitude towards life.

I had an occasion before coming here to review Jeff's C.V. It is only a small exaggeration to say that there are a certain number of economic departments in this country that would be pleased to have a collective C.V. of equal length. There are many distinguished scholars whose lists of articles are not as long as Jeff's list of books and monographs. On topics ranging from migration to factor price equalization to inequality, he has written extremely important and influential books and monographs.

Jeff and I began in the economics department at the same time, and Jeff had a distinguished record at that point. Whatever the general merits of the proposition that most economists are more productive in the first half of their career than in the second half of their career, Jeff's record as a Harvard professor all these years speaks to the enormous contributions that someone makes during the second half of their career.

Jeff has also been a wonderful leader in this community. He and Nancy did a terrific job of serving as masters of Mather House from 1986 to 1993. It is a house that is a bit of a challenge of which to be a master. If you are a Harvard student, your first image of the kind of house you want to live in is not one that is made of concrete; it is not one that is seen as an example of the modernistic architecture of the late 1960s and early 1970s; and it is not one that is a double digit number of stories high. None of that mattered to the students when Jeff and Nancy served as the masters at Mather. The place had great warmth, and students from those periods talked about the Williamsons and the differences that they made in their lives.

More recently, Jeff has been the chairman of our economics department, from 1997 to 2000, and our director of undergraduate studies during the several years since that time. Much more generally than that, he has been a great citizen of the economics department. In contemporary economics departments, the economic historians are not always what other members of the department think of as, to use Schlesinger's phrase, the vital center. But Jeff was someone who has always been involved in the affairs of the department, has always stood up for the importance of economic history, has always worked to collaborate and build connections with others, both within the economics department, and in other parts of the University. His contributions to Harvard are legion.

The third thing to say about Jeff is something that I have had occasion to observe if not every month, then probably every year, over the last couple of decades since he came to Harvard, and I have sometimes wondered why it is so true. I conjecture that it has something to do with his having spent twenty years in the Midwest. *Jeff is a really nice guy.* Not every economist is—and I would not rush to generalize about the correlation between the length of the curriculum vitae and the sunniness of the personality. But to everyone he interacts with, whether it is running into Lisa and me in an airport on the way to St. Thomas, whether it is passing someone in the Yard, whether it is responding to a curious graduate student or undergraduate, Jeff is a remarkably giving person. I am sure that to the economic history profession that is also true.

There are many who make great individual contributions. There are fewer, though also a fair number, who really are giving of themselves to others and to the various communities of which they are a part. There are very few people, in the course of a scholarly career, who manage to do both. Jeff Williamson is one such person. That, I suspect, is part of the reason why there are so many people here for this conference. I am proud to be the President of the University at which he teaches and even more proud to be his friend.

Thank you very much.

Contributors

Gayle J. Allard
Instituto de Empresa, Madrid

Robert C. Allen
Oxford University

Leah Platt Boustan
University of California, Los
Angeles

George R. Boyer
Cornell University

Gregory Clark
University of California, Davis

William J. Collins
Vanderbilt University

Giovanni Federico
European University Institute

Richard S. Grossman
Wesleyan University

Timothy J. Hatton
Australian National University
and University of Essex

Peter H. Lindert
University of California, Davis

Cormac Ó Gráda
University College, Dublin

Alan L. Olmstead
University of California, Davis

Kevin H. O'Rourke
Trinity College, Dublin

Süleyman Özmucur
University of Pennsylvania

Şevket Pamuk
Bogaziçi University, Istanbul

Karl Gunnar Persson
University of Copenhagen

Leandro Prados de la Escosura
Universidad Carlos III, Madrid

Paul W. Rhode
University of Arizona

Alan M. Taylor
University of California, Davis

Jeffrey G. Williamson
Harvard University

Holger C. Wolf
Georgetown University

Tarik M. Yousef
Georgetown University

Index